Career Choice and Development

Career Choice and Development

Fourth Edition

Duane Brown and Associates

JOSSEY-BASS
A Wiley Company
www.josseybass.com

Published by Jossey-Bass
A Wiley Imprint
989 Market Street, San Francisco, CA 94103-1741   www.josseybass.com

Jossey-Bass books and products are available through most bookstores. To contact Jossey-Bass directly call our Customer Care Department within the U.S. at 800-956-7739, outside the U.S. at 317-572-3986, or fax 317-572-4002.

Jossey-Bass also publishes its books in a variety of electronic formats. Some content that appears in print may not be available in electronic books.

Library of Congress Cataloging-in-Publication Data

Brown, Duane.
  Career choice and development / Duane Brown and associates.—4th ed.
    p. cm.—(The Jossey-Bass business & management series)
    Rev. ed. of: Career choice and development / Duane Brown, Linda Brooks,
    and associates. 3rd ed. c1996.
  Includes bibliographical references and index.
  ISBN 0-7879-5741-0 (alk. paper)
  1. Career development. 2. Vocational guidance. I. Career choice and
development. II. Title. III. Series.
  HF5381 .C265143 2002
  331.7'02—dc21
                                                        2002005599

Printed in the United States of America
FOURTH EDITION
HB Printing   10 9 8

The Jossey-Bass
Business & Management Series

Contents

Preface

In the final phases of the preparation of this edition of *Career Choice and Development*, I was talking to an old friend, Tom Harrington, about it. One thing he said to me was, "Make sure you make a strong statement that career development is about change—something that some people seem to overlook." He is right. Career development theories are explanations of how people develop certain traits, personalities, and self-precepts and how these developments influence decision making. These theories are also about the contexts in which people live and how the variables in those contexts interact with personal characteristics to influence development and decision making. In sum, career choice and development theories are about dynamic, ever-changing phenomena. Career counseling, like all forms of counseling, becomes necessary when something goes awry in the natural process of development. Judging by the surveys the Gallup organization has conducted for the National Career Development Association, the course of development gets off-course fairly often.

In Chapter Five, Mark Savickas observes that there is great variation in the theories of career choice and development. He attributes this to the fact that various theorists choose to "explain" different aspects of the developmental process. Few have the courage of Don Super, who tried to explain all facets of the career development process. In the second edition of this book, however, he admitted that the daunting task he had undertaken was not complete and that the "glue" that might hold the segments of his theory together would have to be applied by someone else.

Another approach to theorizing has emerged in the last two decades. This approach simply states that the complexities of the interactions that occur within and among the intrapersonal traits and interpersonal interactions are simply too complicated to understand and, therefore, we should stop trying to do it, except on an individual basis. These people are the constructivists, and their writings have given rise to an oxymoron—constructivist counseling—whether it refers to career counseling or some other type. I call *constructivist counseling* an oxymoron because I eschew the concept of cause-and-effect relationships. People who get "stuck" in their career development often seek help from career counselors, hoping that the counseling process will result in (cause) changes in their development. However, the constructivists have already had one favorable impact on the career choice and development theory and practice. Their criticisms have forced most of us to consider more carefully the economic, social, and cultural context of the individuals we try to understand and help. Some writers have taken this increased recognition of the importance of context as a move toward an integration of the two camps—modern and postmodern. When "dust bowl" empiricists such as John Holland agree that cause-and-effect relationships are unimportant and data collected about large groups of people do not generalize to others, integration is on the way. Until then, integration of these points of view is little more than a gleam in the would-be integrationists' eyes.

Alternative points of view, such as those taken by the modern and postmodern theorists in this book, can be very helpful if readers carefully consider the points of view of the theorists as they read their material. It may be useful to recall that theories are neither true nor false. It may also be useful to examine one's own beliefs about human beings and how they develop and change. If these core beliefs can be combined with one's beliefs about counseling in general and turned into a "What I believe at this time" statement, the reader's journey through this volume will undoubtedly be enriched and, I hope, made more meaningful.

Linda Brooks and I started this project in 1982, and I owe her a debt of gratitude that I will never be able to repay. Her own career development has taken her into retirement. I also owe a debt of gratitude to the many authors who have given of their time and talent to make the four editions possible. Our original vision was to prompt theorists to review their work from time to time and to prompt theory revision and development. We accomplished the first goal, but it is impossible to tell whether this book stimulated any of the new theories that have emerged since the publication of the edition in 1984, with one exception. My work with the authors of the first three editions prompted me to put down my own beliefs about occupational choice. I hope others will be prompted to take a similar path.

Chapel Hill, North Carolina   Duane Brown
May 2002

About the Authors

Duane Brown is professor of education at the University of North Carolina-Chapel Hill. He received his B.S., M.S., and Ph.D. degrees from Purdue University.

His scholarship specialties are career development and consultation. Brown has authored or coauthored twenty-four books and manuals and one hundred research studies, articles, and book chapters. He edited *Counselor Education and Supervision* for three years and has served on the editorial boards of three other journals.

Brown has served on numerous state, regional, and national committees. He has also served as president of the North Carolina Career Development Association, the North Carolina Association of Counselor Educators and Supervisors, the North Carolina Counseling Association, and the National Career Development Association. He is currently serving on the board of the National Career Development Association as trustee-at-large. He has twice received the North Carolina Career Development Association's Roy N. Anderson Award for outstanding contributions to career development. He also received the North Carolina Counseling Association's highest award—the Ella Stephens Barrett Leadership Award—as well as their Distinguished Service Award. He has received numerous other awards for his professional contributions, including the Association of Counselor Education's President's

Award. In 1998, the University of British Columbia selected him to serve in their Noted Scholar's Program.

Brown is a licensed professional counselor in North Carolina and maintains a small private practice. In 2002, he was among the first to become a fellow in the National Career Development Association.

Steven D. Brown is a professor in the Department of Leadership, Foundations, and Counseling Psychology at Loyola University in Chicago. He received a B.A. degree in psychology from Muskingum College in 1969, a master's in experimental psychology from the University of Virginia in 1972, and a Ph.D. in counseling psychology from the University of California, Santa Barbara in 1977.

Brown is also a licensed clinical psychologist in Illinois, specializing in career counseling and consulting. His research focuses primarily on topics of vocational psychology and applied psychological measurement.

Brown was the 1995 recipient of the John L. Holland award for outstanding contributions to career and personality research from the Division of Counseling Psychology of the American Psychological Association. In addition to his collaborations with Robert Lent and Gail Hackett on social cognitive career theory, Brown and Lent are coeditors of three editions of the *Handbook of Counseling Psychology* (Wiley). Brown serves on the editorial boards of vocational, social, and personality psychology journals and is a fellow of the American Psychological Association, American Psychological Society, and the American Association of Applied and Preventive Psychology.

Audrey Collin is professor emeritus of career studies at DeMonfort University, Leicester, U.K. Her interests are in interpretative approaches to career research, mentoring, and the role of organizations in the construction of career. Her publications, including two edited books (with Richard Young), have argued for new approaches to the understanding of career. Her most recent book is *The Future of Career* (Cambridge University Press, 2000).

Rene V. Dawis is professor emeritus in the Department of Psychology, University of Minnesota, where he was director of the Counseling Psychology Program from 1975 to 1985. Previously, he had taught at the University of the Philippines. Among his major publications are *A Psychological Theory of Work Adjustment* (with Lloyd H. Lofquist, 1984) and *Psychology: Realizing Human Potential* (with Rosemary T. Fruehling, 1996). His research has been on individual differences and their application in psychology.

Linda S. Gottfredson is professor of education and affiliate faculty of the Undergraduate Honors Program at the University of Delaware. She earned her B.A. degree (1969) in psychology at the University of California, Berkeley, and her Ph.D degree (1977) in sociology at Johns Hopkins University.

Her research has focused on individual differences in career development and mental abilities and their relation to social inequality. She has also written about the professional challenges that individual and group differences in stable career-relevant traits create for counselors, personnel selection practitioners, social policymakers, and researchers. She has edited or coedited three special journal issues devoted to intelligence and public life, including the validity and fairness of mental tests in employee selection and the social policy implications of individual and group differences in IQ.

Gottfredson is a fellow of the American Psychological Association, the American Psychological Society, and the Society for Industrial and Organizational Psychology. She also serves as codirector of the Delaware-Johns Hopkins Project for the Study of Intelligence and Society.

Gail Hackett received her B.A. and Ph.D. degrees from Pennsylvania State University. She served on the faculty at the Ohio State University and the University of California, Santa Barbara, and is now professor of counseling psychology in the Division of Psychology in Education at Arizona State, where she is also vice provost for academic personnel.

Her research interests include career self-efficacy theory, social cognitive applications to career counseling and development, gender and ethnicity in career counseling and career development, and feminist approaches to counseling and therapy. She has served as associate editor of the *Journal of Counseling Psychology*, vice president for Division E of the American Educational Research Association, and vice president for scientific affairs of Division 17 of the American Psychological Association. She is a fellow of Divisions 17 and 35 of the American Psychological Association.

Monica Kirkpatrick Johnson is a postdoctoral fellow in the Carolina Population Center at the University of North Carolina-Chapel Hill. She received her Ph.D. in sociology at the University of Minnesota in 1999. Her research interests include family and work, social stratification, and the life course. She is particularly interested in the social and psychological antecedents and consequences of work experiences and adult attainment. Johnson's current research focuses on changes in job values during the transition to adulthood, the consequences of adolescent employment, and the dynamic relationship between values and educational attainment.

Robert W. Lent is a professor of counseling psychology in the Department of Counseling and Personnel Services, University of Maryland. He received his Ph.D. in counseling psychology from the Ohio State University in 1979.

Lent has published extensively on applications of social cognitive theory to academic and career behavior. His other research interests include counselor training and development, psychological wellness, relationship adjustment processes, and promotion of health behaviors. Lent is a fellow of Division 17 (Counseling Psychology) of the American Psychological Association and a recipient of the John L. Holland Award for Outstanding Achievement in Career and Personality Research. He is coeditor, with S. D. Brown, of the *Handbook of Counseling Psychology*. Along with M. L. Savickas, he also coedited *Convergence in Career Development Theories:*

Implications for Science and Practice (1994). He serves as associate editor of the *Journal of Social and Clinical Psychology* and is on the editorial boards of the *Journal of Counseling Psychology* and the *Journal of Vocational Behavior*.

Janet G. Lenz is the associate director for career advising, counseling, and programming in the Career Center at Florida State University and a senior research associate in the FSU Center for the Study of Technology in Counseling and Career Development.

Lenz has been a practicing professional in the career services area since 1976. She received her bachelor's degree in sociology from Virginia Commonwealth University. She received her master's degree in student personnel administration in 1977 and her Ph.D. in counseling and human systems in 1990, both from Florida State University.

In addition to her experience at Florida State University, Lenz has worked as the arts and sciences placement coordinator and career counselor in the Career Center at the University of Texas at Austin and as the assistant director in the Career Planning and Placement Center at the University of North Carolina at Greensboro. She is a nationally certified counselor and career counselor.

Erik J. Luchetta is a Ph.D. student in counseling psychology at the University of Houston. He received his M.Ed. in counseling from Lehigh University. His primary research interest involves applications of social cognitive career theory to the vocational development of adolescents.

Jeylan T. Mortimer is professor of sociology at the University of Minnesota and director of the Life Course Center. She received her B.A. degree from Tufts University and her M.A. and Ph.D. degrees from the University of Michigan.

Her research focus is the social psychology of work, including studies of occupational choice, vocational development in the family and work settings, psychological change in response to work, job satisfaction, work involvement, and the links between work and family life. She is now assessing the effects of adolescent work on the timing and patterning of markers of transition to adulthood. Her recent book, *Arenas of Comfort in Adolescence: A Study of Adjustment in Context* (with Kathleen Thiede Call) examines adolescent development in relation to family, school, peer, and work contexts.

Gary W. Peterson received his B.A. degree from Humboldt State University and her M.A. and Ph.D. degrees from Duke University. He is now professor and training director for the academic program titled Psychological Services in Education, in the College of Education, Florida State University. He is also senior research associate in the Center for the Study of Technology in Counseling and Career Development. He teaches courses in personality assessment, research methods, and consultation and organizational development. His research interests include career problem solving and decision making, career assessment, and test construction. He is a licensed psychologist in Florida.

Robert C. Reardon received his B.S. degree from Texas Lutheran College and his M.S. and Ph.D. degrees from Florida State University. He has held full-time counseling and teaching positions at Florida State University since 1966, when he was first employed in the Counseling Center. Today he is a faculty member in the Division of Student Affairs, and his current position is director of instruction, research, and evaluation in the Career Center. He is a professor in the Department of Human Services and Studies and codirects (with Jim Sampson) the Center for the Study of Technology in Counseling and Career Development.

Matthew H. Richwine is currently an academic professional at Dickinson College. He received his M.Ed. in counseling from Lehigh University. He is currently working on research involving motivation in athletes.

James P. Sampson Jr. is currently a professor in the Department of Human Services and Studies at Florida State University, where he has taught courses in career development and computer applications in counseling since 1982. Since 1986 he has served as codirector of the Center for the Study of Technology in Counseling and Career Development, a research center established at FSU to improve the design and use of computer applications in counseling and guidance. He writes and speaks on the appropriate use of computer technology in counseling and on the use of cognitive strategies in the improvement of career counseling and guidance services.

Prior to joining the faculty at Florida State University, he was a senior counselor and the coordinator of the Career Planning Center at the Student Counseling and Career Planning Center, Georgia Institute of Technology. He is a nationally certified counselor and a nationally certified career counselor. He received his Ph.D. in counselor education from the University of Florida in 1977.

Mark L. Savickas is professor and chair in the Behavioral Sciences Department at the Northeastern Ohio University College of Medicine and adjunct professor of counselor education at Kent State University. He has served as editor for the *Career Development Quarterly* (1991–1998) and is currently editor of the *Journal of Vocational Behavior*. In 1994, he received the John L. Holland Award for Outstanding Achievement in Career and Personality Research from the Counseling Psychology Division (17) of the American Psychological Association. In 1996, he received the Eminent Career Award from the National Career Development Association.

Arnold R. Spokane is professor of education and psychology at Lehigh University. He received his B.A. degree from Ohio University, his M.S. degree from the University of Kentucky, and his Ph.D. degree from the Ohio State University. He received the John Holland Award for Oustanding Achievement in Career and Personality Research from the Division of Counseling Psychology of the American Psychological Association in 1987 and the American Association of

Counseling Development Research Award in 1989. His publications include more than forty articles and fifteen books and book chapters. He has served on the editorial boards of four professional journals as well as on numerous committees and commissions.

Ladislav Valach, a psychologist, is currently at the Division of Psychopathology, Faculty of Philosophy, University of Zurich, Switzerland. He received his Ph.D. at the University of Berne in 1984 and has worked at various institutes of the university and at the University Hospital, the Therapy Centre for Victims of Torture of the Swiss Red Cross, and the Rehabilitation Centre of the Medical Clinic, Buerger Hospital, Solothurn, Switzerland. He has pursued the application of action theory in areas such as occupational career, unemployment, coping with illness and the illness career, utilization of medical services, drug abuse, suicide, stroke rehabilitation, health promotion, and the patient-physician encounter. Valach is the coauthor of *Action Theory: A Primer for Applied Research in the Social Sciences* (Praeger, 2002).

Richard A. Young is professor of counseling psychology at the University of British Columbia. A fellow of the Canadian Psychological Association, his interests include career theory, parent-adolescent interaction, and health psychology. With W. A. Borgen, he edited *Methodological Approaches to the Study of Career* (Praeger, 1990) and (with A. Collin) *Interpreting Career: Hermeneutical Studies of Lives in Context* (Praeger, 1992) and *The Future of Career* (Cambridge University Press, 2000). He is the coauthor (with L. Valach and M. J. Lynam) of *Action Theory: A Primer for Applied Research in the Social Sciences* (Praeger, 2002).

Career Choice and Development

PART ONE

Introduction and Cases

1

Introduction to Theories of Career Development and Choice

Origins, Evolution, and Current Efforts

Duane Brown

"In the wise choice of a vocation there are three broad factors: (1) a clear understanding of yourself, your aptitudes, abilities, interests, ambitions, resources, limitations, and knowledge of their causes; (2) a knowledge of the requirements, conditions of success, advantages and disadvantages, compensation, opportunities, and prospects in different lines of work; (3) true reasoning on the relations of these two groups of facts" (Parsons, 1909, p. 5).

Historical Perspective

Efforts to help people identify appropriate careers can be traced to the fifteenth century, and by the nineteenth century at least sixty-five books had been published on the topic (Zytowski, 1972). The first vocational guidance program emerged in this country in San Francisco in 1888—in Cogswell High School—and subsequently in high schools in Detroit in 1897 (Brewer, 1942). However, the roots of career development theory did not emerge until Frank Parsons

Linda Brooks contributed to this chapter during the preparation of the third edition.

advanced the three-step "formula" quoted at the beginning of the chapter. Parsons's schema for successfully choosing a career cannot be called a theory in the strict sense, but it was the first conceptual framework for career decision making and became the first guide for career counselors.

Psychologically Based Theories

Parsons (1909) believed that if people actively engage in choosing their vocations rather than allow chance to operate in the hunt for a job, they are more satisfied with their careers, employers' costs decrease, and employees' efficiency increases. These rather simple ideas are still at the core of most modern theories of career choice and development. Holland (1985, 1997) and, to an even greater degree, Dawis and Lofquist (1984) have made them the cornerstones of their theories.

During the first part of the twentieth century, career counseling practitioners focused on step two of Parsons's tripartite model: increasing people's understanding of the workplace. However, World War I, the Great Depression of the thirties, and World War II produced a great need to classify people in some meaningful way and place them into occupations in which they could perform satisfactorily. The use of tests to measure intellectual functioning began during World War I, accelerated and expanded to include interests, specific aptitudes, and personality in the twenties; it continues to this day. This explosion of technology also provided a new name for Parsons's model: trait-and-factor theory. Trait-and-factor theory dominated the twenties and thirties and went unchallenged until Carl Rogers (1942, 1951) published his books on client-centered counseling and therapy, in which he questioned the directive approaches advocated by E. G. Williamson (1939). Rogers's challenge turned out to be a modest one and did little to lessen the grip of trait-and-factor thinking on the practice of career counseling.

In 1951, Ginzberg, Ginsburg, Axelrad, and Herma set forth a radically new, psychologically based theory of career development that broke with the static trait-and-factor theory. They posited that career development is a lifelong developmental process. They also suggested that career choices are characterized by compromise and, once made, are for the most part irreversible. Ginzberg (1972) later altered both of these propositions. The theory of Ginzberg and others stimulated an initial flurry of research but had little impact on practice, which remained steadfastly loyal to the trait-and-factor model.

In 1953, Donald Super published his theory of career choice and development. Super's theory included propositions relating to trait-and-factor theory, developmental psychology, and personal construct theory (Kelley, 1955), from which Super derived his ideas about self-concepts and sociological theory. Super continued to revise and refine his theory throughout his life. Although a version of Super's theory appeared posthumously in the third edition of this book (Super, Super, & Savickas, 1996), it is probably accurate to note that the last statement by Super himself appeared in 1990. In that statement, he admitted that the disparate segments of his theory had not been properly cemented together and suggested that building a truly comprehensive model of career choice must be left to future theorists. Super and his followers have had, and continue to have, an impact on career development thinking, research, and practice.

In 1956, Anne Roe published a landmark book, *The Psychology of Occupations*, in which she set forth a theory of career development rooted in Maslow's need theory and in personality theory. She theorized that early childhood environments predisposed children to enter certain occupational groups. She also developed a row (fields of interest) by level (occupational level) classification of occupations. Roe's theory stimulated a number of research projects (see Roe & Lunneborg, 1990), but it never became a major influence on practice.

In 1959, John Holland set forth a comprehensive trait-oriented explanation of vocational choice, which extended the trait-and-factor model of the thirties and forties from a static to a dynamic model. In 1973, he published a fuller version of his theory, which he subsequently revised (Holland, 1985, 1997). His theory has provided the impetus for hundreds of research studies. It has had a tremendous impact on practice because of the instruments he developed, and, all in all, is the most influential model of vocational choice making that is currently in existence.

Numerous new theories of career choice and development have emerged since the fifties. In 1963, Bordin, Nachmann, and Segal published a career development theory grounded in psychodynamic thought. In 1969, Lofquist and Dawis published the first version of their work adjustment theory. In 1979, Krumboltz set forth what he termed a social learning theory of career decision making. Two years later, Gottfredson (1981) published her developmental theory of occupational aspirations. In 1991, Peterson, Sampson, and Reardon set forth their theory of career development, which is based on cognitive theory and relies on an information-processing model to explain the processes involved. In 1994, Lent, Brown, and Hackett published their model of career decision making, which is grounded in social-cognitive theory (Bandura, 1986). In 1996, Brown and Crace published the first version of Brown's values-based model of career decision making. A revision that focuses solely on occupational choice, satisfaction, and success and includes both cultural and work values is scheduled for publication (Brown, 2002).

Sociologically Based Theories

The theories mentioned to this point are psychologically based and have dominated the thinking of psychologists and career counselors alike. However, sociologists have been and still are vitally concerned with career choice making. Their concerns about career choice and development have little to do with career counseling, although they do have implications for certain aspects of practice. For the most part, sociologists have focused on the antecedents to status attainment, which include the socioeconomic status of the family and the gender and race of the individual. Hollingshead (1949), Reissman (1953), and Sewell, Haller, and Strauss (1957) studied sociological variables related to career choice and occupational attainment. Others, such as Musgrave (1967), offered sociologically based theories of occupational choice. The status attainment model of Blau and Duncan (1967) was an attempt to include what the authors termed *cognitive variables*, particularly mental ability and social-psychological processes, into the prediction of occupational attainment.

It is clear that there is no shortage of theories of occupational choice and career development. A significant portion of this book is devoted to the theories now considered most influential in terms of stimulating research and improving practice. Obviously, this is a subjective judgment, but there are guidelines for making this determination. These guidelines are discussed later in the chapter.

How to Judge the Value of Career Choice and Development Theory

How can you judge the worth of a theory? Krumboltz (1994), using a map metaphor, suggests that a good theory, like a well-drawn map, provides a representation of reality—in this case the reality of career choice and development. Krumboltz believes that career development theories, also like maps, contain distortions—the chief one being that they oversimplify the phenomenon being described to facilitate understanding of it. Another obvious source of distortion is the view of the theorist or theorists; theories are no more than a description of the nature of reality, pieced together by a single person or a team of persons.

In order to construct a useful (good) map of the career choice and development process, theorists have many tasks to perform. Chief among these tasks is the selection and definition of constructs that are to be used to describe the phenomena involved in measurable terms. Constructs are measurable if researchers can observe them or can construct instruments that can be used to infer their existence.

In the process of selecting and defining constructs, theorists who use existing theories of human functioning as the basis for their theorizing often retain the terms and definitions of the theory from which they deduce their ideas about career choice and development. For example, I (Brown, 1996, 2002) have retained Rokeach's definition of values (Rokeach, 1973) in the construction of my values-based theory of occupational choice and satisfaction. Theorists may also choose to re-label and redefine the constructs of the original theory. Krumboltz (Mitchell & Krumboltz, 1990) chose this route in the development of his social learning theory of career choice. Krumboltz, who used the social learning theory described by Bandura (1971) as the basis of his theory building, employs the terms *associative learning* and *instrumental learning* to replace the standard terms, *classical conditioning, operant conditioning,* and *observational learning,* which Bandura used. Moreover, he defines *associative learning* as subsuming classical conditioning and observational learning, which not only departs from Bandura but from generally accepted ideas about these two types of learning. Finally, theorists may coin new terms. Holland (1997) used an existing term, *congruence,* to describe the relationship between personality and the work environment. However, he offered new definitions of personality and work environment in his theory.

After central constructs are enumerated and defined, theorists identify how these constructs interact in the career development and choice-making process. This is typically done in theories based on modern philosophy by setting forth series of testable hypotheses or propositions. For example, Super (1990) hypothesized that career choice is the implementation of self-concepts. In order to understand this proposition, it is necessary to have a clear definition of *self-concepts* and *career,* as well as a sense of Super's view of the implementation process; few theories of career development or choice have been developed to this level of specificity. The theories included in this volume have well-defined constructs for the most part, and the interrelationships among the constructs included in the theory are carefully explained. Although it sounds a bit contradictory, given what has just been said, all theories, including the ones in this book, contain ambiguities because of the complexities of the phenomena being discussed.

In well-developed theories, constructs are not only carefully defined but they are assigned levels of importance. Super (1990) states in one of his propositions that work and life satisfactions are dependent on the degree to which an "individual finds adequate outlets for abilities, needs, values, interests, personality traits and self-concepts" (p. 208). Unfortunately, it is impossible to discern which of the constructs involved in this proposition is theoretically most important to life and career satisfaction. Super used other propositions to clarify this matter.

Theorists who wish to set forth well-developed theories have many other criteria to consider. Well-constructed theories should be parsimonious, that is, they should incorporate the smallest number of constructs possible to explain the phenomena being addressed. And well-developed theories are comprehensive. A comprehensive theory of career choice and development explains the process for men and women, minorities and majorities, and individuals throughout the world. As will be shown, many of the current theories have been criticized because they fail the test of comprehensiveness.

Another hallmark of a good theory is that it facilitates the understanding of "what" happens and why it happens. Making a career choice is an event—a "what." Why that choice is made is the more crucial question, particularly if we want to influence the antecedents to occupational choice and thus the choice itself. Some theorists, such as Holland (1997), have paid very little attention to why people develop certain personality types, choosing instead to focus on explanations of why the choice occurs and the outcomes of the choice. Others, such as Roe (1956), have paid little attention to the decision-making process itself, electing to emphasize the antecedents of the choice in their theories.

Well-developed theories also facilitate the understanding of past, present, and future events. Why did most middle-class, white women eschew paid work in favor of the work of a homemaker before 1960? Gottfredson's theory (1981) and the research that resulted from it suggests that, early in their lives, children begin to circumscribe their career options based on the information they get from their environment. Moreover, because young women were inundated with information suggesting that the most appropriate role for women was housewifery, girls began to limit their career options. Her theory also helped career counselors develop and understand what was happening in the present (in 1981) and allowed career counselors and vocational psychologists to make predictions about the future of career choices for women.

Traditionally, theories have been developed by white males of European descent; not surprisingly, the theories have been most useful as a basis for understanding the behavior of white males of European descent. Carefully developed theories are useful for males and females, people from all cultural groups, and people from various socioeconomic strata. Few current theories live up to this expectation (Leong, 1995).

To return to Krumboltz's map metaphor, theories provide researchers and practitioners with "directions" that will be useful in exploring career choice and development. As noted earlier, theories are often stated in terms of testable hypotheses or propositions, particularly if the theory is based on the modern or positivist tradition. Postmodern theories are not constructed using testable hypotheses, for reasons that will become obvious later in the chapter. Testable propositions allow researchers to explore theorists' ideas empirically and advance the level of understanding of career development and occupational choice. One indication of how clearly the theorists have conveyed their ideas is the number of research studies that the theory has generated. However, that number is, in all likelihood, related to other factors, including the ease with which the constructs of the theory can be measured and the availability of instruments to measure them. Therefore, a theory that has great promise may languish because the theorist has not provided researchers with the devices needed to test it.

Finally, practitioners, like researchers, need guidelines they can use as they help their clients make career choices and as they design career development programs. As already noted, theories based in sociological thinking have less utility for practitioners, perhaps because sociologists have not taken the time to extrapolate from theory and research to practice. However, all psychologically based theories should be relevant to practice. Theorists vary widely in the extent to which they are able to translate theoretical constructs into practical applications. It is undoubtedly the case that the reason for the widespread acceptance of trait-and-factor ideas such as those of Holland (1997) has been the ease with which his constructs can be implemented. For example, Holland has provided highly useful tools in the form of inventories and linkages to occupational information sources that enable counselors and psychologists to use his theory with clients.

In order to be classified as "well constructed," a theory must meet numerous criteria. At this juncture, no theory meets all of the standards identified. However, most theorists continue to refine their ideas as new data emerge from research studies and as they consider the phenomena they are trying to describe. For example, in Holland's latest statement of his theory (1997), he attempts to clarify and order the constructs in his theory. In 1984, Super altered his hypotheses about the importance of work in the lives of women and, as already noted, in 1972 Ginzberg made substantial changes to the theory he and his colleagues constructed (Ginzberg et al., 1951). People who develop and study theories realize that theories are neither true or false. They are either supported or not supported by the research they generate. To put it differently, theories are approximations of the complex phenomena that influence career choice and development.

The Issue of Theory Convergence

It was suggested earlier that there are many theories of career development and occupational choice. In 1990, Osipow suggested that the most influential ones converge in important ways. He identified the four dominant theories as (1) Holland's theory of personality and vocational choices (1985, 1997), (2) Krumboltz's social learning theory (Krumboltz, 1979; Mitchell & Krumboltz, 1990), (3) Super's developmental theory (1990), and (4) Dawis and Lofquist's work adjustment theory (1984). He went on to suggest that these theories have the same objective: predicting the degree of fit or congruence between people's personalities and their occupations. In addition, Osipow indicated that if certain bridging constructs between and among these theories could be identified and defined, an integrated theory of career choice and development would emerge.

Osipow's ideas are intriguing and raise the question, Are the major theories of career development converging? If they are converging, books such as this one should focus more on building constructs that bridge theories than on presenting individual theories. The papers resulting from a conference to address the issue raised by Osipow (Savickas & Lent, 1994) provide at least partial answers to the question about the convergence of theories. So do the philosophical underpinning of the theory.

Theories Rooted in Logical Positivism

All theories, including those that focus on occupational choice and career development, spring from two philosophical positions—positions for which there is no rapprochement. Most theories of career choice and development are rooted in logical positivism—a philosophical position asserting that foundations in the form of logical proofs and empirical bases can be built—has dominated the philosophy of science for centuries. The assumptions of logical positivism are relatively straightforward and have been summarized as follows (Collin & Young, 1986; Hoshmand, 1989; Passmore, 1967; Wilber, 1989):

- People can be studied separately from their environments; people can be subdivided into categories for study.

- Human behavior can be objectively observed and measured; behavior operates in a lawful, linear fashion; cause and effect can be inferred.

- The tradition of the scientific method is the accepted paradigm for identifying facts about human behavior.

- The contexts (environments) in which people operate are considered neutral or relatively unimportant; thus, the focus of inquiry should be observable actions of human beings.

One of the assertions listed about logical positivism is probably erroneous, at least insofar as it pertains to theories of career choice and development. That error is in the assertion that people who assume the logical positivist position consider the environment to be neutral. Sociological theorists such as Blau and Duncan (1967) and psychological theorist such as Holland (1997) have spoken to the influence of the environment on the individual, and the cultural context in which occupational choice takes place is receiving increasing attention. Blustein and Ellis (2000), writing from a position that diverges from logical positivism—social constructionism—actually drew on the tools of logical positivist thinkers (for example, analysis of variance, item response theory, and generalizability theory) to generate recommendations for making tests more culturally sensitive. They note that the argument they advance is not new. The fact is, as Blustein and Ellis tacitly admit, logical positivists have long been concerned about the impact of the environment on human behavior and the interaction between the two.

Theories Rooted in Social Constructionism

Although logical positivism is still the dominant philosophical position held by social scientists, an increasing number are rejecting it in favor of another philosophical position: social constructionism (Collin & Young, 1986; Hoshmand, 1989; Wilber, 1989). The essential tenet of social constructionism is that people actively construct their own reality; they are not simply passive recipients of it. Wilber (1989) summarizes some of the sentiments of the social constructionists when he indicates that much of the knowledge we possess, including knowledge about music, art, and philosophy, cannot be verified in the sense that logical positivism requires. He goes on to indicate that logical positivists would also have to exclude purpose, values, and meaning from the realm of knowledge because they cannot be empirically determined. The assumptions of the social constructionists position are as follows:

- All aspects of the universe are interconnected; it is impossible to separate figure from ground, subject from object, people from their environments.

- There are no absolutes; thus human functioning cannot be reduced to laws or principles, and cause and effect cannot be inferred.

- Human behavior can only be understood in the context in which it occurs.

- The subjective frame of reference of human beings is the only legitimate source of knowledge. Events occur outside human beings. As individuals understand their environments and participate in these events, they define themselves and their environments.

Passmore (1967) undoubtedly overstates the case when he asserts that positivism is dead in science. Patton (1997), a long-time advocate of the constructivist position, admits that the research methodologies associated with both positions have a place. So logical positivism is very much alive, at least among the theorists and researchers who focus on career development and occupational choice.

The disparate philosophical positions that underpin many of the current theories of occupational choice and career development cannot be bridged as easily as Osipow (1990) suggests if the theories are based on different philosophical positions. However, given that his observations focus on theories that were predicated on logical positivist philosophy, perhaps the possibility of developing an integrated theory within the logical positivist frame of reference exists. Is this possible? Dawis (1994) addresses this issue. He writes, "Although theory convergence and even theory integration is possible, a unified theory is will-o'-the-wisp" (p. 42). Holland (1994), also addressing the idea of a unified theory, states, "It appears more productive to renovate old theories or strategies than to stitch together an integrated theory" (p. 50).

Stitching together theories may not be as easy as it appears on the surface. As noted earlier, theories are made up of constructs that are often borrowed from other psychological theories. Although different theories may employ exactly the same terms (for example, *self-concept*) they may incorporate many different definitions of those terms. As noted earlier, Osipow (1990) indicates that the theories constructed by Holland (1985, 1997), Super (1990), Dawis and Lofquist (1984), and Krumboltz (1979) are all aimed at predicting personality-occupation congruence. The problem is that each theorist employing the term *personality* has a different definition, and it is unlikely that they could agree on a single definition. For example, Holland's conceptualization of personality incorporates his six personality subtypes (Realistic, Investigative, Artistic, Social, Enterprising, and Conventional) (Holland, 1997), whereas Super (1990) focuses on self-concepts as the basis for his ideas about personality (see the contributors to Savickas and Lent [1994] for more on this topic). Moreover, the theorists identified by Osipow do not agree on the definition of *congruence* and may not agree that their primary concern is predicting congruence.

In summary, there seems to be little convergence in theorizing in the area of career development and occupational choice. With the emergence of social constructionism as a viable force in vocational psychology, convergence among theories and the development of an integrated theory seems less likely today than ever.

How Theories Were Selected

This is the fourth edition of *Career Choice and Development*. In 1982, when the idea for the first edition (Brown et al., 1984) began to take form, Brooks and I wanted to encourage leading theorists to present their latest thinking on career choice and development processes. In the second edition, we were more concerned with the application of the theories. Accordingly, contributors, with the exception of Hotchkiss and Borow (1990), were asked to tell how they would provide career counseling to the "Case of K." When considering how to best proceed with the third edition (Brown et al., 1996), we concluded that it would not be possible to include all theories of career choice and development in the book and that only theories that were substantially influencing research or practice would be included, along with some of the theories that were emerging at that time—a conceptualization we have retained for this edition. The most difficult task for those of us working on both the third edition and this edition has been deciding which theories are influential. This was determined, in part, by informally surveying the leading scholars in the field. It was also determined by reviewing leading journals and determining which theories are stimulating current research. On this basis, one theory that was included in the first three editions (Krumboltz's social learning theory) was deleted.

It has also been the intent of this book from the outset to stimulate theory development; thus some space has been dedicated to new or emerging ideas and theories. This was also true in the third edition. We hoped that a second constructivist theory would be included in this edition; unfortunately, the author who initially agreed to provide the chapter found it impossible to do so.

In the first three editions, Brooks and I asked contributors to tell how their theories applied to women and minorities because we hoped to stimulate thinking in this area. I do not think we have been very successful in stimulating theorizing that is applicable to people other than white males. Thus criticism of occupational choice and career development theories for being less than inclusive, such as that of Leong (1995), seems valid. Leong notes that little progress has been made toward making theories of career choice and development applicable to minorities. My chapter in this volume is an attempt to address career choice and development issues of women and minorities using a values-based approach. Additionally, all contributors to this volume have been asked to address issues involved in the career choice and development of women and minorities. As I noted earlier, a good theory is comprehensive in that it is applicable to all types of people. No extant theory meets this criterion.

Readers may wish to return to earlier editions of this book (Brown et al., 1984, 1990, 1996) to review the theories that have been deleted from earlier editions. These are

Ann Roe's theory (1984; Roe & Lunneborg, 1990)

Psychodynamic theory (Bordin, 1984, 1990)

Ginzberg's presentation of the developmental theory developed by Ginzberg, Ginsburg, Axelrad, & Herma (1984)

Krumboltz's learning approach to career decision making (Mitchell & Krumboltz, 1984, 1990, 1996)

The individualistic perspective of David Tiedeman and Anna Miller-Tiedeman (1984, 1990)

Super's theory (1984, 1990)

An interpretation of sociological and economic theory (Hotchkiss & Borow, 1984, 1990, 1996)

Each of these theories has merit, but for the most part none meets the criteria for inclusion into this volume. The exception is Super's life-span, life-space approach to career development. His theory is still influential, and Savickas includes a summary of it in his chapter later in this volume. However, the theory is unique to Super (1990), and, in my view, his own writing is the best source of information about the theory.

As was true in the second and third editions, each author, except for Johnson and Mortimer in this edition and Hotchkiss and Borow in the third edition, has been asked to describe how he or she would proceed to provide career counseling to a client whom we present via a case study. In this edition, two cases are presented. One of the clients, "E," is a white European female; the other is "K," an Asian American male. These case studies can be found in Chapter Two. Readers may wish to read these cases prior to reading the suggestions advanced by the authors operating from various theoretical perspectives.

Finally, one of the most difficult decisions for the editor is how to best organize the book. In this edition, three dynamic trait-and-factor theories are included in the first section, two learning theories in the second section, and two theories rooted in social constructionism in the third section; two chapters devoted to more than one theory can be found in the fourth chapter. These chapters are devoted to developmental theories of career development and to sociological explanations of occupational choice and attainment. It would be easy to infer that there is some status associated with the ordering of the chapter. This is not the case. Holland's theory, as already noted, is extremely important, both from the standpoint of research and practice. However, the cognitive theories included in the second section are generating a great deal of interest among practitioners and researchers alike. Moreover, since the early 1950s when Ginzberg et al. (1951) and Super (1953) set forth their theories, there has been a substantial amount of interest in developmental theory. Although many of the users of this book will be counselors and psychologists, the sociological theory chapter contains information that is not found in the psychological theory chapters—information that deserves the attention of practitioners and researchers alike. In the final analysis, the order of presentation used here is arbitrary.

Summary

Theorizing about career choice and development dates back to the turn of the twentieth century, and the interest in the area has grown steadily over that time period. Although more than a dozen theories have emerged over time, few have stood the test of time, which is the ultimate gauge of a theory's worth. Currently, three or four theories dominate thinking and research, but the trait-and-factor models rooted in the early theorizing of Frank Parsons dominate practice. There has been speculation that perhaps the major theories are about to converge into a single model of career choice and development. This seems unlikely.

References

Bandura, A. (1971). *Social learning theory*. Morristown, NJ: General Learning Press.

Bandura, A. (1986). *Social foundations of thought and action: A social cognitive theory*. Englewood Cliffs, NJ: Prentice Hall.

Blau, P. M., & Duncan, O. D. (1967). *The American occupational structure*. New York: Wiley.

Blustein, D. L., & Ellis, M. V. (2000). The cultural context of career assessment. *Journal of Career Assessment, 8,* 379–390.

Bordin, E. S. (1984). Psychodynamic model of career choice and satisfaction. In D. Brown, L. Brooks, & Associates, *Career choice and development* (pp. 94–137). San Francisco: Jossey-Bass.

Bordin, E. S. (1990). Psychodynamic model of career choice and satisfaction. In D. Brown, L. Brooks, & Associates, *Career choice and development* (2nd ed., pp. 102–144). San Francisco: Jossey-Bass.

Bordin, E. S., Nachmann, B., & Segal, S. J. (1963). An articulated framework for vocational development. *Journal of Counseling Psychology, 10,* 107–116.

Brewer, J. M. (1942). *History of vocational guidance: Origins of early development*. New York: HarperCollins.

Brown, D. (1996). A values-based, holistic model of career and life-role decision making. In D. Brown, L. Brooks, & Associates, *Career choice and development* (3rd ed., pp. 332–337). San Francisco: Jossey-Bass.

Brown, D. (2002). The role of work and cultural values in occupational choice, satisfaction, and success: A theoretical statement. *Journal of Counseling and Development, 80,* 48–56.

Brown, D., Brooks, L., & Associates (1984). *Career choice and development*. San Francisco: Jossey-Bass.

Brown, D., Brooks, L., & Associates (1990). *Career choice and development* (2nd ed.). San Francisco: Jossey-Bass.

Brown, D., Brooks, L., & Associates (1996). *Career choice and development* (3rd ed.). San Francisco: Jossey-Bass.

Brown, D., & Crace, R. K. (1996). Values in life role choices and outcomes: A conceptual model. *Career Development Quarterly, 44*, 211–223.

Collin, A., & Young, R. A. (1986). New directions for theories of career. *Human Relations, 39*, 837–853.

Dawis, R. V. (1994). The theory of work adjustment as a convergent theory. In M. L. Savickas & R. W. Lent (Eds.), *Convergence in career development theory* (pp. 9–32). Palo Alto, CA: CPP Books.

Dawis, R. V. (1996). Work adjustment theory and person-environment-congruence counseling. In D. Brown, L. Brooks, & Associates, *Career choice and development* (3rd ed., pp. 75–120). San Francisco: Jossey-Bass.

Dawis, R. V., & Lofquist, L. (1984). *A psychological theory of work adjustment*. Minneapolis: University of Minnesota.

Ginzberg, E. (1972). Toward a theory of occupational choice: A restatement. *Vocational Guidance Quarterly, 20*, 169–176.

Ginzberg, E. (1984). Career development. In D. Brown, L. Brooks, & Associates. *Career choice and development* (pp. 169–191). San Francisco: Jossey-Bass.

Ginzberg, E., Ginsburg, S., Axelrad, S., & Herma, J. (1951). *Occupational choice: An approach to a general theory*. New York: Columbia University Press.

Gottfredson, L. (1981). Circumscription and compromise. *Journal of Counseling Psychology, 28*, 545–579.

Holland, J. L. (1959). A theory of vocational choice. *Journal of Counseling Psychology, 59*, 35–45.

Holland, J. L. (1973). *Making vocational choices: A theory of careers*. Englewood Cliffs, NJ: Prentice Hall.

Holland, J. L. (1985). *Making vocational choices: A theory of careers* (2nd ed.). Odessa, FL: Psychological Assessment Resources.

Holland, J. L. (1994). Separate but unequal is better. In M. L. Savickas & R. W. Lent (Eds.), *Convergence in career development theory* (pp. 45–52). Palo Alto, CA: CPP Books.

Holland, J. L. (1997). *Making vocational choices: A theory of careers* (3rd ed.). Odessa, FL: Psychological Assessment Resources.

Hollingshead, A. B. (1949). *Elmtown's youth*. New York: Wiley.

Hoshmand, L. (1989). Alternate research paradigms. *The Counseling Psychologist, 17*, 3–80.

Hotchkiss, L., & Borow, H. (1984). Sociological perspectives on career choice and attainment. In D. Brown, L. Brooks, & Associates, *Career choice and development* (pp. 137–168). San Francisco: Jossey-Bass.

Hotchkiss, L., & Borow, H. (1990). Sociological perspectives on work and career development. In D. Brown, L. Brooks, & Associates, *Career choice and development* (2nd ed., pp. 262–307). San Francisco: Jossey-Bass.

Hotchkiss, L., & Borow, H. (1996). Sociological perspectives on work and career development. In D. Brown, L. Brooks, & Associates, *Career choice and development* (3rd ed., pp. 281–336). San Francisco: Jossey-Bass.

Kelley, G. A. (1955). *The psychology of personal constructs*. New York: W. W. Norton.

Krumboltz, J. D. (1979). A social learning theory of career decision-making. In A. M. Mitchell, G. B. Jones, & J. D. Krumboltz (Eds.), *Social learning and career decision-making*. Cranston, RI: Carroll Press.

Krumboltz, J. D. (1994). Improving career development theory from a social learning theory perspective. In M. L. Savickas & R. W. Lent (Eds.), *Convergence in career development theory* (pp. 9–32). Palo Alto, CA: CPP Books.

Lent, R. W., Brown, S. D., & Hackett, G. (1994). Toward a unifying social cognitive theory of career and academic interest, choice, and performance. *Journal of Vocational Behavior, 45*, 79–122.

Lent, R. W., Brown, S. D., & Hackett, G. (1996). Career development from a social-cognitive perspective. In D. Brown, L. Brooks, & Associates, *Career choice and development* (3rd ed.). San Francisco: Jossey-Bass.

Leong, F. T. L. (1995). *Career development and the vocational behavior of ethnic minorities*. Hillsdale, NJ: Erlbaum.

Lofquist, L., & Dawis, R. V. (1969). *Adjustment to work*. East Norwich, CT: Appleton-Century-Crofts.

Miller-Tiedeman, A., & Tiedeman, D. V. (1990). Career decision making: An individualistic perspective. In D. Brown, L. Brooks, & Associates, *Career choice and development* (2nd ed., pp. 308–337). San Francisco: Jossey-Bass.

Mitchell, L. K., & Krumboltz, J. D. (1984). A social learning approach to career decision making: Krumboltz's theory. In D. Brown, L. Brooks, & Associates, *Career choice and development* (pp. 235–280). San Francisco: Jossey-Bass.

Mitchell, L. K., & Krumboltz, J. D. (1990). A social learning approach to career decision making: Krumboltz's theory. In D. Brown, L. Brooks,

& Associates, *Career choice and development* (2nd ed., pp. 145–196). San Francisco: Jossey-Bass.

Mitchell, L. K., & Krumboltz, J. D. (1996). Krumboltz's learning theory of career choice and counseling. In D. Brown, L. Brooks, & Associates, *Career choice and development* (3rd ed., pp. 233–280). San Francisco: Jossey-Bass.

Musgrave, P. W. (1967). Toward a sociological theory of occupational choice. *Sociological Review, 15*, 33–45.

Osipow, S. H. (1990). Convergence in theories of career choice and development: Review and prospect. *Journal of Vocational Behavior, 36*, 122–131.

Parsons, F. (1909). *Choosing a vocation.* Boston: Houghton Mifflin.

Passmore, J. (1967). Logical positivism. In P. Edwards (Ed.), *The encyclopedia of philosophy:* Vol. 5. New York: Macmillan.

Patton, M. Q. (1997). *Utilization-focused evaluation* (3rd ed.). Thousand Oaks, CA: Sage.

Peterson, G. W., Sampson, J. P., & Reardon, R. C. (1991). *Career development and services: A cognitive approach.* Pacific Grove, CA: Brooks/Cole.

Peterson, G. W., Sampson, J. P., Jr., Reardon, R. C., & Lenz, J. G. (1996). A cognitive information processing approach to career problem solving and decision making. In D. Brown, L. Brooks, & Associates, *Career choice and development* (3rd ed., pp. 423–476). San Francisco: Jossey-Bass.

Reissman, L. (1953). Levels of aspiration and social class. *American Sociological Review, 18*, 233–242.

Roe, A. (1956). *The psychology of occupations.* New York: Wiley.

Roe, A. (1984). Personality development and career choice. In D. Brown, L. Brooks, & Associates, *Career choice and development* (pp. 31–53). San Francisco: Jossey-Bass.

Roe, A., & Lunneborg, P. (1990). Personality development and career choice. In D. Brown, L. Brooks, & Associates, *Career choice and development* (2nd ed., pp. 68–101). San Francisco: Jossey-Bass.

Rogers, C. R. (1942). *Counseling and psychotherapy.* Boston: Houghton Mifflin.

Rogers, C. R. (1951). *Client-centered therapy.* Boston: Houghton Mifflin.

Rokeach, M. (1973). *The nature of human values.* New York: Free Press.

Savickas, M. L., & Lent, R. W. (Eds.). (1994). *Convergence in career development theories.* Palo Alto, CA: CPP Books.

Sewell, W. H., Haller, A. O., & Strauss, M. A. (1957). Social status and educational and occupational aspirations. *American Sociological Review, 22,* 67–73.

Super, D. E. (1953). A theory of vocational development. *American Psychologist, 30,* 88–92.

Super, D. E. (1984). A life-span, life space approach to career development. In D. Brown, L. Brooks, & Associates, *Career choice and development* (pp. 192–234). San Francisco: Jossey-Bass.

Super, D. E. (1990). A life-span, life space approach to career development. In D. Brown, L. Brooks, & Associates, *Career choice and development* (2nd ed., pp. 197–261). San Francisco: Jossey-Bass.

Super, D. E., Super, C., & Savickas, M. L. (1996). A life- span, life-space approach to careers. In D. Brown, L. Brooks, & Associates, *Career choices and development* (3rd ed., pp. 121–178). San Francisco: Jossey-Bass.

Tiedeman, D. V., & Miller-Tiedeman, A. (1984). Career decision-making: An individualistic perspective: In D. Brown, L. Brooks, & Associates, *Career choice and development* (pp. 281–310). San Francisco: Jossey-Bass.

Tiedeman, D. V., & Miller-Tiedeman, A. (1990). Career decision-making: An individualistic perspective: In D. Brown, L. Brooks, & Associates, *Career choice and development* (2nd ed., pp. 308–337). San Francisco: Jossey-Bass.

Wilber, K. (1989). Let's nuke these transpersonalists: A reply to Ellis. *Journal of Counseling and Development, 67,* 332–335.

Williamson, E. G. (1939). *How to counsel students.* New York: McGraw-Hill.

Zytowski, D. G. (1972). Four hundred years before Parsons. *Personnel and Guidance Journal, 50,* 443–450.

2

Case Studies

Duane Brown

All contributors to this volume were asked to review the two cases in this chapter and respond to several questions, including how they would provide career counseling to the students described. The questions posed to the contributors were:

What additional assessment data would you want as you provide career counseling to K? To E? Why?

What additional background data would you solicit from K and E as you began the career counseling process, if any? Why would you want these data?

Are there specific cultural or gender issues that you would want to address as you provided career counseling to K? To E?

Based on the data presented, would you be concerned about mental health issues in either case?

How would you proceed to provide career counseling to K and E, using your theoretical explanation of career development as the basis for your answer?

The Case of K

Here are the background data for this case.

Background Data

K is a seventeen-year-old, Japanese-Chinese-American male. He graduated from high school five months ago and will be enrolling in college at the beginning of the spring semester. He did not enroll in the fall because he had applied too late to be admitted. When asked why he decided to go to college, he replied, "A friend of mine thought it would be a good idea." K is bright, with SAT scores of 700 (verbal) and 710 (quantitative), but he is an underachiever in the sense that his grades vary considerably. K's primary hobbies are playing the drums and skateboarding.

K currently works as a librarian's assistant—a job he characterizes as "his best job so far," and the pay is, according to him, "pretty good." He has held other part-time jobs, including that of paperboy, which he liked because he was making money, receptionist, which he liked because it was easy, and book-shelver at the library. He disliked that intensely because it was boring.

K was asked to estimate his chances of finishing college on a 0 to 100 percent scale. He estimated that there is a 60 percent probability that he will complete a college education, not because he cannot do the work but because of his work habits. He admits to being a procrastinator; he gets behind in his schoolwork and then becomes discouraged and discontinues his efforts. However, he is going to college at this time on his own volition because he thinks he will be sorry later in his life if he does not go now. Although K ranks "independence" as one of his most important values, he believes he does better when others set the agenda for him.

K's father is a research scientist, and his mother is a typist. Both have expressed an interest in K attending college, but they are leaving the matter of K's occupational choice strictly up to him. He has one sibling—a brother who is ten years younger.

K admits that he has very little information about careers at this time and expresses an interest in knowing more about technology careers and architecture. He also indicates that he has ruled out all health occupation careers because he doesn't like biology or the idea of working in this field.

Assessment Data

K was asked to rate his confidence in his ability to do well in each of the following subjects, using a 1 to 10 scale, with 1 indicating that he has little confidence in his ability to do well in the subject and a 10 indicating that he is almost totally confident that he could do well if he decided to do so. His self-efficacy ratings follow.

Educational Self-Efficacy Ratings

Math	9
Chemistry	7
Physics	6
English composition	7
English literature	5
Biology	6
History	7
Art (drawing)	6
Music (the study of)	5

K's Self-Directed Search Results

1. Occupational Daydreams

    Something with computers and a lot of money

    Pro skateboarder

    Doing video filming and editing (AES) Architect (AIR)

2. His SDS is CRI/A, with C and R being virtually tied (27 and 26, respectively); I and A were tied (17). His lowest score was on the Social scale (4).

K's Life Values Inventory Results

1. Belonging. It is important to be accepted by others and feel included.

2. Financial Prosperity. It is important to be successful at making money or buying property.

3. Independence. It is important to make your own decisions and do things your own way.

4. Achievement. It is important to challenge yourself and work hard to improve.

5. Privacy. It is important to have time alone.

6. Health and Activity. It is important to be healthy and physically active.

Values Listed as Unimportant (not ranked)

Scientific Understanding. It is important to use scientific principles to understand and solve problems.

Concern for the Environment. It is important to protect and preserve the environment.

Spirituality. It is important to have spiritual beliefs and believe that you are part of something greater than yourself.

Responsibility. It is important to be dependable and trustworthy.

Values That K Expects to Satisfy

1. Job
Financial Prosperity
Achievement
Independence

2. Student

   Independence

3. Family and Important Relationships

   Belonging

   Concern for Others. The well-being of others is important.

   Loyalty to Family or Group. It is important to follow the traditions and expectations of your family or group.

   Responsibility (On the LVI (Life Values Inventory), K said he
   would buy his family a house in Hawaii and pay for his friend's
   car if he won the lottery.)

4. Leisure and Community Activities

   Achievement

   Health and Activity

   Creativity

K responded to a series of open-ended questions in the following manner:

Who do you admire?	Professional skateboarders
Who would you like to pattern your life after?	Professional skateboarders
Who did you admire when you were growing up?	I admire professional skate-boarders and would like to pattern my life after theirs. When I was growing up I admired my cousin because we could do things together. He initiated activities. (K was not sure how he was like or different from his cousin.) However, on the LVI he identified a 10th-grade English teacher as some-one he admired because he had a unique way of teaching and was

well liked. K believes that the values of the person he admired were probably Creativity and Independence.

Do you read any magazines regularly? Which ones? What do you like about these magazines? Do you have any favorite TV programs?

I read skateboard magazines regularly and enjoy the pictures in them the most. "The Simpsons" is my favorite television program.

What do you like to do with your free time? What are your hobbies? What do you enjoy about these hobbies?

Skateboarding is my favorite hobby, although playing drums and video games are also pastimes. I enjoy these hobbies because of the skill it takes to do them.

Do you have a favorite saying or motto? Tell me a saying you remember hearing.

I do not have a favorite saying or motto. The only saying I remember is, "Don't take any wooden nickels." (On the LVI, when asked if he lived his life by a saying or motto, K responded, "I don't live my life by silly sayings.")

What are your favorite subjects in school? Why? What subjects do you hate? Why?

Math is my favorite subject because I am good at it. I hate English because it was hard for me to be creative and thus writing is difficult.

Tell me the earliest recollections you can remember happening in your life.

My earliest recollections were learning to ride a bike (I felt scared); going to pre-school (I felt excited); learning to swim with an instructor (I don't remember an emotional reaction). (From the LVI) My peak experience: graduating from high school.

The Case of E

Here are the background data for this case.

Background Data

E is a twenty-year-old sophomore at a large state-supported university, where she is pursuing a double major in history and religion. Her goal in career counseling is to narrow her choices to a few viable occupational alternatives so that she can feel more comfortable about her educational plans. She feels that the information she has gained thus far from a career exploration class is too general and suggests too many options; the result is that she feels confused. At this time, she has "pretty much ruled out scientific and math paths to careers," partially because these are more difficult for her. However, E is bright and can pursue any career she chooses. Her SAT score was 1350 at the time she graduated from high school, and she has a GPA of 3.8. E has no physical limitations that would limit her career choices.

E has held a number of part-time jobs, including working at Sea World when she was sixteen, serving as an assistant to the VP of a regional grocery store—a job she describes as being a "go-fer"—and as an exercise physiologist at a corporate fitness center. In the latter job, she taught strength training, took blood pressure, assisted in fitness testing, including EKGs, and developed fitness programs for members.

Both of E's parents were trained as attorneys. Her mother stayed at home with the children, although she has done some legal work on an individual basis. Her father is a practicing attorney. They have expressed an interest in her completing a bachelor's degree, but they have not expressed opinions about expected career paths. E has a fifteen-year-old brother and a seventeen-year-old sister.

Assessment Data

E was asked to rate her confidence in her ability to do well in each of the following subjects, using a 1 to 10 scale, with 1 indicating that she has little confidence in her ability to do well in the subject and a 10 indicating that she is almost totally confident that she could do well if she decided to do so.

Educational Self-Efficacy Ratings

Math	6
Chemistry	3
Physics	2
English composition	9
English literature	9
Biology	8
History	10
Art (drawing)	1
Music (the study of)	7

Self-Directed Search Results

1. Occupational Daydreams
   Lawyer (ESI)
   Judge (ESA)
   Writer (AIE)
   Teacher (SAE)
2. Holland Code S (38) E (31) C (27). Lowest score was R (4).

Life Values Inventory Results

1. Responsibility. It is important to be dependable and trustworthy.
2. Concern for Others. The well-being of others is important.
3. Health and Activity. It is important to be healthy and physically active.
4. Spirituality. It is important to have spiritual beliefs and to believe that you are a part of something greater than yourself.

5. Belonging. It is important to be accepted by others and to feel included.

6. Achievement. It is important to challenge yourself and to work hard to improve.

Values That Are Unimportant

Privacy. It is important to have time alone.

Values E Expects to Have Satisfied

Job: Responsibility, Concern for Others, Financial Prosperity

Student: Belonging, Achievement

Family and Important Relationships: Belonging, Concern for Others

Leisure and Community Activities: Health and Activity, Belonging

E responded to a series of open-ended questions as follows:

Who do you admire? Who would you like to pattern your life after? Who did you admire when you were growing up? Who are you like? Who are you different from?

I admire leaders who show compassion and vision for changing things for the betterment of others, such as Pope John Paul II. I would like to pattern my life after my father's female law partner, who has great balance in her family and work life. I wanted to be like Sandra Day O'Connor, a pioneer for women, but I don't know if I could handle a high-stress occupation without taking it out on my family.

Do you read any magazines regularly? Which ones? What do you like about these magazines? Do you have any favorite TV programs?

I usually read *In Style*, which is very glamorous, and *Newsweek*, which keeps me informed on world events. I also read *Fitness for Health* tips and ideas. I don't watch TV that much, but I like the real-life shows like "Wedding Story" and "Dating Story."

What do you like to do with your free time? What are your hobbies? What do you enjoy about these hobbies?

I like to keep in touch with friends by calling or writing them. I'm really a very structured person, so I don't necessarily differentiate between meeting someone for lunch and free time because that is fun for me. I love to listen to music and go to concerts, so that is definitely a hobby. I have a lot of admiration for musicians, and it is also fun to organize and plan for going out with people who like the same kind of music.

Do you have a favorite saying or motto? Tell me a saying you remember hearing?

I love sayings and tidbits of wisdom. I have a daily calendar with sayings about friendship. I love the saying, "Every cloud has a silver lining." The other day my calendar had a good one: "The only people you should get even with are the ones who helped you."

What are your favorite subjects in school? Why? What subjects do you hate? Why?

In high school I always enjoyed English classes because they were the ones that were most open to individual thought. Although I'm not always able to share my opinions verbally, I enjoy thinking and listening to others' opinions. I really don't like chemistry or physics, I think because of all the lab work in them both. I don't always learn best by doing, nor do I easily understand scientific formulas.

Tell me the earliest recollections you can remember happening in your life.

I remember crying in the car when I had to stay at my grandparents' house when my brother was going to be born (three and one-half). At two, I remember having fun hiding my dad's shoes while he was at work and making a game of him finding them when he came home. When I was three, I remember going to a department store with my dad to get a swing set but running off to look at the stuffed animals when he was talking to someone. I didn't realize that I had scared him so much.

PART TWO

Sociological Perspective

3

Career Choice and Development from a Sociological Perspective

Monica Kirkpatrick Johnson, Jeylan T. Mortimer

Sociologists are interested in career choice and development primarily because of their consequences for socioeconomic inequality and mobility. Occupation is a strong determinant of a person's status within the community, earnings, wealth, and style of life. To the extent that young people follow the same or similar occupations as their parents, the inequalities linked to work will be perpetuated from one generation to the next. Thus sociological interest in occupational choice initially focused on mechanisms of intergenerational mobility—what came to be called the process of stratification.

Initial work examined the linkage between fathers' and sons' occupations. Blau and Duncan (1967) identified educational attainment as a pivotal mediating variable, explaining the linkage of fathers' education and occupation and sons' occupational destinations. Subsequent studies in the status attainment tradition have investigated the ways in which gender, race, ethnicity, community size, and features of the family of origin, such as its intact character, the number of siblings, and birth order, influence the process of stratification (see Kerckhoff, 1995b, for a review). Over time, the complexity of the attainment process was increasingly recognized. For example, because of discrimination in the labor market, opportunities are not the same for men and women, whites and minorities, and these must be taken into account in models that purport to represent the attainment process.

A major development in this tradition was the work of Sewell and Hauser (1976; Hauser, 1971). They added achievement-related social psychological variables to the model of attainment (Duncan, Featherman, & Duncan, 1972; Gordon, 1972; Kerckhoff, 1974; Turner, 1962). Their revised model included academic ability and performance, as well as encouragement of educational goals by significant others, including parents, teachers, and friends. Adolescents' aspirations and plans, with respect to future educational and occupational attainment, came to assume central importance (see Mortimer, 1996, for a review). Early on, however, it was also recognized that aspirations may have limited consequences in situations of constrained opportunity. One sociologist questioned the presumed causal process through which aspirations influence achievements. In view of strong constraints on attainment, he concluded that work ambitions are "products of occupations that individuals are entering rather than determinants of patterns that careers take" (Roberts, 1968, p. 176).

Sociological studies have thus focused during the past several decades almost exclusively on the vertical (prestige) dimension of occupational choice, as this is linked most closely to subsequent placement in the socioeconomic hierarchy. Insofar as the individual's motivations and goals are considered, these tend to be restricted to aspirations for educational attainment and the prestige levels of occupational aspirations.

In contrast, psychologically oriented studies of career choice give primary emphasis to the personality characteristics that predispose an individual to seek a career of a given type. Historically, psychologists have exhibited greater interest than sociologists in a person's interests, values, personality type, and orientations, as well as self-concept, as determinants of particular occupational choices (Strong, 1955; Holland, 1964; Super, Starishevsky, Matlin, & Jordaan, 1963; Ginzberg, Ginsburg, Axelrad, & Herma, 1951). Vocational psychologists have been primarily concerned with the degree of "fit" between person and job. If there is a closer fit, in terms of the interests, needs, and personalities of the person and the experiences, rewards, and challenges that a job has to offer, it is expected that there will be greater job satisfaction and fulfillment and a lesser tendency to change jobs over the course of the career. These emphases in the psychological literature are reflected in more recent work (for example, see Vondracek, Lerner, & Schulenberg, 1986, and many of the other chapters in this volume).

In recent decades, these divergent interests have come together to a large extent. Psychologists have become more interested in the social settings that influence and constrain individual action (Bronfenbrenner, 1979), including institutional time tables for important life transitions that make persons who are, for whatever reason, "off time," at a disadvantage (Heckhausen, 1999). Sociologists have recognized that a much broader range of psychological orientations, in addition to educational and occupational aspirations and plans, influence vocational directions and the capacity to be successful in the world of work (Mortimer, 1994, 1996). These include occupational values, that is, preferences with respect to intrinsic, extrinsic, and people-oriented rewards; to a particular work ethic; and to a personal sense of efficacy or control. For example, researchers have recently considered the determinants of efficacy—particularly with respect to future economic matters such as having a well-paying job and owning a home, which are located in the family, the school, and the adolescent workplace (Grabowski, Mortimer, & Call, 2001).

Moreover, these various orientations, including occupational values, have been considered important by sociologists, insofar as they influence nonvertical dimensions of occupational mobility. They have increasingly recognized that a conceptualization of work in terms of a unidimensional hierarchy of occupational prestige is inadequate, both in terms of its characterization of the occupational structure and its representation of intergenerational mobility. For example, the tendency for young people to choose work that is similar in function or context to that of their parents cannot be addressed if only a unidimensional prestige hierarchy is considered. Mortimer (1974) found evidence that occupational "inheritance" occurred along the lines of functional tasks (related to people as opposed to data or things) and was influenced by the entrepreneurial versus bureaucratic character of the work setting. Moreover, her later findings (1976) indicate that intergenerational value transmission is implicated in the tendency for sons of businessmen to enter business and managerial occupations and the sons of professionals to choose professional work.

Whereas psychological and sociological views of career choice have been converging, as Mortimer's work illustrates, sociologists are more likely than psychologists to be concerned with the ways in which location in the social structure, as defined by parental occupation, education, income, gender, race, or ethnicity, influence diverse orientations toward work. Moreover, sociologists are interested in the ways that social institutions affect occupational choices, work orientations, and attainments, as a person moves through the life course.

A life course approach (Elder & O'Rand, 1995) sensitizes us to the fact that occupational choice, as well as vocational development, is not a one-time event or a process that is confined to the early years of life. Instead, people continue to make occupational choices and career decisions as they move through their careers, and this, as we will discuss later, has become increasingly the case among contemporary cohorts. The contexts in which people live their lives and pursue their educational and economic goals (for example, primary and secondary educational institutions, the labor market, and their family circumstances) provide opportunities and challenges, as well as constraints, to their careers. We will examine several of these institutional settings later in this chapter.

The combination of individual action in response to goals, preferences, and values, as well as the workings of institutional settings that determine structural opportunity, yield diverse lifelong career patterns. These may be examined in terms of their continuity, stability, upward versus downward movement, rewards, and eventual attainment.

Vocational Development, Career Choice, and Mobility in Social Context

This section examines some of the most important social contexts that influence vocational development and mobility.

Cross-National Variation

Career choice and development are profoundly affected by broad, cross-national differences in the structure of education and work and the connections between these institutions. As Kerckhoff (1996) points out, educational systems can be characterized by the extent to which they (1) are differentiated by the distinct occupational futures of students and (2) offer vocation-specific credentials. In the United States, most high school students pursue a general sequence of courses that are oriented to college preparation, and all students completing high school, regardless of their track placement or ability grouping or the quality of their schools, receive general high school diplomas. Thus receipt of the general diploma in the American system provides little indication for the job-seeker or the employer about the kinds of vocationally useful skills a young person seeking employment directly after high school graduation might have.

This situation contrasts most vividly with the German educational system. Pupils are channeled at an early age toward educational sequences that lead, for those with the highest test scores, to the university. Those who perform less well are guided toward apprenticeship placement. The apprenticeship is an integrated sequence of experiences that prepare the young person to pursue a particular occupation. It includes part-time work in a firm or business, under the supervision of a worker who is responsible for the apprentice's training and coordinated coursework in a school setting. Those who follow the apprentice route, including about 70 percent of recent cohorts of youth, will obtain, upon completion of their studies, a highly specific occupational certification that provides entry to a specific occupation (see Mortimer & Kruger, 2000).

According to Kerckhoff (1996), the less vocationally specific the training and credential provided by the secondary education structure, the more floundering and turbulent is the early career. In the more general systems, lacking formal differentiation in preparation or credentials, young entrants to the labor force must explore different jobs to find out what they are most interested in doing, and employers must try out a diversity of job-seekers, many of whom might be ill suited for the jobs at hand.

These cross-national differences have much relevance for career choice processes and development. Because high school education is not vocationally specific in the United States, and increasing proportions of young people seek higher education (more than two-thirds of high school graduates in recent cohorts; see Kerckhoff, 2002), contemporary adolescents in the United States tend to have vague notions about occupational choice and little understanding of the kinds of credentials that are necessary to enter particular types of jobs (Schneider & Stevenson, 1999). In Germany, in contrast, adolescents make special efforts to seek information about the various kinds of occupations for which they can be trained, prior to their apprenticeship. The school encourages this process of exploration by providing career information and "trial" apprenticeship placements (Mortimer & Kruger, 2000).

Of course, important cross-national differences constrain career choice—differences in the extent of economic development, the range of occupations and industries a person may choose to enter, and the ensuing prospects for occupational careers. The fit between educational systems and occupational structures is a pervasive, worldwide issue that takes different forms in different contexts (Shanahan, Mortimer, & Kruger, 2002). Some Western commentators worry that young people are given insufficient vocational guidance by their high school teachers and counselors, so they make less effective use of postsecondary educational resources than they would if they had a greater sense of direction (Schneider & Stevenson, 1999). In contrast, young people in some developing countries, such as India, where educational opportunities are very limited, look to employment in the West as a mark of success. This heightens the brain drain (the out-migration of highly educated or skilled workers) and related difficulties in economic development.

The many relevant differences between nations, as contexts for occupational choice and career development, cannot be addressed here. Nonetheless, it is important to point out that national contexts are critical in this regard. At the extreme, there may be no such thing as occupational choice as we know it, if, as in premodern hunting and gathering or even agricultural societies, the work that an adult does is primarily determined by age and sex. Only through comparative study can investigators become aware of the ways particular features of contexts determine the timing, character, and outcomes of vocational development. We now examine particular features of schools and the labor market, with emphasis on the United States.

Structural Features of Schools

Sociologists consider the structure of educational institutions and the labor market as important in shaping careers, so they seek to identify the ways institutional arrangements affect individual experiences, opportunities, and career outcomes. Across the life course, these institutional arrangements link family background and educational attainment, as well as initial and later placements in the occupational structure (Kerckhoff, 1995b). In this section, we describe how this occurs. Occupational goals and preferences are certainly of interest, yet sociologists also look at how the options from which individuals choose, as well as interests and preferences themselves, are subject to structural influences.

Some *educational* structures are thought to perpetuate existing social inequalities in career outcomes across generations and to produce additional inequality as well. Both organizational features within schools and differences between schools shape the distribution of educational outcomes (Lee, Bryk, & Smith, 1993), having implications also for career outcomes. Much of the focus *within* schools has been on "ability grouping" and "tracking" systems. In the case of ability grouping, which is used most often in the elementary grades, students are assigned to separate study groups within the same classroom, based on evaluation of their capacities to learn. Tracking, which is most often used in middle school and high school, consists of separating students into different classes for instruction. Entire programs of study can be distinguished, as when students are assigned to "vocational," "general," or "academic" tracks; furthermore, students can be tracked into ability levels within specific subjects. English and mathematics classes are often offered at "remedial" and "honors" levels, in addition to "general" levels.

Educational outcomes clearly result from long-term trajectories (Dauber, Alexander, & Entwisle, 1996; Alexander, Entwisle, & Horsey, 1997), framed by organizational structures such as ability grouping and tracking. A key characteristic of these arrangements is what Kerckhoff (1993) calls institutional inertia, that is, the tendency for track assignments to be self-perpetuating (Dauber, Alexander, & Entwisle, 1996; Kubitschek & Hallinan, 1996). In other words, placement in the system at one grade level has a strong effect on placement in later grade levels, independent of students' level of academic performance.

A frequent rationale for grouping and tracking is to create relatively homogeneous groups of students, thus enabling teachers to tailor their lessons to students' abilities. Such accommodation to student needs, advocates argue, facilitates learning at all levels. Critics claim that ability grouping and tracking perpetuate inequalities that originate outside the school, including racial and class inequalities (Gamoran, Nystrad, Berends, & LePore, 1995; Kerckhoff, 1993). Because of institutional inertia, any inequity initially introduced by group and track assignments is likely to be sustained over time. Critics also point out that these internal structures widen differences in achievement over time (Rosenbaum, 1976; Entwisle & Alexander, 1992). As educational trajectories diverge, differences in opportunities for higher education and occupational attainment become greater. Kerckhoff (1993) traced the divergence in students' achievement over the life course in a British birth cohort, as initial placements within the school system persisted and had cumulative effects on student learning.

Theorists have argued that track placement is a major mediating factor linking students' backgrounds and academic achievement (Lee & Bryk, 1988; Kerckhoff, 1995b). Because tracking and the ensuing differences in achievement in school provide adolescents with varying levels of skills and opportunities, inequity of track placement is of great concern, along with its implications for career outcomes. Equity issues in tracking arise at multiple levels. There can be inequitable initial access to tracks, inequitable mobility between tracks, and inequitable opportunities for learning in different tracks (Kubitschek & Hallinan, 1996). We discuss each of these—inequities in access, mobility, and learning—in turn.

Inequities in Access. Track placement in middle school and high school is associated with minority status, gender, and socioeconomic status of parents (Jones, Vanfossen, & Ensminger, 1995; Dauber, Alexander, & Entwisle, 1996; Gamoran et al., 1995). There is considerable disagreement, however, about whether this reflects systemic bias or whether it is the result of differences in academic ability and achievements among students at the outset. After taking into consideration students' past academic performance and prior track placements, some studies find that race, class, and gender continue to influence track or ability group placement (for example, Kubitschek & Hallinan, 1996; Kerckhoff, 1993), whereas other studies do not (for example, Dauber, Alexander, & Entwisle, 1996). Based on their review of the research in this area, Entwisle and Alexander (1993) conclude that children from families of lower socioeconomic status do not perform as well in school as those from more advantaged backgrounds, even in the first grade—a time when children are launched into achievement trajectories that persist.

Mobility. Hallinan (1996) points out that there is much more mobility in high school between tracks than has been recognized but that movement between tracks also reflects inequalities, primarily along gender and class lines. Track mobility, which occurs mainly between school years, reflects students' academic achievement, as evidenced by grades and test scores. Yet controlling for these factors, girls, older students, and students from families with fewer socioeconomic resources are at higher risk for changing to lower tracks over time and for dropping out of tracked subjects (Hallinan, 1996).

Learning. In addition to initial inequities in track assignments and inequities in track mobility, academic differentiation across tracks produces differences in achievement. The quality of instruction, for example, is argued to be inferior in the lower tracks (Oakes, Gamoran, & Page, 1992). Track differences in the nature and effects of classroom instruction contribute to the widening achievement gaps among students assigned to different levels (Gamoran et al., 1995). Other features of the tracking system are also important (Gamoran, 1992; Jones, Vanfossen, & Ensminger, 1995; Rosenbaum, 1996). For example, track immobility, or the extent to which students remain in the same track over time, produces greater inequality in verbal and math achievement between tracks and lowers the overall math achievement of students in a school.

Despite widespread criticism of tracking, vocational coursework in high schools may offer some students advantages they might not otherwise have when seeking employment after high school. Vocational education is associated with lower rates of college attendance and thus less likelihood of employment in the professions and managerial occupations. But for students not planning to attend college, it may provide an important safety net (Arum & Shavit, 1995). Vocational education reduces the risk of unemployment and increases the likelihood of employment as a skilled rather than unskilled worker. Vocational education teachers' contacts with local employers may help students enter jobs after high school that put them on a path toward higher earnings over time (Rosenbaum, DeLuca, Miller, & Roy, 1999).

Differences in Schools. In addition to the ways schools operate as internally differentiated institutions, sociologists have been concerned with structural differences *between* schools and their consequences for student achievement and postsecondary opportunities. For example, students in Catholic schools have lower absenteeism rates, are less likely to drop out, and have higher levels of math achievement than students in public schools (Bryk & Thum, 1989; Lee & Bryk, 1988, 1989). The advantages of attending Catholic school are thought to operate through the normative and structural features of these schools, including the greater similarity in course taking across curriculum tracks (in comparison to public schools). Furthermore, students enrolled in smaller schools have higher levels of achievement and lower levels of absenteeism and dropping out than those in larger schools (Finn & Voelkl, 1993; Fowler & Wahlberg, 1991; Lee, Bryk, & Smith, 1993; Lee & Smith, 1995). Variation in the interest and commitment of teachers also produces achievement differences across schools (Lee & Bryk, 1989).

The composition of the student body is another factor influencing individual achievement. For example, the average socioeconomic status composition of schools, above and beyond a student's own socioeconomic status, is linked to absenteeism, dropping out, and achievement (Bryk & Thum, 1989; Fowler & Wahlberg, 1991; Lee & Bryk, 1989). Such compositional effects may influence student outcomes through several possible mechanisms. Socioeconomic status composition may be associated with the fiscal and human resources of a school or may reflect differences in the values and expectations of students, parents, and staff, which in turn shape school organization (Lee, Bryk, & Smith, 1993). The racial composition of schools has also been studied heavily as a possible influence on the achievement of minority students. Several studies indicate that the academic achievement of minority students improves in integrated schools (Bankston & Caldas, 1996; Crain & Mahard, 1978, 1983; Entwisle & Alexander, 1992; Lee, Bryk, & Smith, 1993; Roscigno, 1998; Wortman & Bryant, 1985).

These structural features of schools, like sector, size, and class and race composition, are thought to produce inequities in learning environments and subsequent occupational opportunities. "The unequal distribution of African-Americans and Whites to private and public schools, disparate social class segregation, lower instructional expenditure for non-Whites, and a higher level of crime in the schools attended by African-Americans and Hispanics are, indeed, consequential for persistent racial gaps in performance" (Roscigno, 2000, p. 281).

The jobs people hold, as well as their wages and other rewards, are a function of workers' educational credentials, preferences, and skills (including cognitive and other skills developed through schooling, as well as other job-related skills). Other institutional arrangements likewise shape occupational careers. The labor market is highly structured; workers' positions in this structure influence their current and future occupational attainments. Sociologists have documented that wages and other rewards, as well as mobility patterns, are shaped by the size of the employing organization (Stolzenberg, 1978) and industry (Beck, Horan, & Tolbert, 1978; DiPrete & Nonnemaker, 1997), and by the sex and race composition of the occupation and firm in which one works (Reskin, McBrier, & Kmec, 1999).

One way sociologists have tried to capture the structure of opportunity in the labor market is to distinguish between the more advantageous "core" and less advantageous "peripheral" sectors (Beck, Horan, & Tolbert, 1978). Firms in the core sector are larger, offering higher wages and better opportunities for career advancement. Mobility patterns are institutionalized in many core industries and large organizations through internal labor markets—promotion "ladders" in which employees enter the organization at set entry points and have predictable opportunities for advancement thereafter. Promotions to higher levels are made from lower rungs on the ladder, protecting workers to some extent from competition with those outside the organization (Althauser & Kalleberg, 1990). Firms in the peripheral sector tend to offer jobs with less security, lower wages, and less chance for upward mobility.

Two "ideal types" characterize variation in the structure of control over labor market positions (Sorenson & Kalleberg, 1981; Eliason, 1995). In "open" systems, positions and their rewards are shaped by market mechanisms. Workers compete for wages and other rewards as employers seek to maximize worker productivity. As a result, job rewards are linked to a worker's productivity. In "closed" systems, institutional and organizational rules limit employers' control over access to positions and reward distributions. Job ladders or worker collective action, for example, through labor unions, can tie reward structures more closely to positions than to the productivity or other characteristics of people in those positions. Thus, in a closed structure, the employer cannot easily set wages and other rewards according to individual productivity; for workers, competition is directed to positions, with wage gains made largely through job shifts. Earnings tend to be higher in closed systems (Eliason, 1995).

Although such "dualistic" views of labor market segmentation—core versus periphery, open versus closed—are undoubtedly too simplistic (see, for example, Hodson & Kaufman, 1982), they heighten sensitivity to the systematic links between positions in the labor market and point to the important role of firm, industry, and occupational characteristics in shaping worker outcomes, including earnings and the mobility patterns that constitute careers.

Sociological attention has also been directed to organizational practices that shape career outcomes. For example, organizations that have more formalized personnel practices, that is, procedures for recruiting, hiring, and assigning jobs, as well as for the evaluation and promotion of workers, are more likely to employ racial minorities and women (Reskin & McBrier, 2000; Reskin et al., 1999). More positions go to racial minorities and women when employers actively advertise job openings. In contrast, recruitment through informal networks tends to favor the in-group; for most upper-level positions, this group has consisted of white men (Reskin & McBrier, 2000; Reskin et al., 1999). Because workers generally find jobs through informal channels (Granovetter, 1974), the structure of a worker's social network is, in fact, an important factor affecting job mobility across the career (Podolny & Baron, 1997).

The way in which labor market structures differentially shape the career experiences of men and women has been of particular interest to sociologists of work over the past several decades. Occupational segregation—the tendency for men and women to work in different occupations—is believed to be an important determinant of the wage gap between men and women. Because of an oversupply of women in a small number of female-dominated occupations, occupational segregation depresses all women's wages, even women working in male-dominated occupations (Cotter et al., 1997). Although many women move back and forth between male- and female-dominated jobs (Rosenfeld & Spenner, 1992), women who work in "heavily female" occupations—over 90 percent of incumbents are females—experience a cumulative disadvantage, or what Chan (1999) calls a ghetto effect. Women in such occupations are essentially trapped, with very few moving into other, less female-dominated and higher-paying occupations.

Marini and Fan (1997) examined men's and women's earnings at career entry—a time in which the gender gap in wages ought to be smallest. At this point in their careers, women earned 84 cents for every dollar men earned. About 30 percent of this difference was attributed to gender differences in relevant worker characteristics like skills, credentials, and workers' aspirations. The adult family roles of men and women were of little importance in explaining this early gender gap in wages. Marini and Fan attribute another 42 percent of the earnings gap to the combined influence of the allocation of men and women to different jobs by employers and of social networks that provide job-relevant information and influence to men and women. Such employer and network action leads men and women into different occupations and industries at career entry. They conclude:

> The association between the sex composition of a job and its wage rate within the organizational structure of the labor mar-

ket is perpetuated to some degree by micro-level processes that produce gender differences in the aspirations and qualifications with which workers enter the labor market, but . . . this association is perpetuated even more by micro-level processes that operate at the point of career entry to channel women and men with the same aspirations and qualifications into different, sex-typed jobs. [Marini & Fan 1997, p. 602]

So far, we have focused on sociological contributions to understanding career choice and development by describing the institutional arrangements, both broadly across nations and specifically within the United States, that structure opportunities and constrain decision making. We now turn to the most proximal contexts of individual vocational development and decision making, including the family, the adolescent workplace, and features of the local community.

Contexts of Career Decision Making

We have already considered the family's influence on educational and occupational aspirations in the context of the status attainment model. This section addresses other psychological dimensions that have relevance for occupational attainment.

Family. The socioeconomic position of the family has important implications for the development of occupational reward values (Lindsay & Knox, 1984; Mortimer & Kumka, 1982). These values, also called work or job values, are assessments of the importance of various rewards offered through work.

A major strand of sociological research on occupational choice and attainment has focused on parents' workplaces as a context for the vocational development of children. The characteristics of parents' jobs are thought to influence parents' values and personalities, which, in turn, shape parenting behavior. Through parents' child-rearing orientations and behaviors, parental work conditions affect children's and adolescents' developing interests, values, and aspirations. Kohn and his colleagues' research, the most prominent work in this area, focuses predominantly on the link between fathers' working conditions and their value orientations and psychological functioning (Kohn, 1969; Kohn & Schooler, 1983). Kohn and Schooler argue that the personality traits important to fathers' success at work influence the qualities fathers value most in their children. Men whose work requires them to make independent decisions value self-direction in their children; those whose work places greater emphasis on following directions or the supervision of others are more likely to want their children to be obedient. According to the occupational linkage hypothesis, these values are transferred to children and come to influence their own choice of occupations and capacities to act in a self-directed way, thus perpetuating the class structure intergenerationally. Kohn, Slomczynski, and Schoenbach (1986) have demonstrated, in fact, that the self-directed values promoted by parental jobs are communicated to children, affecting their own values.

There is considerable support for the link between parents' job conditions and their work values. Rewards derived from work, like autonomy and pay, foster the valuing of the same rewards among both men and women (Mortimer & Lorence, 1979; Lindsay & Knox, 1984; Johnson, 2001a). Other research has focused on the links between parents' occupations, their values, and their childrearing practices, demonstrating that the higher the socioeconomic status of parents, the more likely they are to engage in more effective, authoritative parenting and to foster close and communicative parent-child relations (Gecas & Nye, 1974; Greenberger, O'Neil, & Nagel, 1994). Mortimer and her colleagues' research shows that the degree of supportiveness in the parent-child relationship influences various attitudes and behaviors in children that facilitate socioeconomic attainment (Mortimer & Finch, 1986). For example, closer and more communicative relationships with fathers predict greater self-confidence on the part of sons. Other work shows that the quality of parent-child relationships is a central mechanism through which parents' socioeconomic position influences children's work values and eventual occupational attainment (Mortimer, Lorence, & Kumka, 1986).

Research in the 1990s increasingly focused on maternal as well as paternal employment characteristics (Perry-Jenkins, Repetti, & Crouter, 2000). In a study focusing on both mothers' and fathers' occupations and work values, Ryu and Mortimer (1996) found that supportive relationships with fathers fostered sons' intrinsic work values when fathers had higher self-direction in their jobs. Their analysis also suggests that adolescents learn their occupational values more from the same-sex parent than from the opposite-sex parent. Mothers' work histories, in fact, may play an important role in daughters' orientations to work generally. Among young women in the National Longitudinal Study of Youth (NLSY), those whose own mothers were employed outside the home re-entered the labor force more quickly after childbirth and were more likely to be employed one year after childbirth than those whose mothers were full-time homemakers (Wenk & Garrett, 1992).

The conditions of parents' jobs affect several child outcomes that have the potential to shape occupational attainment. For example, the complexity of a mother's job influences the quality of the home environment she can provide for children, ultimately affecting children's cognitive development (Parcel & Menaghan, 1994). Mothers' and fathers' opportunities for self-direction on the job, including the chance to exercise autonomy and engage in substantively complex tasks, affect children's internalization of parental norms, thus lessening behavior problems (Parcel & Menaghan, 1993; Cooksey, Menaghan, & Jekielek, 1997). Whitbeck and colleagues (1997) found that autonomy at work enabled fathers to be more flexible in their parenting styles, fostering a sense of mastery and control in their adolescent children. Mothers' job autonomy, in contrast, had no influence in this study.

Schulenberg, Vondracek, and Crouter (1984) conclude that the family's influence on vocational development lies along two dimensions: (1) by providing opportunities (for example, educational, financial, informational), and (2) through socialization (for example, via parenting practices and parent-child relations). With continuing changes in family life (work-family connections more specifically), the family's influence on vocational development may also change in important ways. Women's increasing labor force participation and contribution to family income, for example, has the potential to alter the historically gendered nature of vocational socialization.

Work. Until recently, adolescent employment has not been given much attention by researchers (Stone & Mortimer, 1998). Yet adolescents' work experiences are important as one part of a larger configuration of activities outside of school. The large majority of adolescents work at some time during high school (Manning, 1990; Bachman & Schulenberg, 1993; Ruhm, 1995); many devote a larger amount of time to this pursuit. Estimates vary, but approximately 20 percent of high school juniors and seniors work more than twenty hours per week during the school year (Stone & Mortimer, 1998).

Adolescent employment has the potential to influence career choice and development in a variety of ways. Early jobs serve as first-hand introductions to employment and thus have the potential to shape work habits, attitudes, and occupational interests. For example, working may help clarify an adolescent's work interests and values and encourage the adolescent to consider what he or she may be "good at." Even undesirable jobs may inspire thinking about the kind of work one would like to do and the credentials needed to obtain a satisfying job or career. Moreover, work experience can build human capital, enabling young people to command higher wages as they move from job to job, and may serve as a buffer against unemployment as they learn how to look for and keep jobs. Finally, adolescent work experience can influence career choice and development by affecting school performance and attainment. If time spent in paid work hinders adolescents' school performance or draws them out of school entirely, occupational opportunities will diminish.

Parents and teens alike have favorable assessments of adolescent employment, viewing it as an important site for vocational development. Parents express considerable enthusiasm about their own early jobs (Aronson, Mortimer, Zierman, & Hacker, 1996). Many feel that what they learned served them well in adulthood, including gaining a sense of responsibility and learning money management skills. Consistent with this positive evaluation of their own early work experiences, parents also hold positive attitudes about their own teenagers' employment (Phillips & Sandstrom, 1990; Aronson et al., 1996). Parents believe that employment fosters responsibility, independence, and good work attitudes and habits, and that it teaches skills that adolescents would not learn in school.

Adolescents also evaluate their employment experiences favorably. Nearly all working adolescents in the St. Paul-based Youth Development Study felt they benefited from their jobs, learning responsibility and social skills (Aronson et al., 1996). Most adolescents also felt their jobs helped teach them basic skills like following directions and being on time. Such skills have the potential to set young people on courses that will benefit them across their working lives. However, only about one-fourth of the adolescents felt their work experience had a direct influence on their career choice. Although less commonly reported than the benefits, some adolescents perceived costs to their employment, such as having less leisure time and feeling tired.

Consistent with teens' and parents' perceptions, studies indicate developmental gains for working adolescents, including higher punctuality, personal responsibility and dependability, and (for girls only) self-reliance (Greenberger & Steinberg, 1986). Other studies point to the importance of the nature of the work experience for vocational development rather than just working per se. Findings from the Youth Development Study indicate that adolescents who have opportunities for advancement, who perceive little conflict between school and work, and who feel they are paid well increase in self-efficacy over time (Finch, Shanahan, Mortimer, & Ryu, 1991). Furthermore, adolescents who report having an opportunity to learn skills on the job develop stronger intrinsic and extrinsic occupational reward values (Mortimer et al., 1996), which contribute to vocational development and affect career decision making.

In addition to these social-psychological outcomes of adolescent employment, working may teach young people important job-seeking skills, like where and how to look for a job and how to behave during a job interview. Earnings also rise as young people accumulate work experience. Consistent with these ideas, adolescent employment has been found to have positive effects on adult occupational attainment, as measured by weeks of employment and wages (Committee on Child Labor, 1998). Hours of work during high school reduce the risk of unemployment in the early years following high school (Marsh, 1991; Steel, 1991). High school work experience also affects women's employment in young adulthood, with early experience promoting labor force attachment (Alon, Donahoe, & Tienda, 2001). And controlling for educational attainment, high school employment has positive effects on wages up to a decade following high school (Carr, Wright, & Brody, 1996).

In contrast to this positive view of adolescent work and adult labor market outcomes, other research points to harmful consequences of employment that may interfere with successful adolescent development (Greenberger & Steinberg, 1986). For example, long hours of employment during the teen years are linked to substance use and other delinquent behaviors (Greenberger & Steinberg, 1986; Mortimer et al., 1996; Steinberg & Dornbusch, 1991; Bachman & Schulenberg, 1993; Mihalic & Elliot, 1997). In addition, the educational consequences of employment are a matter of great concern. Studies have produced mixed findings as to whether adolescent employment hinders students' academic performance. The issue is complicated by the fact that adolescents who are less academically engaged and doing less well in school tend to invest more time in paid work. Longitudinal studies that control earlier performance and academic orientations do not produce consistent findings (Mortimer

& Finch, 1986; Marsh, 1991; Mihalic & Elliot, 1997; Mortimer et al., 1996; Warren, LePore, & Mare, 2000; Schoenhals, Tienda, & Schneider, 1998). *Long* hours of work in adolescence may ultimately hinder educational attainment. Carr and colleagues (1996) found that hours of work per week during high school predict a small decrement in educational attainment measured at ages twenty-eight to thirty-one. The duration of work during high school also reduces boys' educational attainment. To the extent that adolescent employment interferes with educational attainment, it could have important implications for career opportunities. In their review, however, Stone and Mortimer (1998) note that exclusive focus on educational attainment ignores other important routes to building human capital that may be more attractive for some youth.

Among those who limit their hours, employment may enable higher levels of educational attainment (Tienda & Ahituv, 1996; D'Amico, 1984). Examining the "career" of work during the high school years, Mortimer and Johnson (1998) point to the significance of long-term working patterns. They found that a "balanced" work pattern, involving employment of long duration at an intensity of twenty or fewer hours per week (on the average), was particularly beneficial to boys. Boys who pursued this pattern of employment during high school accumulated more months of postsecondary schooling than other boys, including those who had never worked. Students who learn how to successfully combine work and school appear to continue this pattern as they move to postsecondary schooling, ultimately achieving higher levels of postsecondary attainment. By their mid-twenties, they outstrip the initial earnings advantage of youth who worked at greater intensity (more than twenty hours per week on the average) during high school (Mortimer, in press).

Not all youth are equally likely to work, nor do they have the same experiences in the labor force. Adolescents in well-educated, middle-class families are most likely to be employed (Carr et al., 1996; Schoenhals, Tienda, & Schneider, 1998). When they do work, youth from lower-income families are likely to be employed more intensively during high school (Mortimer, in press; Committee on Child

Labor, 1998). Non-white adolescents are less likely to be employed at all during high school; when they are, they tend to be employed for fewer months than white adolescents (Carr et al., 1996; D'Amico, 1984; Marsh, 1991; Schoenhals, Tienda, & Schneider, 1998; Mortimer & Johnson, 1998). Mortimer and Johnson (1998) also find in the Youth Development Study that school orientation and achievement in 9th grade predict work investment patterns in 10th through 12th grade. Students with higher academic self-esteem, intrinsic motivation to school, and grades worked fewer hours per week. Students with high educational goals were most likely to work rather continuously over the high school years at low intensity. Thus youth from advantaged backgrounds and those who are academically oriented tend to invest in work experience during adolescence in ways that have beneficial outcomes. Youth who have fewer resources, coming from lower socioeconomic backgrounds and with less promising initial attitudes toward schooling, pursue more highly intensive work during high school, reducing their educational attainment.

As a result of these patterns, the meaning of adolescent work experiences can vary considerably. The consequences of working, for example, can depend on whether any earnings are saved for college (Marsh, 1991). McNeal (1997) reports that sophomores in high school who work more hours are more likely to subsequently drop out of high school, but the relationship only held for certain types of jobs. Intensity of employment mattered little for those young people working on farms or in retail jobs but had substantial effects for jobs in manufacturing or service. Adolescents' motivations for working and the individual or community factors involved in selecting particular types of jobs likely help to explain these patterns. Paralleling the finding in McNeal's study that working on a farm has unique meaning for school persistence, rural-urban differences in the consequences of work have also been observed (Shanahan et al., 1996).

Community. Occupational choice and attainment are shaped by community labor market conditions. These are particularly important at the time of labor force entry, as initial placements influence subsequent occupational career trajectories. The types of industry present in communities vary widely, and both the presence of particular industries and the range of industries affect the occupations in which men and women can be employed. Both the probability of employment and the level of earnings achieved are, in part, determined by local unemployment rates, local wage levels, and the size and racial composition within central cities. Non-Hispanic whites are more subject to these local labor market conditions, as minority workers' opportunities are more restricted; however, they earn lower wages, regardless of local conditions (Farkas, Barton, & Kushner, 1988; Barton, Farkas, Kushner, & McCreary, 1985).

Sociologists have been particularly concerned with employment opportunities and the vocational development of young people in high poverty areas of major urban centers. In his recent book *When Work Disappears* (1996), William Julius Wilson argues that the nationwide decline in manufacturing jobs and the movement of jobs and more advantaged families to the suburbs have created a new form of urban poverty in which the majority of adults in a neighborhood do not work in the formal economy. Under such conditions, young people grow up in families without a steady breadwinner and in neighborhoods with high levels of joblessness. As they reach employment age, young people face not only limited opportunities for work but have not developed the disciplined habits associated with stable employment. Such extreme conditions are a reminder that possibilities for "choosing" one's career can range from the extremely limited to the wide open. In such circumstances, even marginal jobs, such as those in the fast-food industry, assume great importance in the process of vocational development (Newman, 1999).

Many rural areas also face rising unemployment and the outmigration of young people. Moreover, rural areas offer less diversified labor markets, and opportunities for meaningful employment can be limited. In addition to the local labor market conditions of rural areas, rural youth face some additional complexities in making career choices. With greater geographic isolation, rural youth may have less access to information about higher education and the qualifications needed for various occupations. Most young people in rural areas do not have local access to a postsecondary educational institution.

For rural youth, pathways out of school into work are more closely tied to decisions about whether to leave one's home community. Rural residents often feel strong ties to their communities and families, and moving disrupts such bonds (Looker, 1992; Elder & Conger, 2000; Shaffer, Seyfrit, & Associates, 2000). Yet those young people who want to "get ahead" tend to leave. For many rural youth who want to pursue college degrees, they must face having to move out of their communities to achieve this goal, and they may not be able to return if they are to find suitable jobs (Elder, King, & Conger, 1996). In part because they have fewer options to "take over the farm" or work in other rural industries like their fathers, more young women than young men aspire to migrate out of rural areas, and in fact more do so (Hamilton & Seyfrit, 1994; Elder, King, & Conger, 1996).

Growing up in different kinds of communities influences what young people seek in their work lives, as their values are shaped by those of the people around them, as well as local conditions of life. Perhaps reflecting an overarching difference in the value of materialism, young people from farms and rural communities attach less importance to extrinsic rewards than young people from other community types (Johnson, in press). Young people from farms, in particular, whose families are often more heavily involved in community service, are most oriented toward altruistic job rewards like the chance to help others, though they are also more concerned about job stability than other young people.

Work-Family Connections

Career choices are often made in tandem with decisions regarding other arenas of life, including schooling and family. Career choices, as we have noted, not only involve decision making about what sort of occupation in which to work but also involve accompanying decisions about education and training and, later, where, how much, and when to work. All of these decisions may be shaped by one's other roles, including spouse (or partner) and parent. Most sociology of work-family connections has focused on the way in which work influences family life (Perry-Jenkins, Repetti, & Crouter, 2000). Some attention, however, has been directed toward the way careers are shaped by what sociologists call the family of destination (to distinguish it from the family of origin)—a subject to which we now turn.

To be sure, men's traditional responsibility to provide economically for a wife and children influences their work lives. Yet in many ways, women's careers are affected even more by their family roles. But contrary to what is popularly believed, there is no convincing evidence that women choose their occupations to facilitate their roles as mothers (Rosenfeld & Spenner, 1992). Men's jobs have more flexible schedules and more benefits like unsupervised breaks, paid sick leave, and vacation, making them more "parent friendly" (Glass, 1990). Budig and England (2001) report that mothers are no more likely than non-mothers to be in female-dominated jobs and conclude that "there is no evidence that women select female jobs because they are more mother-friendly" (p. 216). In recent times, without housewives to attend to household management and care of children, fathers as well as mothers are increasingly experiencing tension between work and family roles (Gerson, 1993). So although much of sociological research on work-family connections focuses on women, men's careers are increasingly influenced in important ways by their family involvement.

Adolescents' aspirations and other orientations toward the future reflect some awareness of how career and family life influence one another. In a variety of ways, those young people with high ambitions expect to coordinate the timing of their family formation with their career investments. In a recent study of high school seniors, Johnson and Mortimer (2000) found that adolescents who expect to marry at older ages (compared to their peers) anticipate less interference between their family and work roles. The pursuit of some careers can be facilitated by delaying family formation, and decisions may be made with this in mind. Moreover, for young women, who are still often the primary caretakers for their young children, there was further evidence of "timing" or "sequencing" strategies. Young women who had higher educational and occupational achievement ambitions planned to marry at older ages than did their male peers. High-aspiring young women placed no less importance on their future family lives than those who had lower aspirations, yet they did plan to allocate more time to the non-married state, perhaps in order to achieve their career goals.

Educational, career, and family formation pathways are woven together in the early adult years. Educational attainment and fertility timing, for example, are interrelated for women in the United States (Marini, 1984; Martin, 2000), and the effects are bidirectional. Educational attainment has a delaying effect on childbearing, but entry into parenthood also limits women's educational attainment. The age at which young men and women enter family roles has historically had important consequences for occupational attainment. For example, earlier age at entry into family roles promoted men's earnings and limited women's earnings (Marini, Shin, & Raymond, 1989). Evidence from recent cohorts indicates that relatively early family formation continues to have gender-specific effects on adult attainment. Over the first few years after high school, young women who marry are less likely to be attending postsecondary education and to be working part-time (Mortimer & Johnson, 1999). Early parenting limits both young men's and women's investments in postsecondary education and part-time work and further limits women's participation in full-time work. Most jobs in early adulthood are short in duration, and job exits (to attend school, take another job, or for other reasons) are tied to young men's and women's family status (Koenigsberg, Garet, & Rosenbaum, 1994). Such early work histories can leave long-lasting imprints on prestige and earnings trajectories.

Beyond the initial timing of entry into work and family roles and the ways families shape the early career, decision making in each domain has ongoing implications for the other. And family roles continue to affect careers across the life course. One way this occurs is in the daily interactions at home that influence the worker's behavior. Family-to-work conflict and distress in family relationships can affect job performance and tenure (Glass & Estes, 1997; Perry-Jenkins, Repetti, & Crouter, 2000). Women's work patterns, in particular, are tied to changes in their family roles (Brewster & Rindfuss, 2000). Mothers who return to work on a part-time basis after childbearing lose pay and seniority, and often benefits and job security as well (Cocran et al., 1984). For women pursuing careers, time spent out of the labor force negatively influences occupational advancement (Brewster & Rindfuss, 2000; Rindfuss, Cooksey, & Sutterlin, 1999; Rosenfeld, 1992). Moreover, even when labor force experience, hours spent at work, and other relevant factors are controlled, women who have children suffer a wage penalty compared to nonmothers (Waldfogel, 1997; Taniguchi, 1999; Budig & England, 2001). This penalty is larger for white women than African American women, for women with lower levels of education, and for women who bear children relatively early. In addition to caretaking responsibilities for children, many workers care for their aging parents or other older family members, and this also shapes their performance and satisfaction with work (Singleton, 1998). Performance of housework limits wages, more so for women than men, because the type of household tasks women typically perform are those that have negative effects on wages (Noonan, 2001).

Another way family roles affect careers is through a spouse's preferences and opportunities. Individuals' work and family trajectories are linked to those of their spouses, and individual career development can be tied to the career development of one's spouse. For example, career advancement often involves relocation, and for men and women in dual-earner couples, this can affect the spouse's career opportunities as well. Because husbands have more frequently been the higher earner in the family, women's work lives more often have been shaped by their husbands' work lives than vice versa. Wives in dual-earner couples are less willing to relocate for a better job when it detrimentally affects their husbands' work, but wives' potential work sacrifices do not deter husbands from relocating quite as often (Bielby & Bielby, 1992). These gender differences are weaker, however, among men and women with less traditional gender role beliefs (Bielby & Bielby, 1992), which are becoming increasingly common. In a recent examination of dual-career couples in upstate New York, Pixley and Moen (in press) found that men were still somewhat more likely than women to report having taken advantage of a major career opportunity that required a spouse to move or change jobs. Still, a good proportion of both men and women had turned down opportunities of this kind (42 and 56 percent, respectively).

A Look to the Future

A most prominent feature of vocational development in the United States, which may become exacerbated in the future, is its extension to later life phases. In an earlier era, occupational choice and development were expected to take place during the teen years. Adolescence was considered to be a time of vocational exploration and of the formation of vocational identity; after completing high school, most people entered the full-time labor force and, after some further exploration, gravitated toward jobs that would become their full-time careers.

This scenario has become much less frequent, given the increasingly individualized, "destructured," and unpredictable early life course (Shanahan, 2000). Beginning in high school, young people combine and alternate school and work. Many leave school, only to return a short time later. Some who drop out later pursue GEDs (general educational diplomas). Although more than two-thirds of high school graduates enter some form of higher education, less than half of these eventually obtain baccalaureate degrees. Many drop out of college, only to return some time later as they become more focused in their interests or realize the occupational advantages that would accrue from higher educational credentials. Women tend to have more unstable work careers than men, as many move in and out of the labor force, or alternate periods of more or less intensive work in response to the needs of their children and families. Some return to full-time schooling in midlife to obtain higher educational degrees and to prepare themselves for new occupational pursuits.

These trends mean that vocational development is more extended and perhaps more indeterminate than in previous historical periods. Policy implications may therefore be fruitfully considered by phase of the life course, as vocational development may increasingly come to be a lifelong phenomenon.

With respect to the period of adolescence, we have noted many students' general lack of interest in thinking about their adult occupational choices. Moreover, youths' difficulties in making the school-to-work transition have been increasingly recognized and linked to the absence of institutional bridges. The School-to-Work Opportunity Act was set forth to find ways to remedy this situation through stronger connections between schools and workplaces, opportunities for young people to pursue internships in work organizations of their choice, high school–based enterprises, and so forth (Borman, Cookson, Sadovnik, & Spade, 1996). We have argued elsewhere (Mortimer & Johnson, 1998), however, that schools have not yet taken full advantage of the fact that most teenagers are, in fact, in the labor market. Much more could be done to integrate their experiences in the workplace and in school. For example, young people might be encouraged to discuss the rewards and challenges, as well as the problems that they encounter on their jobs, to increase awareness of the various opportunities that are present in the workplace. They might be offered the opportunity to write about their experiences at work in their term papers and other school assignments, to reflect, especially, on what they like and dislike about their jobs, so as to become increasingly aware of their own vocationally relevant interests, preferences, and abilities.

In adulthood, a major obstacle to vocational achievement is the need to simultaneously care for children and household while pursuing a career. The burden of family work has, up to this point, fallen most heavily on women. Coordinating work and family roles, however, is made more or less difficult by the policy context, both at the level of the employer as well as the community and nation. Employer policies regarding parental leave, flexible scheduling of work hours, and support for child care are diverse in the United States and often do not cover the men and women most in need of family accommodations (Glass & Estes, 1997). "Family friendly" policies can decrease tardiness, absenteeism, and turnover and increase job satisfaction and productivity among women and men (Glass & Estes, 1997). Employer policies shape the work careers of women, in part, through the rate at which women return to work after childbearing (Hofferth, 2000). Access to part-time work and on-site child care promote a faster return to work. Many part-time employees would have left the labor force after childbearing had part-time work not been available to them (Rogers, 1992). The availability of good-quality, affordable child care is a particularly important factor in work-family decisions (Rindfuss & Brewster, 1996; Mason & Kuhlthau, 1992). Mothers with liberal unpaid leave and flexible spending accounts (allowing the option of pre-tax payroll deduction for insurance premiums, medical expenses, or child-care expenses) return more quickly to full-time work.

Cross-national differences in family policies influence women's fertility and labor force participation (Brewster & Rindfuss, 2000). Parental leave policies, state support of child care and elder care, and the age at which children start school vary across nations and form the contexts in which both mothers and fathers navigate their work and family lives. Examining the life histories of four birth cohorts (1929–1961) living in East Germany, Trappe (2000) documents how the availability of state-supported child care in the later cohorts allowed women to pursue work opportunities and family roles simultaneously. Earlier cohorts more often sequenced their efforts in employment and child rearing. With reunification, the coordination of work and family roles has become more difficult, as many of these supports have diminished or disappeared.

As this review indicates, sociologists are as likely (or more likely) to be concerned with the ways in which career choices are facilitated or constrained by ascribed characteristics, educational and labor market institutional arrangements, and local contexts as they are to be concerned with personal choice of jobs and occupations. Most of the theory and research of sociologists of work is therefore far removed from vocational counseling and career decision-making processes. Nonetheless, it has some important implications for career counseling, however uncultivated they are to date.

> Guidance and career counselors can recognize, and help their clients recognize, that career choice is not a one-time event but that some decisions do have long-term implications for ongoing career opportunities.

With rapid change in the employment sector, occupational options cannot be predicted far into the future. Occupational interests and values can also change considerably over the life course (Johnson, 2001b). With the nature of jobs and personal interests both changing, searching for a good fit between the two has the potential to be a lifelong project. At the same time, it is important for clients to understand that some choices they make with respect to their career will close doors on other opportunities or make other career possibilities more difficult to pursue later. Clients may need help in seeing the complex, interconnected nature of early and later work experiences, as well as the structural constraints they are likely to encounter in pursuing their goals.

The prolongation of the transition to adulthood, as we have noted, has been associated with delay in serious vocational consideration and decision making. As a result, many youth are left to make consequential decisions at a time when opportunities have narrowed and they have moved out of the protective institutions of childhood and adolescence—family and school—where there were adults whose primary objective it was to guide them. Engaging young people in thinking about work and making tentative explorations (but not necessarily deciding on a career path) earlier rather than later would be highly desirable (Mortimer, in press).

Guidance and career counselors can work to build their clients' knowledge about the educational, training, and skill requirements of different occupations.

Sociological research in the status attainment tradition identifies aspirations for the future as centrally important for career outcomes. Contemporary generations of teenagers have high aspirations for educational and occupational attainment but have greater difficulty making clear plans for reaching their ambitions (Schneider & Stevenson, 1999). The focus of guidance counseling for youth has mostly been about getting into college, and although this is clearly a worthy objective, given the economic and social benefits of higher education, there is a downside. Adolescents are left largely on their own to find out about work possibilities, and many are not sufficiently motivated to do so (Schneider & Stevenson, 1999). Counselors can assist young people in developing coherent plans, identifying the steps that can be taken to achieve their goals, and connecting their often-vague ideas about their future work life to actual educational and career paths.

Guidance and career counselors can encourage young people to take a constructive approach to their early employment experiences by providing opportunities to discuss what they like and dislike about their jobs, as well as what skills or experience a job provides that might be useful to them in the future. When possible, counselors can encourage youth to select jobs that provide meaningful experiences in these ways.

As we noted earlier, opportunities exist for schools to take greater advantage of the fact that their students are working by integrating employment and school experiences to the benefit of adolescents' vocational development. Guidance counselors can play a key role in spearheading such efforts. Many youth do not see their jobs as connected with their future work lives or as having any influence on their occupational preferences. More can be done to develop internships and work-school cooperative programs that might involve workplace visits or job shadowing, for example. Through such programs, youth are exposed to the possibilities of working in particular kinds of settings; they can learn about the requirements to fill certain kinds of jobs and do particular types of tasks (see also Hamilton & Hamilton, 2000).

Guidance and career counselors can assist individuals in disadvantaged positions with navigating career paths and facing common barriers to achieving their educational and occupational goals.

Individuals face many structural barriers in pursuing their occupational goals, some of which we have described in this chapter; some are related to students' race or ethnicity, class background, and gender. Although labor market structures are not under the immediate control of career counselors, assistance can be provided, for example, in terms of (1) identifying sources of financial aid for education and job training and helping clients with application materials and procedures, (2) discussing and rehearsing a range of job-searching strategies, and (3) encouraging the accumulation of meaningful skills and credentials, including the completion of high school and potentially postsecondary certificates or degrees.

The sociological perspective on career choice and development becomes increasingly necessary as a vehicle for understanding the diverse societal, institutional, and microcontextual environments of the modern world that influence these processes, the mechanisms of both intergenerational and intragenerational mobility, and the determinants of adult socioeconomic well-being. It is also necessary to inform social policies that will enable people to make satisfying occupational choices and to obtain fulfilling occupational careers that will extend throughout the lives.

References

Alexander, K. L., Entwisle, D. R., & Horsey, C. S. (1997). From first grade forward: Early foundations of high school dropout. *Sociology of Education*, *70*, 87–107.

Alon, S., Donahoe, D., & Tienda, M. (2001). The effects of early work experience on young women's labor force attachment. *Social Forces*, *79*, 1005–1034.

Althauser, R. P., & Kalleberg, A. L. (1990). Identifying career lines and internal labor markets within firms: A study in the interrelationships of theory and methods. In R. L. Breiger (Ed.), *Social mobility and social structure* (pp. 308-356). Cambridge, UK: Cambridge University Press.

Aronson, P. J., Mortimer, J. T., Zierman, C., & Hacker, M. (1996). Generational differences in early work experiences and evaluations. In J. T. Mortimer & M. D. Finch (Eds.), *Adolescents, work, and family: An intergenerational developmental analysis* (pp. 25–62). Newbury Park, CA: Sage.

Arum, R., & Shavit, Y. (1995). Secondary vocational education and the transition from school to work. *Sociology of Education*, *68*, 187–204.

Bachman, J. G., & Schulenberg, J. (1993). How part-time work intensity relates to drug use, problem behavior, time use and satisfaction among high school seniors: Are these consequences or merely correlates? *Developmental Psychology*, *29*, 220–235.

Bankston, C. L., III, & Caldas, S. J. (1996). Majority African American schools and social injustice: The influence of de facto segregation on academic achievement. *Social Forces*, *75*, 535–555.

Barton, M., Farkas, G., Kushner, K., & McCreary, L. (1985). White, black, and Hispanic male youths in central city labor markets. *Social Science Research*, *14*, 266–286.

Beck, E. M., Horan, P. M., & Tolbert, C. M., II. (1978). Stratification in a dual economy. *American Sociological Review*, *43*, 704–739.

Bielby, W. T., & Bielby, D. D. (1992). I will follow him: Family ties, gender-role beliefs, and reluctance to relocate for a better job. *American Journal of Sociology*, *97*, 1241–1267.

Blau, P. M., & Duncan, O. D. (1967). *The American occupational structure*. New York: Wiley.

Borman, K. M., Cookson, P. W., Jr., Sadovnik, A. R., & Spade, J. Z. (1996). *Implementing educational reform: Sociological perspectives on educational policy*. Norwood, NJ: Ablex.

Brewster, K. L., & Rindfuss, R. R. (2000). Fertility and women's employment in industrialized nations. *Annual Review of Sociology, 26*, 271–296.

Bronfenbrenner, U. (1979). *The ecology of human development: Experiments by nature and design*. Cambridge, MA: Harvard University Press.

Bryk, A. S., & Thum, Y. M. (1989). The effects of high school organization on dropping out: An exploratory investigation. *American Educational Research Journal, 26*, 353–383.

Budig, M. J., and England, P. (2001). The wage penalty for motherhood. *American Sociological Review, 66*, 204–225.

Carr, R. V., Wright, J. D., and Brody, C. J. (1996). Effects of high school work experience a decade later: Evidence from the National Longitudinal Survey. *Sociology of Education, 69*, 66–81.

Chan, T. W. (1999). Revolving doors reexamined: Occupational sex segregation over the life course. *American Sociological Review, 64*, 86–96.

Cocran, M., Duncan, G., & Ponza, M. (1984). Work experience, job segregation, and wages. In B. F. Reskin (Ed.), *Sex segregation in the workplace* (pp. 171–191). Washington, DC: National Academy Press.

Committee on the Health and Safety Implications of Child Labor. (1998). *Protecting youth at work: Health, safety and development of working children and adolescents in the United States*. Washington, DC: National Academy Press.

Cooksey, E. C., Menaghan, E. G., & Jekielek, S. M. (1997). Life course effects of work and family circumstances on children. *Social Forces, 76*, 637–667.

Cotter, D. A., DeFiore, J. Hermsen, J. M., Marsteller-Kowalewski, B., & Vanneman, R. (1997). All women benefit: The macro-level effect of occupational integration on gender earnings equality. *American Sociological Review, 62*, 714–734.

Crain, R. L., & Mahard, R. E. (1978). Desegregation and black achievement: A review of the research. *Law and Contemporary Problems, 42*, 17–56.

Crain, R. L., & Mahard, R. E. (1983). The effect of research methodology on desegregation-achievement studies. *American Journal of Sociology, 88*, 839–854.

D'Amico, R. J. (1984). Does employment during high school impair academic progress? *Sociology of Education, 57,* 152–164.

Dauber, S. L., Alexander, K. L., & Entwisle, D. R. (1996). Tracking and transitions through the middle grades: Channeling educational trajectories. *Sociology of Education, 69,* 290–307.

DiPrete, T. A., & Nonnemaker, K. L. (1997). Structural change, labor market turbulence, and labor market outcomes. *American Sociological Review, 62,* 386–404.

Duncan, O. D., Featherman, D. L., & Duncan, B. (1972). *Socioeconomic background and achievement.* New York: Seminar Press.

Elder, G. H., Jr., & Conger, R. D. (2000). *Children of the land: Adversity and success in rural America.* Chicago: University of Chicago Press.

Elder, G. H., Jr., King, V., & Conger, R. D. (1996). Attachment to place and migration prospects: A developmental perspective. *Journal of Research on Adolescence, 6,* 397–425.

Elder, G. H., Jr., & O'Rand, A. M. (1995). Adult lives in a changing society. In K. S. Cook, G. A. Fine, & J. S. House (Eds.), *Sociological perspectives on social psychology* (pp. 452-475). Boston: Allyn & Bacon.

Eliason, S. R. (1995). An extension of the Sorensen-Kalleberg theory of the labor market matching and attainment process. *American Sociological Review, 60,* 247–271.

Entwisle, D. R., & Alexander, K. L. (1992). Summer setback: Race, poverty, school composition, and mathematics achievement in the first two years of school. *American Sociological Review, 57,* 72–84.

Entwisle, D. R., & Alexander, K. L. (1993). Entry into school: The beginning school transition and educational stratification in the United States. *Annual Review of Sociology, 19,* 401–423.

Farkas, G., Barton, M., & Kushner, K. (1988). White, black, and Hispanic female youths in central city labor markets. *Sociological Quarterly, 29,* 605–621.

Finch, M. D., Shanahan, M. J., Mortimer, J. T., & Ryu, S. (1991). Work experience and control orientation in adolescence. *American Sociological Review, 56,* 597–611.

Finn, J. D., & Voelkl, K. E. (1993). School characteristics related to student engagement. *Journal of Negro Education, 62,* 249–268.

Folwer, W. J., & Wahlberg, H. (1991). School size, characteristics, and outcomes. *Educational Evaluation and Policy Analysis, 13,* 189–202.

Gamoran, A. (1992). The variable effects of high school tracking. *American Sociological Review, 57*, 812–828.

Gamoran, A., Nystrad, M., Berends, M., & LePore, P. C. (1995). An organizational analysis of the effects of ability grouping. *American Educational Research Journal, 32*, 687–715.

Gecas, V., & Nye, I. F. (1974). Sex and class differences in parent-child interaction: A test of Kohn's hypothesis. *Journal of Marriage and the Family, 36,* 742–749.

Gerson, K. (1993). No man's land: Men's changing commitments to family and work. New York: Basic Books.

Ginzberg, E., Ginsburg, S. W., Axelrad, S., & Herma, J. L. (1951). *Occupational choice: An approach to a general theory.* New York: Columbia University Press.

Glass, J. L. (1990). The impact of occupational segregation on working conditions. *Social Forces, 68,* 779–796.

Glass, J. L., & Estes, S. B. (1997). The family responsive workplace. *Annual Review of Sociology, 23,* 289–313.

Gordon, C. (1972). *Looking ahead: Self-conceptions, race and family as determinants of adolescent orientation to achievement.* Washington, DC: Rose Monograph Series. American Sociological Association.

Grabowski, L. S., Mortimer, J. T., & Call, K. (2001). Global and economic self-efficacy in the educational attainment process. *Social Psychology Quarterly, 64,* 164–179.

Granovetter, M. S. (1974). *Getting a job.* Cambridge, MA: Harvard University Press.

Greenberger, E., O'Neil, R., & Nagel, S. K. (1994). Linking workplace and homeplace: Relations between the nature of adults' work and their parenting behaviors. *Developmental Psychology, 30,* 990–1002.

Greenberger, E., & Steinberg, L. D. (1986). *When teenagers work: The psychological and social costs of teenage employment.* New York: Basic Books.

Hallinan, M. T. (1996). Track mobility in secondary school. *Social Forces, 74,* 983–1002.

Hamilton, L. C., & Seyfrit, C. L. (1994). Resources and hopes in Newfoundland. *Society and Natural Resources, 5,* 561–578.

Hamilton, S. F., & Hamilton, M. A. (2000). Research, intervention, and social change: Improving adolescents' career opportunities. In L. J. Crockett & R. K. Silberensen (Eds.), *Negotiating adolescence in times of social change* (pp. 267–283). Cambridge, UK: Cambridge University Press.

Hauser, R. M. (1971). *Socioeconomic background and educational performance.* Washington, DC: Rose Monograph Series, American Sociological Association.

Heckhausen, J. (1999). *Developmental regulation in adulthood: Age normative and sociocultural constraints as adaptive challenges.* Cambridge, UK: Cambridge University Press.

Hodson, R., & Kaufman, R. L. (1982). Economic dualism: A critical review. *American Sociological Review, 47,* 727–739.

Hofferth, S. L. (2000). Effects of public and private policies on working after childbirth. In T. L. Parcel & D. B. Cornfield (Eds.), *Work and family: Research informing policy* (pp. 131–159). Thousand Oaks, CA: Sage.

Holland, J. L. (1964). Major programs of research on vocational behavior. In H. Borwow (Ed.), *Man in a world of work* (pp. 259–284). Boston: Houghton Mifflin.

Johnson, M. K. (2001a). Change in job values during the transition to adulthood. *Work and Occupations, 28,* 315–345.

Johnson, M. K. (2001b). Job values in the young adult transition: Stability and change with age. *Social Psychology Quarterly, 64,* 297–317.

Johnson, M. K. (in press). Social origins, adolescent experiences, and work value trajectories during the transition to adulthood. *Social Forces.*

Johnson, M. K., & Mortimer, J. T. (2000). Work-family orientations and attainments in the early life course. In T. L. Parcel & D. B. Cornfield (Eds.), *Work and family: research informing policy* (pp. 215–248). Thousand Oaks, CA: Sage.

Jones, J. D., Vanfossen, B. E., & Ensminger, M. E. (1995). Individual and organizational predictors of high school track placement. *Sociology of Education, 68,* 287–300.

Kerckhoff, A. C. (1974). *Ambition and attainment. A study of four samples of American boys.* Washington, DC: Rose Monograph Series, American Sociological Association.

Kerckhoff, A. C. (1993). *Diverging pathways: Social, structure and career deflections.* Cambridge, UK: Cambridge University Press.

Kerckhoff, A. C. (1995a). Institutional arrangements and stratification processes in industrial societies. *Annual Review of Sociology, 15,* 323–347.

Kerckhoff, A. C. (1995b). Social stratification and mobility processes: Interaction between individuals and social structures. In K. S. Cook, G. A. Fine, & J. S. House (Eds.), *Sociological perspectives on social psychology* (pp. 467–496). Boston: Allyn & Bacon.

Kerckhoff, A. C. (1996). Building conceptual and empirical bridges between studies of educational and labor force careers. In A. C. Kerckhoff (Ed.), *Generating social stratification: Toward a new research agenda* (pp. 37–56). Boulder, CO: Westview Press.

Kerckhoff, A. C. (2002). The transition from school to work. In J. T. Mortimer & R. Larson (Eds.), *The changing adolescent experience: Societal trends and the transition to adulthood*. Cambridge: Cambridge University Press.

Koenigsberg, J., Garet, M. S., & Rosenbaum, J. E. (1994). The effect of family on the job exits of young adults. *Work and Occupations, 21*, 33–63.

Kohn, M. (1969). *Class and conformity: A study in values*. Homewood, IL: Dorsey.

Kohn, M., & Schooler, C. (1983). *Work and personality: An inquiry into the impact of social stratification*. Norwood, NJ: Ablex.

Kohn, M., Slomczynski, K. M., & Schoenbach, C. (1986). Social stratification and the transmission of values in the family: A cross-national assessment. *Sociological Forum, 1*, 73–102.

Kubitschek, W. N., & Hallinan, M. T. (1996). Race, gender, and inequity in track assignments. *Research in Sociology of Education and Socialization, 11*, 121–146.

Lee, V. E., & Bryk, A. S. (1988). Curriculum tracking as mediating the social distribution of high school achievement. *Sociology of Education, 61*, 78–94.

Lee, V. E., & Bryk, A. S. (1989). A multilevel model of the social distribution of high school achievement. *Sociology of Education, 62*, 172–192.

Lee, V. E., Bryk, A. S., & Smith, J. B. (1993). The effects of high school organization on teachers and students. In L. Darling-Hammond (Ed.), *Review of research in education* (pp. 171–268). Washington DC: American Educational Research Association.

Lee, V. E., & Smith, J. B. (1995). Effects of high school restructuring and size on early gains in achievement and engagement. *Sociology of Education, 68*, 241–270.

Lindsay, P., & Knox, W. E. (1984). Continuity and change in work values among young adults. *American Journal of Sociology, 89*, 918–931.

Looker, E. D. (1992). Interconnected transitions and their costs: Gender and urban/rural differences in transitions to work. In P. Ansief & P. Axelrod (Eds.), *Transitions: Schooling and employment in Canada* (pp. 43–64). Toronto: Thomson Educational Publishing.

Manning, W. D. (1990). Parenting employed teenagers. *Youth and Society, 22*, 184–200.

Marini, M. M. (1984). Women's educational attainment and the timing of entry into parenthood. *American Sociological Review, 49*, 491–511.

Marini, M. M., & Fan, P-L. (1997). The gender gap in earnings at career entry. *American Sociological Review, 62*, 588–604.

Marini, M. M., Shin, H-C., & Raymond, J. (1989). Socioeconomic consequences of the process of transition to adulthood. *Social Science Research, 18*, 89–135.

Marsh, H. W. (1991). Employment during high school: Character building or subversion of academic goals? *Sociology of Education, 64*, 72–89.

Martin, S. P. (2000). Diverging fertility among U.S. women who delay childbearing past age 30. *Demography, 37*, 523–533.

Mason, K. O., & Kuhlthau, K. (1992). The perceived impact of child care costs on women's labor supply and fertility. *Demography, 29*, 523–544.

McNeal, R. B., Jr. (1997). Are students being pulled out of high school? The effect of adolescent employment on dropping out. *Sociology of Education, 70*, 206–220.

Mihalic, S. W., & Elliot, D. (1997). Short- and long-term consequences of adolescent work. *Youth and Society, 28*, 464–498.

Mortimer, J. T. (1974). Patterns of intergenerational occupational movements: A smallest-space analysis. *American Journal of Sociology, 79*, 1278–1299.

Mortimer, J. T. (1976). Social class, work, and the family: Some implications of the father's occupation for familial relationships and sons' career decisions. *Journal of Marriage and the Family, 38*, 241–256.

Mortimer, J. T. (1994). Individual differences as precursors of youth unemployment. In A. C. Petersen & J. T. Mortimer (Eds.), *Youth unemployment and society* (pp. 172–198). Cambridge, UK: Cambridge University Press.

Mortimer, J. T. (1996). Social psychological aspects of achievement. In A. C. Kerckhoff (Ed.), *Generating social stratification: Toward a new research agenda* (pp. 17–36). Boulder, CO: Westview Press.

Mortimer, J. T. (in press). *Work and growing up in America*. Cambridge, MA: Harvard University Press.

Mortimer, J. T., & Finch, M. D. (1986). The effects of part-time work on self-concept and achievement. In K. Borman & J. Reisman (Eds.), *Becoming a worker* (pp. 68–89). Norwood, NJ: Ablex.

Mortimer, J. T., Finch, M. D., Ryu, S., Shanahan, M. J., & Call, K. T. (1996). The effects of work intensity on adolescent mental health, achievement, and behavioral adjustment: New evidence from a prospective study. *Child Development, 67*, 1243–1261.

Mortimer, J. T., & Johnson, M. K. (1998). Adolescent part-time work and educational attainment. In K. Borman & B. Schneider (Eds.), *The adolescent years: Social influences and educational challenges* (pp. 183–206). National Society for the Study of Education. Chicago: University of Chicago Press.

Mortimer, J. T., & Johnson, M. K. (1999). Adolescent part-time work and post-secondary transition pathways: A longitudinal study of youth in St. Paul, Minnesota. In W. Heinz (Ed.), *From education to work: Cross national perspectives* (pp. 111–148). Cambridge, UK: Cambridge University Press.

Mortimer, J. T., & Kruger, H. (2000). Transition from school to work in the United States and Germany: Formal pathways matter. In M. Hallinan (Ed.), *Handbook of the sociology of education* (pp. 475–497). New York: Plenum.

Mortimer, J. T., & Kumka, D. (1982). A further examination of the "occupational linkage hypothesis." *The Sociological Quarterly, 23*, 3–16.

Mortimer, J. T., & Lorence, J. (1979). Work experience and occupational value socialization: A longitudinal study. *American Journal of Sociology, 84*, 1361–1385.

Mortimer, J. T., Lorence, J., & Kumka, D. (1986). *Work, family and personality: Transition to adulthood*. Norwood, NJ: Ablex.

Mortimer, J. T., Pimentel, E. E., Ryu, S., Nash, K., & Lee, C. (1996). Part-time work and occupational value formation in adolescence. *Social Forces, 74*, 1405–1418.

Newman, K. S. (1999). *No shame in my game*. New York: Knopf and the Russell Sage Foundation.

Noonan, M. C. (2001). The impact of domestic work on men's and women's wages. *Journal of Marriage and the Family, 63*, 1134–1145.

Oakes, J., Gamoran, A., & Page, R. N. (1992). Curriculum differentiation: Opportunities, outcomes, and meanings. In P. W. Jackson (Ed.),

Handbook of research on curriculum (pp. 570–608). Washington, DC: American Educational Research Association.

Parcel, T. L., & Menaghan, E. G. (1993). Family social capital and children's behavioral problems. *Social Psychology Quarterly, 56,* 120–135.

Parcel, T. L., & Menaghan, E. G. (1994). Early parental work, family social capital, and early childhood outcomes. *American Journal of Sociology, 99,* 972–1009.

Perry-Jenkins, M., Repetti, R. L., & Crouter, A. C. (2000). Work and family in the 1990s. *Journal of Marriage and the Family, 62,* 981–198.

Phillips, S., & Sandstrom, K. L. (1990). Parental attitudes toward youth work. *Youth and Society, 22,* 160–183.

Pixley, J. E., & Moen, P. (in press). Prioritizing his and her careers. In P. Moen (Ed.), *It's about time: Couples' career strains, strategies, and successes.* Ithaca, NY: Cornell University Press.

Podolny, J. M., & Baron, J. N. (1997). Resources and relationships: Social networks and mobility in the workplace. *American Sociological Review, 62,* 673–693.

Reskin, B. F., & McBrier, D. B. (2000). *American Sociological Review, 65,* 210–233.

Reskin, B. F., McBrier, D. B., & Kmec, K. A. (1999). The determinants and consequences of workplace sex and race composition. *Annual Review of Sociology, 25,* 335–361.

Rindfuss, R. R., & Brewster, L. L. (1996). Childrearing and fertility. *Population and Development Review, 22*(Suppl.), 258–289.

Rindfuss, R. R., Cooksey, E., & Sutterlin, R. A. (1999). Young adult occupational achievement. *Work and Occupations, 26,* 220–263.

Roberts, K. (1968). The entry into employment: An approach toward a general theory. *Sociological Review, 16,* 165–184.

Rogers, C. S. (1992). The flexible workplace: What have we learned? *Human Resources Management, 31,* 183–199.

Roscigno, V. J. (1998). Race and the reproduction of educational disadvantage. *Social Forces, 76,* 1033–1060.

Roscigno, V. J. (2000). Family/school inequality and African-American/Hispanic achievement. *Social Problems, 47,* 266–290.

Rosenbaum, J. E. (1976). *Making inequality: The hidden curriculum of high school tracking.* New York: Wiley.

Rosenbaum, J. E. (1996). Policy uses of research on the high school-to-work transition. *Sociology of Education, 69,* 102–122.

Rosenbaum, J. E., DeLuca, S., Miller, S. R., & Roy, K. (1999). Pathways into work: Short- and long-term effects of personal and institutional ties. *Sociology of Education*, *72*, 179–196.

Rosenfeld, R. A. (1992). Job mobility and career processes. *Annual Review of Sociology*, *18*, 39–61.

Rosenfeld, R. A., & Spenner, K. I. (1992). Occupational sex segregation and women's early career job shifts. *Work and Occupations*, *19*, 424–449.

Ruhm, C. J. (1995). The extent and consequences of high school employment. *Journal of Labor Research*, *16*, 293–303.

Ryu, S., & Mortimer, J. T. (1996). The "occupational linkage hypothesis" applied to occupational value formation in adolescence. In J. T. Mortimer & M. D. Finch (Eds.), *Adolescents, work, and family: An intergenerational developmental analysis* (pp. 167–190). Thousand Oaks, CA: Sage.

Schneider, B., & Stevenson, B. (1999). *The ambitious generation: America's teenagers, motivated but directionless*. New Haven: Yale University Press.

Schoenhals, M., Tienda, M., & Schneider, B. (1998). The educational and personal consequences of adolescent employment. *Social Forces*, *77*, 723–762.

Schulenberg, J. E., Vondracek, F. W., & Crouter, A. C. (1984). The influence of the family on vocational development. *Journal of Marriage and the Family*, *46*, 129–143.

Sewell, W. H., & Hauser, R. M. (1976). Causes and consequences of higher education: Models of the status attainment process. In W. H. Sewell, R. M. Hauser, & D. Featherman (Eds.), *Schooling and achievement in American society* (pp. 9–27). New York: Academic Press.

Shaffer, L. S., Seyfrit, C. L., & Associates. (2000). *Rural youth and their transitions and pathways connecting school and work: A white paper*. Report from the conference, Rural Youth and Their Transition from School to Work. Norfolk, VA: Old Dominion University.

Shanahan, M. J. (2000). Pathways to adulthood in changing societies: Variability and mechanisms in life course perspective. *Annual Review of Sociology*, *26*, 667–692.

Shanahan, M. J., Elder, G. H., Jr., Burchinal, M., & Conger, R. D. (1996). Adolescent earnings and relationships with parents: The work-family nexus in urban and rural ecologies. In J. T. Mortimer & M. D. Finch (Eds.), *Adolescents, work, and family: An intergenerational developmental analysis* (pp. 97–128). Newbury Park, CA: Sage.

Shanahan, M. J., Mortimer, J. T., & Kruger, H. (2002). Preparation for adult work in the twenty-first century. *Journal of Research on Adolescence*.

Singleton, J. (1998). The impact of family caregiving to the elderly on the American workplace: Who is affected and what is being done? In D. Vannoy & P. J. Dubeck, *Challenges for work and family in the twenty-first century* (pp. 201–214). New York: Aldine De Gruyter.

Sorenson, A. B., & Kalleberg, A. L. (1981). An outline for a theory of the matching of persons to jobs. In I. Berg (Ed.), *Sociological perspectives on the labor market* (pp. 49–74). New York: Academic Press.

Steel, L. (1991). Early work experience among white and non-white youths: Implications for subsequent enrollment and employment. *Youth and Society, 22*, 419–447.

Steinberg, L., & Dornbusch, S. M. (1991). Negative correlates of part-time employment during adolescence: Replication and elaboration. *Developmental Psychology, 27*, 304–313.

Stolzenberg, R. M. (1978). Bringing the boss back in: Employer size, employee schooling, and socioeconomic achievement. *American Sociological Review, 43*, 813–828.

Stone, J. R., & Mortimer, J. T. (1998). The effect of adolescent employment on vocational development: Public and educational policy implications. *Journal of Vocational Behavior, 53*, 184–214.

Strong, E. K. (1955). *Vocational interests 18 years after college*. Minneapolis: University of Minnesota Press.

Super, D. E., Starishevsky, R., Matlin, N., & Jordaan, J. P. (1963). *Career development: Self-concept theory*. Princeton, NJ: College Entrance Examination Board.

Taniguchi, H. (1999). The timing of childbearing and women's wages. *Journal of Marriage and the Family, 61*, 1008–1019.

Tienda, M., & Ahituv, A. (1996). Ethnic differences in school departure: Does youth employment promote or undermine educational attainment? In G. Magnum & S. Magnum (Eds.), *Of heart and mind: Social policy essays in honor of Sar A. Levitan* (pp. 93–110). MI: Upjohn Institute Press.

Trappe, H. (2000). Work and family in women's lives in the German Democratic Republic. In T. L. Parcel & D. B. Cornfield (Eds.), *Work* and family: Research informing policy (pp. 5–29). Thousand Oaks, CA: Sage.

Turner, R. H. (1962). Some family determinants of ambition. *Sociology and Social Research*, 46(July), 397–411.

Vondracek, F. W., Lerner, R. M., & Schulenberg, J. E. (1986). *Career development: A lifespan developmental approach.* Hillsdale, NJ: Erlbaum.

Waldfogel, J. (1997). The effect of children on women's wages. *American Sociological Review*, 62, 209–217.

Warren, J. R., LePore, P. C., & Mare, R. D. (2000). Employment during high school: Consequences for students' grades in academic courses. *American Educational Research Journal*, 37, 943–969.

Wenk, D., & Garrett, P. (1992). Having a baby: Some predictions of maternal employment around childbirth. *Gender and Society*, 6, 49–65.

Whitbeck, L. B., Simons, R. L., Conger, R. D., Wichrama, K. A. S., Ackley, K. A., & Elder, G. H., Jr. (1997). The effects of parents' working conditions and family economic hardship on parenting behaviors and children's self-efficacy. *Social Psychology Quarterly*, 60, 291–303.

Wilson, W. J. (1996). *When work disappears.* New York: Vantage Books.

Wortman, P. M., & Bryant, F. B. (1985). School desegregation and black achievement: An integrated review. *Sociological Methods and Research*, 13, 289–324.

PART THREE

Developmental and Postmodern Theories

PART THREE

Developmental and
Contextual Theories

4

Gottfredson's Theory of Circumscription, Compromise, and Self-Creation

Linda S. Gottfredson

Career choice is both an option and a responsibility in modern democratic societies such as the United States. People have far more freedom in fashioning their work lives than has been typical in other times and places. This developmental task is not a clear or easy one, nor does it always end well. However, it most assuredly affects the broader welfare of individuals, families, and communities. Hence the continuing concern, both inside and outside of vocational psychology, over the degree to which individuals and groups have sufficient freedom and support in fashioning their careers.

The theory I am describing is directed to that concern. Its original emphasis was on explaining gender and class differences in career development, with particular attention to the barriers that individuals face. The puzzle it addressed was this: Why do children seem to re-create the social inequalities of their elders long before they themselves experience any barriers to pursuing their dreams? The theory's elaboration here turns from the puzzle of between-group differences to the puzzle of *within*-group differences: Why do individuals from the *same* circumstances tend to have such *different* aspirations and success in implementing the self they prefer? The elaboration therefore turns to *why individuals differ*, regardless of

I would like to thank Duane Brown and Richard Sharf for their helpful comments on earlier versions of this chapter.

group membership. My new theory pays particular attention to the powers an individual has, but may not always exercise, to create a public self that resonates better with his or her unique internal self.

Evolution of the Theory

I revised the circumscription and compromise theory in 1981 (Gottfredson, 1981) and revised it again, slightly, in 1996 (Gottfredson, 1996); this chapter extends the scope of the theory considerably. Research testing of the theory since 1995 has not been extensive but consistently supports the components tested (for example, dimensions of compromise, Armstrong & Crombie, 2000; young people's images of the occupational world, Shivy, Phillips, & Koehly, 1996; internalized constraints on career exploration, Flum & Blustein, 2000). Users have continued to find its focus on childhood development, as well as gender differences (for example, McLennan & Arthur, 1999), helpful. Criticisms of the theory have concerned what it fails to discuss, particularly adult development. But because there are theories that deal with adult development, I have chosen to address a lacuna shared by all theories of careers: Where do interests, abilities, and other determinants of vocational choice themselves come from? How would knowledge about these determinants assist counselors and counselees, especially with the processes of circumscription and compromise?

All career theories in psychology stress the importance of a good match between person and job. For instance, my own theory concerns the process by which people unnecessarily circumscribe and compromise their career options, often sacrificing fulfillment of their "internal unique selves" in order to meet expectations for job prestige and sextype. The theory's aim is to help people prevent or reverse unwarranted constriction in early career development and thereby be more likely to obtain the "best fits" within their reach. The assumption in career psychology—indeed, in all of differential psychology—is that people embody inherent characteristics that distinguish them from others and that help make them who they are. We convey this sense of individuals having their own unique core when we speak of "trying to find yourself" and or say "life is a journey of self-discovery."

But when and from what does that discoverable self germinate? Are we but products of other people's actions, from parents to politicians, who would shape us this way or that? Or are we born into the world already unique and with stubborn proclivities that propel us toward some ends rather than others? Were vocational psychologists to make their assumptions on the nature-nurture question explicit, their views would probably range widely. But the field of vocational psychology has been mostly silent on this fundamental issue. That silence is probably due, in part, to the fact that until recently it has lacked the necessary information. However, there is now much new evidence that is relevant to career development professionals, and I will highlight it shortly.

Another reason the field has been silent is that it has lacked a comfortable ethical perspective on the nature-nurture debate. Neither side has seemed consistent with the ethos of counseling psychology. On the one hand, if we want only what others train us to want (nurture), what does it mean for counselors to help us discover and implement those externally manufactured selves? On the other hand, what if counselors are merely the handmaidens of biological fate? What if people are driven blindly by their genetic heritage (nature) to be who they are?

Behavioral genetic research reveals this grim choice to be a false one, as I will show. The new evidence is entirely consistent with career psychology's traditional view of individuals as active agents in creating themselves and shaping their own destiny. I have therefore extended my theory to incorporate behavioral genetic evidence on interests and other career-relevant human traits. I have also tried to illustrate how career counseling might take advantage of resulting insights about the way we create our public selves from the raw materials that both nature and nurture provide us.

The Core Theory

Next I outline the core concepts and propositions of the theory as of 1996 (Gottfredson, 1996). Supporting evidence for that core can be found in Gottfredson (1981, 1996; Gottfredson & Lapan, 1997). Following this review, I describe extensions of the theory that incorporate pertinent research from behavioral genetics.

Major Concepts

Self-concept refers to one's view of oneself—of who one is both publicly and privately. It has many elements, including appearance, abilities, personality, gender, values, and place in society. Some elements are more central to one's sense of self than others. People may not be able to articulate their self-concepts, nor may their self-perceptions always be accurate, but they act on them and protect them just the same. The self-concept is the object of cognition (the "me"), but it also reflects the person as actor (the "I").

People also hold *images of occupations* (often called occupational stereotypes), including the personalities of people in those occupations, the work they do, the lives they lead, the rewards and conditions of the work, and the appropriateness of that work for different types of people. Americans from all segments of society share basically the same images of occupations and their incumbents, for example, of personality type and prestige level.

These common images are organized into a meaningful, shared *cognitive map of occupations*. Adolescents and adults distinguish occupations along a few major dimensions: masculinity-femininity, occupational prestige level (overall desirability), and field of work. These distinctions can be represented in a two-dimensional map (Sextype by Prestige Level), as shown in Figure 4.1. Differences in occupations' rated prestige mirror differences in the intellectual complexity of their duties (Gottfredson, 1997), which means that the occupational prestige hierarchy is also a ladder of demands for intelligence on the job.

FIGURE 4.1. Map of Occupations According to Prestige and Sextype Ratings

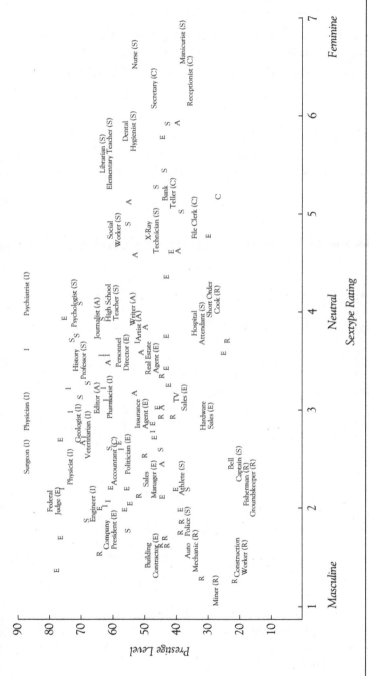

Note: Occupations are denoted by a letter indicating their Holland types: R = Realistic, I = Investigative, A = Artistic, S = Social, E = Enterprising, C = Conventional.

Figure 4.1 is from Gottfredson, 1981; Copyright © 1981 by the American Psychological Association. Reprinted with permission.

Jobs in different fields of work tend to cluster in different parts of this shared cognitive map. This clustering can be seen more clearly in Figure 4.2, where a large sample of common occupations is classified by Holland type, as well as by sextype and prestige level. This map of occupations constitutes, most generally, a map of the larger social world—of the "places" or ecological niches in society that different occupations offer.

Children have a ready facility to construct common social maps, illustrating "a remarkable skill for perceiving, remembering, accumulating, and organizing concrete social information" (Cairns

FIGURE 4.2. Prestige and Sextype Ratings of Occupations in the Different Holland Fields of Work

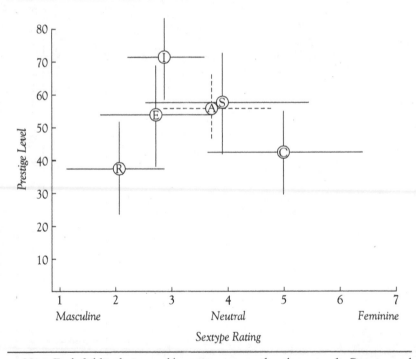

Note: Each field is designated by a cross centered at the mean for Prestige and Sextype and showing one standard deviation on either side of the mean; letters denote Holland fields.

Figure 4.2 is from Gottfredson, 1981; Copyright © 1981 by the American Psychological Association. Reprinted with permission.

& Cairns, 1988, p. 198). Their maps are primitive early in life, but with increasing cognitive maturity they come to perceive the same occupational map of the social order as adults do. The overall map is probably common to all groups in the developed world (for example, see Treiman, 1977, for an international occupational prestige scale) but ought not be assumed so for impoverished or disorganized nations in the Third World. When social orders differ, so too will their members' perceptions of them.

Individuals identify the occupations they most prefer by assessing the *compatibility* of different occupations with their images of themselves. Compatibility is what is usually meant by the terms *congruence* and *person-environment fit*. The greater the perceived compatibility (suitability), the stronger the person's preference. Individuals may seek out but rarely achieve compatibility with all elements of self. Occupations that conflict with core elements of the self-concept will be most strongly rejected. The theory postulates that (1) public presentations of masculinity-femininity will be most carefully guarded, (2) protecting social standing among one's fellows will be of considerable but lesser concern, and (3) ensuring fulfillment of activity preferences and personality needs via occupation will be of least concern.

One's most preferred occupations are not necessarily realistic or available. Many barriers may stand in the way of implementing them. Individuals therefore must also assess the *accessibility* of occupations when choosing which vocational alternatives to pursue.

What vocational psychologists typically refer to as *occupational aspirations* are the joint product of assessments of *compatibility* and *accessibility*. Aspirations are called *expectations* or *realistic aspirations* when they are tempered by knowledge of obstacles and opportunities. They are called *idealistic aspirations* when they are not.

Social space refers to the range of alternatives within the cognitive map of occupations that the person considers acceptable, although the person may much prefer some of these alternatives to others, as is illustrated in Figure 4.3. This *zone of acceptable alternatives* may be large or small but reflects the individual's view of where he or she fits best into society.

FIGURE 4.3. Circumscription of Aspirations According to Perceptions of Job-Self Compatibility

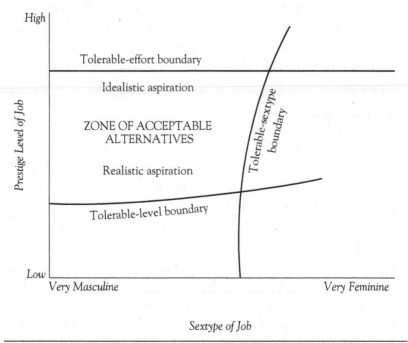

Note: This example represents a hypothetical middle-class boy of average intelligence.

Figure 4.3 is from Gottfredson, 1981; Copyright © 1981 by the American Psychological Association. Reprinted with permission

An occupational aspiration is simply the one alternative within this space that the individual happens to voice at a particular time, and it may change quickly as individuals adjust their perceptions of suitability and accessibility. In the theory, then, single aspirations are but shifting and fallible indicators of the center of a set or array of occupational niches that the individual is willing or eager to consider. The theory thus requires thinking in terms of (and measuring) territories rather than single points of preference.

Circumscription is the process by which youngsters narrow that territory. They progressively eliminate unacceptable alternatives in order to carve out a social space (their zone of acceptable alternatives) from the full menu that a culture offers. Choosing one particular occupation is but the end of a long process in which youngsters have greatly constrained that final choice, knowingly or not.

Compromise is the process by which youngsters begin to relinquish their most preferred alternatives for less compatible ones that they perceive as more accessible. Individuals often discover, when the time comes, that they are unable to implement their most-preferred choices. In a sense, they have to reverse the choice process and reconsider their less-preferred alternatives, perhaps even ones they had earlier ruled out as unacceptable. Compromise can occur either in anticipation of external barriers (anticipatory compromise) or after they are encountered (experiential compromise).

Circumscription Process

The circumscription of aspirations from early childhood through adolescence can be described by several principles, which play themselves out in four stages of development. However, it is first essential to describe how the entire process is conditioned on cognitive development. It is widely recognized, of course, that cognition and human limits in information processing are essential to understanding career development. However, age changes and individual differences in general cognitive ability (intelligence) remain underappreciated.

Forming occupational aspirations is a process of comparing one's self-image with images of occupations and judging degree of match between the two. This is a very demanding cognitive process that requires perceiving and understanding properties of self, occupations, and the place of both in the social world. Young children, however, hold only primitive images of themselves and the world around them. They nonetheless begin to draw conclusions about which kinds of work are suitable—and distinctly unsuitable—for them. Simplistic or not, their conclusions can have lasting consequences because they lead youngsters to rule out from further consideration progressively more sectors of the occupational world of which they may as yet be only dimly aware. Young people circum-scribe their options before they fully understand them.

Principles of Circumscription. The delineation of one's self-concept and associated social space (the zone of acceptable alternatives) proceeds by five principles:

1. Increasing capacity for abstraction
2. Interactive development of self and aspirations
3. Overlapping differentiation and incorporation
4. Progressive elimination of options
5. Taken for granted and lost for sight

1. Increasing capacity for abstraction. With age, children become increasingly able to apprehend and organize complex, abstract infor-mation about themselves and their world. They progress from mag-ical and intuitive thinking to recognizing highly concrete elements of the world (gender differences in clothing, occupations with uni-forms, gross motor activity) and then to perceiving the more abstract (personality traits, values). Children progress through this sequence at different rates because they differ in mental ability. By early ado-lescence, some youngsters will function mentally like college stu-dents but others more like children in the fourth grade or below.

2. Interactive development of self and aspirations. Self-concept and vocational preferences develop closely in tandem, each influencing the other as children understand more about both. Occupational preferences reflect an effort to both implement and enhance the self-concept. Occupational preferences are so tightly linked with self-concept because individuals are very concerned about their place in social life, and occupations are a major signal and con-straint in the presentation of self to society.

3. Overlapping differentiation and incorporation. Children appre-hend and integrate information about self and occupations in order of complexity. They begin to catch on to the more complex distinctions among individuals (for example, social class) while they are still incorporating the more concrete (sex roles) into their concepts of self. In turn, they may still be incorporating notions of social status into the self-concept when they start to perceive more abstract distinctions such as in temperament and values. They begin developing new insights before they finish acting on prior ones.

4. *Progressive elimination of options.* As youngsters incorporate more abstract elements (first gender, then social class, and so on) into their images of self, their self-concepts become more complex and more clearly delineated. Simultaneously, they rule out as incompatible an ever-greater range of occupations, for example, as the "wrong" sextype, too low level, too difficult. This narrowing of options is, in effect, irreversible because the rejected options are seldom reconsidered spontaneously. People reconsider options they have previously ruled out as unacceptable in sextype or prestige only when they are prompted to do so by some formative new experience or some notable or consistent change in their social environment. For example, a teacher might encourage a working-class child to consider an occupation the child has always presumed to be intellectually beyond her grasp.

5. *Taken for granted and lost to sight.* The joint process of delineating self and circumscribing vocational choices is so fundamental, gradual, and taken for granted that people typically cannot spontaneously "see" or report on it, despite its having a continuing and profound effect on their beliefs and behaviors. Some strong external stimulus, such as switching schools and peer groups, generally seems required to illuminate what's been taken for granted.

Stages of Circumscription. The development of self-images and occupational aspirations can be usefully segmented into four stages. Each successive stage requires and reflects a higher level of general mental development and personal integration. Each stage leads to further narrowing of the potential social space, relative to a culture's full menu of possibilities, as youngsters begin to understand more complex aspects of themselves and occupations. Each new step in psychological integration is also a step in creating a public self—that is, in integrating the self into society and vice versa.

The following age and grade delineations between the four stages are somewhat arbitrary because youngsters differ considerably in mental maturity at any given chronological age.

Stage 1: Orientation to size and power (ages three to five). Children in preschool and kindergarten progress from magical to intuitive thinking and begin to achieve object constancy (for example, they know that people cannot change their sex by changing their outward appearance). They begin to classify people in the simplest of ways—as big (and powerful) versus little (and weak). They also come to recognize occupations as adult roles and cease reporting that they would like to be animals (bunnies), fantasy characters (princesses), or inanimate objects (rocks) when they grow up.

Children at this stage do not have stable or coherent conceptions of sex roles or an abstract concept of male versus female. But they are laying the groundwork for such conceptions, because they now apprehend the concrete, observable differences in gender (both appearance and behavior), prefer to play with same-sex peers, orient to same-sex adults, and report same-sex preferences for adult activities, including employment. Their achievement is to have recognized that there is an adult world and that working at a job is part of it.

Stage 2: Orientation to sex roles (ages six to eight). Children at this age have progressed to thinking in concrete terms and making simple distinctions. They are dichotomous thinkers, however, and tend to rank everything simply as good versus bad. They have begun to understand the concept of sex roles but focus primarily on their most visible cues such as overt activities and clothing. Being particularly rigid and moralistic, they often treat adherence to sex roles as a moral imperative. Vocational aspirations at this stage reflect a concern with doing what is appropriate for one's sex. Both sexes believe their own sex is superior. Although the predominance of same-sex occupational preferences in Stage 2 may be primarily a by-product of children's orientation to same-sex adults and their knowledge that adult activities are sextyped, in Stage 2 it clearly reflects an active rejection of cross-sex behavior. Youngsters have now erected their *tolerable-sextype boundary* (see Figure 4.3).

Children exhibit no concern over occupational prestige at this age and show but a "preawareness" of distinctions in social class. They will speak of social status but simply collapse the distinctions of "rich versus poor," "clean versus dirty," and "own versus other" into a single dichotomy between "good" and "bad." Girls report fewer but higher-status occupational preferences than do boys, but this is an artifact of which same-sex occupations are most visible to young children because of equipment (truck driver), gross motor activity (athlete), uniforms (police officer, nurse), or personal contact (teacher).

In summary, children have now ruled part of the occupational world out of bounds for being the wrong sextype. They may have a developing sense of other social distinctions, but the nature and relevance of these distinctions is not yet clear to them.

Stage 3: Orientation to social valuation (ages nine to thirteen). At this stage, youngsters become very sensitive to social evaluation, whether by peers or the larger society. The issue is no longer just male versus female but higher versus lower. By age nine (grade 4), youngsters become harsher judges of low-status occupations and cease to mention them as preferences. They start to recognize the more concrete symbols of social class (clothing, rough behavior, possessions brought to school). By age thirteen (grade 8), most rank occupations in prestige the same way adults do, and they understand the tight links among income, education, and occupation. It has become clear to them that there is an occupational hierarchy that affects how people live their lives and are regarded by others.

They and the important adults in their lives have also formed perceptions of the adolescent's own general level of ability (intelligence) relative to that of schoolmates and thus of their competitiveness for more difficult and more desirable occupations. Adolescents have also learned which occupations their own families and communities would reject as unacceptably low in social standing. In short, they have begun to sense a ceiling and a floor for their attainments.

As youngsters incorporate considerations of social class and ability into their self-concepts, they reject occupational alternatives that seem inconsistent with those newly recognized elements of self. In particular, they reject options that are of unacceptably low prestige in their social reference group, thus establishing a *tolerable-level boundary* below which they will not voluntarily venture again (see Figure 4.3). They also ignore options that seem too difficult to obtain with reasonable effort or that pose too high a risk of failure. Schools have perhaps the biggest impact today on children's perceptions of occupational difficulty, because they starkly illuminate students' differences in intelligence and thus their prospects for rising socially via higher education. Such perceptions lead children to set a *tolerable-effort boundary*, above which they are not apt to look again unless their self-conceptions of ability and competitiveness change.

Teachers, parents, and others encourage brighter youngsters to aim higher in education and occupation, which these children actually do relative to peers of the same socioeconomic status background. Similarly, youngsters from higher social class (wealthier, better educated) families are subject to higher occupational expectations, and they must achieve a higher minimum occupational status level in order to avoid being considered a failure in their social group. Thus both high-social-class background and high ability elevate aspirations—the former by raising the floor of what is acceptable and the latter by raising the ceiling of what is possible. By the same token, low-social-class background and low ability dampen aspirations by, respectively, lowering what is acceptable and what is possible.

These zones of acceptable alternatives can vary by size, location, clarity, and stability across individuals and over time. For example, a low-ability child from a high-status family is likely to perceive far fewer acceptable alternatives than will a high-ability child from a lower-status family. The ceiling and floor on aspirations will be much closer together for the former than the latter.

Not all acceptable alternatives are equally preferred. Rather, there are gradients of preference, from high to low, across the zone of acceptable alternatives. For example, a young woman might pre-fer a sex-neutral job of moderate prestige, but she will find other possibilities somewhat attractive too. Attractiveness might fall off gradually for jobs that are successively lower in prestige, more intel-lectually demanding, or more gender-stereotyped.

By the early teen years, youngsters largely take their broad social identities for granted. Although they may be confused or undecided about which particular occupations they prefer, they have devel-oped firm conceptions of their place in the broad social order and narrowed their vocational options accordingly. Teens will soon intensify their exploration of specific alternatives but only within the restricted range they have delimited for themselves.

Stage 4: Orientation to the internal, unique self (ages fourteen and above). Adolescents now take their desired place in society more or less for granted. In addition, most are keenly concerned with their attractiveness to the opposite sex, which can reinforce their adherence to sex and status stereotypes. The unsettled and unset-tling question for many relates instead to who they are as individu-als. This is the fourth stage of development.

Adolescents have become better able to apprehend and inte-grate highly abstract, complex information. Orienting to more internally defined goals and internally based concepts of self (for example, personality), they begin to forge a more personal sense of self. A focus on the external similarities of self with others becomes modulated by a growing concern for their own unique attributes. Their unreflecting attempt to "fit into" the right social crowd becomes a more discerning quest for a more personally compatible set of activities and interpersonal relations. However, abstract char-acteristics are less directly observable, so adolescents struggle, often confused and insecure, to ascertain just what their interests, abili-ties, personality traits, and values really are. In fact, many of their interests and values may still be largely unformed. Individuals often require experience in new activities and unfamiliar settings in order to diagnose and develop their specific strengths and weaknesses, likes and dislikes, and stance toward life. Few of us know the limits of our abilities or courage, for instance, until they are actually tested. And many an education or business major has solidified—or changed—career plans after taking a course that gives them actual field experience. This, then, is a period of learning more about one's psychological profile, especially as it affects one's *public* self, that is, the public presentation of who we can and want to be.

Occupational exploration is confined to the zone of acceptable alternatives circumscribed at earlier stages. It now focuses, in particular, on fields of work within that space that seem most congruent with the more internal, unique sense of self that the individual wishes to implement and project. Youngsters also begin to contemplate occupational preferences within a broader life plane—one that comes with social obligations as well as personal fulfillment—for example, as "good providers" (economic or nurturant) for their future families.

Whereas the first three stages are devoted to rejecting unacceptable alternatives, this stage is devoted to identifying which of the acceptable choices are most preferred and most accessible. Gradients of preference shift as youngsters learn more about and reflect on their personality, values, special aptitudes, and family needs. For example, as a result of recent volunteer work, a young man may realize that he is more attracted to artistic work than to the midlevel social service or entrepreneurial occupations that he had been considering.

Preference gradients also shift as young people consider probable barriers and opportunities in implementing different choices. The young man, for instance, might begin to rethink his new-found interest in artistic work as he learns how much competition there is for so few artistic jobs. Stage 4 thus initiates the process of compromise.

Compromise of Aspirations

Whereas circumscription is the process by which individuals reject alternatives they deem unacceptable, compromise is the process by which they abandon their most-preferred alternatives. Compromise is adjusting aspirations to accommodate an external reality. Anticipatory compromise takes place when people begin to moderate their hopes (assessments of compatibility) with their perceptions of reality (assessments of accessibility). As they do, the aspirations they voice will shift away from their ideal and toward the expected. Experiential compromise takes place when individuals meet a barrier in implementing their most-preferred choices.

The barriers and opportunities in implementing different aspirations include, for example, the local availability of particular kinds of education and employment, hiring practices (including discrimination), and family obligations. They also include the fact that not all combinations of sextype, prestige, and vocational interest type are readily available in the labor market. As Figures 4.1 and 4.2 show, for example, there is more high-prestige work that is distinctively masculine than feminine, and some combinations do not even exist (low-level investigative work). These external constraints restrict virtually everyone to some degree; few have unrestricted choices.

Perceptions of Accessibility. As I described earlier, vocational aspirations are a function of people's assessments of what is accessible as well as what is compatible. The relative accessibility of different jobs is hardly obvious, however; it can vary greatly across time and place, depending on many factors. Information on accessibility degrades quickly as time passes, and it may always be difficult to obtain for some occupations.

Notions of accessibility depend on both the information to which individuals are exposed and the information they themselves seek out. Monitoring and seeking out information demand time and effort.

Three principles govern the accumulation and influence of information on accessibility, all emphasizing economy in search:

1. Selective attention
2. Need to implement as spur to action
3. Ease and proximity of search

1. *Selective attention.* People normally attend to information about the accessibility of occupations they deem suitable for themselves and the alternatives within their perceived social space. The more preferred the occupation, the more likely an individual is to attend to information about it.

2. *Need to implement as spur to action.* People attend to information primarily when they must begin to implement an occupational aspiration. The closer the time of implementation (say, the nearer graduation) or the more serious the commitment (choosing a job versus a college major), the more realistic idealistic aspirations become.

3. *Ease and proximity of search.* People actively seek information and guidance on where to get it primarily from sources that are convenient and trusted. Parents, friends, teachers, colleagues, and others in one's social network thus play a key role in shaping our perceptions of accessibility as well as our perceptions of suitability. Economy of search thus tends to promote stability rather than change in one's social space.

Degrees of Compromise. Compromises can range from minor to wrenching. They are not especially difficult when they involve highly acceptable alternatives. Indeed, because they involve the "balancing" or "trading off" of different values and interests in order to identify one's best overall option, they are viewed more as choices than compromises. Figure 4.4 illustrates this point (ignore the three curves for now). Degree of compromise (deviation from the ideal) can range from low to high for one or more of the three dimensions of compatibility. The greater the compromise, the higher the level of concern over it.

Compromises become more difficult and seem less voluntary as one depletes the more acceptable alternatives within one's social space. They can be very painful when the choice is among alternatives that the individual deems unacceptable, that is, outside the person's social space. Although a choice among acceptable alterna-

FIGURE 4.4. Concern Over Degrees of Compromise

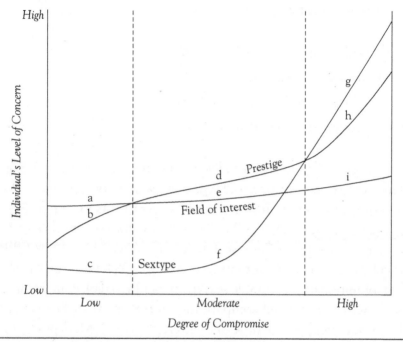

Note: The graph shows sensitivity to different degrees of compromise in sex-type, prestige, and field of interests.

tives (a minor compromise) can limit the degree to which the preferred self-concept can be fully implemented via career, the prospect of taking a frankly unacceptable job (a major compromise) can deeply threaten the self-concept. As will be discussed shortly, a major compromise along some dimensions of compatibility is more upsetting than others.

Principles of Compromise. The theory proposes four principles by which compromise proceeds. They all emphasize the greater importance to individuals of protecting one's visible social self than the more private psychological self. We are social beings, so crafting a "good enough" public self is essential; fulfilling the private self is more discretionary, at least until later in life.

The principles of compromise, which are discussed in the sections to follow, are:

1. Developing conditional priorities
2. Opting for "the good"
3. Staving off the "not good enough"
4. Accommodating to compromise

Principle 1: Developing conditional priorities. The relative importance of sextype, prestige, and type of work activity depends on the severity of the compromise required. Severe threats to sextype (segment g in Figure 4.4) will be warded off before severe threats to either prestige (h) or interests (i), because a "wrong" sextype (g) is usually the greater threat to the self-concept. As long as the threshold for minimally acceptable sextype is met (avoid g), compromises will sacrifice increased compatibility of sextype (c or f) to avoid losses in either prestige (b or d) or interests (a or e). Moderate compromise in prestige (d) will be avoided before moderate compromise of interests (e). If that threshold for prestige is met (avoid d), then trade-offs will favor greater compatibility in interests (a) rather than in either prestige (b) or sextype (c). To summarize, if compromises are severe, protect sextype; if compromises are moderate, sextype is good enough so favor prestige; if compromises are minor, that means both sextype and prestige are good enough, so favor interests.

These successive thresholds lead to the following predictions about priorities in compromise. They reflect a reversal in priorities (in salience) as severity of compromise increases and different thresholds of concern are crossed.

- When individuals are trading off small discrepancies from their ideal field of interests (a), prestige (b), and sextype (c), they give highest priority to interests (avoiding a rather than b or c); the latter two are good enough to indulge the former.

- When moderate trade-offs are required within the social space (d, e, or f), people will most avoid the compromise in prestige (d). By contrast, they will have little or no concern with sextype unless it verges on the unacceptable (g, which means for most people a cross-sextyped job).

- When faced with major compromises (g, h, and i), people will sacrifice interests (i) before transgressing either their tolerable prestige level (h) or sextype (g) boundaries. Although avoiding an unacceptably low-level job (h) is of great concern, avoiding a cross-sextyped job (g) is of yet higher concern.

- Vocational interests are always of moderate concern (a, e, and i), but they are overshadowed by concerns for either prestige or sextype, except when both of the latter are close to optimal (b and c).

Many combinations of compromise are possible, of course, and only sometimes is it clear what the priorities in compromise will be. For example, a traditional middle-class woman with Realistic interests might have a choice between carpentry and social work—that is, between a cross-sextyped job (g) of moderately unsatisfactory prestige (d) in her field of interest (a) and a slightly feminine job (f) of fairly desirable prestige level (b) in an incongruent field of work (i). The model in Figure 4.4 suggests that she will probably be more concerned with avoiding the wrong sextype (g) than the wrong field of work (i) and thus choose social work—a decision that would be reinforced by its more satisfactory prestige (b versus d).

The curves in Figure 4.4 for the three types of compatibility can be conceptualized as sensitivity curves that depict how sensitive the average individual is to different degrees of compromise along a particular dimension of compatibility. The curves are not parallel; they intersect. Prestige overtakes vocational interest type as the major concern when compromises are moderate in degree; sextype overtakes both when compromise is severe. The most important implication of such intersection is that the most central elements of self-concept (for which the highest *absolute* levels of concern can be aroused) are not necessarily the most salient (of most *relative* concern) in any particular circumstance. Salience and centrality have frequently been conflated in research on compromise.

One last prediction on priorities in compromise concerns gender differences:

- The sextype threshold is more relaxed for women than for men, because research suggests that women currently are more willing to perform cross-sextyped work than are men. It may be like clothing, where women are freer to dress like men than men are to dress like women. Stated in terms of Figure 4.4, the curve for sextype is more often displaced to the right for women.

Principle 2: Opting for the "good enough." Individuals settle for a good choice, not the best possible choice. Individuals are generally satisfied by the former and typically unable or unwilling to go through the demanding process of gathering and balancing the often-vague (their own values) and uncertain (accessibility) information necessary for identifying the best possible choice.

Principle 3: Staving off the "not good enough." If the individual is not satisfied with the available choices within the social space, he or she will avoid becoming committed to any, if possible. Avoidance may take many forms, including searching for more alternatives, persevering with an untenable choice, reconsidering the tolerable-effort boundary, or simply delaying decisions or commitments (remaining "undecided") for as long as possible.

Principle 4: Accommodating to compromise. Individuals accommodate psychologically to even major compromises in field of work activity, less to compromises in prestige that threaten social standing, and least of all to shifts in sextype that undermine the implementation of an acceptable gender identity. Overall satisfaction with one's occupation will depend on the degree to which the compromise allows one to implement a desired social self, either through the work itself or the lifestyle it allows self and family.

It should be stressed that these principles of compromise apply to people just launching their adult lives. After adults have established a life trajectory, solidified a public self, and discharged most of their family responsibilities, they may reflect on the compromises they have made. Freed from early life concerns, older adults who feel they have sacrificed their private selves to fulfill their duties as public selves may now alter course to pursue their "true calling" in life.

Extensions of the Theory

The principles of circumscription and compromise just described represent the development of the average person. However, there is much variability among individuals. Indeed, that is the message of counseling psychology—that we are all unique individuals, regardless of the circumstances of our birth and upbringing and, moreover, that satisfaction and achievement flow from finding life roles and activities that accord with our uniqueness.

Career theorists, myself included, have often focused on group differences in career development, particularly gender differences, but seemed to lose sight of the far greater variation among individuals *within* groups. Our theories have tended to take key individual differences for granted rather than try to explain them. However, not knowing how nature and nurture work together to govern the direction of personal growth hinders our ability to help counselees thrive. Why do some young people circumscribe their choices more narrowly or compromise them less wisely? Why do children from similar environments, even the same households, often have different interests and abilities and follow quite different career trajectories? To what extent did they encounter—or create—different opportunities? To what extent did they always march to different drummers, and why?

As noted earlier, different career theories tend to make different assumptions about the origins of individual differences in abilities and interests, but behavioral genetic research suggests that many common assumptions are mistaken. I review next a family of mistaken theories that Scarr (1997) has summarized as *socialization theory*. I then describe a new family of theories called *nature-nurture partnership theory* by Eysenck (1998) that has emerged from several decades of genetically sensitive family studies. Whereas socialization theory sees us mutely following the life compasses that our culture sets for us, the latter theory points to the quiet but persistent genetic compasses with which nature equips each of us at birth and which vie with culture in shaping our travels through life. In the closing section of this chapter, I describe the implications of this biosocial perspective for career counseling.

"Mistaken" Socialization Theory of Individual Differences

Although often giving lip service to the role of genes, most if not all career theories seem to assume that our parents and teachers, friends and enemies, and socioeconomic circumstances make us who we are most fundamentally. This socialization theory of development is shown in the top half of Figure 4.5. According to the theory, the differences among us may be highly genetic at birth, but (the theory continues) we are increasingly shaped and reshaped by the different environments to which we are exposed. So, for instance, the theory predicts that children from advantaged, supportive environments will be more self-confident, brighter, and achieve more, owing to the successive good experiences that their environments provide. Children who are continually exposed to art and high culture will develop Artistic interests, just as those raised by entrepreneurs will develop Enterprising interests. In like manner, the theory predicts that children who grow up in neglectful or intellectually impoverished environments will tend to develop unfavorable traits owing to their unfavorable experiences.

FIGURE 4.5. Mistaken Versus Modern Views of Nature-Nurture

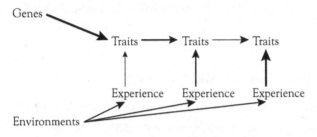

Mistaken socialization theory: Nurture gradually dilutes and replaces early genetic influence

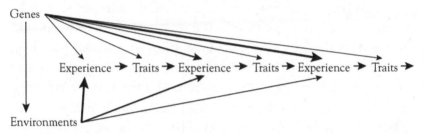

Modern nature-nurture partnership theory: Both genes and environments drive experience, and (increasingly gene-driven) experience consolidates traits

Under socialization theory, external forces create our experiences and our experiences create us. A person's profile of attributes thus arises from the profile of social influences that have constructed the person. Stated in terms of learning processes, socialization theory suggests that we passively learn to be what we are taught to be. So a person becomes smart if given many opportunities to learn, abusive if reared amidst abuse, and interested in mechanical activities if encouraged to engage in them. It suggests that we come to prefer one Holland field of work to others because we are more often exposed to and reinforced for it.

The expectation from socialization theory is therefore that the longer we live in the world, the more fully we become the products of our social circumstances, with different circumstances yielding different products. By this theory, individual differences should become less genetically heritable—perhaps insignificantly so, as environ-mental influences accumulate with age. This expectation is shown in the top panel of Figure 4.5 by the successively thicker arrows from "experience" to "traits" but a waning influence for genes with advancing age.

Research Disproving Socialization Theory

Although most social scientists still favor socialization theory for explaining the differences among us, behavioral genetic research has nonetheless decisively disproved it. The theory's Achilles heel is that it rests on correlations between relatives without regard to their genetic relatedness. However, no conclusions whatsoever can be drawn about environmental effects from correlations between chil-dren and the biological parents or siblings with whom they live, because those correlations reflect some unclear mix of genetic and nongenetic influences on the children. The two sorts of influence can be disentangled only by studying pairs of family members that reflect different degrees of environmental and genetic relatedness, for instance, identical twins raised apart (they share 100 percent of their genes but 0 percent of their family environments, meaning that any similarity between them is owing to genes) and adopted children raised together (they are no more genetically alike than strangers but 100 percent alike in family environment, meaning that any similar-ity is owing to shared environments). The following seven replicated findings from genetically sensitive family studies (primarily from families of working class or higher in Western countries) suffice to illustrate that socialization theory is false (for reviews, see Bouchard, 1998; Plomin, DeFries, McClearn, & McGuffin, 2001; Wachs, 1992; in the context of vocational interest theory, see Gottfredson, 1999, and Betsworth & Fouad, 1997). The sixth and seventh findings have shocked even behavioral geneticists.

1. *Heritability of highly general traits.* Individual differences in all broad psychological traits studied so far (mental abilities and dis-

abilities, personality traits, psychopathology) are at least moderately heritable, that is, genetic in origin (usually 40–70 percent). *Heritability*, or h^2, is the ratio of *genotypic* to *phenotypic* variation in a trait in the population studied. Stated another way, it is the proportion of variation in an observed trait such as IQ (the denominator) that can be traced to genetic variation in the population (the numerator). Heritability is a characteristic of groups in specific times and places and does *not* reflect the proportion of an *individual's* IQ score, for instance, that is genetic in origin.

2. *Heritability of more culturally specific attitudes and behaviors.* Individual differences in more culturally channeled attitudes, beliefs, and behaviors (including religious beliefs, political preferences, social attitudes, vocational interests, and self-perceived competence) also tend to be somewhat heritable, with degree of heritability ranging widely (0–60 percent). For instance, the heritabilities of traditionalism, sexual attitudes, and religious attitudes have been estimated at 50 percent; attitudes about taxes, the military, and politics are lower (15–30 percent; Plomin et al., 2001, p. 246). Individual differences in vocational interests are about 40 percent heritable (Betsworth et al., 1994), and differences in self-rated competence are even more heritable (50–60 percent for self-rated physical appearance and social, athletic, and scholastic competence; McGuire et al., 1994). People obviously do not have genes for attitudes on taxes or the military, but being more conservative than other citizens on such matters may stem, for example, from more basic differences in personality, such as traditionalism.

3. *Heritability of life outcomes.* It may seem surprising at first, but individual differences in life events and adult outcomes also tend to be moderately heritable. Examples are level of education (60–70 percent), occupation (50 percent), and income (40–50 percent). More controllable events (for instance, conflicts with children or a change in financial status) tend to be more heritable than less controllable ones (death or major illness of child or spouse; estimates are 40 percent for controllable events versus 20 percent for less controllable ones; Plomin, Lichtenstein, Pedersen, McClearn, & Nesselroade,

1990). These findings are less surprising when one considers that all the outcomes in question are influenced by heritable traits such as intelligence, impulsiveness, conscientiousness, and the like.

4. *Heritability of personal environments.* We tend to think of environments as "out there," as external factors impinging on us, but they too are shaped somewhat by our genetic proclivities. This is especially so for our close interpersonal settings. For instance, both our perceived and actual rearing environments are somewhat heritable. Behavioral genetic analyses of scores on standard measures of early rearing environments, such as the Home Observation for the Measurement of Environment (HOME), routinely show that parents' behavior (warmth, toys provided, and so on) is shaped in part by their children's genetic differences. Scores on the HOME are about 40 percent heritable. Behavioral genetic research "consistently shows that family environment, peer groups, social support, and life events often show as much genetic influence as do measures of personality" (Plomin, DeFries, McClearn, & Rutter, 1997, pp. 203–204). The reason is that people with different genotypes are exposed—and expose themselves—to different environments and experiences. Environments can differ for (that is, correlate with) different genotypes because parents transmit both their genes (say, aesthetic) and their environments (art-laden) to offspring, which is called *passive gene-environment correlation.* More important, however, is that differences in our personal environments are somewhat heritable because we both evoke and seek out different experiences based on our genetic proclivities: *reactive* (or evocative) and *active gene-environment correlation.* For instance, teachers often inform bright students of special scholarship opportunities, and bright students often actively seek out tougher intellectual challenges. Proximal environments, then, are not just externally imposed but are self-selected and self-generated.

5. *Differential susceptibility to the same environments based on genotype.* Some genotypes are more benefited (or harmed) by the same environment or experience (medications, education, delinquent peers, musical training, and the like) than are others. Take criminal behavior, for example. Adopted children whose adoptive parents

have criminal convictions have no higher rate of criminal behavior than other adoptees *unless* their biological parents also have criminal records—that is, unless the children are at genetic risk (Plomin et al., 2001). This is called *gene-environment interaction*. In like manner, the same vocational encouragement (say, toward Realistic interests) will bear most fruit with the genetically most receptive.

6. *Age-related increase in the heritability of (at least some) general traits.* Perhaps the greatest surprise for behavioral geneticists has been their discovery that the heritability of intelligence rises from 20 percent in infancy, to 40 percent in early childhood, to 60 percent in adolescence, and then to 80 percent in late adulthood. In other words, differences in developed intelligence come to more closely reflect underlying genetic differences as people age. Less definitive evidence suggests that the heritability of its close correlates (for example, academic achievement), broad mental abilities (for example, verbal and spatial abilities), and personality disorders (for example, antisocial personality) also rise with age, whereas shared environmental effects wane (Plomin et al., 2001; shared environmental effects will be discussed next). This unexpected age trend in heritabilities has prompted behavioral geneticists to develop new theories of child and adult development that, as will be described later, emphasize people's lifelong efforts to find environments that are compatible with and reinforce their genetic tendencies.

7. *Importance of nonshared, rather than shared, environmental influences for the development of general traits.* There are two types of nongenetic influences on development: shared and nonshared environmental effects. *Shared* influences, by definition, result from environments that family members experience in common (family income, schools, and so on) and that make siblings more alike. *Nonshared* influences are ones that affect one family member but not another (say, illness) and that make siblings *less* alike. Scientists had long assumed that shared influences have large, lasting influences on general traits such as intelligence, but research has strongly suggested otherwise. Shared environments turn out *not* to create similarity among siblings in either mental ability (except

temporarily in childhood) or in personality. This fact is illustrated by biological siblings who are no more alike phenotypically by adolescence in these respects than their genetic similarity (50 percent, on the average) would predict. It is also shown by adoptive siblings who are phenotypically no more alike than strangers by adolescence. In fact, while adoptees *lose* their early similarity in IQ with adoptive relatives as they age (a similarity that could have arisen only from living in the same home), they become *more* similar to the genetic relatives they have never met. Surprisingly, it is only the environments that siblings do *not* share that permanently affect their general mental abilities and personality traits. Behavioral geneticists have therefore concluded that "[e]nvironmental influences largely operate in a nonshared manner, making children growing up in the same family different from one another" (Plomin et al., 2001, p. 304). Researchers have yet to identify specifically what those nonshared factors are, but some suggest that they are random and thus uncontrollable. It should be noted, however, that many *narrower* skills and behaviors might be subject to shared environmental effects. This has been shown true of vocational interests, for example, as will be discussed shortly.

8. *Polygenic nature of complex heritable attributes.* Finally, behavioral geneticists believe that, with the exception of certain single-gene disabilities, individual differences in complex traits and behaviors arise from the cumulative action of many genes. Having shown that all complex traits yet studied are substantially heritable, researchers are now looking for the genes involved.

In short, socialization theory is false. We are not passive lumps of clay merely to be molded by chance or others' artifice; we are active agents in our own creation. We help to create our own environments and experiences—and hence our selves—based on our genetic tendencies. To the extent that our most central, stable traits are permanently shaped by nongenetic forces, those forces are not the ones that even behavioral geneticists had once assumed. Namely, they are not the environments that we experience in common with family members but environments that affect us one individual at a time. Both genes and environments thus contribute to our uniqueness. Moreover, it is the genetic influences on our behavior, not the nongenetic ones, that seem to cumulate over time, meaning that the phenotypes for some of our core traits move ever closer to our genotypes with advancing age (for instance, the genotype-phenotype correlation, h, for intelligence rises from 0.4 in early childhood to 0.9 by late adulthood, on a scale from 0 to 1.0). Behavioral geneticists theorize that this increase results from individuals seeking and creating environments that bring out and reinforce their genetic proclivities. Career theories that emphasize shared family influences and passive learning as the source of individual differences in career-related behavior cannot, therefore, explain the most important precursors to career development (Rowe, 1997).

Modern Nature-Nurture Partnership Theory of Individual Differences

The nature-nurture partnership theory rejects the view that individuals are effects and that rearing environments are their causes. Instead, it conceives of both individuals and environments as mutual creations of the other and as emerging simultaneously from an individual's stream of experience. This view is illustrated in the bottom panel of Figure 4.5 by the alternating succession of "traits" and "experiences." The "genes-drive-experience" version of nature-nurture partnership theory (Bouchard, Lykken, Tellegen, & McGue, 1996) emphasizes how people's genetic individuality shapes their experiences (shown by the arrows in Figure 4.5 from genes to environments and experiences). Genetically distinct individuals evoke and create different environments for themselves, as noted earlier. Scarr's "niche-seeking" version of the theory (Scarr, 1997; Scarr & McCartney, 1983) emphasizes the cumulative life-course ramifications of ceaselessly tending toward experiences that comport better with one's genetic individuality, that is, the pursuit of a congruent ecological "niche" or place in the world.

Nature-nurture partnership theory thus stresses that humans are self-directed and self-creating from birth but that only through experience do we take form as psychologically distinct beings. It departs from socialization theory by recognizing that environments are both causes and effects—that people shape the environments that shape them. After all, our environments are typically other people, and we constantly nudge and activate, accept and reject, these others in our encounters. Social learning versions of socialization theory are correct to emphasize that behavior is shaped by our reinforcement histories, but they err in seeming to assume that the same stimuli induce the same degree of comfort and discomfort and hence the same responses in all of us. Large, loud social gatherings may be strong stimuli for all high school students, but they are as painful for some genotypes (shy) as they are pleasurable for others (sensation seekers) and will therefore always repel some individuals while attracting others. (Both shyness and sensation-seeking are substantially heritable.)

This biosocial perspective on individual differences suggests some principles that can help explain the development and implementation of career-relevant traits and behaviors, including circumscription and compromise. It does so by suggesting that individual differences in career-relevant attributes vary in their nearness to the genetic substrate and the manner in which experience crystallizes them into stable, measurable tendencies to behave in certain ways. This distinction in degrees of genetic embeddedness, in turn, illuminates which of our various dimensions of individual difference may reflect culturally channeled or canalized behaviors that can be shaped and packaged to some extent by parents, schools, and economies and that are deep, inherent aspects of individuality that we might be able to redirect socially but not remanufacture. The biosocial perspective also helps to explain which cultural pathways we follow or avoid in life and to what extent our paths deviate from those trod by our social peers.

Trait Development Principles. Nature-nurture partnership theory suggests the following five propositions about how individual differences in traits develop:

1. Genetic individuality as wellspring of experience
2. Universally available human experiences as consolidator of general (culture-independent) traits
3. Culturally channeled activity as consolidator of ends-specific (culture-dependent) trait combinations
4. Ends-specific traits as bridges between general traits and social niches
5. Niche development as culmination of a gene-driven, culturally constrained trait development process

Figure 4.6 schematizes the successive levels of trait development to which the principles refer. More background for these principles can be found in Gottfredson (1999).

1. Genetic individuality as wellspring of experience. Individuals are self-activating, self-directed experience instigators, selectors, and evaluators. The genetic propensities with which we are born, including temperament, are the precursors of the general personality and ability traits that will soon take form (Funder, 2001; Lykken, Bouchard, McGue, & Tellegen, 1993). These propensities act like an internal compass, inclining us toward or away from possible forms of experience that we might encounter or create (for example, risky versus safe, people-related versus things-related). We tend toward those we resonate with and away from those that discomfit us. Emitting a constant stream of mostly preconscious feedback, this compass colors our past experiences and influences our future choices. Our genotypes thus help shape both the perceived and actual environments in which we develop. In other words, nature activates and shapes nurture.

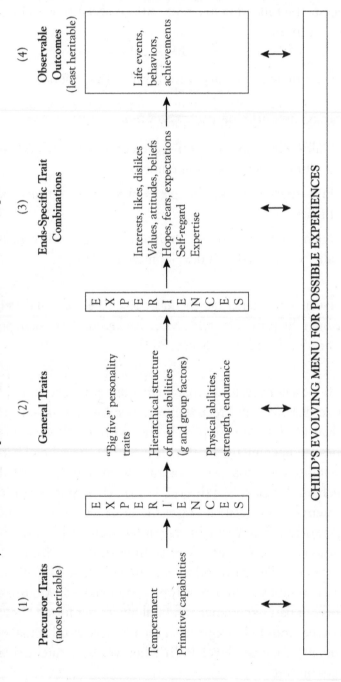

FIGURE 4.6. Crystallization and Expression of Individual Differences with Experience

(1)	(2)	(3)	(4)
Precursor Traits (most heritable)	**General Traits**	**Ends-Specific Trait Combinations**	**Observable Outcomes** (least heritable)

E X P E R I E N C E S

"Big five" personality traits

Hierarchical structure of mental abilities (g and group factors)

Physical abilities, strength, endurance

Temperament

Primitive capabilities

E X P E R I E N C E S

Interests, likes, dislikes
Values, attitudes, beliefs
Hopes, fears, expectations
Self-regard
Expertise

Life events, behaviors, achievements

CHILD'S EVOLVING MENU FOR POSSIBLE EXPERIENCES

2. *Universally available human experiences as consolidator of general (culture-independent) traits.* The flow of small experiences in everyday life provides myriad testing and training grounds that, by revealing and reinforcing genetic proclivities, catalyzes and consolidates our most basic, most general traits (intelligence, personality) in childhood. These are represented in column 2 in Figure 4.6. In this manner, nurture (experience) begins to build the core self from the raw materials that nature provides us. Researchers describe the resulting stable differences among us as the "structure" of ability or personality. With regard to mental abilities, factor analyses have revealed a "hierarchical" structure in which all abilities can be ordered according to their generality versus specificity. Only one mental ability has been found at the most general level, which is called g, for the general intelligence factor. The g factor, in turn, is the core ingredient of all 8-12 abilities at the next lower level of generality: broad abilities such as verbal ability and spatial ability. These, in turn, are the major components of yet more specific abilities, such as lexical knowledge and spatial scanning, that are useful in much narrower domains of activity. With regard to personality, factor analyses generally reveal five independent dimensions of personality (extraversion, agreeableness, conscientiousness, neuroticism [or emotional stability], and openness to experience), which researchers refer to as the "big five." The most general dimensions of personality (the big five) and ability (g) are culture-independent, because all cultures offer enough species-typical experiences (with people, objects, problem solving, and so on) to crystallize the relevant genetic differences into stable, organized, observable—"traited"—distinctions among us (for example, Lykken et al., 1993).

3. *Culturally channeled activity as consolidator of ends-specific (culture-dependent) trait combinations.* Cultures organize human activity by providing typical forms of activity that are directed toward culture-specific ends, such as producing particular goods and services or promoting allegiance to specific actors, activities, or ideals, whether they be economic, social, religious, or political. This cultural organization

is not arbitrary, for not all imaginable cultures would comport with human nature (our collective genotype). Each culture, however, represents a somewhat distinct way of organizing its members' activities relative to their human and nonhuman environments.

No ends-directed cultural activity draws forth only one trait, however; they all mobilize and reinforce some mixture of personality and ability. Teachers, mechanics, politicians, parents, and pole-vaulters, for instance, all need certain combinations of mental ability, personality, and physical competence to be effective. Recurring call for such specific, ends-targeted trait combinations fosters the development (or least the recognition) of derivative, multifaceted individual differences that are defined primarily by the cultural objects and ends being sought or renounced. They are represented in column 3 of Figure 4.6. These ends-directed trait combinations include vocational interests (interest *in* scientific work), social attitudes (opposition *to* the death penalty), goals and expectations (aspiration *for* a high income), and forms of expertise (skill *in* writing). These culture-specific traits correlate in meaningful ways with various dimensions of personality or ability (or both) but seem to constitute a different psychological domain than either personality or ability (Ackerman & Heggestad, 1997; see also Holland, 1997, for correlations between personality dimensions and Holland scales).

Ends-specific trait compounds such as vocational interests are culture-dependent in the sense that they are trait combinations that a culture regularly calls on for specific purposes. For instance, the particular mix of abilities and personality traits that typify clerical or mechanical interests would not crystallize as distinct, observable interests in a society that had neither paperwork nor machines.

Career psychology has focused on the flux and interplay among these ends-directed traits, specifically, on the processes by which young people gradually learn more about themselves in relation to the world (their interests, values, attitudes, self-concept) and orient to some fates rather than others (hopes, fears, aspirations, expectations). This theoretical focus is understandable, because these ends-directed trait combinations reflect young people's most self-conscious efforts to launch themselves into adult roles. Career psychologists have accordingly put much effort into developing inventories to assess people's interests, aspirations, self-efficacy, and other ends-specific traits but have paid relatively little attention to the more general traits of ability and personality, despite the many instruments already available for measuring them.

4. *Ends-specific traits as bridges between general traits and social niches.* The different ends-specific traits emerge when people pursue personal ends (amusement, status, well-being) along established cultural pathways (sports, employment as accountant or auto mechanic). Ends-specific trait compounds are thus the bridges linking highly general traits with particular social niches—the bridges across which genes and culture do commerce within us and thereby orient our behavior to life within a particular culture. Because we are inherently social beings, personal development involves our entering into society and society into us across these bridges (for example, by our taking on social roles that shape our activities, skills, and self-perceptions while simultaneously integrating us into the culture).

To clarify, the culture does not create the most basic differences among us (personality, physique, intelligence), but it both constrains and facilitates their expression. It does so by packaging these largely independent general differences into useful trait sets or profiles—distinct cultural toolkits, so to speak. Multivariate behavioral genetic analyses might, for instance, reveal Holland's typology of vocational interests to be one such collection of trait compounds in the post-industrial West. For example, Social interests might have genetic roots in both verbal facility and agreeableness, among other traits, and Investigative interests might have genetic roots in openness to experience, moderately high general intelligence, and perhaps spatial ability. Ends-specific trait compounds may also be more susceptible than are general traits to shared family influences. Whereas no general trait has been found to be permanently affected by shared environmental influences, some of the ends-specific traits have been. For instance, roughly 10 percent of differences in all the

General Occupational Themes and Basic Interest Scales of the Strong Interest Inventory appear to stem from shared environmental effects (Betsworth et al., 1994).

5. *Niche development as culmination of a gene-driven, culturally constrained trait development process.* Our different social niches and outcomes in adulthood—including careers—can also be conceptualized as part of the trait development process, because they too are shaped somewhat by our genotypes. These are represented in column 4 of Figure 4.6. Behavioral geneticists often describe the personal events and circumstances of our lives as our "extended phenotypes," that is, as factors seemingly outside ourselves but actually rooted partly in our own genes. We know that these seemingly external factors have a genetic component because, as noted before, many broad life outcomes are moderately heritable. Moreover, multivariate genetic analyses show that their heritable components overlap those for general traits of personality or intelligence. For example, from one-half to two-thirds of the heritable differences in education, occupation, and income level share the same genetic origins as intelligence (Lichtenstein & Pedersen, 1997; Rowe, Vesterdal, & Rodgers, 1998), perhaps because phenotypic intelligence has such strong effects on career attainment. (The outcomes' genetic overlap with other traits has not yet been assessed.) Because our environments do not carry our genes, they correlate with our genotypes only because we select, create, and act on those environments.

An important difference between the development of life niches and of general traits such as intelligence, however, is that general traits develop relatively independently of cultural variation. In contrast, individual differences in life roles, activities, and niches—our extended phenotypes—are less heritable, on average, because cultures channel and constrain the use of even the most heritable traits. Cultures limit our actions on the world around us. Depending on the cultural era or ends in question, then, our genetic compass or gyroscope may have less influence and cultural forces more influence on which activities we undertake and which niches we actually occupy. Individual differences in level of education, occupation, and income, for instance, can all be traced in part to shared family influences (roughly 10 to 25 percent; Lichtenstein & Pedersen, 1997; Rowe et al., 1998); this was probably more the case in generations past. Heritabilities of different life outcomes can be expected to range widely at any one time, depending on which roles and activities a culture or subculture currently coerces or allows its members to entertain. Variation in life outcomes will be more heritable (more influenced by genetic proclivities) in settings where people are free to pursue whichever jobs and life styles they prefer than in settings where people essentially have no choice.

In short, niche development is the gene-driven but culturally constrained development of our most global social roles, activities, and life achievements, with occupations being perhaps most key among them in the world today. It is the process by which we help create and take our place in society. The next question is, How does this process proceed, and what determines how well it turns out.

Niche Development Principles. The foregoing five-trait development process suggests how people become unique psychological and social beings, partly by creating and seeking culturally valued but genetically compatible niches in society. But why are some individuals more successful than others in doing so? Although we cannot know anyone's genotype from observing their phenotype, people certainly do seem to differ in the degree of person-environment fit they achieve. Is this owing to internal factors, external ones, or both? Nature-nurture partnership theory suggests the following five principles of niche development for explaining why some individuals are more likely than others to attain congruent life niches. All the principles relate to the menus of life niches and formative experiences to which individuals are exposed (or expose themselves to) during development.

1. Culture as a finite minute of possible life choices
2. Life course as a gradual, uncertain journey from birth niche to adult niche

3. Personal freedom as a major external factor governing the subset of experiences actually available to us

4. Temperament or personality as a major internal factor governing the subset of experiences actually available to us

5. Development as increasingly gene-directed, person-centered, and insightful

1. *Culture as a finite menu of possible life niches.* The ability to express or implement one's abilities, interests, and other traits on a sustained basis—to create a life niche comporting with them—depends on the availability of cultural channels for their expression. Stated another way, cultural roles and activities are the raw materials that genetically distinct individuals have for building their preferred social niches. We must be public selves to be ourselves in human society, but we must work within the menu of possible public selves (jobs, family roles, and so on) that our particular culture provides or allows. This point is made clearer by noting that traditional versus modern and agricultural versus postindustrial societies provide very different such menus. Cultures provide many, but still limited and Procrustean, possibilities for lives and selves.

2. *Life course as a gradual, uncertain journey from birth niche to adult niche.* In democratic societies, we believe that people's social origins should not determine their destinies. The circumstances into which we are born constitute, however, our *default niche* in life. In biological families, people's default niches are correlated to some extent with their genotypes by virtue of receiving both genes and rearing environments from their parents (passive gene–environment correlation). Although this circumstance is likely to build in some degree of person-environment fit from birth, the fit is often far from comfortable. We are, after all, genetically distinct from our parents, because we share only 50 percent of our (segregating) genes with each parent.

Were we to select randomly from the experiences available in our default environments and resonate equally with all of them, we would never drift far from our birth niche over time. But recall that neither individuals nor their environments are neutral with regard to the other. They inevitably modify or redirect each other to some extent. The developmental task, then, is to shift from one's birth niche, with its particular possibilities and expectations, toward a life niche that resonates better with one's inner self. The task is neither clear nor straightforward, however. It may require extricating one-self from old circumstances as well as entering or creating new ones. Moreover, the destination—a genetically congenial niche—may never be clear. As discussed next, the success of this gradual, incre-mental, typically winding and unreflective journey—usually but not inevitably toward a more congruent life niche—depends on both internal (largely genetic) and external (largely nongenetic) factors. These factors affect the number and type of opportunities we have, recognize, and actually use from the full cafeteria that the culture embodies (Lykken et al., 1993).

It is to these factors we now turn. Figure 4.7 helps to illustrate these final three niche development principles.

3. *Personal freedom as a major external factor governing the subset of experiences actually available to us.* Regardless of the size and con-tent of a culture's full menu of possible life roles, activities, and social niches, not all individuals have equal access to them. Rather, all cultures tend to steer different kinds of people down different paths. Age is one such factor. As we move from infancy through childhood and past adolescence, we have increasing freedom to sample the panoply of experiences our culture offers, not just the ones that our birth niche provides. Access to that panoply will dif-fer, however, depending on one's particular birth niche. Not all jobs and lives are visible or available from our particular places of origin. The freer we are, however, to explore the full range of possible ac-tivities and roles, regardless of our birth status (religion, race, class, gender, and so on), the broader the range of formative experiences we will tend to have. The wider-ranging our experiences, in turn, the better able we will be to consolidate and recognize our individ-ual interests, values, attitudes, and capabilities (that is, ends-specific

FIGURE 4.7. Influences on Child's Menu of Possible
Developmental Experiences

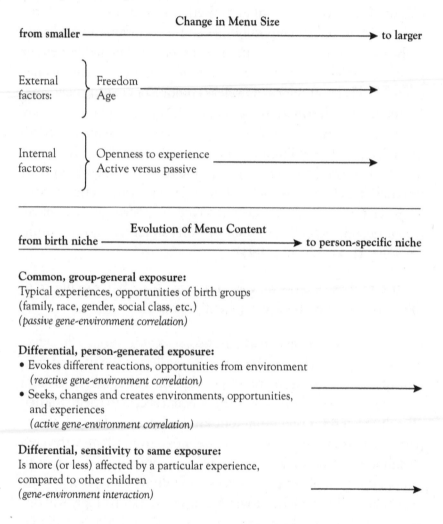

traits) and thereby identify more genetically congenial activities
and social niches. But with the benefits of freedom come costs; the
same freedom that allows some people to climb to the heights of
human possibility allows others to descend to its depths of despair
and depravity. The same freedom that some individuals experience
as a release from social bondage others experience as chaos.

4. *Temperament or personality as a major internal factor governing the subset of experiences actually available to us.* People differ greatly in their inclination to exploit the cultural pathways that are, in fact, available to them. All children are required to engage in certain common activities, such as attending school, but many activities and experiences in life are discretionary, so many individuals never sample them. Relatively few are spread before us, buffetlike, to pick and choose among. Conversely, relatively few are forced upon us, like the peas, spinach, or piano lessons we tried to avoid as children. Rather, as we enter and leave childhood, it is increasingly left up to us to scan the horizon for possible activities and reference groups, to explore and experiment with the unfamiliar, and to discover what might activate or resonate with our genetic proclivities.

Initiative may open doors, but stepping through can be difficult. If nothing else, moving toward a more compatible niche means moving *away* from a birth niche. Rejecting and shedding key elements of one's life to that point, whether they be activities, daily rhythms, ways of thinking, or friends, can be difficult no matter what the potential benefits may be. Moving away from poor-fitting birth niches may be all the more difficult to contemplate if individuals have worked hard to adjust to them, perhaps by suppressing or twisting themselves to fit in.

However, some temperaments facilitate this niche-shifting, self-development process more than others. Individuals who are more active, imaginative, self-confident, or "open to experience" (one of the big five personality dimensions) tend to sample more of the possible experiences that a culture provides. Individuals who are chronically passive, pessimistic, or fearful or who for other reasons have less taste for exploring, experimenting, and deviating from the crowd will end up sampling less of what life offers and of what they could be. They will learn less about themselves, develop fewer interests, recognize fewer talents, less often challenge inappropriate expectations and guidance, and venture less far from their birth niches toward more congruent ones. Failing to exploit their environments, they remain underdeveloped and risk unnecessary circumscription and compromise.

5. *Development as increasingly gene-directed, person-centered, and insightful.* The larger our submenus of life possibilities, the more likely we are to discover and practice what is rewarding—to discover ourselves. But what tends to be in those subsets? What paths in life do they open up to us, or close? The subsets evolve with age but in what direction and why? And to what extent do we consciously guide that evolution rather than just drift with the tide?

The bottom panel of Figure 4.7 illustrates that a child enters the world into a generic set of social influences over which it had no control. This birth niche is likely to be somewhat compatible for most children, owing to passive gene–environment correlation. But, as noted before, both social circumstances and the laws of genetic inheritance guarantee that many people will be born into less-than-optimal niches. With age, individuals create an increasingly personalized niche via the processes of gene-environment correlation and interaction. The shy, reticent child evokes different caregiving and selects different toys and friends than does his aggressive, impulsive brother (respectively, evocative and active gene–environment correlations). Some children are genetically more responsive to the same temptations or guidance and are thus more easily led in new directions, good or bad (gene-environment interaction). In this way, even siblings in the same household come to inhabit increasingly different—surprisingly different—worlds (Dunn & Plomin, 1990). In other words, life trajectories become increasingly gene-directed and person-centered when people are free to be themselves, find the kinds of people with whom they are most compatible, and seek their own places in life.

Beginning at birth, the self-directed individuation proceeds mostly outside conscious awareness. Our genotypes operate more like whispers than shouts, nudges than shoves, and their messages are hard to distinguish from the other influences on our behavior. Genetic propensities may typically provide only faint directional signals and seldom decide any of the single actions among the myriad constituting daily life. But no matter how faint they may seem at any single moment, those signals are the most constant and consistent directional force in our behavior and thereby become dis-cernible by the patterns they create. Its emergent pattern of effects gradually makes our inner compass somewhat available to conscious reflection.

Perceiving the orderliness in our interactions with the world is the essence of self-insight, but it is hard-won to the extent that it is gleaned at all. It is precisely for these patterns that adolescents and young adults grope in order to discover and come to terms with themselves, their internal unique selves, in Stage 4 of the circum-scription process. Although always elusive, such insight is nonethe-less essential for individuals to be able to direct their lives in a more deliberate and wise manner—to distinguish their internal selves from the externally imposed, and to shape their environs for a bet-ter personal fit. In short, it is only with the dawning and cultivation of self-knowledge that individuals become more the director and less the directed in their own lives.

Relation of Inner Compass to Circumscription and Compromise

Circumscription and compromise are two processes by which we nar-row our life choices and begin to take some paths in life rather than others. This progressive narrowing reflects the constraints imposed on us but also the ways we have identified and used the opportunities available to us. Circumscription and compromise therefore represent processes of self-definition and self-creation.

Figure 4.8 helps to make this point by summarizing the relation of these two processes to the ten principles of trait and niche devel-opment just outlined. The core theory of circumscription and com-promise (denoted in italics) focuses on how people's *perceptions* of themselves (self-concept) and the larger social world (cognitive map) develop during childhood and adolescence. The five trait-development principles help to describe the empirical *reality* of the individual—the unique self from which self-perceptions arise and with which self-environment fit must be achieved.

FIGURE 4.8. Summary of Biosocial Basis of Circumscription and Compromise

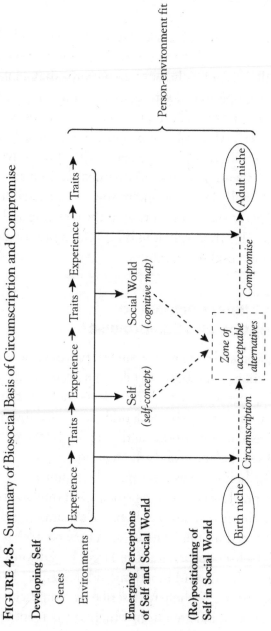

Turning to the last row in Figure 4.8, people act on their self-perceptions, accurate or not, to position themselves in the social world. When perceptions are inaccurate, fit may be impeded. The core theory describes, in particular, how young people compare their perceptions of certain *aspects* of self (such as academic ability) to their perceptions of parallel *aspects* of the occupational world (jobs' intellectual demands) in order to identify a range of occupational niches that is suitable for themselves (their social space, or zone of acceptable alternatives). As indicated in Figure 4.8, visualizing this zone is part of the broader, increasingly self-conscious process of moving from a birth niche toward a congenial adult niche.

Individual-Level Differences

Circumscription refers to the fact that youngsters never seriously entertain the full menu of niches that a culture offers but rather begin eliminating whole segments from consideration as soon as they are able to perceive essential distinctions among people and lives. Their zone of acceptable alternatives is the submenu of life niches that individuals perceive as fitting for themselves. This subset, however, largely reflects the person's birth niche, that is, the mélange of beliefs, expectations, activities, roles, and opportunities characteristic of the near environment into which the person is born. During the first three stages of circumscription, it is as if children were downloading successive bundles of the nearest cultural software as their mental hardware grows in capacity—first on adult roles, then sex roles, then the social hierarchy. Most children, moreover, seem to download it with the standard options (expectations), as it were, and only gradually customize their social space as they come to recognize its deficiencies for someone like themselves.

Moreover, they seldom seriously question that social space as long as it serves them "well enough." As the earlier principles of circumscription, compromise, and accessibility indicate, inertia and economy of effort keep individuals oriented to the major reference groups of their birth niche until some force turns them in a new direction. First, individuals are not apt to spend the effort and risk the consequences of venturing too far afield as long as their niche is "good enough." In addition, people tend to glean information about their options from people in close proximity and who thus populate their birth niche, which constitutes a recipe for minor adjustment rather than major change. It should come as no surprise, then, that people's adult niches tend to resemble their birth niches, that children re-create the society—and social inequalities—of their elders. The more pertinent question may therefore be, Why do some people venture further away from their birth niche toward more congenial ones? If stability is the norm, what accounts for mobility?

The likelihood of movement depends, first, on degree of fit with the birth niche. Many people can be quite happy remaining in the social circumstances of their birth. Only when the fit between individuals and their actual or expected environments becomes uncomfortable are they likely to envision or seek a more congenial environment. The shift is likely to be more dramatic, however, when individuals encounter something new (for example, a particular hero, book, activity) to which they resonate powerfully or when they behave in ways (illegal, duplicitous, obnoxious) that evoke protest from their niche-mates.

Second, even when people recognize that they face a poor fit, they differ in their ability and willingness to seek more congenial circumstances. As described earlier, and as the two arrows extending from the first row to the last row in Figure 4.8 indicate, both internal (personality) and external factors (degree of personal freedom) govern the subset of options we have and exploit. For instance, although we might possess the necessary ability and personality for some particular vocational interest, we may not know this if we never have—or make—the opportunity to experience the pertinent activities. Without that formative experience, we may never reconsider suitable occupations that we unreflectively rejected many years before but that might be accessible if we now took appropriate action. Lack of self-knowledge acts much like social barriers; by limiting options unnecessarily, it renders both circumscription and compromise non-optimal.

Group Differences

The same ambiguities that plague the interpretation of so much research on individual differences also plague research on group differences. Although there are now statistical methods to decompose average group differences into their genetic and nongenetic components, few such analyses have yet been done. It seems likely, however, that many group differences in career-related traits and behaviors—particularly sex differences—have genetic as well as nongenetic origins.

Specifically, we might expect some gene-based sex differences in profiles of interests, abilities, and temperaments related to dealings with people versus things. The sexes overlap greatly in most abilities and interests, but the same fundamental sex differences in interests and abilities tend, in fact, to exist the world over. It is also highly likely that cultures either magnify or suppress any gene-based sex differences in behavior. For instance, some traditional societies may suppress individual differences among men or among women, and some may even enforce adherence to cultural roles that exaggerate natural differences between the sexes. No matter how well a culture's sex roles may fit the average man or woman, however, the fit will pinch for many. Some modern societies are attempting to mute or eradicate sex differences in behavior, thereby perhaps enforcing an unnatural similarity that may pinch a different subset of men and women—but pinch equally painfully.

Nature-Nurture Partnership
Approach to Career Counseling

The original circumscription and compromise theory directed attention to two underappreciated problems in career development. First, many young people unnecessarily and unwittingly narrow their career options long before they begin sorting through their possibilities in adolescence. By adolescence, most individuals may therefore be dealing only with the remnants of vocational choice. Counseling with the circumscription and compromise theory therefore focuses attention on career options that young people *reject* as well as on options they say they prefer. The aim is to ascertain whether individuals have unthinkingly eliminated good options at earlier ages and to expose the bases for their rejection (sextype and so on).

The second problem to which the theory draws attention is that many young people unnecessarily compromise, or give up, their most-preferred choices by failing to come to grips with reality (availability of jobs and training, lack of required skills, and so on), either by ignoring that reality or not dealing with it effectively. Counseling with circumscription and compromise theory therefore focuses on how to encourage "constructive realism," that is, realism not only about the constraints on choice (job requirements and availability) but about the ways to expand choice (actions one can take to become more competitive for a preferred job).

These strategies are pursued in a five-step diagnostic sequence for determining whether individuals have unnecessarily circumscribed or compromised their options. The five steps, or sequence of diagnostic questions, which are more fully described elsewhere (Gottfredson, 1986b, 1996), are as follows:

1. Is the counselee able to name one or more occupational alternatives?

2. Are the counselee's interests and abilities adequate for the occupation(s) chosen?

3. Is the counselee satisfied with the alternatives he or she has identified?

4. Has the counselee unnecessarily restricted his or her alternatives?

5. Is the counselee aware of opportunities and realistic about obstacles for implementing the chosen occupation?

The examination of occupational alternatives that are inside and outside an individual's zone of acceptable alternatives is facilitated by a one-page map of the occupational world, such as the Occupational Aptitude Patterns Map (Gottfredson, 1986a).

Nature-nurture partnership theory provides counselors additional tools for preventing or reversing unwarranted circumscription and compromise. It does so by showing how people's zones of acceptable alternatives—indeed, their selves—are shaped in large measure by their progress in finding or creating healthy, genetically congenial life niches within their cultural settings. The new challenge that this theory poses for counseling psychology is this: How do we work with our natures to fashion sound, congenial environments when we cannot fully know what our natures are? The research gives us a few facts to work from. The vast majority of counselors may already practice what I suggest next, but nature-nurture partnership theory helps illuminate the basis for their collective wisdom.

Fact 1: For all practical purposes, we cannot purposefully change individual differences in general traits such as intelligence and personality. Modifying environments (administering "treatments") will likely have no lasting effect on these highly general tendencies.

Therefore work with, not against, core traits. Although we cannot create or erase career-relevant general traits, we can train and constrain their expression, that is, respond wisely to them. So, although we cannot eradicate the unfavorable ones (extreme impulsivity, aggressiveness, timidity, low intelligence), we may be able to suppress, mute, constructively channel, or even disguise them, just as we can highlight, train, and capitalize on more favorable attributes (gregariousness, high quantitative ability, conscientiousness). Moreover, habits for highly specific forms of behavior (say, in how we cope with shyness or impulsiveness in specific settings) *can* be ingrained or eradicated. In short, we can respond wisely by bringing out the best and suppressing the worst in ourselves.

Fact 2: In contrast to the general traits, the ends-specific traits such as vocational interests seem to be more context-dependent and thus somewhat more amenable to intervention. In particular, their consolidation and activation seems to depend somewhat on exposure to specific kinds of environments and experiences. This fact suggests that administering or withdrawing environments, so to speak, can catalyze and even somewhat modify individual differences in these more specific, culture-bound constellations of personal traits. At the very least, exposure to relevant environments can bring them forth.

Therefore, help young people develop and sample a broader menu of possible experiences so they can better discover and develop their vocational interests and values. It is hard to know whether individuals have inappropriately circumscribed their zones of acceptable alternatives until their interests and aptitudes have actually been put to the test, that is, exposed to potentially resonant and discordant environments. Experience is never sufficient to develop specific interests and skills, but it is essential. Both nature and nurture must be present in sufficient measure for an interest to emerge.

Fact 3: People shape the environments they inhabit and the lives they lead to a much greater degree than they imagine. This is not to say that individuals are responsible for all the good and bad that befalls them, only that they have considerable leverage for improving their circumstances, their lives, themselves. We shape our selves by choosing with whom and what to surround ourselves or avoid and by the activities in which we immerse ourselves or refuse to participate.

Therefore, help counselees to understand which kinds of people, activities, and settings bring out the best or worst in themselves, that is, which environments make it easier or harder for them to be who they want to be, to act in the ways they wish, to evoke positive responses from intimates. It is often easier to change the way one behaves by modifying the external stimuli to which one reacts than by struggling to muffle one's genetic propensities. It is empowering to recognize that one has many opportunities to shape one's self and life by changing even the little things—perhaps especially the little things—in one's environment. Put another way, counselors may be able to foster personal development, not just by "treating" the individual in question but by having the person "treat" (modify) their own environments. Self-insight means insight into self in context.

Fact 4: We cannot know the differences in people's genotypes, only that such differences will frequently lead individuals to respond differently to the same stimuli. As in medicine, people often respond differently to the same treatment for genetic reasons. What is a healing dose for some may be ineffective or even toxic for others. Although we can make educated guesses, often only trial-and-error will tell us which treatments—which changes in environment and experience—are most effective for an individual. The more calculated the experimentation, however, the quicker we learn. Moreover, some people are less able or less willing to accept treatment, no matter how effective we know it to be. Of those who accept treatment, some will undermine its effectiveness by misunderstanding or misapplying it.

Therefore, be alert for and respectful of individuality in response to the same experiences, including counseling treatments. The readiness to experiment and explore, the ability to gather and integrate relevant information, and other strengths and weaknesses in vocational development are somewhat genetically conditioned. Counselors therefore should expect young people to differ considerably in both the degree and type of support and guidance they need, and may always need, even when they are dealing with exactly the same vocational problem (anxiety, indecision, lack of information, family pressures, and so on). Effective counseling is like a good life niche in the sense that both require that we fashion experiences and environments that resonate constructively with genetic individuality.

Fact 5: We can know only people's phenotypes, that is, the observable but ceaselessly evolving results of the nature-nurture partnership within an individual. Thus, although we must respect the force of the genotype, we can cooperate with it only indirectly through the phenotype—the joint emissary representing both nature and nurture.

Therefore, keep an open mind about the sources of an individual's vocational interests, abilities, and attitudes. Make no assumptions about either the person's malleability or lack of malleability, about roots in nature or nurture. Counselors can look for patterns in how an individual seeks, avoids, and experiences different environments, and they can experiment and theorize. But they can never clearly distinguish the genetic from the cultural in any person's career behavior. Only the individual involved is directly privy to the signals of the inner compass, so only the individual can decide in which direction it points. Counselors can, however, be the midwives to self-insight. They can help counselees distinguish the internal and external forces propelling them, the ways in which one force becomes transmuted into the other (the internal externalized and the external internalized), and, finally, how our temperament affects our ability to develop and use self-knowledge.

Likewise, make no assumptions about the sources of group differences in interests, abilities, and attitudes. They too have both genetic and nongenetic components, in all likelihood, so group disparities are no guide to the sources of difference among individuals or to how a particular individual should be counseled.

Case Studies

K, a seventeen-year-old male Japanese-Chinese-American high school graduate, and E, a twenty-year-old female college sophomore, are at different stages of career development. (Their cases are discussed in Chapter Two.) This can be seen by applying the five-step diagnostic scheme described earlier. E has named a reasonably coherent set of options (Step 1) for which she seems to have adequate interest and ability (Step 2) but is not clearly satisfied with them (Step 3). K has named a motley set of options that has little consistent relation to his assessed interests and abilities. Both E and K, however, may have unnecessarily restricted their alternatives, although for different reasons. Both are still struggling to move further from the non-optimal birth niches that they are unable to fully accept (E) or reject (K), perhaps owing to close family ties.

The Case of K

K is a study in contradictions. His SAT scores show that he is very bright, yet he performed poorly in high school and put off going to college. He values independence but rates belonging just as highly and likes others to "set the agenda for him." His assessed Holland interests (SDS scores) are Conventional and Realistic, but his expressed interests (occupational aspirations) are mostly Artistic, which are opposite on Holland's hexagon. K is at least moderately confident that he could do well in any school subject, but he has spent most of his time and energy in nonintellectual, often juvenile endeavors such as skateboarding, playing video games and the drums, and watching animated TV programs like "The Simpsons." He knows that schooling is important if he is to meet his goals, but he consistently avoids it by procrastinating. He lists responsibility as an *unimportant* life value but then rates it very highly when it involves family. Perhaps most important, he seems not to recognize the contradictions in which he is enmeshed. He has no self-insight.

1. *Additional assessment data to collect?* K's assessed and expressed vocational interests are not very informative, partly because he has done little to test and consolidate them. A personality assessment might, however, help resolve some of the foregoing contradictions and indicate what kind of counseling might work best with him. Where does he stand on the big five personality dimensions? Might he be, for example, relatively "agreeable" and "conscientious" but somewhat "introverted" and not "open to experience"? Does it show that his apparent anxiety is dispositional ("neuroticism"), or should we look to his situation to explain his near paralysis in career development? K's chronic procrastination and resulting discouragement suggest that he should be assessed for depression and anxiety.

2. *Additional background data to collect?* K reports that his parents are leaving his occupational choice "strictly up to him." Although this is a very Americanized parental stance toward a child's career development, K still acts as if he belongs to a fairly traditional Asian family. For instance, he stresses the importance of belonging and

being loyal to family, and he would spend any lottery winnings on his family and friends. But whether accurately or not, he may sense mixed messages about what he is expected to do. Are his parents recent immigrants? Does he belong to an extended family with many traditional members? Do his two parents bring different Asian traditions with them (Japanese and Chinese)? It might be especially helpful to ask K about the occupations and activities his parents or extended family would *reject* as *unacceptable* for him, and why. Whose value is it that he earn lots of money?

I would also be interested in knowing more about K's performance and interest in the various courses he took in high school and college. What resonated with him, and why? What did he dislike? He is young for his grade level, so was he accelerated in school at some point? If so, why and with what consequences (say, rendering him less physically and socially mature than his classmates)?

3. *Any cultural issues to address?* Yes (see 2).

4. *Any mental health issues involved?* K's immaturity in interests and reluctance to develop academically and occupationally raise the possibility of disabling anxiety or depression. Such maladies might result from K being unable to recognize and resolve conflicting desires and social pressures. But whatever their origin, they are probably impeding development.

5. *What career counseling to provide?* The challenge in counseling K is to foster more insight and exploration. He probably does not know what his interests and abilities really are, because he has confined himself to juvenile activities. His route to understanding will not be through talk but through structured exercises, concrete experience, and immediate, clear feedback (as occurs with video games and skateboarding).

The most immediate challenge, however, is that he has come to counseling for information about particular occupations, not for insight and exploration—both of which he seems to have avoided so far. K's lack of insight, probable anxiety, impatience with talk (recall his comment about "silly sayings"), and (reserved) Realistic-Conventional Holland type will make it difficult to engage him in sustained dialogue unless the counselor first resonates with his practical, less reflective side.

The counselor could begin by probing what has attracted him to "technology careers and architecture" and repelled him from health occupations. The aim would be to begin mapping the social space he has constructed for himself and understanding to what extent it mirrors his birth niche (for example, what his family or friends consider acceptable or unacceptable) but does not resonate with his own likes and dislikes. And (this is very important) what *specifically* has convinced him—if anything has—that he likes one career option but dislikes another? Has he had experiences that would actually test or reveal interests and abilities in the broad occupational areas he has rejected or ignored? If not, how can he get the relevant missing experience or exposure? In short, how can he leverage his experiences to reveal better who he is and can be?

The key question is whether K's evolving social space is progressing toward a congenial adult niche, albeit haltingly, or whether that progression has stalled because K is unable or unwilling to reject or resolve the incongruent aspects of his birth niche. Sampling more of the culture's menu of possibilities will help K in either case, because it can both clarify and expand his options. It is not clear at the moment that he sees any that truly satisfy him. If, however, he is unable or unwilling to deal with ill-fitting family expectations, then personal counseling may be needed in addition to career counseling in order to ameliorate any cultural conflicts and confusions or mental health problems.

The Case of E

E's profile is highly consistent and differentiated. Virtually all of her assessed and expressed interests are in Social and Enterprising occupations, which are adjacent on Holland's hexagon. Her life values, two college majors, and the leaders she admires are Social in character, and her hobbies, memories, and favorite saying all reflect the importance she places on affiliation. Consistent with this, E rejects math, science, and lab work and generally has less confidence in her ability in those areas. Despite this apparent consistency, she seems a bit unsure about continuing to major in history and religion without clear occupational alternatives upon graduation. The key question here is whether she is really in the right major and, if not, why not.

1. *Additional assessment data to collect?* What are E's separate SAT-math and SAT-verbal scores? Her personal history is consistent with having higher verbal than math abilities. Even the most mathematically gifted women tend to favor nonscientific over scientific careers when their verbal scores are higher, even when they have great confidence in their mathematical abilities (Lubinski, Webb, Morelock, & Benbow, 2001). If E's math score were significantly higher than her verbal score, however, it would be important to understand why she is not favoring her strongest suit. Although unlikely, this possibility should be examined. If her SAT-math score is not near 700, she probably is *not* competitive for all careers.

2. *Additional background data to collect?* What is E's perception of her mother's experience in combining—or not being able to combine—law and family? To what, in particular, does she attribute the ability of her father's law partner to combine career and family? These questions relate not only to her sense that law may not be accessible to her as a career, owing to its stressful demands, but to her regard for her mother. She speaks often and warmly about her father but not of her mother. While taking several female lawyers as role models, E seems to view her mother as a cautionary tale.

In addition, how broad a selection of courses has she taken in college? Which ones did she like least and most, and why? That is, how sure can we be that she has had sufficient experience to consolidate and reveal all her interests?

3. *Any cultural issues to address?* No, except for the gender issues discussed in 2 and 5.

4. *Any mental health issues involved?* None that are apparent.

5. *What career counseling to provide?* E seems to have identified an appropriate social space for herself, although that conclusion

could be quickly confirmed by questioning her about the occupations falling outside the sextype, prestige, and effort boundaries she seems to have set. The biggest question is whether E truly is interested in law and other Enterprising activities (on the SDS, she was higher on E than S) or whether law is a fairly superficial interest developed from living among lawyers. Being surrounded by the law, so to speak, could have artificially boosted her score on the Enterprising scale, because there is nothing else in her profile suggesting that she likes to lead, persuade, or manipulate people (Enterprising) rather than serve and help them (Social). Although some types of lawyering can satisfy Social interests, practicing law tends to be a very high-pressure way of indulging them. It is a highly prestigious occupation, however, whereas Social occupations tend to be lower in prestige and more stereotypically feminine. Indeed, the gender equity movement has often targeted the legal profession as key to women's advancement. It is therefore worth exploring whether concerns over occupational prestige (is it high enough?) and sextype (is it too traditional?) are inclining E toward law and away from occupations that would seem to offer activities more in keeping with her stated interests (writing and teaching).

E could test her interests in Social versus Enterprising occupations by taking a course that is characteristic of each or by shadowing women in Social and Enterprising occupations that she and the counselor might together identify as potential options. She should shadow women workers, because any career will have to comport with her goals as a wife and mother.

Returning to Figure 4.8, the strategy with both K and E is to assess their progress from birth niche to adult niche by having them try to distinguish their internal from their external compasses. Probing the basis for their zone of acceptable alternatives is one means of doing so: Why do they or their families find some options acceptable but others not? K and E can also develop greater self-insight by reviewing their "selves in context," that is, how well they resonate with different environments. Besides reflecting on past experiences, they must also fashion new ones, because only through experience do people test, consolidate, and reveal their interests, values, and other ends-specific traits.

Perhaps the most important thing they could both learn is that when they shape and shift the environments they experience, they are engaging in acts of self-discovery and self-creation. It is in grasping these many small, daily opportunities that they take the power—and the responsibility—to create better lives and selves from the raw materials that circumstance provides them.

Summary

The theory of circumscription and compromise described here tries to explain what might seem to be a paradox. On the one hand, children of different genders and social class backgrounds tend to aspire to careers that are typical of what they perceive as their gender and social class. This apparent cross-generational transmission of inequality suggests that many young people are influenced by social stereotypes or other restrictions on personal choice. On the other hand, individuals often respond differently to the same external forces, as seen in the fact that even same-sex siblings tend to differ greatly in their career-relevant aptitudes, interests, and choices. That is, although constrained by circumstance, young people are not simply creatures of it. Rather, they are ceaselessly active agents who, working with the raw materials that God, nature, and social circumstance have blessed or burdened them, have (or could have) a strong hand in creating who they become. Behavior genetic research helps to explain this interplay between nature and nurture, between the inner compass and external forces that influence behavior. It also shows why each of us is unique, for both genetic and environmental reasons.

Circumscription and compromise in career choice are especially important in this partly self-directed development process, because both reflect individuals selecting and rejecting some life paths rather than others. Their choices, however, are conditioned by genetic proclivities and cultural forces of which they are generally only dimly aware. Counselors can use the nature-nurture-partnership perspective on career development to help young people develop greater self-insight into both sorts of influence and thereby make wiser, more satisfying career and life decisions. Specifically, the case studies of K and E illustrate how counselors can help young people (1) become aware of the fuller menu of opportunities available to them in their culture, (2) gain additional relevant experience in order to learn more about their (genetically conditioned) strengths and weaknesses, abilities, and interests, and (3) better recognize how they gradually help create themselves by the sorts of experience they seek out, reject, and evoke from others in the daily stream of their lives.

References

Ackerman, P. L., & Heggestad, E. D. (1997). Intelligence, personality, and interests: Evidence for overlapping traits. *Psychological Bulletin*, 121(2), 219–245.

Armstrong, P. I., & Crombie, G. (2000). Compromises in adolescents' occupational aspirations and expectations from Grades 8 to 10. *Journal of Vocational Behavior*, 56, 82–98.

Betsworth, D. G., Bouchard, T. J., Jr., Cooper, C. R., Grotevant, H. D., Hansen, J-I. C., Scarr, S., & Weinberg, R. A. (1994). Genetic and environmental influences on vocational interests assessed using adoptive and biological families and twins reared apart and together. *Journal of Vocational Behavior*, 44, 263–278.

Betsworth, D. G., & Fouad, N. A. (1997). Vocational interests: A look at the past 70 years and a glance at the future. *The Career Development Quarterly*, 46, 23–47.

Bouchard, T. J., Jr. (1998). Genetic and environmental influences on adult intelligence and special mental abilities. *Human biology*, 70(2), 257–279.

Bouchard, T. J., Jr., Lykken, D. T., Tellegen, A., & McGue, M. (1996). Genes, drives, environment, and experience: EPD theory revised. In C. P. Benbow & D. Lubinski (Eds.), *Intellectual talent: Psychometric and social issues* (pp. 5–43). Baltimore: Johns Hopkins University Press.

Cairns, R. B., & Cairns, B. D. (1988). The sociogenesis of self-concepts. In N. Bolger, A. Caspi, G. Downey, & M. Moorehouse (Eds.), *Persons in context: Developmental processes* (pp. 181–202). Cambridge, UK: Cambridge University Press.

Dunn, J. F., & Plomin, R. (1990). *Separate lives: Why siblings are so different.* New York: Basic Books.

Eysenck, H. J. (1998). *Intelligence: A new look.* New Brunswick, NJ: Transaction Press.

Flum, H., & Blustein, D. L. (2000). Reinvigorating the study of vocational exploration: A framework for research. *Journal of Vocational Behavior, 56,* 380–404.

Funder, D. C. (2001). Personality. *Annual Review of Psychology, 52,* 197–221.

Gottfredson, L. S. (1981). Circumscription and compromise: A developmental theory of occupational aspirations [Monograph]. *Journal of Counseling Psychology, 28,* 545–579.

Gottfredson, L. S. (1986a). Occupational Aptitude Patterns Map: Development and implications for a theory of job aptitude requirements. *Journal of Vocational Behavior, 29,* 254–291.

Gottfredson, L. S. (1986b). Special groups and the beneficial use of vocational interest inventories. In W. Walsh & S. Osipow (Eds.), *Advances in vocational psychology. Vol. 1: The assessment of interests* (pp. 127–198). Hillsdale, NJ: Erlbaum.

Gottfredson, L. S. (1996). Gottfredson's theory of circumscription and compromise. In D. Brown, L. Brooks, & Associates (Eds.), *Career choice and development* (3rd ed., pp. 179–232). San Francisco: Jossey-Bass.

Gottfredson, L. S. (1997). Why g matters: The complexity of everyday life. *Intelligence, 24*(1), 79–132.

Gottfredson, L. S. (1999). The nature and nurture of vocational interests. In M. L. Savickas & A. R. Spokane (Eds.), *Vocational interests: Their meaning, measurement, and use in counseling* (pp. 57–85). Palo Alto, CA: Davies-Black.

Gottfredson, L. S. (in press). g, jobs, and life. In H. Nyborg, *The scientific study of general intelligence: Tribute to Arthur R. Jensen.* New York: Pergamon.

Gottfredson, L. S., & Lapan, R. T. (1997). Assessing gender-based circumscription of occupational aspirations. *Journal of Career Assessment*, 5(4), 419–441.

Holland, J. L. (1997). *Making vocational choices: A theory of vocational personalities and work environments* (3rd ed.). Odessa, FL: Psychological Assessment Resources.

Lichtenstein, P., & Pedersen, N. L. (1997). Does genetic variance for cognitive abilities account for genetic variance in educational achievement and occupational status? A study of twins reared apart and twins reared together. *Social Biology*, 44(1–2), 77–90.

Lubinski, D., Webb, R. M., Morelock, M. J., & Benbow, C. P. (2001). Top 1 in 10,000: A 10-year follow-up of the profoundly gifted. *Journal of Applied Psychology*, 86(4), 718–729.

Lykken, D. T., Bouchard, T. J., Jr., McGue, M., & Tellegen, A. (1993). Heritability of interests: A twin study. *Journal of Applied Psychology*, 78, 649–661.

McGuire, S., Neiderhiser, J. M., Reiss, D., Hetherington, E. M., & Plomin, R. (1994). Genetic and environmental influences on perceptions of self-worth and competence in adolescence: A study of twins, full siblings, and step-siblings. *Child Development*, 65, 785–799.

McLennan, N. A., & Arthur, N. (1999). Applying the cognitive information processing approach to career problem solving and decision making to women's career development. *Journal of Employment Counseling*, 36, 82–96.

Plomin, R., DeFries, J. C., McClearn, J. E., & McGuffin, P. (2001). *Behavioral genetics* (4th ed.). New York: Worth.

Plomin, R., DeFries, J. C., McClearn, J. E., & Rutter, M. (1997). *Behavioral genetics* (3rd ed.). New York: W. H. Freeman.

Plomin, R., Lichtenstein, P., Pedersen, N. L., McClearn, G. E., & Nesselroade, J. R. (1990). Genetic influence on life events during the last half of the life span. *Psychology and Aging*, 5(1), 25–30.

Rowe, D. (1997). A place at the policy table? Behavior genetics and estimates of family environmental effects on IQ. *Intelligence*, 24, 133–158.

Rowe, D. C., Vesterdal, W. J., & Rodgers, J. L. (1998). Herrnstein's syllogism: Genetic and shared environmental influences on IQ, education, and income. *Intelligence*, 26(4), 405–423.

Scarr, S. (1997). Behavior-genetic and socialization theories of intelligence: Truce and reconciliation. In R. J. Sternberg & E. L. Grigorenko (Eds.), *Intelligence, heredity, and environment* (pp. 3–41). Cambridge: Cambridge University Press.

Scarr, S., & McCartney, K. (1983). How people make their own environments: A theory of genotype-environment effects. *Child Development, 54,* 424–435.

Shivy, V. A., Phillips, S. D., & Koehly, L. M. (1996). Knowledge organization as a factor in career intervention outcome: A multidimensional scaling analysis. *Journal of Counseling Psychology, 43*(2), 178–186.

Treiman, D. J. (1977). *Occupational prestige in comparative perspective.* New York: Academic Press.

Wachs, T. D. (1992). *The nature of nurture.* Newbury Park, CA: Sage.

5

Career Construction

A Developmental Theory of Vocational Behavior

Mark L. Savickas

Vocational behavior encompasses a large domain of inquiry—too large to comprehend all at once, too vast a sphere of thought and action for one theory to conceive fully. Accordingly, vocational theorists and researchers usually identify a specific range of vocational behaviors that they wish to study. The question, Which units of vocational thought and action shall we study? is answered inherently by the theories explicated in this book. Each theory concentrates on a particular problem and proposes a different unit of study. So the first thing to know about any theory is what problems it addresses. This defines the scope and usefulness of the theory. The present chapter describes career construction theory by explaining what problems it addresses and which clients it can help. The chapter begins by describing the theory's place in the structure of vocational psychology and its function as a developmental perspective in that disciplinary discourse.

A Developmental Perspective on Vocational Behavior

The "individual differences" view of occupations and the "individual development" view of careers are the two grand perspectives in vocational psychology, one focusing on vocational behavior and the other on its development. Within each perspective are different theories, whose distinctions are made compelling by the use to which they are put. Because of their overriding importance, it is worth comparing the differential and developmental perspectives within vocational psychology, starting with the individual differences perspective.

The first project for vocational psychology, pioneered by Frank Parsons (1909) at the beginning of the vocational guidance movement, concentrates on occupations and the types of people who fill them. This approach to vocational guidance identifies a few stable traits or personality types that differentiate people in meaningful ways relative to occupational requirements. It then uses tests to measure these traits and systematically match individuals to fitting occupations. Job success and satisfaction are the twin outcomes of a congruent match between a person's abilities and interests and a position's requirements and rewards.

The second project for vocational psychology, pioneered by Donald Super (1953) after World War II, concentrates on how individual work lives unfold. This approach to career counseling elicits work autobiographies from individuals and then identifies the schema and thema that shape the narrative. It uses these patterns of meaning to encourage individuals to implement their vocational self-concepts in work roles, including movement to increasingly more congruent occupational positions. This person-centered method permits counselors and researchers to recognize the processes that construct and develop an individual's career through the life course. The career perspective takes a longitudinal view of adaptational patterns; in contrast, the occupational perspective takes a cross-sectional view of personality types. Metaphorically, we might liken the differential approach to comparing the characteristics revealed in photographs of six different people and the developmental approach to noting the changes in six photographs of the same person taken at different times.

The developmental vantage point of constructing careers situates the meaning of *career* in vocational psychology—the study of vocational behavior and its development. The term *vocational* refers to the responses an individual makes in choosing and adapting to an occupation. Crites (1969) distinguishes vocational behavior from other types of behavior by requiring that the stimulus be occupational rather than physical or social. He enjoins researchers to systematically use the word *occupational* to designate stimulus variables and the word *vocational* to denote response variables as, for example, in *occupational information* and *vocational choice.* Vocational psychology's basic unit of study is vocational behavior. The developmental perspective on vocational behavior evokes the construct of career.

Career is the development of vocational behavior over time. Instead of the stimulus-response (S-R) paradigm for studying vocational behavior, the response-response (R-R) paradigm is used for studying career and identifying the antecedents of behavioral patterns. Vocational behavior, or response, remains the basic unit of study, but instead of studying differences in vocational behavior among individuals, the career perspective concentrates on changes in vocational behavior by the same individual across time. Vocational development is inferred and career denoted by changes in vocational behavior observed across three or more points in time—the minimum required to notice a trend.

Objective Versus Subjective Career

"Life course" is the meaning sociologists inscribe on *career* when they define it as a sequence of occupations in the life of an individual. This sequence can be objectively observed, as well as analyzed for patterns. Studies that analyze occupational sequences and concatenations in careers originated in the research of Davidson and Anderson (1937) on occupational mobility. A few years later, the sociologists Form and Miller (1949) coined the term *occupational career pattern* to denote the sequence and duration of work positions occupied by an individual—a definition similar to Shartle's conceptualization of career (Shartle, 1959). He indicated that one's career involves stages, including preparation, participation, and withdrawal from one's occupation.

At about the same time that Davidson and Anderson (1937) and Form and Miller (1949) were studying objective careers, other sociologists were studying subjective careers. These studies involved life histories and were originally called "own story" research. Sociological life-history research seeks to draw an intimate portrait of the sequence of events in the course of a person's life and illuminate how this sequence expresses a trend in behavior. During the 1930s, life-history research was enthusiastically promoted by the University of Chicago Sociology Department, led by Clifford Shaw (1930, 1931). Shaw's use of the term *career* focused explicitly on the subject's point of view, particularly how individuals conceptualize their social roles and interpret their experiences. This subjective perspective on private meaning stands in contrast to the public pattern of occupations in a work history. It coincides with Hughes's definition (Hughes, 1958) of *subjective career* as an evolving notion from which people see their lives as a whole and interpret the meaning of their attributes, actions, and experiences. It is this subjective meaning—the one individuals use to orient themselves to their society's occupational structure—that Super (1954) assessed with a technique that identified the preoccupations (for example, themes) that shape a career and the concept that Miller-Tiedeman and Tiedeman (1985) denoted. They suggested that career should be defined as the meaning one places on behaviors related to their careers.

The premise of career construction theory is that *career* denotes a reflection on the course of one's vocational behavior, not vocational behavior itself. This reflection can focus on actual events such as one's occupations (objective career) or on their meaning (subjective career). From this perspective, a subjective career is a reflexive project that transforms individuals from actors of their career to subjects in their own career story. It tells one's "own story," usually by emphasizing a sense of purpose that coherently explains the continuity and change in oneself across time, which is similar to McAdams's conception of identity (McAdams, 1993).

All of this is to say that the developmental approach shares with the differential approach an interest in how individuals fit into different occupations at a particular point in their lives. Yet the developmental approach emphasizes how individuals fit work into their lives. Harry Dexter Kitson, one of the first vocational psychologists, recognized the potential value that life history research might add to vocational guidance. Kitson (1926) proposed that researchers study vocational histories, which eventually propelled his protégé, Donald Super, to launch an influential program of research to construct and test his theory of vocational development. This commitment to learning about how careers unfold led, in due course, to three of Super's major contributions: the Career Pattern Study, a classic book, and a theory of vocational development (Savickas, 1994a). The momentous Career Pattern Study (Super, 1985) followed the careers of one hundred 9th-grade students for more than twenty years and produced four books, scores of journal articles, three psychometric inventories, and dozens of dissertations. The second major product was an authoritative book titled *The Psychology of Careers* in which Super (1957) refocused vocational psychology by expanding its attention to occupational choice as an event to include career decision making as a process. The third product of Super's study of careers was his journal article titled "A Theory of Vocational Development" (Super, 1953).

Career Construction Theory

The ten propositions in Super's original (1953) statement of vocational development theory have been repeatedly modified for clarity and expanded to incorporate new research (Super & Bachrach, 1957; Super, 1981; Super, 1984; Bell, Super, & Dunn, 1988; Super, 1990; Super, Savickas, & Super, 1996). Students of career development should read Super's initial (1953), definitive (1984), and final (1990) statements of his theory, as well as Salomone's (1996) critique of the theory's evolution. The developmental theory of constructing careers, described herein, is an undated and expanded version of Super's theory of vocational development. In crafting this update of the theory, I have adopted Super's suggestion that "self-concept theory might better be called personal construct theory" (Super, 1984, p. 207). Career construction theory adheres to the epistemological constructivism that says we construct representations of reality but diverges from the ontologic constructionism that says we construct reality itself.

A second important update is the switch from an organismic worldview to a contextualist worldview—one more attuned to conceptualizing development as driven by adaptation to an environment than by maturation of inner structures. Careers do not unfold; they are constructed. Viewing careers from constructivist and contextual perspectives prompted several innovations, the most noticeable being the replacement of the maintenance stage in vocational development theory with the management stage in career construction theory. In the end, these changes have more tightly integrated the segments of the theory and incorporated contemporary developments from mainstream psychology.

Career construction theory consists of the following sixteen propositions:

1. A society and its institutions structure an individual's life course through social roles. The life structure of an individual, shaped by social processes such as gendering, consists of core and peripheral roles. Balance among core roles, such as work and family, promotes stability, whereas imbalances produce strain.

2. Occupations provide a core role and a focus for personality organization for most men and women, although for some individuals this focus is peripheral, incidental, or even nonexistent. Then other life roles such as student, parent, homemaker, "leisurite," and citizen may be at the core. Personal

preferences for life roles are deeply grounded in the social practices that engage individuals and locate them in unequal social positions.

3. An individual's career pattern—that is, the occupational level attained and the sequence, frequency, and duration of jobs—is determined by the parents' socioeconomic level and the person's education, abilities, personality traits, self-concepts, and career adaptability in transaction with the opportunities presented by society.

4. People differ in vocational characteristics such as ability, personality traits, and self-concepts.

5. Each occupation requires a different pattern of vocational characteristics, with tolerances wide enough to allow some variety of individuals in each occupation.

6. People are qualified for a variety of occupations because of their vocational characteristics and occupational requirements.

7. Occupational success depends on the extent to which individuals find in their work roles adequate outlets for their prominent vocational characteristics.

8. The degree of satisfaction people attain from work is proportional to the degree to which they are able to implement their vocational self-concepts. Job satisfaction depends on establishment in a type of occupation, a work situation, and a way of life in which one can play the types of roles that growth and exploratory experiences have led one to consider congenial and appropriate.

9. The process of career construction is essentially that of developing and implementing vocational self-concepts in work roles. Self-concepts develop through the interaction of inherited aptitudes, physical make-up, opportunities to observe and play various roles, and evaluations of the extent to which the results of role playing meet with the approval of peers and

supervisors. Implementation of vocational self-concepts in work roles involves a synthesis and compromise between individual and social factors. It evolves from role playing and learning from feedback, whether the role is played in fantasy, in the counseling interview, or in real-life activities such as hobbies, classes, clubs, part-time work, and entry jobs.

10. Although vocational self-concepts become increasingly stable from late adolescence forward, thus providing some continuity in choice and adjustment, self-concepts and vocational preferences do change with time and experience as the situations in which people live and work change.

11. The process of vocational change may be characterized by a maxicycle of career stages characterized as progressing through periods of growth, exploration, establishment, management, and disengagement. The five stages are subdivided into periods marked by vocational development tasks that individuals experience as social expectations.

12. A minicycle of growth, exploration, establishment, management, and disengagement occurs during transitions from one career stage to the next, as well as each time an individual's career is destabilized by socioeconomic and personal events such as illness and injury, plant closings and company layoffs, and job redesign and automation.

13. Vocational maturity is a psychosocial construct that denotes an individual's degree of vocational development along the continuum of career stages from growth through disengagement. From a societal perspective, an individual's vocational maturity can be operationally defined by comparing the developmental tasks being encountered to those expected, based on chronological age.

14. Career adaptability is a psychological construct that denotes an individual's readiness and resources for coping with current and anticipated tasks of vocational development. The adap-

tive fitness of attitudes, beliefs, and competencies—the ABCs of career construction—increases along the developmental lines of concern, control, conception, and confidence.

15. Career construction is prompted by vocational development tasks and produced by responses to these tasks.

16. Career construction, at any given stage, can be fostered by conversations that explain vocational development tasks, exercises that strengthen adaptive fitness, and activities that clarify and validate vocational self-concepts.

The next three sections of this chapter explain these propositions, first by addressing developmental contextualism (propositions 1–3), then vocational self-concepts (propositions 4–10), and, finally, developmental tasks as the nexus of career construction (propositions 11–16).

Developmental Contextualism

Individuals construct their careers in a particular social ecology. This context is multilevel, including such variables as the physical environment, culture, racial and ethnic group, family, neighborhood, and school. Historical era represents an additional contextual dimension in career construction. As a social activity, work links the individual to the group because it provides a way of connecting to, cooperating with, and contributing to one's community. The link is actively encouraged by institutions such as the family, school, and religious institutions, and by the media; all communicate to infants and children within a given culture a more or less unified view about how social relationships should be conducted and how life should be lived. Thus people are embedded in environments that affect them. A male born into an Asian family living in Manhattan might be encouraged to become a physician or an engineer while a female with the same genetic potential living in Harlem may be socialized to become a waitress. Of course, this situation is often unfair to an individual and detrimental to the community.

Development in a Social Context

Although initial statements of vocational development theory ignored the fact that careers evolve in a social context, starting in the 1980s there was a push to elaborate theory to situate careers in social context and define their relation to historical era, geographic location, race, and culture. Vondracek, Lerner, and Schulenberg (1986), in articulating a new model of vocational development, emphasized that careers develop in a particular time and place. Previous theorists had recognized that careers evolve in response to societal demands, but these theorists had concentrated on an individual's responses to societal tasks. Vondracek and his colleagues redressed this oversight by amending career theory to highlight the context of development, especially the stimulus demands of a particular culture in a specific historical era. They asserted the importance of social ecology in their life-span approach to careers called developmental contextualism. This view synthesizes the ideas that "contextual change is probabilistic in nature, and that development proceeds according to the organism's activity" (p. 32). The result is that, in the model of developmental contextualism, the individual's own organization and coherence interact with contextual opportunities and constraints to produce development. While the context shapes the individual, the individual shapes the context. Based on this principle of reciprocity in development, Vondracek and his colleagues articulated two recommendations of great import. First, they urged that career professionals appreciate plasticity in development, that is, the potential for change in the individual and in the context. Second, they enjoined career professionals to view individuals as producers of their own development and, as a consequence of this belief, to help clients consciously influence their own development.

The Concept of Life Space

One very important dimension of the context in which careers develop is social roles, that is, the duties and rewards a culture assigns and ascribes to its members based on variables such as sex and race. The term *life space* denotes the collection of social roles enacted by an individual, as well as the cultural theaters in which these roles are played. The work role, albeit a critical role in contemporary society, is only one among many roles that individuals may occupy. While making a living, people live a life. The social elements that constitute a particular life space coalesce into a pattern of core and peripheral roles. This arrangement of roles, or "life structure," organizes and channels the person's engagement in society, including occupational choice. Usually two or three core roles hold a central place, and other roles are peripheral or absent. For example, a medical student indicated that her major roles are student, child, and sibling. These three roles constitute the core of who she is; they are fundamental to her identity and essential to her life satisfaction. She values and finds meaning in her peripheral roles as a friend, companion, and church member, yet she can vacate these peripheral roles, and sometimes does, when her core roles require more of her time.

A person's core roles interact to reciprocally shape each other. Thus individuals make decisions about their work role, such as occupational choice and organizational commitment, within the circumstances imposed by the social roles that give meaning and focus to their lives. To understand an individual's career, it is important to know and appreciate the web of life roles that connects the individual to society. Accordingly, counselors must determine the constellation of roles that an individual plays and the relative importance placed on the work role. Sometimes examination of a life structure will reveal that the career problem is not occasioned simply by a work-role transition, such as college graduation, but that the problem is spun in another strand of the web. For example, some students' indecision problems are wrapped in their role as children because they cannot make a choice for fear of disappointing a parent. More often than not, career clients seek counseling when they are changing elements in their life structure or rearranging the pattern of roles. During such a transition, individuals redesign their lives as they adopt new roles, drop outdated roles, and modify continuing roles. Although career counseling is a major intervention in its own right, it should be embedded in the larger intervention of life planning so that it fully responds to the particulars of a client's concerns and circumstances (Brown, 1988; Hansen, 1997; Savickas, 1991a). Rather than automatically privileging the work role in promoting "career development," counselors must concentrate on fostering "human development through work and relationships" (Richardson, 1999).

Vocational Self-Concepts

Having discussed social context and life roles, I turn now to the "person" half of the person-environment transaction. Propositions 4–7 deal with vocational behavior from an objective perspective. By *objective* I mean the consensus, shared by members of a society, that (1) defines an occupation's requirements, routines, and rewards, (2) judges an individual's abilities and interests, and (3) matches people to positions. This rational paradigm (Parsons, 1909) for guiding people to fitting occupations has been one of vocational psychology's most significant contributions to the human sciences. To save space, I do not discuss these propositions herein but refer readers to other theories that concentrate on these ideas, such as the preeminent statements of person-environment psychology devised by Holland (1997) and by Lofquist and Dawis (1991).

Here I concentrate on the phenomenological perspective of vocational self-concepts in propositions 8–10 of career construction theory. In concentrating on the development and implementation of vocational self-concepts, these propositions provide a subjective, personal, and ideographic framework for comprehending career construction—one that augments the objective, public, and normative framework for comprehending vocational behavior.

Development of a Self-Concept

A self consists of symbolic representations that are personally constructed, interpersonally conditioned, and linguistically communicated. Perceptions of the self originate with the awareness that one is distinct from the mothering person. Although newborns display consciousness, or the ability to direct attention, they require several months to become self-conscious in directly attending to themselves. Infants form the idea of a self and develop that self-idea by viewing themselves as an object, particularly in social situations. Ironically, to develop a self that resides inside the body, individuals must view the self from the outside. This view leads to objectification of the self in the form of self-perceptions, which the individual interprets and invests with meaning using the tool of language. A forming self-concept can be viewed as a collection of percepts that is neither integrated nor particularly coherent. The child draws on this disjointed repertoire of attributes and fragmented selves as needed in different situations. This accounts for a child's rapidly changing interests and ambitions. Later in childhood and early adolescence the individual, through reflection, generalizes the rather concrete self-percepts into more abstract self-descriptions and then weaves them together to fabricate a more or less unified and cohesive self-concept. Thus reflective self-awareness constitutes the process that develops a self-concept and self-descriptions compose its content. Once formed, an organized self-concept functions to control, guide, and evaluate behavior. The self-concept also organizes the way in which the individual processes and understands new self-percepts, until disconfirming percepts force a revision in the self-concept.

Role of Parents. The content that constitutes vocational self-concepts originates in the home as children learn to view themselves and the world through their parents' eyes. Children look to their parents as guides when they begin to explore how they will prioritize social roles and rewards. For example, the dramatic play of dressing in parents' clothes and imitating them is particularly influential as an architect of the self. The prototypical concepts learned from observing and imitating parents are elaborated as children extend their interaction into the wider environment of the neighborhood and school. When children engage in play, hobbies, chores, and schoolwork, they form self-perceptions and make social comparisons that build the attributes and characteristics that will constitute their vocational self-concepts, as well as conceptions of the work role. Childhood play is particularly important in learning about and forming preferences for the roles and rewards that can be pursued in the community theaters of work, love, friendship, leisure, and spirituality. The imagination and initiative shown in behaviors such dressing in costumes, imitating characters in books and movies, and participating in games enables children to learn about both themselves and their society. Unfortunately, the guiding lines drawn by parents and by cultural scripts also produce preoccupations and tensions. Career construction theory asserts that the themes that will eventually structure a career emerge as an individual turns these tensions into intentions.

Role Models. The process of transforming a preoccupation into an occupation relies greatly on identifying role models who show a path forward from the family to the community (Lockwood & Kunda, 1997). In what may be considered a very important career choice, children choose role models who portray solutions to their problems in growing up. As children imitate desirable qualities of their models for self-construction, they rehearse relevant coping attitudes and actions, form values about and interests in certain activities, and exercise abilities and skills as they engage in these activities. Playing selective roles, with increasing attention to the results, enables a reality testing that strengthens or modifies vocational self-concepts. Furthermore, choosing and pursuing hobbies accelerates reality testing, because hobbies lay halfway between play and work (Freud, 1965). Of course, schoolwork also contributes mightily to the growth of vocational self-concepts, particularly through the influence of one's student-role self-concept.

Classification of Self-Concepts

Super worked to make more precise and operational the overly mystical language of phenomenology used in traditional discourse on self-concept. Devising a scientific lexicon for vocational self-concepts made his theory more useful because it identified different aspects of self-concepts and organized them into a taxonomy. Super (1963) started by describing the self-concept as a "picture of the self in some role, situation, or position, performing some set of functions, or in some web of relationships" (p. 18). Then he asserted that people have multiple self-concepts, not just one self-concept, thus distinguishing between a self-concept and a self-concept system. Within their multidimensional self-concept system, or self-structure, individuals have conceptions of self in each life role they enact. These distinct self-concepts, which are activated in different roles, remain stable in particular types of situations and relationships, and facilitate information processing during decision making (Tunis, Fridhandler, & Horowitz, 1990).

Having articulated the self-concept system in general, Super concentrated next on a particular self-concept. He defined a *vocational self-concept* as the conception of self-perceived attributes that an individual considers relevant to work roles. Finally, he devised a taxonomy to classify the elements that constitute vocational self-concepts.

One important outcome of this taxonomic work was the distinction between, on the one hand, attributes called self-concept dimensions (for example, gregariousness and dogmatism) and, on the other hand, characteristics called self-concept metadimensions (for example, consistency and stability) that describe the arrangement and structure of self-concept dimensions. The usage typical of writers on self-concept can be criticized for confusing dimensions and metadimensions—a confusion that has resulted in use of the term *self-concept* as a synonym for, and even instead of, the term *self-esteem*. Career construction theory asserts that self-concept dimensions influence the content of choice alternatives, whereas the metadimensions shape the process of choosing. Particularly useful in comprehending decisional processes are the metadimensions of esteem, clarity, consistency, realism, complexity, and efficacy. In this regard, research (Super, 1982) has shown that those who lack self-esteem are less likely to make good matches between vocational self-concepts and occupational roles. Similarly, it is difficult to see how people who have vague self-concepts can adequately picture themselves in any occupational role. A person whose self-percepts are contradictory—who sees herself, for example, as both gregarious and solitary or as friendly and hostile—must also have difficulty translating that inconsistent self-concept into fitting occupations. One whose vocational self-concept is unrealistic is likely to make unwise choices, and one whose concept of self is limited to a few dimensions seems likely to have an inadequate basis for making matching decisions. And finally, an individual with weak self-efficacy for career construction may avoid making choices and remain undecided or indecisive (Betz & Taylor, 1994).

To this point, I have stressed the role of the family, neighborhood, and school in providing self-ideas to fill developing vocational self-concepts. Implicit in this discussion has been the view that the content of self-concepts emerges from the interpersonal world that children inhabit.

Career Choice Within Social Networks

The social networks that engage individuals impose cultural scripts about gender, race, ethnicity, and class that condition the development of children's vocational self-concepts. Career attitudes and aspirations are tightly tied to the social practices in which they are forged. Ignoring this contextualist idea of "habitus" leads to an exaggerated belief in agency. Although self-determination plays a role, careers are deeply grounded in "status identity," that is, an individual's internal representation of his or her location among unequal social positions. Linda Gottfredson (1996), in her sociological theory of vocational development, sagaciously describes how the social order, with its gender and class differences in employment, shape children's occupational aspirations. She explains how society encourages children to circumscribe the range of occupational alternatives that they consider and how, in making compromises between the vocational self-concept and the social order, they learn to let conceptions about an occupation's prestige and sextype overshadow their own vocational interests.

Thinking about the development of vocational behavior from the self-concept perspective led to Super's heuristic postulate (Super, 1951) that in expressing vocational preferences, people put into occupational terminology their ideas of the kind of people they are; that in entering an occupation, they seek to implement a concept of themselves; and that after stabilizing in an occupation, they seek to realize their potential and preserve self-esteem. This core postulate—that vocational self-concepts interact with work roles—leads to the conceptualization of occupational choice as implementing a self-concept, work as a manifestation of selfhood, and vocational development as a continuing process of improving the match between the self and situations.

Viewing occupational choice as an attempt to implement a self-concept (see Super, 1951) was a simple formulation, yet the notion of translating one's self-view into occupational terms and then preparing for and performing in that occupation had, and still has, widespread appeal. It fits the developmental model in portraying a career as a sequence of matching decisions. With a changing self and changing situations, the matching process is never really completed. The series of changing preferences should progress, through successive approximations, toward a better fit between worker and work. Thus a career can be viewed as the life course of a person encountering a series of social expectations and attempting to handle them in such a way as to attune her or his inner world to the outer world. The overriding goal toward which career construction moves is a situation in which the occupational role validates the individual's self-concept, or as Super states, "The occupation thus makes possible the playing of a role appropriate to the self-concept" (1963, p. 1). Ideally, an occupational role enables an individual to cooperate with and contribute to the community in ways that both substantiate and confirm that individual's self-concept. In this manner, an occupational role enables an individual to become the person he or she wants to be, and, in fact, likes.

Developmental Tasks in Career Construction

The previous sections have introduced the two variables that interact to produce careers, namely, self and society. The essence of constructing careers lies in recursive transactions between vocational self-concept and work role—a process prompted by community expectations about how life should be lived. As an individual extends the self into the community through enacting work roles, there must be effective transactional adaptation for both to flourish. The vocational self-concept, usually in the form of integrative and self-defining narratives, guides adaptation by negotiating cultural opportunities and constraints. Each transaction should both strengthen the group and improve the individual's adaptive fitness. In pursuit of these twin goals, the transactional adaptations required to mesh vocational self-concept and work role produce vocational development.

The never-ending process of transactional adaptation and career construction evolve in probabilistic ways. These alternative pathways are socially constructed, conditioned by local situations, and contingent on time, place, and socioeconomic status. In the United States during the second half of the twentieth century, the approach Super (1957) took to recounting the social tasks of vocational development concentrated on one main path through life. His recital of career stages highlights changes in goals across five periods of life as an individual moves from one stable condition to another stable condition. Each stage has a different goal, and the name of a stage indicates that goal: growth, exploration, establishment, maintenance, and disengagement. Each career stage can be further delineated as a sequence of major developmental tasks. Although the career stages emphasize change, the vocational development tasks within them detail how stability is reestablished and continuity maintained. These vocational development tasks are expectations imposed by society and experienced by individuals as career concerns. Success in adapting to each developmental task results in more effective functioning as a student, worker, or retiree and lays the groundwork for progressively mastering the next task along the developmental continuum. At each age, vocational development tasks and career concerns should mesh, and the degree of mesh indicates level of vocational maturity. Skipping a task in the normative sequence may result in difficulties at a later stage. For example, failure to explore during adolescence can cause unrealistic occupational choices in early adulthood. Let us examine in detail the ontogenetic progression of the five career stages, each with its own set of vocational development tasks.

Career Stage One: Growth

The years of career growth, generally defined as ages four to thirteen, involve forming a vocational self-concept. This life stage has been the subject of thousands of psychological studies, many pertinent to vocational behavior. Only a select few, however, have been incorporated into conceptual models of vocational development. In practice, career researchers, with their interest in continuity and change, have concentrated on four lines of development (Freud, 1965), which I call concern, control, conception, and confidence. Each of these developmental lines brings forward into adolescence a syndrome of attitudes, beliefs, and competencies that are critical in determining how people choose their work and construct their careers (Super, 1990; Savickas & Super, 1993). I conceptualize the four syndromes as constituting response readiness and coping resources for dealing with the four major tasks of vocational development that society imposes on children:

1. Become *concerned* about one's future as a worker.
2. Increase personal *control* over one's vocational activities.
3. Form *conceptions* about how to make educational and vocational choices.
4. Acquire the *confidence* to make and implement these career choices.

1. *Career concern* is the line of vocational development rooted in dependence on parents and plotted by the coordinates of interpersonal trust and intrapersonal hope (Erikson, 1963). Recent scholarship directed to constructing a relational theory of vocational development has focused on how attachment to parents enables infants to initiate and children to form a conception of self and other people that extends into later life in general and into occupational life in particular (Blustein, 2001; Flum, 2001). Infants and children who establish secure attachments to their caregivers learn to trust themselves and other people. This positive conception of both self and others forms an "internal working model" of human relationships that enables children and adolescents to feel secure as they explore the work world and daydream about their place in it. Later, as adults, this felt security allows individuals to interact positively with mentors, supervisors, and coworkers (Hazen & Shaver, 1990), as well as to commit themselves to their occupations and stabilize in their organizations (Meyer & Allen, 1997).

In contrast, insecure attachments produce negative conceptions of self or others (Bartholomew & Horowitz, 1991) that characterize three less adaptive styles of career construction: (1) a preoccupied style (negative self, positive others) of anxiety and ambivalence regarding vocational development tasks, (2) a dismissive style (positive self, negative others) of dissocial attitudes toward vocational development tasks, and (3) a fearful style (negative self, negative other) of career indifference. The secure attachment style fosters a future orientation and optimism, as well as daydreaming about possible selves and alternative futures. These childhood behaviors prefigure an adolescent's acquisition of foresightful attitudes toward anticipated tasks of vocational development, as well as competence at planning how to master them. If one is not (or does not feel) safe, then surviving the present is more compelling than planning tomorrow. Adolescents who are unable to plan their work and work their plan are less likely to transform their occupational daydreams into reality. The fundamental function of concern in constructing careers is reflected by the prime place given to it by prominent theories of vocational development, denoted by names such as Ginzberg's *time perspective*, Super's *planfulness*, Tiedeman's *anticipation*, Crites's *orientation*, and Harren's *awareness* (Savickas, Silling, & Schwartz, 1984).

2. *Career control* is the line of vocational developmental rooted in independence from parents and plotted by the coordinates of interpersonal autonomy and intrapersonal willpower (Erikson, 1963). This developmental line has been, and remains, the subject of extensive research in vocational behavior, including studies of locus of control, causal attributions, sense of agency, assertiveness, and decisional styles, competencies, and strategies. Much of this extensive literature on the initiation and regulation of intentional behavior is brought to bear on vocational behavior in a model of self-determination devised by Blustein and Flum (1999). Suffice it to say, for our purposes here, career control is a major developmental construct—one particularly important to viewing individuals as producers of their own development. During childhood, proactive behaviors such as making decisions, delaying gratification, negotiating, and asserting one's rights increase a sense of interpersonal autonomy and personal agency. These behaviors prefigure an adolescent's attitudes of decisiveness and competence at making career choices. Individuals who do not feel in control allow luck, fate, or powerful others to make their career choices.

3. *Career conception* is the line of vocational development rooted in interdependence with other people and plotted by the

coordinates of interpersonal initiative and intrapersonal purpose (Erikson, 1963). This developmental line starts when the curiosity that prompts children to explore who they are and what they want eventually leads to questions about the meaning of life and how it should be lived. Conceptualizing how life should be led includes forming ideas about how career choices should be made. Career concepts, as well as the considerations and convictions that accompany them, involve the expectations and explanations that individuals use to comprehend how to make choices and construct their careers.

These conceptions affect choices by determining the bases for choosing. For example, some people believe that "you should choose the occupation that you are good at," whereas other people believe that "you can become anything you want as long as you try hard." Once employed, some people believe that "you must stick with the job you have chosen"; others believe that "if you stay too long in a job, the boss will take you for granted." Research on people's assumptions about career construction has focused on career choice misconceptions (Crites, 1965), ordinary explanations (Young, 1986), and career beliefs (Krumboltz & Vosvick, 1996). Exploration of how choices are made in one's family and culture, followed by an interrogation of these processes, prefigures adolescents' contrivances for making career choices and fund of information about self and occupations. Distorted career conceptions can derail the career choice process, leading to decisional difficulties such as indecision and unrealism. Adaptive conceptions about the career choice process lead to suitable and viable choices throughout one's career, not just during adolescence.

4. *Career confidence* is the developmental line rooted in feelings of equality with other people and plotted by the coordinates of interpersonal industriousness and intrapersonal confidence (Erikson, 1963). Self-confidence denotes the anticipation of success in encountering challenges and overcoming obstacles (Rosenberg, 1979). Confidence can move one from play acting to setting goals and actualizing roles. In career construction theory, confidence denotes feelings of self-efficacy concerning one's ability to success-

fully execute a course of action needed to make and implement suitable educational and vocational choices. Career confidence arises from solving problems encountered in daily activities such as household chores, schoolwork, and hobbies. Moreover, recognizing that one can be useful and productive at these tasks increases feelings of self-acceptance and self-worth. These behaviors and feelings prefigure adolescents' confidence about constructing their careers and competence at problem solving. The resulting career confidence facilitates performing behaviors that lead to developmental task mastery.

Progress along the four developmental lines discussed herein arises from the daily experiences of children. For example, an experience such as saving part of the money earned from household chores to purchase a birthday present for a friend lets a child rehearse and develop a future orientation and the willpower to delay gratification, as well as plan a strategy and feel confident about pursuing it. At the end of childhood, the four development lines coalesce into the ABCs of career construction—attitudes, beliefs, and competencies. When development is on schedule, adolescents approach the tasks of the exploration stage with a concern for the future, a sense of control over it, adaptive conceptions about how to make career decisions, and the confidence to engage in designing their occupational future and executing plans to make it real. In addition to these developing dispositions and increasing competencies, individuals enter adolescence with a collection of self-percepts and identifications with idols, images, and ideals. The next career stage requires that they activate their dispositions and competencies to weave these images into a cohesive representation of the self and then use that fabric to clothe the vocational self in an occupation.

Career Stage Two: Exploration

The years of vocational exploration, generally defined as ages fourteen to twenty-four, involve fitting oneself into society in a way that unifies one's inner and outer worlds. During the years of exploration, society expects young people to learn who and what they might become. Over time, adolescents should gradually translate their vocational self-concept into a vocational identity—one substantiated by "the tangible promise of a career" (Erikson, 1963, pp. 261–262). Society presents this task to individuals in the concrete form of expectations to make an occupational choice. As indicated by its name, the chief coping behavior of this stage is vocational exploration, that is, attempts to acquire information about the self and about occupations in order to make the matching choices that construct a career. This information-seeking behavior provides experiences and expertise for dealing with the three vocational development tasks that move an individual from occupational daydreams to employment in a job: (1) crystallization, (2) specification, and (3) actualization.

Crystallization. The first task of the exploration stage—*crystallizing vocational preference*—requires that individuals explore broadly to form tentative ideas about where they fit into society. Exploration-in-breadth is a quest for a more complete sense of self—a search that also develops the attitudes, beliefs, and competencies needed to crystallize a vocational self-concept. Tiedeman and O'Hara (1963) explain that vocational exploration propels a process of differentiation by which one conceptualizes new distinctions about role-related self-attributes. When individuals look at their own "me," they develop their self-concepts. Each look invites further differentiation of self-percepts. Self-differentiation is fostered by educational and leisure experiences and can be accelerated by psychometric testing that helps individuals draw an objective portrait of their vocational interests, occupational abilities, and work values. During adolescence, differentiation expands the number and increases the abstractness of dimensions used for self-description. In due course, the differentiated percepts and identifications must be integrated into a stable and consistent structure.

As self-clarity increases, so should clarity about the world. The formation of occupational conceptions follows the same developmental course as self-perceptions, which Neimeyer (1988) charted well. First, through differentiation the adolescent characterizes various occupations according to their requirements, routines, and rewards. After sufficient differentiation of occupations, the adolescent integrates the distinct occupations into a cognitive map of occupations, usually articulated by fields of interests or levels of ability. This process of integration can be facilitated by learning a pre-existing schema such as Holland's hexagon (Holland, 1997) or the world-of-work map that Prediger (2001) described. These schemas specify the location of occupations in a common social space, thus helping individuals synthesize and interpret the occupational information they have accumulated.

Following the unification of self-percepts into a vocational self-concept and the unification of occupations into a cognitive map, the next step is to match, initially randomly and later systematically, the vocational self-concept to fitting positions on the occupational map. These trial matches are experienced as occupational daydreams about possible selves (Dunkel, 2000). Visions of possible selves instill the courage needed to enter the adult world. The more attractive possible selves become the focus of exploration. In addition to drawing more exploration, these important possibilities sensitize the individual to relevant information and feedback. Using the self-knowledge and occupational information gained from reality testing, the individual forms provisional preferences for a select group of occupations.

Mastering the task of crystallizing preferences is facilitated by the ripening of the attitudes, beliefs, and competencies brought forward from the years of career growth. Recall that the lines of development involved career concern, control, conception, and confidence. Development along the four lines progresses at different rates, with possible fixations and regressions. Delays within or disequilibrium among the four developmental lines produce problems in coping with the task of crystallization—problems that career counselors diagnose as unrealism, indifference, indecisiveness, and indecision. Moderate disharmony among the developmental lines produces individual differences in readiness to crystallize and explains variant patterns of development. Strong disharmony produces deviant patterns of development. Accordingly, the four developmental lines sketch a framework that can be used to assess career adaptability and diagnose vocational decision-making difficulties.

The assessment framework arranges variables from the four developmental lines into a structural model that can be used to recognize individual differences in the readiness and resources for the task of crystallizing preferences. The variables in the structural model of career adaptability are dichotomized into dispositions and competencies. Dispositions refer to attitudes and beliefs that orient an individual's frame of mind, response tendencies, and inclinations toward constructing career choices. The dispositions include career concern, control, conception, and confidence as they emerge from the growth stage and develop during the exploration stage.

The cognitive competencies, that is, comprehension and problem-solving abilities, denote the resources brought to bear on making career choices. In the structural model, the competencies are knowledge about self and occupations, as well as skill at relating the two through matching, planning, and problem solving.

The development and use of competencies is shaped by the dispositions, with each disposition facilitating development of a particular competency. Concern generates planning competence; control enhances decisional competence; conception engenders knowledge of self and occupations; and confidence breeds problem-solving competence. The cognitive competencies modulate career choice behavior, whereas the dispositions, lying between competence and action, mediate the use of competencies (Savickas, 2000a). These cognitive competencies are measured by the *Career Maturity Inventory* (Crites & Savickas, 1996), whereas confidence about executing the corresponding behaviors is measured by the *Career Decision-Making Self-Efficacy Scale* (Betz & Taylor, 1994).

Specification. As tentative preferences are formed and readiness for making choices increases, the individual encounters the second developmental task of the career exploration stage. *Specifying an* *occupational choice* requires that individuals explore deeply to sift through tentative preferences in preparation for declaring an occupational choice. Exploration-in-depth requires that role playing become more purposive and reality testing become more systematic. It can include obtaining further education and training, as well as moratorium periods used to explore self and world through travel and work experiences. Eventually, advanced exploration results in specifying a particular occupation that one wants to enter and making a commitment to do so.

Specifying an occupation choice involves more than just the psychological activity of mentally comparing and suitably coupling self and occupational concepts. It consists of constructing a story that engages the larger sociocultural context by organizing self-percepts and then positioning the resulting self-concept in society. An individual's career story crystallizes how that person sees him- or herself in relation to the world. Vocationally relevant traits such as abilities and interests constitute the substance of this story, yet the story's essence is the narrative theme that shapes the story's meaning, continuity, and distinctiveness. The theme imposes narrative structure on the choices made and, in so doing, constructs a unified self from an individual's often-contradictory views, baffling behaviors, and inconsistent desires. This unity makes the vocational self-concept whole by stating its ruling passion and describing how the occupational choice transforms this lifelong obsession into a profession. The theme also stakes a claim to uniqueness, an assertion that distinguishes "me" from others in the same community and identifies the way in which "I" can be a resource for the group (Hogan, 1983). The declaration of an occupational choice confirms who we are and wish to become. Moreover, the choice announces the controlling idea for our working lives, sometimes even revealing a secret we have hidden. The career story we tell authorizes entry into the adult world of work and enables us to add our voice to it. The more we tell the story, the more real we become. In short, translating private vocational self-concepts into public occupational roles involves the psychosocial process of vocational identity formation.

Berzonsky (1989) describes three distinct behavioral strategies by which people construct, maintain, and revise their psychosocial identities. When applied to the formation of vocational identities, these strategies represent three different patterns of dispositions and competencies for thinking about self in relation to the world of work.

The *informational* style uses exploration and problem-focused coping to integrate role models into a cohesive and unitary whole and then make suitable and viable choices. The informational style springs from secure attachment in the growth stage and leads to identity achievement. It can be conceptualized as steady development and application of the dispositions and competencies in the structural model of career choice. There are, of course, individual differences in the rate and trend of this steady development.

The *normative* style, often leading to identity foreclosure and pseudo-crystallization of vocational preferences, conforms to the prescriptions and expectations of significant others. This style springs from a preoccupied attachment and seeks to preserve the existing identification as part of a family. Rather than explore the self, individuals who use the normative style protect the self from external threats by adhering to the family's occupational specifications. In cultures that prioritize individual desires over family needs, the normative style may be conceptualized as delayed development of adaptive dispositions toward career construction, thereby inhibiting the use of choice competencies and forgoing performance of choice behaviors. The *avoidant* style overuses delay and procrastination in an effort to ignore, for as long as possible, problems and choices. Those who use the avoidant style prefer emotionally focused coping and seem to lack role models. This style springs from negative perceptions of others that leads to diffuse identity and, if self is also evaluated as negative, to a disorganized identity. Diffuse and disorganized identities generally produce unstable work histories. The avoidant style can be conceptualized as disrupted development of both dispositions and competencies.

Actualization. The third and final task of the exploration stage—*actualizing an occupational choice*—requires that the individual realize a choice by converting it into actions that make it a fact. Actualizing a choice usually involves trial jobs in the specified occupation. The initial occupational position allows individuals to try on the occupation for fit and then move to other positions so as to zero in on a suitable job. The period during which choices are actualized is often referred to as the school-to-work transition (Blustein, Juntunen, & Worthington, 2000). The quality of vocational coping behavior during that transition appears to be more important than actual success in the first, second, or even third job.

The critical vocational coping behaviors during the disjunctive transition from school to stable employment consist of actions that move one to increasingly more congruent occupational positions (Super, Kowalski, & Gotkin, 1967). The goal of this movement is to arrive at a situation in which the person can function optimally, or at least effectively. The ideal progression starts with *developing skills* that prepare one to enter an occupation through further schooling, training, or apprenticeships. This training should be followed by *experimenting* with a series of related jobs in a process of elimination that leads to a more or less permanent position. Having found such a position, the individual begins the process of *stabilizing* to make the job secure. Obviously, this progression can be delayed or disrupted by maladaptive attitudes, beliefs, and competencies for crystallizing preferences, by vocational identity styles that distort the specification of an occupational choice, and by external barriers that thwart actualizing a choice. These delays and disruptions can be manifested in *drifting* from one unsuitable position to the next, *floundering* performance in a position, or *stagnating* in an inappropriate or blind-alley job. In the Career Pattern Study (Super et al., 1967) about one-third of the participants drifted and floundered during the bulk of the seven years after high school; another one-sixth started off drifting and, after three or four years, began to stabilize. At age twenty-five, 80 percent were stabilizing. Consequently, effective coping with the tasks of the exploration stage should not be conceptualized as predicting early stabilization in a position; rather, it ensures continuing movement to more congruent positions, with eventual establishment in a suitable and viable position.

Career Stage Three: Establishment

The years of vocational establishment, generally defined as ages twenty-five to forty-four, involve the implementation of a self-concept in an occupational role. The goal of the establishment years is to effect a cohesion between one's inner and outer worlds. The work performed, in addition to making a living, should contribute to making a life. It should be a vocational manifestation of self—ideally, a manifesto that proclaims the passions that move one and the proclivities that direct this movement. When work is just a job done for hire—a travail—then outlets for self-concepts must be sought from other life roles in the theaters of family, friendship, and leisure.

The three vocational development tasks of the establishment stage outline how society expects one to both hold a job and be held in community. Implementation of a self-concept first means stabilizing in an occupational position that allows self-expression. Stabilizing requires that one take hold of a position and make one's place secure by assimilating the organizational culture and performing job duties satisfactorily. The middle years of the establishment stage involve consolidating one's position by demonstrating positive work attitudes and productive habits, as well as cultivating congenial relationships with coworkers. Consolidation includes refinement of the self-concept in response to the requirements of reality. Refinements in one's conception of self add depth and substance to one's life story and enhance its viability by clarifying purpose, recognizing subtleties and imperfections, and increasing coherence. Refining one's self-portrait can reveal, for the first time, glimpses of an untapped potential for leadership, creativity, entrepreneurship, or adventure. This vision may lead individuals to face the third task of the establishment stage, namely, advancement to new or different responsibilities. With a refined view of self, they may seek better opportunities for self-expression in their current organization, other organizations, or even in different occupations. Advancement can sometimes come from a lateral move if the movement increases person-environment fit.

Whether or not one advances to more responsible positions, late in the years of establishment most every worker, at one time or another, thinks about what remains of her or his work life. Sometime during midlife, individuals reach a point where taking care of what they have established, that is, maintaining, becomes more important than advancing in new directions. This concern introduces the next career stage: *maintenance* in Super's vocational development theory or *management* in career construction theory.

Career Stage Four: Maintenance or Management

As individuals begin to concentrate on maintaining what they have established, they typically encounter the midlife question: Do I want to do this for the next twenty-five years? Essentially, they ask themselves and their family and friends if they should hold on or let go. This vocational development task of renewal requires that individuals reevaluate work experiences and revise their vocational self-concept accordingly. This is a question of re-finding, not refining, the self. If reevaluation leads them to change organizations, occupations, or fields, then they must recycle through exploration and establishment by crystallizing and specifying a different choice and then stabilizing in a new position (Williams & Savickas, 1990). If they decide to remain in the established occupation and organization, then they enter the stage of career maintenance, generally defined as ages forty-five to sixty-four or from midlife to retirement. Society expects mature adults to hold steady in the positions they occupy by remaining interested in their work and committed to their organization. The goal of this maintenance is to sustain oneself in an occupational role and preserve one's self-concept.

Because the chief task of maintenance is self-concept preservation, the focus is on style of maintaining one's position, not on coping with a predictable sequence of age-related tasks. Super (1984) conceptualized three styles of positive functioning during the maintenance stage: (1) holding, (2) updating, and (3) innovating. In *holding* a position, individuals must meet the challenges presented by competing workers, changing technology, increasing family demands, and diminishing stamina. To conserve what they have established, if not improve it, individuals must continue to do what they have done before, and do it well. This requires that they avoid the stagnation of just holding on until retirement. Stagnating—a negative style of maintenance—implies that the worker *holds on* by exerting minimal effort, responding obsequiously to authority, and bending the rules. *Updating*, the second style of maintaining, involves more than just doing tasks; it means striving to do tasks better by keeping current in the field and renewing skills and knowledge. Workers who stay fresh remain committed to meeting normative expectations and achieving goals. *Innovating*, the third maintenance style, means breaking new ground by doing tasks differently, doing different tasks, or discovering new challenges. Of course, the ground they break may lead innovators to construct a new path—one that leads to changing jobs. Each of these three positive styles of maintaining vocational self-concepts during later adulthood (doing tasks, doing tasks better, and doing different tasks) can create a successful and satisfying life, especially when harmoniously integrated with other life roles.

Many readers may be wondering why they do not know more people who are maintaining their positions. This raises an important point. An increasing number of workers are recycling through exploration and establishment, then losing their positions and doing it again, and then yet again. The social expectation that older adults maintain a productive society harkens back to bureaucratic organizations wherein the worker, once stabilized, was expected to put in thirty years and retire. The maintenance stage is the mainstay of careers that unfold in bureaucratic organizations. However, today, as many of the large organizations that sustain career maintenance disappear, fewer people experience the maintenance stage as it was once conceptualized. Some workers experience a shortened version of the maintenance stage; others experience only a brief period of stability before being forced to recycle to new positions; still others are perpetual establishers who enjoy the adventure of starting anew.

One wonders if the maintenance stage itself is disappearing, as the corporations that once provided lifetime employment shift to new methods of organizing their labor (Collin & Young, 2000). New models of protean (Hall & Mirvis, 1993) and boundaryless (Arthur & Rousseau, 1996) careers are emerging in conjunction with the revised psychological contract (Rousseau, 1989) between employer and employee. With a new focus on constructing and managing careers (Savickas, 2000b; Watts, in press), these models emphasize resilience and starting over, not maintenance and preservation. Given these social changes, I have replaced the maintenance stage in Super's vocational development theory with the management stage in career construction theory.

Career construction theory asserts that coping with change and managing transitions involves re-exploration and re-establishment. Having secured a new role, the individual typically recycles—a minicycle—through one or more of the career-stage maxicycles (Super, 1984). Thus the high school graduate entering her first job usually progresses through a period of growth in the new role, including exploration of the nature and expectations of that role. She becomes established in it, manages the role if successful, and then experiences disengagement if, with further growth, she becomes ready to change jobs or even switch occupational fields. Similarly, the established worker, frustrated or advancing, may experience growth and explore new roles and seek to get established in one of them. As workers manage their careers, they sometimes wish they could experience a long period of maintenance in which their future, with a solid pension, was secure. But now even the role of pensioner is being reconstructed by societies that once viewed age sixty-five as the time of mandatory retirement.

Career Stage Five: Disengagement

The career stage of disengagement (sixty-five and older) involves the vocational development tasks of decelerating (reorient vocational self-concept), retirement planning (disengage vocational self-concept), and retirement living (reflect on vocational self-concept; life review). After a long period of maintenance, workers eventually experience a decline in energy for and interest in their occupation. Accordingly, they start to disengage from it by decelerating, that is, slowing down on the job, starting to turn over tasks to younger colleagues, and contemplating retirement. In due course, retirement planning becomes a central activity that leads eventually to separation from the occupation and commencement of retirement living with its challenges of organizing a new life structure and different lifestyle. The developmental tasks of retirement living, such as life review, are best addressed in gerontology textbooks, not books that tell the story of careers.

This story of the career stages, with their maxicycles and minicycles, tells a grand narrative about psychosocial development and cultural adaptation. Maybe no one individual ever lived all of it, yet the narrative serves as an organizing story that people use to understand themselves and others. Nevertheless, Super's account is not *the* account; it is *an* account of vocational development tasks for one culture in one historical era. It was written at midcentury to portray the then-current corporate culture and societal expectations for a life, especially a male life. Other accounts are being narrated today as the global economy, information technology, and social justice challenge dominant narratives and rewrite the social organization of work and the meaning of career. These rich narratives chronicle untold stories and voice complexity. Although postindustrial societies are revising master narratives about work, the new story lines for contemporary lives are far from being clear, coherent, and complete. These new stories, rather than focusing on progress through an orderly sequence of predictable tasks, will increasingly focus on adaptability for transitions, especially coping with changes that are unexpected and traumatic.

Evaluations of Career Construction Theory

Career construction theory embodies the essential elements in the functionalist system of psychology. It emphasizes empirical research, focuses on relations among variables, stresses the provisional and tool character of its propositions, and avoids premature attempts at stating explanatory postulates and devising logico-deductive super-structures. The theory addresses functionalism's main concern, that is, adaptive patterns rather than personality traits, in asking two central questions: What do people do? and Why do they do it? (Marx & Hillix, 1963). To answer these questions, the theory formulates data-oriented propositions that, as a series of summarizing statements, remain closely tied to empirical findings. The theory then organizes these propositions into an interpretive schema that aims to be heuristic, not predictive.

A review of the theory's evaluation by critics necessarily concentrates on prior versions of career construction theory, namely vocational development theory and life-span, life-space theory. In general, evaluations of the theory conclude that it provides a useful description of vocational behavior and its development—one that incorporates research findings from the main streams of psychology and sociology and summarizes these results in the form of propositions (Borgen, 1991; Hackett, Lent, & Greenhaus, 1991; Osipow & Fitzgerald, 1996). These two strengths relate to the theory's greatest weakness. Although it easily incorporates mainstream research and comprehensively describes vocational development, the theory's propositions lack the fixed logical form needed to test its validity and generate new hypotheses (Betz, 1994; Brown, 1990; Swanson & Gore, 2000). More often than not, the theory is invoked retrospectively to explain and interpret research findings, not to structure a study prospectively (Hackett, Lent, & Greenhaus, 1991). Nevertheless, the theory does successfully provide a cogent framework for post hoc interpretation and integration of empirical facts.

Most reviews of the empirical research on the theory (for example, Hackett & Lent, 1992; Osipow & Fitzgerald, 1996) reach three conclusions: (1) the data generally support the model, (2) the developmental segment is well documented, and (3) data relative to the self-concept segment generally agree with the theory. The data about success in earlier tasks predicting success in later tasks have been viewed as more equivocal (Hackett & Lent, 1992), yet the problems of selecting appropriate predictive validity criteria for these studies suggest that the results are stronger than first believed (Savickas, 1993a). Reviewers have expressed concern that each year only a few new empirical tests of the theory are published (Osipow & Fitzgerald, 1996; Swanson & Gore, 2000). In recent years, these research studies have concentrated on the vocational development tasks, exploratory behavior, vocational identity, and the school-to-work transition. Also there have been important applications and extension of the theory to gender and sexual orientation, as well as to other cultures such as South Africa and Australia (Swanson & Gore, 2000).

Given the current status of career construction theory, I believe that three topics merit priority for future research. First, there is a pressing need for a project that delineates specific aspects of the vocational self-concept and how they relate to vocational behavior (Betz, 1994; Super, 1990). This project would aim to improve definitional specificity and organizational parsimony among the self-concept dimensions and metadimensions. For example, such work could investigate how career self-efficacy relates to vocational self-concept metadimensions such as self-esteem, clarity, consistency, and realism. It should also relate vocational self-concepts to vocational identities by building on the foundation of contemporary research about identity style. Finally, it could prompt a switch from studying self-concepts to investigating the process of self-conceptualizing by applying the narrative paradigm of career as story (Savickas, 1998).

A second research priority calls for linguistic explication and operational definition of career adaptability (Savickas, 1997a). This construct has improved the theory in recent years, from envisioning mainly a maxicycle to involving minicycles of growth, exploration, establishment, management, and disengagement, linked in a series within the maxicycle. With the addition of the adaptability construct, the process of transition through re-exploration and re-establishment merits greater attention. Discontinuities in psychosocial adaptation frame the dialectic of development, which occurs when encounters between an individual's thesis and society's antithesis produce a new synthesis. Development of potentials and construction of new meaning arises from actively adapting to changes and difficulties in the real world. Research on transitions and the dialectic they engender, beginning with the school-to-work transition, should apply the metatheoretical model of selective optimization with compensation (Baltes & Baltes, 1990) to examine the actual mechanisms of vocational development and career construction (Savickas, 2001; Vondracek & Porfeli, in press).

The third research priority requires extensive attention to diverse groups as well as socioeconomic factors (Osipow & Fitzgerald, 1996). The original statement of vocational development theory (Super, 1953) was formulated at midcentury during an era when many men spent a career in one company and many women worked as homemakers or in sexually segregated occupations. Accordingly, practitioners have, on occasion, rightly criticized the theory for emphasizing white men to the neglect of women and racial-ethnic minorities. This criticism seems valid from our perspective at the beginning of the twenty-first century (Richardson, 1993; Savickas, 1994b). Additions to the original theory, including perspectives such as developmental contextualism and constructs such as role salience, respond to the gender context of work, better comprehend women's careers, and increase the theory's usefulness for multicultural and cross-cultural research and counseling. To continue enhancing the usefulness of career construction theory, research and reflection must identify its biases and rectify the resulting distortions. Similar to the careers it conceptualizes, the theory itself must continue to innovate, not stagnate.

Application of Career Construction Theory

The assessment and counseling model that stems from career construction theory is designed to help individuals develop and implement their self-concepts in their society. Its mission is to help clients construct a career path that moves them toward the community, not climb a career ladder that elevates them above it (Savickas, 1993b). This section explains the constructivist career counseling model by first describing its assessment methods, then discussing its counseling interventions, and finally illustrating its application using the cases of K and E.

Assessment

Constructivist career assessment begins with an intake interview that identifies the vocational development tasks that concern the client. These career concerns can be identified during the interview or by administering the *Adult Career Concerns Inventory* (Super, Thompson, & Lindeman, 1988), which measures degree of concern with the tasks of exploration, establishment, management, and disengagement. Once identified, assessment of the client's concern proceeds through four phases that, in turn, focus on (1) life space, (2) career adaptability, (3) vocational self-concept and career themes, and (4) vocational identity, including work values, occupational interests, and vocational abilities.

Assessing Life Space. The first phase in the assessment model locates the career concern in a client's life space. A counselor should initiate this assessment by determining the cultural context that embeds the client's career concern. Part of this assessment should turn the spotlight from the stage on which the career story is performed to the audience—imagined and real, internal and external— that reacts to the unfolding drama. Following this discussion of relational resources and significant others, attention should focus on the client's life structure and the salience of the work role. If the work role appears important in that structure, then further vocational development and occupational assessments will mean a great deal. However, if the work role appears unimportant to a client, then progressing to assessment of adaptability, vocational self-concept, and vocational identity may not be meaningful or accurate because occupations and their roles play little part in that client's life. When circumstances suggest that the work role should be more important, then career orientation is called for (Savickas, 1991a); if not, then counseling may concentrate on preparation for other roles, such as those of parent, homemaker, or volunteer.

Assessing Career Adaptability. After situating the career concern in the client's life space, the counselor turns to assessing the client's adaptive fitness for coping with that concern. Generally, adaptability assessment evaluates dispositions toward and competencies for making educational and vocational choices (that is, crystallizing, specifying, and actualizing) or implementing them (that is, stabilizing, consolidating, and advancing). Career adaptability can be efficiently measured in high school students using the *Career Maturity Inventory* (Crites & Savickas, 1996) and in college students using the *Career Development Inventory* (Savickas & Hartung, 1996). Alternatively, counselors can assess career adaptability by using a structured interview (Savickas, 1990). In such an interview, I use four general categories of questions to elicit information about the client's dispositions and competencies. I start by asking clients how often and what they think about their future. Then I assess their career concern by listening for responses that show optimism, awareness of imminent and future tasks, and involvement in actively preparing to deal with these tasks. Second, I ask how they have made important choices and negotiated transitions in the past. Then I assess career control by listening for responses that indicate the audience for their career story, self-determination beliefs, attitudes of decisiveness and compromise, and decisional competence for handling the developmental task, transition, or problem that concerns them. Third, I ask about the alternative strategies they have considered for coping with their career concern. Then I assess career convictions by listening for responses that show a curious attitude and information-seeking behavior, as well as reveal decisional styles and strategies. I also ask clients to tell me what they know about their preferred occupation and how it suits them. Then I listen to the response to assess the fund of occupational information and matching competence. Fourth, and finally, I ask clients to describe how they solved an important problem they have faced.

Then I assess career confidence by listening for self-efficacy beliefs and problem-solving competence. This assessment of career choice dispositions and competencies allows me to understand how clients construe their career concern, as well as their readiness and resources for coping with it. If the concern is about stabilizing rather than choosing, then I assess dispositions toward and competence for adapting to an organizational culture, performing job tasks, forming congenial relationships with coworkers, maintaining productive work habits and attitudes, and planning to advance both within one's organization and career (Dix & Savickas, 1995). This assessment of work adaptation can be performed using data elicited from an inventory such as the *Career Mastery Inventory* (Crites, 1996) or in conversations about work (Hirsch, Jackson, & Kidd, 2001).

Having collected data about the client's life space and career adaptability, the first half of the assessment is finished. Attention turns naturally from assessing the *process* of career construction to assessing its *content*, as contained in vocational self-concepts and expressed in vocational identities.

Assessing Vocational Self-Concept and Career Themes. The third step in constructivist career assessment investigates vocational self-concepts and career themes. In contrast to the assessment of vocational identity with objective, quantitative measures, the assessment of vocational self-concepts relies on subjective, qualitative methods (Watkins & Savickas, 1990). The constructivist career assessment model examines two perspectives on subjective experience: (1) a cross-sectional view of vocational self-concepts and (2) a longitudinal view of career themes. The view from the cross-sectional perspective on self-concepts may be looked at through adjective checklists (Johansson, 1975), card sorts (Hartung, 1999), or the repertory grid technique (Neimeyer, 1989). These methods reveal the content of a self-concept, as well as the attributes used to construe occupations. As an alternative to elicitation methods, counselors can use procedures such as those devised by Mathewson and Rochlin (1956) to appraise clients' vocational self-concepts directly from their oral behavior during an interview.

To complement the cross-sectional view of self-concept content, the longitudinal perspective characterizes themes that organize this content for the purpose of autobiographical reasoning. Biographical themes provide an architecture to guide thinking about the continuity of a self across the past, present, and future. The essence of a career theme does not lie in reporting past experiences. To the contrary, themes interpret past facts to make them fit present needs. Themes illuminate what experience alone cannot; they convey a message that supports present goals and shapes the future. As such, themes are "created meaning" that resides in the present and explains the essential impulse of the self. Accordingly, career-theme assessment uses an individual's autobiography to identify threads of continuity in the work history, then uses this fabric to interpret the past, explain the present, and foresee the future. Counselors can use autobiographies (Annis, 1967; Mumford, Stokes, & Owens, 1990) and genograms (Okiishi, 1987) to elicit career narratives. In addition, the career-theme interview (Savickas, 1989), included in the case materials reported for K and E (see Chapter Two) was designed specifically to prompt autobiographical reasoning and produce career narratives. The five questions, in conjunction with three early recollections, produce narratives that express psychological truths and lessons learned from self-defining events during different career periods.

To identify patterns and projects from these career-defining stories, the counselor tries to learn about the origin of the career theme, the career path's trajectory and turning points, and prior experiences that might apply to the current concern. To do this, I use a method called extrapolation based on thematic analysis (Super, 1954; Jepsen, 1994). As an example of thematic analysis in constructivist career assessment, Savickas (2000c) has shown how articulating the connection between the problem stated in the first early recollection and the solution portrayed by the role models identifies the thread that weaves a career theme. Other techniques for thematic analysis of career autobiographies have been elaborated by Cochran (1997), Jepsen (1994), and Neimeyer (1989). The themes in a client's career narratives, especially those that maintain consistency across repeated tellings, will figure prominently in her or his vocational identity.

Assessing Vocational Identity. The fourth step in constructivist career counseling uses traditional person-environment procedures, such as interest inventories, to draw an objective picture of a client's vocational identity and then to sketch out how particular occupations might validate that identity. Counselors who do constructivist career counseling typically measure interests with the *Self-Directed Search* (SDS; Holland, 1985) or *Strong Interest Inventory* (SII; Harmon, Hansen, Borgen, & Hammer, 1994). The RIASEC summary code from the SDS or the SII and the occupational scales in the SII indicate "degree of resemblance" to workers employed in different occupations. Rather than measuring expressed interests, resemblance scores suggest identifications, if not possible identities. These indicators of similarity paint an objective picture of a client's vocational identity—a life portrait that can be appreciated best in the light of the client's unique vocational self-concept and career themes. Accordingly, counselors seek to comprehend how the objectively identified occupations might manifest a client's vocational self-concept and career themes.

Integrating Data and Interpreting Narrative. As a transition from assessment to intervention, the counselor organizes the data about life space, career adaptability, vocational self-concept, and vocational identity and interprets them to the client. Depending on the counselor's style, this interpretation may take the traditional form, which presents results from each assessment separately, or it may take an integrated form, which blends all of the interview data and test results into a narrative (Crites, 1981). I prefer an integrative interpretation that realistically and sensitively narrates the client's "own story." The narrative should reconstruct the client's character with greater agency and self-consciousness, as well as focus the script on a generativity plot of imagined steps along existing thematic lines. The narrative should be told in dramatic form, using metaphoric language to describe the client's career concern, and then situated in the context of the client's life space. Having described the predicament and its setting, the narrative then portrays the protagonist, balancing how an "audience" sees the client (vocational identity) and how the client views the self (vocational self-concept). The story leading the client to the current predicament is presented as yet another example of the client's career theme. Finally, the predicament is again linked to the career theme in speculating about the client's possible selves and future scripts.

Speculation about the future always includes at least three alternative scenarios. In the first scenario, the client remains the same by doing nothing—making no choices or adjustments. In the second scenario, the client follows his or her theme and does what he or she has usually done in the past. The third scenario depicts the client actively mastering the tasks being encountered and anticipated and, in so doing, better implementing the self-concept. This third scenario concentrates on self-development by portraying how particular variations or key changes in the career theme might be useful, as well as by delineating the coping attitudes, beliefs, and competencies that could be effective in handling the developmental task, transition, or problem. How counseling can modulate career themes and attune career adaptability is described in some detail so that the client can make an informed choice when the counselor invites the client to collaborate in constructing a better future for the client.

Discussion of the assessment results, whether in integrative narratives or in test score interpretations, necessarily leads to counseling. At their best, assessment and counseling blend into and overlap each other. Excellent presentation of the assessment work involves the client in reflecting on vocational self-concepts and work roles, considering career themes and developmental tasks, and estimating interests, values, and talents. When the client is involved in this self-interrogation, she or he develops some self-understanding and even self-acceptance; thus counseling has begun and assessment has merged with intervention.

Counseling

Constructivist career counseling engages clients in autobiographical reasoning that articulates their vocational interests as a psychosocial link between self and society (Savickas, 1999). It seeks to write and rewrite a career story that relates vocational self-concepts to work roles. The career narrative should explain how clients can use occupations to become more complete (Savickas, 1993b). As stated earlier, this means helping clients fit work into their lives rather than fitting people into occupations. In general, constructivist career counseling helps clients construct and manage their careers so that they may experience self-fulfillment at work and contribute to the welfare of the community. In particular, constructivist career counseling fosters self-concept clarification and implementation, along with handling the developmental tasks. It helps clients articulate and integrate their vocational self-concepts and career themes, clarify and validate their vocational identities, relate their preferences to the opportunity structure, and increase their realism in making educational and vocational choices. Relative to handling the encountered and anticipated vocational development tasks, constructivist career counseling helps clients form adaptive attitudes, beliefs, and competencies.

The narrative paradigm for constructivist career counseling helps clients to author self-enhancing and generative career autobiographies, especially vocational stories that allow them to see clearly what is at stake, what the alternative choices are, and what decision needs to be made (Savickas, 1992). Connecting today's indecision to yesterday's experiences and tomorrow's possibilities serves to clarify meaning, allow comprehension, and enhance the ability to choose. This central task of enhancing narratability requires that counselors help clients rewrite and edit their career narratives in a way that invests work with personal meaning and charts a future course. When discussing a career transition, the counselor helps clients to personalize their experience of discontinuity by fitting the problem into the larger pattern of meaning. This narrative shaping of transitional discontinuities engenders meaning that bridges the separation, reduces confusion, and resolves doubt. The reward for looking at the past to construct a story about the present is the ability to move forward into the future.

The constructivist career counseling model regards narrative work as "bricolage," that is, constructing something new with whatever is at hand. The accumulation of everyday experiences provides the building blocks with which to construct careers. The source of materials for new construction, or for deconstruction and reconstruction, are old events that are transportable to the new situation, as well as current and concrete stories of daily survival. Using biographical bricolage (Savickas, 2000c), clients apply ordinary language and concrete thinking to make sense out of the work world and construct career narratives that authenticate their choices and improve their adaptive fitness. This is the process of career decision making as experienced by individuals; it is one of roundabout means, not the technical rationality prescribed by Parsons's paradigm of "true reasoning" (Parsons, 1909).

The interview is the counselor's prime procedure for enabling career construction through narrative means, as well as for creating a safe space from which clients can seek growth and exploratory experiences. Meaningful conversation brings change. During the conversation, constructivist career counselors apply the narrative paradigm by using generic counseling processes such as coaching, educating, facilitating, guiding, influencing, mentoring, modifying, organizing, planning, and restructuring (Stone, 1986). These counseling processes should be selected and applied systematically, because some counseling processes work better than others in preparing clients to cope with different developmental tasks (Savickas, 1996). For example, guidance may work better for crystallizing a group of vocational preferences to explore, whereas coaching may work better for conducting a job search. Constructivist career counseling, of course, also uses homework assignments that help clients form new attitudes, beliefs, and competencies. These assignments or experiences can include consulting pamphlets and books, viewing filmstrips, interacting with computerized guidance systems, talking with school or college officials, observing workers discuss or demonstrate their occupation, taking an exploratory course, joining an occupationally relevant club or association, shadowing someone at work, performing volunteer work, and working at a part-time or vacation job.

Case Studies

The career stories of K and E (see Chapter Two) serve to show the contrast between the informational and avoidant styles of forming a vocational identity and constructing a career. E displays the informational style, supported by well-developed career concern, control, conceptions, and competence. In contrast, K displays the avoidant style, in his case showing underdeveloped concern and confidence with somewhat better developed control and conceptions. Both of these lives merit a novel, but herein they receive only a paragraph.

For economy of presentation, I state my impressions without the qualifications and tentativeness that I employ during a counseling interview. In counseling, my overriding goal is to be useful to the client, not be right. The following narratives about K and E are created meaning, not discovered fact. Their "truth" is grounded in their utility to K and E. Maybe career conversations that discuss the following ideas would be useful to K, as he tries to crystallize vocational preferences, and to E, as she tries to specify an occupational choice.

The Case of K

K evinces the avoidant style in his emotional approach to coping, procrastinating, and academic underachieving. There are indications that K can work hard; for example, his SAT score in mathematics is 10 points higher than his verbal score. It is not apparent what career concern K brought to the counselor. It appears that a counselor has solicited K's "own story" for use in this book rather than K seeking career counseling.

K's degree of career control suggests he has developed some autonomy and sense of agency in negotiating his situation; nevertheless, he prefers structure from others, as suggested by his accepting a friend's recommendation that he attend college and by his work in the organized environment of a library. Achievement through conformity is common among only children; frequently they are independent yet still need reassurance. K holds vague conceptions about how to make a career choice and convictions concerning preferred roles and rewards. He reports an interest in technology and architecture, maybe because they structure his creativity. His father's Investigative-Realistic vocational personality type and his mother's Conventional-Realistic type suggest the possibility that K might resemble an IRC type, which is consistent with the interview data.

The career theme interview reveals a vocational self-concept that portrays someone who is on the move and likes to learn. His line of movement seems to go from being scared to being excited. His choice of role models indicates that he wants to develop from procrastinating and moving hesitantly to being an initiator of activity. He wants to launch new projects and even lead, yet also wants a partner available to provide reassurance and structure. His competence at self-knowledge and occupational information appears weak, and he now uses an intuitive decision-making style.

In counseling, I would invite K to stop skating across the top of life. I would encourage him to take hold, to explore other ways to move—ways that use his talents and gratify his needs. The first goal would be to help him take initiative; I would, at first, provide structure and reassurance as he explored technology occupations, especially jobs wherein he could design movement, maybe of vehicles or other machines that move. I would deal with the anxiety that makes him procrastinate and reinforce any initiative he showed. And I would be sure to help him envision his career theme as moving from a preoccupation with being scared by new challenges to an occupation in which he is excited about taking initiative, learning, testing his abilities, designing technology, and solving problems. I would also make sure he understood the importance of recruiting a mentor who will provide structure and encouragement. I would prompt occupational exploration by discussing his interest in architecture and then reviewing occupations classified as IRE and RIE as well as RIC and IER. We would build a plan of exploration and make an appointment to meet in two weeks to discuss the results of his information-seeking behavior. In the end, I would hope he became better able to structure his own initiative and more coura-geous in moving forward in life.

The Case of E

Whereas K feels anxious about constructing his career, E worries. E evinces the informational approach to constructing her career. She shows adaptive fitness in her concern, control, conceptions, confidence, and competence. Her concern is with "narrowing" her ambition. Unlike K, E wants in now but fears being left out. Her ambition shows in wanting "more" for her life and in "pursuing" a double major in history and religion—two activities that require attention to details and doing the correct thing (in contrast to the problem solving required in math and science). Similar to other oldest children with two siblings, E is dutiful and rule-oriented. However, E is also a "conscientious rebel" who dislikes the current state of affairs in the United States, where sexism and racism limit the opportunities and thwart the activities of much of the population. She wants to move from her preoccupation with feeling sad about being left out of "a man's world" to moving to an occupation in which she can enact her compassionate vision, be a pioneer, work for change, and yet balance other life roles and keep stress low. To do so she needs to turn her tension into intention. She is conflicted about staying versus going. Staying put in a traditional role makes her depressed, but running off in a pioneer role scares the people who care for her, so for now she stays put. She needs to integrate these two—to learn to be a pioneer without scaring other people, maybe in a structured job such as a professor of law or history.

E and I would start exploration by discussing occupations classified as ESA and SEA. In the end, she needs to realize that her project in life is to fight for the rights of those whom society leaves out and to use her intellect to work as a conscientious objector to sexism and racism. In counseling, I would also invite her to explore the purpose that crying serves in her life and to discuss the power of her sensitivity, as well as its potential for becoming depression. She needs all the courage she can muster to be a pioneer who fights the good fight yet does not sacrifice herself in the process.

Readers who want to read more case examples may consult reports by Savickas (1988, 1989, 1995a, 1995b, 1997b), as well as detailed descriptions of constructivist career counseling methods and materials written by Bimrose (2000), Cochran (1997), Csikszentmihalyi and Beattie (1979), Peavey (1998), and Savickas (1997c). I invite the reader to add to this literature.

References

Annis, A. (1967). The autobiography: Its uses and value in professional psychology. *Journal of Counseling Psychology, 14*, 9–17.

Arthur, M. B., & Rousseau, D. M. (1996). *Boundaryless careers: A new employment principle for the new organizational era.* New York: Oxford University Press.

Baltes, P. B., & Baltes, M. M. (1990). Psychological perspectives on successful aging: The model of selective optimization with compensation. In P. B. Baltes & M. M. Baltes (Eds.), *Successful aging: Perspectives from the behavioral sciences* (pp. 1–34). Cambridge, UK: Cambridge University Press.

Bartholomew, K., & Horowitz, L. M. (1991). Attachment styles among young adults: A test of a four-category model. *Journal of Personality and Social Psychology, 61*, 226–244.

Bell, A. P., Super, D. E., & Dunn, T. B. (1988). Understanding and implementing career theory: A case study approach. *Counseling and Human Development, 20*, 1–19.

Berzonsky, M. D. (1989). Identity style: Conceptualization and measurement. *Journal of Adolescent Research, 4*, 268–282.

Betz, N. E. (1994). Self-concept theory in career development. *Career Development Quarterly, 43*, 32–42.

Betz, N. E., & Taylor, K. M. (1994). *Career Decision-Making Self-Efficacy Scale manual.* Columbus, OH: The Ohio State University.

Bimrose, J. (Ed.). (2000). *Career guidance: Constructing the future.* Stourbridge, England: Institute of Career Guidance.

Blustein, D. L. (2001). The interface of work and relationships. *The Counseling Psychologist, 29,* 179–192.

Blustein, D. L., & Flum, H. (1999). A self-determination perspective of interests and exploration in career development. In M. L. Savickas & A. R. Spokane (Eds.), *Vocational interests: Meaning, measurement, and counseling use.* Palo Alto, CA: Davies-Black.

Blustein, D. L., Juntunen, C. L., & Worthington, R. L. (2000). The school-to-work transition: Adjustment challenges of the forgotten half. In S. D. Brown & R. W. Lent (Eds.), *Handbook of counseling psychology* (3rd ed., pp. 435–470). New York: Wiley.

Borgen, F. H. (1991). Megatrends and milestones in vocational behavior: A 20-year counseling psychology retrospective. *Journal of Vocational Behavior, 39,* 263–290.

Brown, D. (1988). *Life-role development and counseling.* Paper presented at the meeting of the National Career Development Association, Orlando, FL.

Brown, D. (1990). Summary, comparison, and critique of the major theories. In D. Brown, L. Brooks, & Associates, *Career choice and development* (2nd ed., pp. 338–363). San Francisco: Jossey-Bass.

Cochran, L. (1997). *Career counseling: A narrative approach.* Thousand Oaks, CA: Sage.

Collin, A., & Young, R. (Eds.). (2000). *The future of career.* Cambridge, UK: Cambridge University Press.

Crites, J. O. (1965). Measurement of vocational maturity in adolescence: I. Attitude test of the Vocational Development Inventory. *Psychological Monographs, 79,* (2, Whole No. 595).

Crites, J. O. (1969). *Vocational psychology.* New York: McGraw-Hill.

Crites, J. O. (1981). Integrative test interpretation. In D. H. Montross & C. J. Shinkman (Eds.), *Career development in the 1980s: Theory and practice* (pp. 161–168). Springfield, IL: Charles C. Thomas.

Crites, J. O. (1996). Assessment and counseling for career mastery. In M. L. Savickas & W. B. Walsh (Eds.), *Integrating career theory and practice.* Palo Alto, CA: Davies-Black.

Crites, J. O., & Savickas, M. L. (1996). Revision of the Career Maturity Inventory. *Journal of Career Assessment, 4,* 131–138.

Csikszentmihalyi, M., & Beattie, O. V. (1979). Life themes: A theoretical and empirical exploration of their origins and effects. *Journal of Humanistic Psychology, 19,* 45–63.

Davidson, P. E., & Anderson, H. D. (1937). *Occupational mobility in an American community.* Palo Alto, CA: Stanford University Press.

Dunkel, C. (2000). Possible selves as a mechanism for identity exploration. *Journal of Adolescence, 23,* 519–529.

Dix, J. E., & Savickas, M. L. (1995). Establishing a career: Developmental tasks and coping responses. *Journal of Vocational Behavior, 47,* 93–107.

Erikson, E. H. (1963). *Childhood and society* (2nd ed.). New York: W. W. Norton.

Flum, H. (2001). Relational dimensions in career development. *Journal of Vocational Behavior, 59,* 1–16.

Form, W. H., & Miller, D. C. (1949). Occupational career pattern as a sociological instrument. *American Journal of Sociology, 54,* 317–329.

Freud, A. (1965). *Normality and pathology in childhood: Assessments of development.* New York: International Universities Press.

Gottfredson, L. S. (1996). Gottfredson's theory of circumscription and compromise. In D. Brown, L. Brooks, & Associates (Eds.), *Career choice and development* (3rd ed., pp. 179–232). San Francisco: Jossey-Bass.

Hackett, G., & Lent, R. W. (1992). Theoretical advances and current inquiry in career psychology. In S. D. Brown & R. W. Lent (Eds.), *Handbook of counseling psychology* (2nd ed., pp. 419–451). New York: Wiley.

Hackett, G., Lent, R. W., & Greenhaus, J. H. (1991). Advances in vocational theory and research: A 20-year retrospective. *Journal of Vocational Behavior, 38,* 3–38.

Hall, D. T., & Mirvis, P. H. (1993). The new career contract: Developing the whole person at midlife and beyond. *Journal of Vocational Behavior, 47,* 269–289.

Hansen, L. S. (1997). *Integrative life planning: Critical tasks for career development and changing life patterns.* San Francisco: Jossey-Bass.

Harmon, L., Hansen, J. C., Borgen, F., & Hammer, A. (1994). *Strong Interest Inventory manual.* Palo Alto, CA: Consulting Psychologists Press.

Hartung, P. J. (1999). Interest assessment using card sorts. In M. L. Savickas & A. R. Spokane (Eds.), *Vocational interests: Meaning, measurement, and counseling use.* Palo Alto, CA: Davies-Black.

Hazen, C., & Shaver, P. R. (1990). Love and work: An attachment-theoretical perspective. *Journal of Personality & Social Psychology, 59,* 270–280.

Hirsch, W., Jackson, C., & Kidd, J. M. (2001). *Straight talking: Effective career discussions at work.* Cambridge, England: National Institute for Careers Education and Counseling.

Hogan, R. (1983). A socioanalytic theory of personality. In M. Page (Ed.), *Nebraska symposium on motivation 1982: Personality—Current theory and research* (pp. 55–89). Lincoln: University of Nebraska Press.

Holland, J. L. (1985). *The Self-Directed Search professional manual.* Odessa, FL: Psychological Assessment Resources.

Holland, J. L. (1997). *Making vocational choices: A theory of vocational personalities and work environments* (3rd ed.). Odessa, FL: Psychological Assessment Resources.

Hughes, E. C. (1958). *Men and their work.* Glencoe, IL: Free Press.

Jepsen, D. A. (1994). The thematic-extrapolation method: Incorporating career patterns into career counseling. *Career Development Quarterly, 43,* 43–53.

Johansson, C. B. (1975). *Self-Description Inventory.* Minneapolis: National Computer Systems.

Kitson, H. D. (1926). The scientific compilation of vocational histories as a method to be used in vocational guidance. *Teachers College Record, 27,* 1–8.

Krumboltz, J. D., & Vosvick, M. A. (1996). Career assessment and the Career Beliefs Inventory. *Journal of Career Assessment, 4,* 345–361.

Lockwood, P., & Kunda, Z. (1997). Superstars and me: Predicting the impact of role models on the self. *Journal of Personality and Social Psychology, 73,* 91–103.

Lofquist, L. H., & Dawis, R. V. (1991). *Essentials of person-environment correspondence counseling.* Minneapolis: University of Minnesota Press.

Marx, M. H., & Hillix, W. A. (1963). *Systems and theories in psychology.* New York: McGraw-Hill.

Mathewson, R. H., & Rochlin, I. (1956). Analysis of unstructured self-appraisal: A technique in counselor education. *Journal of Counseling Psychology, 3,* 32–36.

McAdams, D. P. (1993). *Stories we live by: Personal myths and the making of the self.* New York: Morrow.

Meyer, J. P., & Allen, N. J. (1997). *Commitment in the workplace: Theory, research, and application.* Thousand Oaks, CA: Sage.

Miller-Tiedeman, A., & Tiedeman, D. (1985). Educating to advance the human career during the 1980s and beyond. *Vocational Guidance Quarterly, 34,* 15–30.

Mumford, M. D., Stokes, G. S., & Owens, W. A. (1990). *Patterns of life history: The ecology of human individuality.* Hillsdale, NJ: Erlbaum.

Neimeyer, G. J. (1988). Cognitive integration and differentiation in vocational behavior. *The Counseling Psychologist, 16,* 440–475.

Neimeyer, G. J. (1989). Applications for repertory grid technique to vocational assessment. *Journal of Counseling and Development, 67,* 585–589.

Okiishi, R. W. (1987). The genogram as a tool in career counseling. *Journal of Counseling and Development, 66,* 139–143.

Osipow, S. H., & Fitzgerald, L. F. (1996). *Theories of career development* (4th ed.). Boston: Allyn & Bacon.

Parsons, F. (1909). *Choosing a vocation.* New York: Agathon Press.

Peavy, R. V. (1998). *Sociodynamic counseling: A constructivist perspective.* Victoria, British Columbia: Trafford.

Prediger, D. J. (2001). *ACT's world-of-work map revised.* Iowa City, IA: ACT.

Richardson, M. S. (1993). Work in people's lives: A location for counseling psychologists. *Journal of Counseling Psychology, 40,* 425–433.

Richardson, M. S. (1999, August). Discussant in S. Phillips (Chair) *Relational perspectives on career decisions.* Symposium at annual conference of the America Psychological Association, Boston.

Rosenberg, M. (1979). *Conceiving the self.* New York: Basic Books.

Rousseau, D. M. (1989). Psychological and implied contracts in organizations. *Employee Responsibilities & Rights Journal, 2,* 121–139.

Salomone, P. R. (1996). Tracing Super's theory of vocational development: A 40-year retrospective. *Journal of Career Development, 22,* 167–184.

Savickas, M. L. (1988). An Adlerian view of the Publican's pilgrimage. *Career Development Quarterly, 36,* 211–217.

Savickas, M. L. (1989). Career-style assessment and counseling. In T. Sweeney (Ed.), *Adlerian counseling: A practical approach for a new decade* (3rd ed., pp. 289–320). Muncie, IN: Accelerated Development Press.

Savickas, M. L. (1990, March). *Developing career choice readiness.* Paper presented at the meeting of the American Association for Counseling and Development, Cincinnati. Abstract in *Resources in Education, 25*(8), August 1990.

Savickas, M. L. (1991a). The meaning of work and love: Career issues and interventions. *Career Development Quarterly, 39,* 315–324.

Savickas, M. L. (1991b). Improving career time perspective. In D. Brown & L. Brooks (Eds.), *Techniques of career counseling* (pp. 236–249). Boston: Allyn & Bacon.

Savickas, M. L. (1992, March). Using the narrative paradigm in career counseling. In M. Savickas (Chair), *Career as story*. Symposium conducted at the meeting of the American Association for Counseling and Development, Baltimore.

Savickas, M. L. (1993a). The predictive validity of career development measures. *Journal of Career Assessment, 1*, 93–104.

Savickas, M. L. (1993b). Career counseling in the postmodern era. *Journal of Cognitive Psychotherapy: An International Quarterly, 7*, 205–215.

Savickas, M. L. (1994a). Donald Edwin Super: The career of a planful explorer. *Career Development Quarterly, 43*, 4–24.

Savickas, M. L. (1994b). Vocational psychology in the postmodern era: Comments on Richardson's proposal. *Journal of Counseling Psychology, 41*, 105–107.

Savickas, M. L. (1995a). Examining the personal meaning of inventoried interests during career counseling. *Journal of Career Assessment, 3*, 188–201.

Savickas, M. L. (1995b). Constructivist counseling for career indecision. *Career Development Quarterly, 43*, 363–373.

Savickas, M. L. (1996). A framework for linking career theory and practice. In M. L. Savickas & W. B. Walsh (Eds.), *Handbook of career counseling theory and practice* (pp. 191–208). Palo Alto: Davies-Black.

Savickas, M. L. (1997a). Adaptability: An integrative construct for life-span, life-space theory. *Career Development Quarterly, 45*, 247–259.

Savickas, M. L. (1997b). The spirit in career counseling: Fostering self-completion through work. In D. P. Bloch & L. J. Richmond (Eds.), *Connections between spirit and work in career development: New approaches and practical perspectives* (pp. 3–25). Palo Alto: Davies-Black.

Savickas, M. L. (1997c). Constructivist career counseling: Models and methods. In R. Neimeyer & G. Neimeyer (Eds.), *Advances in personal construct psychology* (Vol. 4, pp. 149–182). Greenwich, CT: JAI Press.

Savickas, M. L. (1998, January). *Career as story: Using life themes in counseling*. Paper presented at the 24th National Consultation on Career Development, Ottawa, Canada.

Savickas, M. L. (1999). The psychology of interests (pp. 19–56). In M. L. Savickas & A. R. Spokane (Eds.), *Vocational interests: Their meaning, measurement, and counseling use*. Palo Alto, CA: Davies-Black.

Savickas, M. L. (2000a). Assessing career decision making. In E. Watkins & V. Campbell (Eds.), *Testing and assessment in counseling practice* (2nd ed., pp. 429–477). Hillsdale, NJ: Erlbaum.

Savickas, M. L. (2000b). Renovating the psychology of careers for the 21st century. In A. Collin & R. Young (Eds.), *The future of career* (pp. 53–68). Cambridge: Cambridge University Press.

Savickas, M. L. (2000c, June). *Career choice as biographical bricolage*. Paper presented at the Ninth National Career Development Association Conference, Pittsburgh.

Savickas, M. L. (2001). Toward a comprehensive theory of careers: Dispositions, concerns, and narratives. In F.T.L. Leong & A. Barak (Eds.), *Contemporary models in vocational psychology: A volume in honor of Samuel H. Osipow*. Mahwah, NJ: Erlbaum.

Savickas, M. L., Briddick, W. C., & Watkins, C. E., Jr. (in press). The relation of career maturity to personality type and social adjustment. *Journal of Career Assessment*.

Savickas, M. L., & Hartung, P. J. (1996). The Career Development Inventory in review: Psychometric and research findings. *Journal of Career Assessment, 4*, 171–188.

Savickas, M. L., Silling, S. M., & Schwartz, S. (1984). Time perspective in career maturity and decision making. *Journal of Vocational Behavior, 25*, 258–269.

Savickas, M. L., & Super, D. E. (1993). Can life stages be identified in students? *Man and Work: Journal of Labor Studies, 4*, 71–78.

Shartle, C. L. (1959). *Occupational information* (3rd ed.). Englewood Cliffs, NJ: Prentice Hall.

Shaw, C. (1930). *The jack-roller: A delinquent boy's own story*. Chicago: University of Chicago Press.

Shaw, C. (1931). *The natural history of a delinquent career*. Chicago: University of Chicago Press.

Stone, G. L. (1986). *Counseling psychology perspectives and functions*. Monterey, CA: Brooks/Cole.

Super, D. E. (1951). Vocational adjustment: Implementing a self-concept. *Occupations, 30*, 88–92.

Super, D. E. (1953). A theory of vocational development. *American Psychologist, 8*, 185–190.

Super, D. E. (1954). Career patterns as a basis for vocational counseling. *Journal of Counseling Psychology, 1*, 12–20.

Super, D. E. (1957). *The psychology of careers*. New York: Harper & Row.

Super, D. E. (1963). Self-concepts in vocational development. In D. E. Super, R. Starishevsky, N. Matlin, & J. P. Joordan, *Career development: Self-concept theory* (pp. 17–32). New York: College Entrance Examination Board.

Super, D. E. (1981). A developmental theory: Implementing a self-concept. In D. H. Montross & C. J. Shinkman (Eds.), *Career development in the 1980s: Theory and practice* (pp. 28–42). Springfield, IL: Charles C. Thomas.

Super, D. E. (1982). *Self-concepts in career development: Theory and findings after thirty years.* Paper presented to the International Association for Applied Psychology, Scotland.

Super, D. E. (1984). Career and life development. In D. Brown & L. Brooks (Eds.), *Career choice and development* (pp. 192–234). San Francisco: Jossey-Bass.

Super, D. E. (1985). Coming of age in Middletown: Careers in the making. *American Psychologist, 40,* 405–414.

Super, D. E. (1990). A life-span, life-space to career development. In D. Brown, L. Brooks, & Associates, *Career choice and development* (2nd ed., pp. 197–261). San Francisco: Jossey-Bass.

Super, D. E., & Bachrach, P. B. (1957). *Scientific careers and vocational development theory.* New York: Teachers College Press.

Super, D. E., Kowalski, R. S., & Gotkin, E. H. (1967). *Career pattern study monograph IV: Floundering and trial after high school.* New York: Teachers College, Columbia University.

Super, D. E., Savickas, M. L., & Super, C. M. (1996). The life-span, life-space approach to careers. In D. Brown, L. Brooks, & Associates (Eds.), *Career choice and development* (3rd ed., pp. 121–178). San Francisco: Jossey-Bass.

Super, D. E., Thompson, A. S., & Lindeman, R. H. (1988). *Adult Career Concerns Inventory: Manual for research and exploratory use in counseling.* Palo Alto, CA: Consulting Psychologists Press.

Swanson, J. L., & Gore, P. A., Jr. (2000). Advances in vocational psychology theory and research. In S. D. Brown & R. W. Lent (Eds.), *Handbook of counseling psychology* (pp. 233–269). New York: Wiley.

Tiedeman, D. V., & O'Hara, R. P. (1963). *Career development: Choice and adjustment.* Princeton, NJ: College Entrance Examination Board.

Tunis, S. L., Fridhandler, B. M., & Horowitz, M. J. (1990). Identifying schematized views of self with significant others: Convergence of quantitative and clinical methods. *Journal of Personality and Social Psychology, 59,* 1279–1286.

Vondracek, F. W., Lerner, R. M., & Schulenberg, J. E. (1986). *Career development: A life-span developmental approach.* Hillsdale, NJ: Erlbaum.

Vondracek, F. W., & Porfeli, E. (in press). Life-span developmental perspectives on adult career development: Recent advances. In S. G. Niles (Ed.), *Adult career development: Concepts, issues, and practices* (3rd ed.). Alexandria, VA: National Career Development.

Watkins, E., & Savickas, M. L. (1990). Psychodynamic career counseling. In B. Walsh & S. Osipow (Eds.), *Career counseling: Contemporary topics in vocational psychology* (pp. 79–116). Hillsdale, NJ: Erlbaum.

Watts, A. G. (in press). Career education for young people: Rational and provision in the U.K. and other European countries. *International Journal of Educational and Vocational Guidance.*

Williams, C. P., & Savickas, M. L. (1990). Developmental tasks of career maintenance. *Journal of Vocational Behavior, 36,* 166–175.

6

A Contextualist Explanation of Career

Richard A. Young, Ladislav Valach,
Audrey Collin

Virtually all theories of career choice and development attempt to account for context in one way or another. Indeed, Parsons's pioneering formulation of a process of vocational guidance (Parsons, 1909) was his response to the social and economic conditions of early twentieth-century Boston. In this chapter, we extend the career theorists' concern with context by offering an integrative explanation of career that addresses context extensively. This explanation is informed by a way of looking at the world that is very different from the way many traditional—and even many contemporary—career theorists see it. Our explanation is in accord with recent developments in the social sciences and other fields, some of which are referred to as postmodern. Using this perspective, we reconceptualize the nature of "career" and hence of career counseling, with significant implications for theory, research, and practice.

The purpose of this chapter, then, is to offer a contextualist explanation of career based on action theory. We begin by examining the meaning of *context* and *contexture* and positing properties of context based on these meanings. Several approaches to career development and counseling that address the context of career (for example, Vondracek, Lerner, & Schulenberg, 1986) focus on one or more of these properties. Nevertheless, although the approaches are *contextual*, most are not grounded in contextualism. In contrast, we introduce action theory (Polkinghorne, 1990; von Cranach &

Harré, 1982), which has roots in a number of broad contextualist approaches, notably Dewey (1890/1969), Mead (1934), and Vygotsky (1978), as a means of integrating the properties of context. This approach has been developed for the field of career by Young and Valach (Valach, 1990; Young & Valach, 1996; 2000; Young, Valach, & Collin, 1996; Young, Valach, et al., 2001) and reported to offer alternative and valuable ways of addressing counseling issues, in particular through the constructs of joint action and project (for example, Issacson & Brown, 2000; Niles & Hartung, 2000; Patton & McMahon, 1999; Zunker, 1998).

In using the term *action*, we are focusing on human intention, processes, and change in context rather than on context as a setting (environment) for action. The use of that term also enables us to address the continuity of meaning in the middle and long term, in contrast to focusing on unconnected episodes, and we can establish the relation between action and career. Finally, we apply the contextualist explanation to career research and career counseling, illustrating the latter through the cases of E and K (introduced in Chapter Two).

Context and Contextualism

To understand contextualism, it is useful to begin with a definition of *context*, generally recognized as a complex whole constituted of many interrelated and interwoven parts. *New Webster's Dictionary of the English Language* (1975) defines it as "the parts of a written or spoken communication which precede or follow a word, sentence, or passage, and affect its meaning; as distortion by quoting out of context. The surrounding environment, circumstances or facts which help give a total picture of something" (p. 345). The meaning of the Latin root of the word—*texere* (to weave)—is even more explicit in the cognate noun *contexture*, that is "the act, process or manner of interweaving several parts into one body" (p. 345).

Contextualism interprets the world in terms of the complexity and interrelatedness of context. One formulation of it is one of

Pepper's four mutually exclusive world hypotheses or theoretical frameworks in Western thinking (Pepper, 1942; the others are organicism, mechanism, and formism). To understand the hypotheses that people make about the world, Pepper uses root metaphors or analogies from "some area of common sense fact" (p. 91). The root metaphor for contextualism is the "historic event" (p. 232). By this, he does not mean a past event but "the event in its actuality . . . going on *now*, the dynamic, dramatic active event" (p. 232; Pepper's emphasis). It may also be called an act: "not an act conceived as alone or cut off" but "an act in and with its setting, an act in its context" (p. 233). Pepper suggests that "acts or events are all intrinsically complex, composed of interconnected activities of continuously changing patterns" (p. 233). He further indicates the immediacy of an act by using the present participle of verbs, such as doing, enduring, and enjoying—the type of language that, incidentally, resonates readily with people's everyday experiences of career.

Basing themselves to a greater or lesser extent on Pepper (1942), more recent authors have provided further understanding of contextualism (Capaldi & Procter, 1999; Hayes, Hayes, Reese, & Sarbin, 1993). For example, Gillespie (1992) suggests that contextualism is "an interactive, dynamic worldview" and that "the contextualist focuses on the readiness of experience and shared meaning that arise out of interaction with others" (p. 18).

Contextualism conceives of the wholeness of an event and the interpenetration of its features. We can use the metaphor of weaving a tapestry and creating a pattern by the interweaving of threads to illuminate the different ontological and epistemological assumptions of contextualism. Much social science research and theory, including that on career, breaks phenomena into their component parts in order to understand and analyze them. To the contextualist, to analyze events in their various strands would be to start to unravel the tapestry (Collin, 1994).

This chapter develops a contextual action, theoretical explanation of career for which several aspects of contextualism are particularly relevant. First, the goals of actions rather than their causes are emphasized. "Studying for an examination" is an action that career counselors can readily understand, not so much because it is caused by certain factors but because it embodies the individual's and others' (for example, family members' and teachers') understanding of and response to their context. Second, actions are embedded in their context, which has implications for the client-counselor relationship and the interpretation they engage in together. Third, change has a prominent role in career. Fourth, because events take shape as people engage in practical action with particular goals, analysis and interpretation are always practical. Researchers and counselors look at an action for a particular purpose. What is crucial here is that goal, end, and purpose define the practicality of action and our understanding of it. Finally, just as contextualism works from the present event outward, so counselors work from their clients' present outward.

As a world hypothesis or root metaphor, contextualism addresses ontology, epistemology, and practice. We can illustrate these domains by using everyday statements about career. Ontology deals with questions of being. It addresses the "What is it?" of an object. For example, the statements "I have a job that is meaningful to me" and "Globalization is a new aspect of the world we live in" apply to the "What it is" of career. Other statements reflect the way we know about career, that is, epistemology or knowledge. "I count a lot on what I learn from experience" and "You can't believe everything you read in the newspapers about how jobs are changing" are examples of such statements. Finally, there is the domain of how we do things (for example, "Making connections with others is the way I am going to find a job" and "Career counseling involves the assessment of interests"). This is the domain of practice or doing, or of achieving changes. We identify and illustrate these domains to indicate that a contextual explanation of career, to be inclusive, has to address what career is, how we know about it, and how we intervene, facilitate, and guide it.

Context in Career and Counseling
Theory, Research, and Practice

As we noted at the outset, context is well recognized in career theory and counseling, although it is conceptualized in various ways (Holland, 1997; Krumboltz, 1998; Lent, Brown, & Hackett, 2000; Leong & Serafica, 2001; Savickas, 2001). Contextualism is also recognized in explanations of career (Richardson, 2000; Patton & McMahon, 1999). Richardson (2001) notes that counseling psychologists and, by implication, counselors have always been contextualists, in that they have always been interested in the significant contexts of people's lives, although many have not used explicitly contextual conceptualizations. However, to our knowledge, no career theorist has espoused contextualism as defined in this chapter. Thus we believe it would be helpful to establish how a range of career development and counseling theories, research, and practices represent and address context.

We stated earlier that theories of career and counseling usually address one or more of the properties of context. We said that the properties of context are (1) a multiplicity and complexity of parts, (2) the inextricable weaving together of these parts, and (3) the meaning of events or phenomena. We now illustrate how these career theories often address one or the other of the properties of context and how they include counseling applications fitting that property. We then propose that our contextualist action theory integrates the properties of context with the domains of ontology, epistemology, and practice identified earlier.

The career theories that incorporate the first of these properties emphasize the complexity of the career world, the institutional structures that must be accommodated to, and the myriad of variables that are at play in career development. In two discussions (Hotchkiss & Borow, 1996; Maranda & Comeau, 2000), the authors identify a number of sociological approaches that attempt to account for the complexity of the variables that contribute to career. These variables include structural factors such as the nature of the labor market, race, and gender, as well as family socioeconomic status. Maranda and Comeau show how various schools of sociology interpret these structural factors differently, with contrasting implications for the person and for career. Some approaches to context that emphasize multiplicity and complexity also draw implications for counseling practice. Hotchkiss and Borow identify a range of counseling practices to help clients address the structural dimensions of their contexts, including informing clients about the labor market and combating gender stereotyping. They also cite Gottfredson's career theory of circumscription and compromise (Gottfredson, 1981) as a particularly good explanation of career that incorporates the gender and status dimensions of occupational aspiration.

Other career theories address context by looking specifically at how things (for example, roles) are woven together. Rather than focus on the list of variables as Hotchkiss and Borow (1996) did, these theorists suggest that career should be looked at as a kind of interlocking system. Vondracek and colleagues' contextual-developmental approach to career (Vondracek, Lerner, & Schulenberg, 1986) addresses the dynamic interaction between the context and the person, using the concept of affordances. Patton and McMahon (1999) also examine the interlocking nature of career systems by explicitly labeling their approach as a systemic approach to career development; they propose it "as a potential overarching framework for career theory" (p. 134). Leong and Hartung (2000) provide a particular example of the interlocking nature of factors that pertain to career. In discussing multicultural career and counseling issues, they suggest that the demographics of increasing cultural diversity are in the process of producing a multicultural mind-set, in other words, the reciprocal influence of people from different ethnic groups living in the same groups and societies affects the way we know and think about multicultural issues. Leong and Hartung go on to propose counseling interventions in career that are culturally functional, that is, procedures that fit for the joint undertaking that is multicultural counseling.

Finally, we know that context reveals the meaning of events or phenomena that would otherwise be ambiguous or unavailable to us. Meaning is not always explicitly addressed in the systemic approaches just described. Brown's values approach (Brown, 1995, 1996a) and Cochran's narrative approach (Cochran, 1990, 1998) are good examples of career theories that incorporate context by addressing meaning. Brown, for example, suggests that values serve as standards by which people evaluate their own actions and the actions of others. In his view, values, which are influenced by contextual factors, are the fundamental unit of meaning. Cochran's "sense of vocation" is also an explanation that incorporates context by focusing on meaning of the life-career. Later he extended this to include a narrative approach to career counseling (Cochran, 1998). As Cochran maintains, meaning reveals itself through narrative that incorporates both time and place. In Young and Collin's edited book (Young & Collin, 1992), the studies described used natural language, text, and interpretation as a means of constructing meaning and generating contextual knowledge about career.

Savickas (2001) relies on the action-theoretical work of Baltes (1997) as an explanation integrating other career theories that deal with the multiplicity of variables, the interaction among them, and the meaning they have for individuals and groups. In other words, Savickas suggests that career theorists have to go beyond previous explanations. In particular, we have to have a theory that addresses not only the "what" of career but the "how"—the process of career.

We are heeding Savickas's call for an integrative theory that explains career process, and, as did Baltes (1997) and his colleagues, we are relying on the construct of *action*, which is central to our explanation of career in this chapter. Our explanation integrates the three domains and the three properties of career into a contextualist explanation. Along with addressing the properties of context in terms of what career is, our explanation includes our assumptions about psychological processes, about knowledge generation processes, and about psychological practice in the career field. In our explanation, what career is, knowledge generation about career, and career practice, as well as the properties of context, not only coexist but mutually influence and gain meaning from each other.

A Contextualist Action Theory Explanation of Career

The contextualist explanation of career development and counseling proposed here is founded on the notion of action as goal-directed, intentional behavior. Career is full of goals, plans, and intentions, but these are virtually meaningless without reference to context. Similarly, career behavior and associated contexts only gain substance and importance when understood in relation to the person's intentions.

Action is conceptualized as being cognitively and socially regulated and steered. It is organized as a system that has hierarchical, sequential, and parallel dimensions. *Hierarchy* pertains to the super- and subordination of actions toward goals; for example, quitting this job and finding another may be part of a superordinate action of working in a field that is consistent with one's values. *Sequence* refers to the temporal ordering of actions; for example, applying for a job may involve reading the advertisement, preparing a résumé, and being interviewed. Actions can also be parallel, that is, different actions for different goals can coexist.

The simplest way to understand action is to consider it from three perspectives: *manifest behavior*, *internal processes*, and *social meaning*. Because these are perspectives on what is essentially a single phenomenon, their order here is arbitrary rather than causally or temporally related. Studying for an examination is a career-related action that is embodied in *manifest behavior* (for example, sitting at one's desk, making notes). These behaviors can be observed by others. Studying for an examination is also experienced by the student as cognitive and emotional *internal processes* (for example, in identifying topics needing more work, feeling anxious). Finally, studying for an examination expresses and is couched in *social meaning* (for example, studying results in making good grades and being successful in a chosen field). Thus anyone drawing on social meaning can understand this action and will attribute conventional short- and long-term goals and intentions to the student, or the student will attribute them to herself. Thus the social and cultural understanding of this action is anchored in its social representation, and the context of action is manifested.

Our approach to action on which our contextualist explanation of career is based uses a language for dealing with people in their everyday lives. In observing another's behavior or in acting in relation to that behavior, people attribute goals and thus make sense of the stream of behavior. This process serves as an aid not only to understanding others but to framing one's interaction with them. The language of action reflects everyday experience and the results of empirical research, as well as a conceptualization of the person, indicating that intentions and goals are significant dimensions of human behavior, that human actions are social processes, and that actions produce each person's social and cultural world. In discussing the concept of action, we will explain its contextual characteristics.

Action and Context

It is important to distinguish the simple phrase "studying for an examination" from engaging in the action itself. The phrase appears to decontextualize this action, but it is the action itself that contextualizes: given all the variables, in this time and place and for this purpose, this person acts. The dictionary assigns several meanings to most words. But when words are used in sentences and speech, we have no difficulty in knowing which meaning is intended. Those who wish to understand "a career" for professional or personal reasons will want to keep together as much information as is pertinent. We propose goal-directed human action as the construct that allows us to keep all the pertinent information together so we can understand the meaning of our own and others' behavior. As we attempt to make sense of actions with others, sequences of actions across time, or actions that have goals and subgoals, we need broader and more encompassing constructs. To do this, we propose three constructs that extend the notion of action: (1) joint action, (2) project, and (3) career.

Joint Action. The term *joint action* refers to the action that people take together, and it too is made up of manifest behavior, internal processes, and meaning. It is based on the assumption that many actions occur between and among people; for example, couples have conversations about career issues. Although individuals have their own intentions, a dyad or group also develops joint goals and joint action. One might say that these joint goals and actions are co-constructed, although this should not be taken to mean that all parties have an equal role in their construction.

Shotter (1993) characterizes joint action as having an intentional quality that is not fully accounted for by summing up the individual intentions of the participants. He suggests that people engaging in action together create a new "third thing" that is neither individual action nor an external event. He also recognizes the primacy of conversation in joint action and the creation of a "practical-moral" domain in which personal and social identity is constructed and influenced. Given this point of view, the relevance of joint action in a career explanation is substantial.

Many counseling theorists and researchers take into account what is happening between the client and counselor and have some conceptualization for it. The working alliance (Meara & Patton, 1994) is one such conceptualization. Our approach focuses on the action of the dyad rather than the interaction between them. We gain particular access to the context in which counselor and client are acting. In the joint action of counseling, as in life generally, career identity, values, interests, and behaviors are not shaped from the outside "in"; rather, they are constructed, perhaps largely through language, in conversation with others. The concept of joint action represents a particularly notable and new way of addressing context.

Joint action in career differs from individual action in the following components: task and group structure, knowledge processing and energizing, and execution (von Cranach, Ochsenbein, & Valach, 1986). When a counselor and client rehearse a hypothetical employment interview, they are engaged in this as a socially defined task related to a goal. The action is also informed by the group structure of the client and counselor: who will introduce the topic, who will provide information, who will role play the applicant, who will evaluate, and so forth. Unlike individual action, in which knowledge processing is internal, the energizing and processing of information occurs in a joint action through communication. The demand for effective communication in the dyad increases as the complexity of the task and the dyad's structure increase. Finally, there may be differences in the execution when the client engages in an actual employment interview.

Project. The example of a couple discussing career issues illustrates the idea of a superordinate construct—the *project*. Imagine a young couple interested in developing an egalitarian relationship with regard to education, occupation, and family roles and tasks. They might construct such a project in terms of alternating who will attend school while the other works, deciding about moving to take a position, and determining the child-care responsibilities. As their project develops, other concerns and tasks may arise for the couple, for example, responding to an employment layoff, or the equal sharing of the care of their children or elderly parents. This egalitarian relationship project is developed by the couple as part of their anticipated life together and is implemented by them. We can readily imagine that both parties contributed to defining the goals and the tasks, although the project may have been initiated by one of them. It is likely that neither the goal nor the tasks were fully defined in advance. Rather, the project goals are defined and redefined as the couple actually engages in actions and activities and are confronted by life circumstances. We can also see the possibility that this project may become the subject of counseling at some point in the relationship, should either party's understanding of the shared goal or tasks break down.

In this example, we see the use of a construct that is broader than action but involves action. Nevertheless, it is individual and joint actions, which include manifest behavior, internal processes, and social meaning, that contribute to the project. We recognize in this example that the project has social meaning derived from its context, which our very use of it as an example illustrates. This project is socially constructed; the couple and others can readily understand and interpret the couple's behavior in light of the project.

Career. Like project, *career* is a superordinate construct that allows people to construct connections among actions; to account for effort, plans, goals, and consequences; to frame internal cognitions and emotions; and to use feedback and feed-forward processes (Young & Valach, 1996). As a construct, career can extend over longer periods of time than project and encompass a greater range of actions. As the construct one uses to link action broadens, it involves an increasingly complex interaction of internal processes, particularly emotion, social meaning, and manifest behavior. Here, career begins to approximate Cochran's idea of vocation (Cochran, 1990), which entails intrinsic motivation, purpose, and meaningfulness. For some, career represents a form of meaning according to which they can readily interpret their own and others' behavior. However, as Richardson (1993) points out, the use of the term *career*, as it is widely understood, does not have personal relevance for everyone. Nevertheless, what is important is not the term itself but the constructs used to account for purpose and meaning over the long term and to connect actions. As Boesch (1991) remarks, it is not sufficient that action has a goal representation and motivation; it must have a superordinate goal structure and be embedded in a network of meaning at the social level. Such is the function of career and allied constructs, such as biography and life narrative.

The Organization of Action

There are three levels of action: (1) elements, (2) functional steps, and (3) goals. Actions are organized at their lowest level by their elements: physical and verbal behavior such as words, phrases, movements, and environmental structures. However, elements never exist by themselves; if they did, they would be quite difficult to interpret. The phrase "I don't feel like working any longer" can be understood quite differently if uttered by a chronically unemployed person or one who has been intensively involved with a challenging task for an extended period of time. That a phrase or other physical or verbal behavior is subject to different interpretations does not imply that they are meaningless but that they have to be contextualized to find their potential meanings.

The second level of action is the *functional step*. An element of action can be contextualized by seeing it as one of a series of contiguous behaviors that comprise a step. A mother's statement, "Please go to school," can be one statement in a sequence in which a mother pleads with her teenage son not to drop out of school, or it may be a reminder to a child that if she does not leave the house soon, she will miss her bus. The same element can be part of two quite different functional steps: pleading or reminding.

These functional steps are further contextualized by the actor's *goals*, which are the highest level of the organization of action, joint action, project, and career. Goals represent the general intention of the actor (individual or group). Thus in a parent-adolescent conversation about career, the mother's goal of attempting to keep her teenage son from dropping out of school contextualizes the conversation to some extent. As a reminder not to be late for school, the element and functional step are also contextualized. In the case of dropping out of school, one might think of the mother-son conversation as part of career, whereas the reminder about being late may be confined to action or project. The former may have more long-term implications for a student than the latter. Hence it can be constructed as part of project (keeping the kids in school at all costs) or career (completing high school being one of several ways to overcome a life of poverty and unemployment).

Figure 6.1 summarizes the main constructs of action theory that we have just described. Each aspect in the table is related to all the other aspects in a complex and dynamic way. Their relationship is highlighted in the following discussion of several salient issues related to career and counseling.

FIGURE 6.1. Main Concepts of Action Theory

Action Systems	Perspectives on Action		Levels of Action Organization
Career Project Joint action Action	can be seen from the perspective of	Manifest behavior Internal processes Social meaning and defined as	Goal Functional steps Elements

Interpretation and Narrative

Interpretation refers to the process by which people make sense of action and context. People tend to interpret others' actions, for the most part, as intentional and goal-directed, but it is these constructs of intentionality and goal orientation that are particularly subject to and salient for interpretation. Interpretation connotes making sense of something that already exists, that is, finding its meaning, as one "interprets" the already spoken words of a foreign language. Even in this act, however, there is meaning that projects forward in time. The interpreter translates according to her or his present and antic-ipated context ("What and how will the listener understand?"). Interpretation also addresses issues of meaning over the long term. Telling a story that involves the long term serves to integrate the lis-tener in the long-term process of project or career. The narrative is not a reproduction of events but a construction that the teller thinks the other should know about for some reason. Collin and Young (1992) address the notion and importance of the long-term mean-ing that one makes of one's life. They link interpretation, in part, to the development of a sense of identity through the construction of narratives. The development of the narrative is enhanced by artic-ulating it (Taylor, 1989). Collin and Young observe that narrative "is built from history, culture, society, relationships and language. It embodies context" (p. 8).

Linde (1993) refers to coherence as the process used to repre-sent context. Cochran (1990) uses the phrase *holistic construction* to identify the process of constructing "a coherent and reasonably well-founded whole to serve as a basis for further refinements, extensions, and revisions" (pp. vii–viii). A coherent narrative is one in which there is a sequence or temporal ordering of events that makes sense to the person. However, coherence does not precede other dimensions of the narrative; it is constructed simultaneously with them. In the construction of career narratives, people frequently use continuity and causality as criteria for the judgment of adequacy (Linde). The narrator seeks to provide good reasons for what has happened in her or his life. Among the acceptable reasons recognized in our society from which individuals and groups can draw in their construction of career narratives are those related to ability, personality, socioeconomic class, and economic conditions. Goals and intentions, constructed through social discourse, also serve to establish coherence.

We identified narrative as an important feature of interpretation in some earlier works (Collin & Young, 1992; Young & Valach, 1996); others have considered narrative as central to meaning and interpretation as well. Sarbin (1992) suggests that narrative is equivalent to Pepper's "historic act" (Pepper, 1942) as the appropriate root metaphor for contextualism. Hermans (1992) equates the contextual and the narrative metamodels of development, and Savickas (2001) includes narrative as one level of a comprehensive theory of career development. Narrative is also seen as pivotal in construing and communicating among people (Bruner, 1986; Polkinghorne, 1988; Sarbin, 1986).

Young and Valach (1996) identify a number of features of narrative relevant to career and action. First, narrative can create coherence and continuity out of separate, unrelated actions. It serves to construct and enable intentional, goal-directed action. Second, narrative provides a guide for action (Sarbin, 1992). The overall story or narrative supplies a framework within which to understand the particular and act in the present. In this way, career is constructed and the future of the career is suggested. Finally, as Shotter (1993) points out, we do not live wholly in narratives. The action-theoretical explanation addressed in this chapter underlines the fact that people are required to take action in their daily lives that is both practical (that is, dealing with objects) and symbolic (that is, dealing with signs and symbols).

The Role of Emotion

Kidd (1998) makes a strong case for the increased recognition of emotion in career theory, research, and practice. Her argument is that emotion, rather than being intrapsychic, is highly interpersonal and contextual. The separation of emotion and cognition in both psychology and vocational counseling may be another reason for the insufficient attention paid to emotion. For example, in a number of vocational counseling texts, emotion is not indexed (for example, Luzzo, 2000; Zunker, 1998). The recent social approaches to emotion, as well as a number of neuropsychological studies, speak against the distinction between cognition and emotion, which appears to be more logical than psychological (for example, Forgas & Bower, 1987; Mayer, McCormack, & Strong, 1995). The characterization of emotion as passive—something that happens to us and limits our ability to act (Averill & More, 1993)—may be another reason for its devaluation in agency-oriented career counseling.

In the contextualist action theory of career, emotion assumes a more central place. Emotion and cognition are internal processes that regulate and guide action; both are connected to the interpersonal and contextual. Emotion is critical in this explanation because it concerns action. Brown (1996a), basing his work on that of Rokeach (1973), also sees emotion as one of three components of values that, in turn, determine goals and action. But as Kidd (1998) points out, emotion is present, not only in single actions but in career as well. If one considers career as becoming more responsive to changing contexts, emotion has a significant place in it. Clients in counseling have feelings not only about specific events in their lives but about longer and more complex segments such as projects and careers.

Recent neuropsychological research indicates substantial links among emotion, stress, and memory-related prospective and retrospective constructions of events (for example, Cahill, Babinsky, Markowitch, & McHaugh, 1995; Isen, 2000; McFarland & Buehler,

1998). Considering the importance of these processes for individual activity and for career and project maintenance and development, the role of emotion in career processes at the level of project and career becomes obvious. It is even more pronounced in organizing our interactive action related to our substantial personal and identity projects and careers.

Averill and Nunley (1992) refer to emotions as being constructed in much the same way that language is constructed; thus they are not primarily products of our biology but of social and individual development. In many theories of emotion (for example, Solomon, 1993), emotions and cognitions are considered together as internal processes, as we have identified them in our discussion. Although the internal processes have a cognitive component, action cannot be undertaken without emotion. As Epstein (1993) notes, a cognitive system by itself cannot drive action. Thus emotion is motivational or energizing. Emotions are also *about* something; that is, they can be considered intentional (Solomon).

Frijda (1986) distinguishes between emotions that are closely linked to the readiness to act and more complex emotions such as pride and jealousy. These are related to the context and to superordinate frames such as project and career. Emotion is related to context and arises out of it. Frederickson (2001) suggests, based on substantial evidence, that positive emotions are vehicles for individual growth and social connection. Thus emotion is connected to needs, goals, plans, and purposes. Grimstad (1992) provides an excellent example of pride in relation to the careers of home economics teachers. For the women in her study, pride was constructed interpersonally and contributed to the complex events that supported their careers as teachers and provided cultural continuity for their narratives. Further, Averill and More (1993) note the importance of long-term plans and goals and, in turn, a sense of happiness. They suggest that happiness is linked to one's overall ability to form some sense of what one's life should be.

There are three reasons why emotion is important in this contextualist action explanation of career and counseling. First, emotion serves to energize and motivate action. Specific career actions and projects can be frustrating, difficult, or dull; one must be energized by emotions in order to carry out the specific action and also to transcend it. It is difficult to imagine that a career or project can be engendered or maintained over the long term without the emotion to sustain it. For example, a pianist may be motivated by love of music to repeatedly practice a piece that she wants to master. Second, emotions serve to regulate and control actions, projects, and careers. People rely on internal processes to make moment-to-moment decisions about their actions. Finally, emotion provides the key to narratives of project and career. Career and project are constructed from issues of concern in a person's life. Because emotion is associated with needs, desires, purposes, and goals, it is able to access, develop, and orient narratives about project and career. Not only do emotions cue the person to the narrative but they are used when the person is constructing and developing narrative. Young, Paseluikho, and Valach (1997) illustrate the place of emotion in the construction of career in parent-adolescent conversations. They found that emotion regulates the action in the conversations and is implicated in the goals and strivings of the parents and adolescents; thus emotion serves as the basis of the narratives they construct together. Simply put, our emotional processes regulate our actions, and these processes are social in nature. At the same time, to a certain extent our emotions are constructed by our actions, projects, and careers.

The Validity of the Explanation

In addressing the validity of this contextualist action theory of career, we are concerned about how sound it is, about its breadth and its applicability; we know it has considerable range and applicability. As we pointed out, it addresses the three properties of context, multiplicity, the interweaving function, and the meaning of career itself. Moreover, it addresses these properties for knowledge generation about career and for career practices, as well as in its focus on human action.

Bronfenbrenner (1979, 1993) identifies three conditions of ecologically valid research. These conditions are not just related to methods but must remain central to theorizing as well. Extending these conditions to explanations, the conditions are that the explanation must (1) maintain the integrity of real-life situations, (2) be faithful to social and cultural contexts, and (3) be consistent with the person's description of experiences and events. The explanation set out in this chapter meets these conditions by (1) identifying goal-directed action as the central unit of our approach, thus maintaining the integrity of real-life situations, (2) recognizing the structural, functional, and meaning properties of context that incorporate the social and cultural contexts, and (3) using language and concepts that are close to human experience and localized at the level of action, project, or career. Thus the cultural, gender, and intergenerational validity of the explanation is based on the same conditions and can be addressed in particular.

Culture and Career

The theme of this chapter represents the substantial relationship between career and culture; context subsumes culture. We have already suggested that career is enacted in a given time and place. It is linked to a culture and a history. Career includes plans, intentions, goals, and actions that incorporate time and place in both their specificity and breadth. Boesch (1991) is particularly insightful on this point when he refers to action as situated in a cultural field. Similarly, career is situated in a cultural field, and it is this field that affords and constrains career possibilities. Because of the complexity of career and its extension over time, culture is more explicit in career than in a single action. For example, we can think of some actions that might have similar meanings in different cultures, but it is much more difficult to imagine careers having the same meaning in different cultures.

The contextual explanation of career also addresses the increased ethnic diversity of societies in which career is constructed and career services are provided. Leong and Hartung (2000) use the term *multicultural mind-set* to highlight the contrast with an earlier monocultural perspective. Although recognition of the importance of multiculturalism is on the rise, they note that the multicultural mind-set is not the dominant frame of reference in many disciplines and professional practices. Their point is important. It suggests that cultures change, continually providing different affordances and constraints for career. We also have to recognize that the affordances and constraints of a culture are confined neither to ethnicity nor to the ethnic dimension of a multicultural society.

What, then, is the intercultural validity of our contextual explanation of career? Collin (2000) recognizes that *career* itself is a term that is loaded with cultural specificity. It has been tied in significant ways to the individualism, capitalism, and bureaucratic organization that flourished in midcentury America. In the explanation offered in this chapter, we attempt to pull "career" away from the specific occupational, organizational, and economic factors that encapsulated it at one time. We recognize, however, that the specifics of career (for instance, career practices such as counseling), like the specifics of action, are always tied to specific times and places. They are culturally specific, which is not to say that career and counseling cannot be used in a range of cultural contexts. They are. But in each case, they adapt to the specific cultural context. Not only is it not possible to extricate ourselves from the cultural specificity of career, it is the strength of our explanation. However, when discussing the cross-cultural validity of this explanation, one needs to recognize that we are proposing an explanation that helps in collecting and understanding ecologically valid data at both the research and practice levels. Unlike traditional science, we have not proposed a theory based on causal propositions that are assumed to be universal but are challenged to prove their validity in different contexts.

Gender and Career

Career is a gendered construct, that is, gender is inextricably interwoven into the structure, functions, and social meaning of career. The efforts of many feminists working in the career field have been to have the gender properties of career explicitly recognized rather than have them subsumed under male assumptions. Some of the literature on women's career development has focused on structural features like, for example, the rate of labor market participation or the role of women in institutions such as marriage and child rearing. The implication for practice is to help women bypass or remediate structural disadvantages or to change the structures themselves.

Another subset of the literature on gender addresses the issue of how women interact or function within various career-related systems. This literature ranges from parental influence on women (for example, O'Brien & Fassinger, 1993) to women's relationship with the organizations in which they work (for example, Cleveland, Stockdale, & Murphy, 2000; Kilduff, 2001). One implication for practice is to address systemic change by involving women in the career system. Finally, the gendered nature of career and counseling has been addressed as meaning, for example, that "career success" can have different meanings for men and women (Höpfl & Atkinson, 2000), that feminism has fostered a radical reconsideration in the ways we know (for example, Riger, 2000), and that relationship has unique considerations in counseling for meaning for women (Miller & Stiver, 1997).

The Applicability of the Theory

Does the explanation presented in this chapter apply as well to the new workplace as to traditional forms of occupations and work? Young and Valach (2000) address this intergenerational validity by arguing that this explanation of career has reconceptualized career from a construct that was based exclusively in organizations, industries, and institutions (the bureaucratically based career) to one that is anchored broadly in society and in the social connections we have as people (the socially anchored career). For example, Kanter's entrepreneurial career is "one of several alternatives to the bureaucratic career, standing between the bureaucratic career and the socially anchored career" (Young & Valach, 2000, p. 190; Kanter, 1989). Our reconceptualization of career also involves not only the long term but the short- and midterm as well. For example, *project* is increasingly being recognized as a heuristic construct that can be used to describe various work periods and tasks, which Jones (1996) did for the film industry, paths for adolescents to adult occupations (Larson, 2000), and as the basis for vocational identity (Riverin-Simard, 2000), and for effective functioning (Richardson, 2000). Clearly, the social basis of career, the conceptualization of the midterm in the form of projects, and the attention to change and change processes increase the value of this explanation to address career in the information-oriented, technological, global, and networked society of the twenty-first century.

Contextualizing Career Research

Young and Valach (1996) argue that one of the strengths of the contextualist action approach is the fluid relations among theory, research, and practice. The principle that underlies this fluidity is that action, project, and career are everyday concepts that are close to human experience, not abstracted from it. One of the primary purposes of career research from a contextualist action theory approach is to describe career processes more fully. The perspectives on action, manifest behavior, internal processes, and social meaning are the same perspectives for research access to a single integrated action, a joint project, or a career of one or more persons. Although other research uses one or more of these perspectives, the full understanding of action, project, or career requires that all perspectives be considered.

Since the initial formulation of this approach (Young & Valach, 1996; Young, Valach, & Collin, 1996), a number of authors have commented on the need for supporting research (for example, Brown, 1996b; Niles & Hartung, 2000). We have undertaken a line of research that examines the actions and projects that occur in conversations between parents and adolescents and other family activities that contribute over time in the construction of career (for example, Young, Valach, Dillabough, Dover, & Matthes, 1994;

Young, Valach et al., 1997; Young, Valach, Ball et al., 2001). We have been able to identify, monitor, and subsequently describe joint, goal-directed action at the level of project, specifically in the form of the family career development project. These studies illustrate how career is socially constructed through joint goal-directed actions and projects. They lay the groundwork for the investigation of other microsystem dyads and small groups that contribute to the construction of career.

We have also been able to develop and refine the Qualitative Action-Project Method, which involves collecting data for each of the perspectives of action: manifest behavior, internal process, and social meaning (Young, Valach, Ball et al., 2001; Young, Lynam, Valach et al., 2000, 2001). This method allows for the qualitative examination of projects over time. In this method, we collect data representing the perspective of manifest behavior in the form of videotaped conversations between parents and adolescents. We collect data on internal processes and social meaning through the self-confrontation procedure in which the participants are asked to recall their feelings and thoughts during the conversation by seeing a videotape of the conversation immediately after it is completed. We also collect data on social meaning, internal processes, and manifest behavior through interviews with the participants, logs of their activities, and regular telephone calls that monitor the project across time.

We use narrative feedback to participants that summarizes, from an action perspective, our analysis of their common activities based on the videotapes and transcripts. These procedures neither decontextualize the phenomenon being studied, because both action and intention are involved, nor falsely contextualize it, for example, by pretending that our research method is unobtrusive. These procedures also contextualize the data so the need to gather a lot of supporting information is reduced; the procedures actually highlight what is notable to the participants. This method departs from much research that addresses the researcher's a priori constructs, usually measured through paper-and-pencil inventories or questionnaires. Thus we maintain that our research pays tribute to the proposition that we take part in processes relevant in the participants' everyday lives.

The results illustrate how a number of the constructs used in this chapter are created: career, goal (Young et al., 1997), task structure, functions, roles and responsibilities (Young et al., 1999), group action, emotion (Young, Paseluikho, & Valach, 1997), information processing, project, and its embeddedness in other family projects (Young, Lynam, Valach et al., 2001, Young, Valach, Ball et al., 2001). Shotter (1993) suggests that research such as we have described, which focuses on language and conversation, has the effect of pointing our attention to "crucial features of the context, features that 'show' connections between things that would otherwise go unnoticed" (p. 34). This approach has greater potential to identify the phases or sequences involved in action and thus address people's everyday career experience than many methods based on a priori constructs.

Action theory is used explicitly in research in social, personality, and developmental psychology that has relevance for career. It is impossible to review this literature extensively here, but pertinent sources are Brandtstädter and Lerner (1999) and Gollwitzer and Bargh (1996). Although not unequivocal on all aspects of action theory, the researchers contributing to these volumes conceptualize and use constructs, such as *life tasks, project, life planning,* and *identity goals,* that have relevance for career. For example, Wiese, Freund, and Baltes (2000) take an action-theoretical view in postulating processes that contribute to successful life management, based on contextual conditions. They found that action-related strategies are efficient means for planning and managing occupational and partnership challenges of adult life. Little's work on personal projects (Little, 1999) lends support to the hypotheses that they provide meaning, community, and structure. He and his colleagues (Phillips, Little, & Goodine, 1996, 1997) found important relationships between the projects of senior-level managers, gender, and organizational life, as well as implications for the relevance of community-oriented projects during retirement.

Finally, research from a contextual, if not a contextualist, perspective can take a variety of forms, as the discussion earlier in this chapter indicates. For example, Blustein (2001) contextualizes work and career behavior by examining the connections between work and relationships more closely. Using qualitative methods that allow research participants to share the meaning of lived experiences, he and his colleagues provide significant evidence for the embeddedness of work and career in human relationships (Blustein et al., 2001; Phillips, Christopher-Sisk, & Gravino, 2001; Schultheiss, Kress, Manzi, & Glasscock, 2001). The challenge of their work, as Flum (2001) notes, is the conceptualization of the complexity of relationship and career—an observation that is addressed in action theory. In the language of action theory, these studies point to the construction of career as a joint project, as well as its embeddedness in other life projects.

Other research has attempted to contextualize career by using retrospective accounts. The studies in the edited text by Young and Collin (1992) adopt an interpretative and contextualist approach. However, although these studies describe social meaning, as well as behavior and internal processes recalled retrospectively from the perspective of social meaning, they address less well the career-related action that occurs in the present. Approaches like these recognize the importance of working with social meaning, without which research and theory are much less responsive to, and beneficial for, practice.

Contextualizing Career Counseling

Young and Valach (1996) point out that *career* is first and foremost a practice construct. It represents the actions that people take in the world as they engage in projects and realize their goals. Counseling, though clearly involving action and career, can be most readily thought about as a project: the counselor and client working together over a given period of time. This view suggests that practitioners should look to their clients' everyday experiences and constructs in formulating their own understanding and practice of counseling. The desire of practitioners to meet their clients on equal terms and the knowledge that their own activity as counselors, as well as their clients' activity, is intentional focuses on the need for an explanation of goal-directed, intentional action that addresses the counselor's and client's activity alike. The career counselor is also confronted by a broad range of client behavior, from the cognitive-adaptive regulation of a specific action to long-term life planning. For example, a teacher's long-term career interests and goals may be jeopardized by a short-term process such as stage fright. Similarly, performing a relatively short-term action, such as filling out a job application, may be at risk because of a long-term experience of anxiety in situations where paper credentials are scrutinized. Although the source of neither the stage fright nor the anxiety needs to be identified to illustrate the difference between long term and short term, both types of issues fall within the purview of career counseling. A helpful explanation must include and integrate them.

Counseling is constructed in the language of goal-directed action. Feltham and Dryden (1993) note that all counseling is implicitly goal-directed; the broadest possible goals are, for example, to be happy or to understand oneself better. Egan (1998) has enunciated one of the clearest models, in which he refers to goals as a consequence of counseling. What is added here is the conception of goals as part of the ongoing process of counseling itself, embedded in what the counselor and client are doing together.

Working with Interpretation and Narrative

Counseling involves interpersonal communication between counselor and client in which interpretation has a central role. *Interpretation* refers specifically to a constructionist sense making of one's experiences and goals (for example, Sexton & Griffin, 1997). This meaning-making process applies equally to the long-term career and to the immediate action between the counselor and client. The counselor can approach interpretation by

- Becoming aware of client conceptualizations, concepts, and constructs
- Helping clients become aware of their constructs and recognize those that are workable
- Supporting clients in their use of their constructs
- Not abandoning the use of these constructs in favor of other "more scientific" or "more therapeutically oriented" ones

For example, a counselor would probably prefer to work with the client's concepts that may be descriptive, such as referring to emotional states as warm or cold or using the client's metaphors, than to use explanatory concepts.

When used judiciously in counseling, narratives can help people reconfigure their pasts and futures and thus make different action possible (Cochran, 1998; Russell & van den Broek, 1992; White & Epston, 1990). Narratives are not, nor should they be treated as, a retreat to unreality. Rather, as Efran (1994) points out, narratives are of central relevance to the construction of action. Cochran describes narratives as life stories that have a temporal organization, synthesize spheres of meaning, and convey a point. Basing his work on McAdams (1995), Savickas (2001) refers to the narrative life story that "brings overall unity, purpose, and meaning to a life" (p. 310). Although such narratives serve an important function in understanding career, counselors should not expect clients to begin counseling with such a narrative nor necessarily arrive at one as a counseling outcome. When using narratives in counseling, the counselor and client can look for more than one theme, goal, or intention that might serve to create a tapestrylike pattern in the narrative. A narrative that lacks coherence can be problematic because it does not enable the variety and range of a person's actions to be pulled together. However, a highly coherent or "tight"

narrative may be as problematic to a client as one that lacks coherence. For example, a story that has a client becoming a research
scientist as the only option for her future is one that may require
attention in counseling, just as one in which the client describes a
wide range of ambitions in terms of both level and focus. We, as
counselors, should also be wary of a single grand theme or life story
that does not give adequate attention to the uniqueness of context.
One expects that clients will pay attention to the details of context that make their narratives and their lives unique. When they
don't, clients can be helped to elaborate their narratives.

In addition to revealing the way the clients want to disclose
their construction of their career, projects, and actions, the strength
of a narrative is in its telling. Conveying a personally relevant story
with the close emotional monitoring of its telling is an important
part of the narrative process. Clients can steer and regulate their
emotional involvement in the telling of a personal narrative.

Themes—frequently referred-to topics, problems, or perspectives—are another characteristic of narratives. Counselors may find
that what was previously thought of as an interest, trait, attribute, or
personality characteristic may emerge as a construct and theme of
the person's life; the person may then assume the agent's role. The
purpose of looking for and working with themes is not to attribute a
greater or lesser role to them than they already have but to help the
client construct them so as to retain more control over their themes.

Interpretation, which we defined earlier in this chapter as the
process by which people make sense of action and context, also
takes place in the discourse that is constructed between the client
and counselor. As we pointed out earlier, narratives do not just happen; they are the intentional, goal-directed product of the group (in
this case the client and counselor). Frequently, clients approach
counselors with stories and constructions of their lives or parts of
their lives that are dysfunctional and problematic. This discourse is
usually understood within the context of their lives. It must also be
understood within the context of counseling. In a sense, a narrative
of a problem or a dysfunction is often an accepted discourse to begin

negotiations with counselors. Counselors should "interpret" them as narratives about clients' lives and as narratives that are functional in counseling to negotiate the counseling process. This interpretation serves to set up a joint action between the client and counselor that would be a suitable part of the client's long-term career or project. Thus counselors need to be aware that, in addition to the narratives shared in counseling, clients have other discourses about their lives as lived in relation to other people and events.

Goals

The emphasis on goals and goal-directedness in contextualist action theory may lead some counselors to reject the approach as too rational, too predetermined, too calculated, or too disconnected from emotion. It is important to state that these are misunderstandings of action. Goals are only one part of action that, to some extent, are set prior to action but largely emerge from action, project, and career. Thus in action theory, action is the product of some goals and the precursor of others; it is the basis for goal development and enhancement. Once counselors and clients address real-life events, which inevitably involve goals, they recognize that goals involve emotions and cognitions, arise from events in our lives, can be spontaneous, and, although conscious, are not always available for reflection.

The counselor can also recognize that goals represent one level in the organization of action (Figure 6.1) but not the entirety of action, project, or career. Rather than dealing with goals in an isolated way, the counselor and client are encouraged to work on the action, project, and career. This includes addressing internal processes as well as behavioral components. Although not a new idea in counseling, the connection of action, project, and career proposed in this explanation allows goals to be seen in a more integrated way across the dimensions and stages of one's life. The counseling itself is a joint project that serves as a basis and model for developing and practicing changes at any of the levels.

Joint Action

The notion of joint action between counselor and client contrasts with the way counselor and client are regarded separately in much of counseling. For example, about 35 percent of the entries in Feltham and Dryden's *Dictionary of Counselling* (1993) concern the client, whereas 55 percent address the counselor. The entries concerning clients deal with distressful and dysfunctional emotion and imply passive processes and negative consequences, whereas counselor-related concepts often have a cognitive focus and are related to active steering and controlling. The conceptualization of joint action between the counselor and client offers the opportunity to consider counseling as a unitary action rather than disparate systems. The counselor, client, and others who may be involved participate in the same venture.

Most counselors are familiar with the idea of the working alliance between client and counselor. Writing from a psychoanalytic perspective, Meara and Patton (1994) identify three characteristics of the working alliance in career counseling: goal, task, and bond. Joint action adds something to the accepted view of each of these. Not only should goals be explicit and agreed-on by the client and counselor but the notion of joint action also suggests that joint goals can emerge by virtue of their action together. Examples of joint goals in counseling may include developing and sharing the client's narrative, exploring the client's occupational concerns, and identifying related goals and projects in the client's life. It is important to reiterate that the counselor's and client's joint goals are not determined in advance. They develop as a result of the counseling itself. These are the dyad's goals, which are only in a limited way identical to the goals of the individual participants; these joint goals are unique and do not conform entirely to the preconceived goals of either party. Similarly, in addition to individual tasks, joint tasks (which will be largely verbal) arise by virtue of the action between the two actors. Finally, Meara and Patton's third characteristic—bond—refers to the affective component between them. However, this is only part of the energizing and direction needed for the joint action between them; joint action is also energized by the communication between them.

It is at the level of joint action that counseling overcomes any inherent limitations of a strictly narrative or retrospective approach. In counseling, as in career and human life generally, one is required to act.

Other Counseling Practices

A new conceptualization of how to gather data and what data are gathered in counseling is part of this contextualist explanation.

Data Gathering.   Data gathering is not an isolated event within counseling, nor are data gathered as if the person were isolated from everyday life. The three perspectives (manifest behavior, internal processes, and social meaning; see Figure 6.1) provide the basis for ongoing assessment in counseling. Although developed for research purposes, the use of video self-confrontation (Young, Valach, Dillabough, Dover, & Matthes, 1994; Young et al., 2001) represents an example of data gathering that can also be used in counseling. Having clients engage in salient career-related actions, such as discussing career plans with partners and then having them identify internal processes and meaning associated with the action, brings relevant contextual information into counseling.

Involving Others in Counseling.   A central feature of the explanation of career provided in this chapter is that career, project, and action develop in and through social exchange. We have shown in our research how significant others are involved in the construction of career (for example, Young et al., 2001). The involvement of others and their communication are aspects particularly amenable to counseling.

Case Studies

Both E and K, college students in the early adult stage of life (see Chapter Two), are involved in individual and joint action, in projects, and to some extent in career. Both the client and the counselor can and will look at these systems of action from the perspectives of the client's manifest behavior, internal processes, and meaning, and will address one or more of the levels of action organization, that is, goals, steps to realize goals, and specific behavioral elements that contribute to the steps. Thus we consider this approach broad and inclusive—counseling E and K will involve more strategies than can be discussed here. However, understanding these cases from an action perspective is a critical step in using and applying appropriate strategies and techniques.

These cases seem to require that some type of initial occupational decision be addressed, although this is more tacit in the case of K than of E. Sometimes clients assume that there is a critical one-time occupational decision to which prior education should be tailored. College students making this assumption sometimes want to use a firm occupational decision as a motivator for their studies. These assumptions are not new, but they may not be as valid as they once were.

We need to recognize at the outset that both cases are constructions. The data distinctly represent E and K, but the data were abstracted from larger data sets and assembled by a counselor. In some ways, these cases represent a negotiated construction or exchange between the client and the counselor, as well as a construction for the purposes of providing these case analyses. Each action in the process, such as taking the tests, talking to the counselor, and writing the case study, contextualizes the material.

As we described earlier, the counseling itself can be considered a joint project between the client and the counselor, with the counselor drawing the client into a project that is characterized by goal, task, and bond (Meara & Patton, 1994).

The Case of E

E engages in a range of actions. Not only is she a sophomore at the university, she has had summer jobs, stays in touch with friends, watches TV, goes to concerts, and comes to counseling. Many other activities are implied. For example, she is likely to be involved in a number of activities with her family that are not one-time events. Sequences of goal-directed actions that have meaning for E and for her counselor are described. However, it is too early to say what meaning they have; inasmuch as E described these actions, they have meaning for her.

Because these actions are more than one-time events, they can be described as projects. In other words, they contribute to longer-term broad goals that E may have. They are also constructed as she engages in the actions themselves. Actions and projects are guided by goals, and goals emerge from actions and projects. For the purposes of explicating our position in this chapter, we tentatively name three projects that these actions may be a part of; however, naming projects has to be integral to the counseling process and depends on E's participation in it (as in the case of K that follows).

E is involved in a number of tasks pertinent to academic achievement, attending university being a major one. These tasks come together for her at the level of goals, as she frames a narrative around these academic tasks. It is from this narrative that an understanding of the relevant projects to which her particular actions contribute will be clarified. But we can initially identify an educational project.

E also seems quite interested in her relationships with her family. One would suspect that there is a family relational project of considerable importance; moreover, this family project may be related to her concerns about occupation. For example, she seems to reflect her parents' own occupational preferences. She is taking courses that would lead to a career in law (like her parents); law is an occupational daydream, and she admires women lawyers and would like to pattern her life after them. One may speculate that she may feel overembedded in the family project and unsatisfied that she cannot differentiate her own goals as distinct from the family project. Indeed, her goals for counseling, which seem so focused, may reflect some need to satisfy parental pressure for closure around educational and career goals. These are hypotheses that could be tested in counseling.

Finally, there is evidence of an identity project based on her self-referent statements, including having an image for herself. Watching real-life TV shows and admiring others (musicians, the Pope, her father's law partner) may represent a lack of personal realization. E may be experiencing a block in taking who she is from the level of images to the level of implementing them. She may have difficulty recognizing the projects in which she is participating. There may also be a gap between these images and the actions and projects that are required to realize whatever aspects of them can be used in her own life. This identity project is understandably gendered, reflected particularly in E's identification of women as models. The place of gender for her and in her particular contexts (culture) can profitably be explored in counseling.

Action theory recognizes that significant others usually have an important role in how the person constructs career. In is unclear in the case of E who, other than her family, has contributed to this construction and how they have contributed to it. E mentions friends only briefly, and significant others are not referred to.

What we have suggested at the level of project seems also to apply to career. At the present time, E appears to limit her understanding of career to an occupational career. The actions and projects in her life do not contribute to her occupational career to the extent that she would like or expects. She also expresses confusion about the relation of her occupational images to their implementation.

There is no evidence that a clinical diagnosis of psychopathology is warranted in this case, but all of the issues are relevant to E's overall positive mental health. We suggest that having short-, middle-, and long-term goals that connect individuals to their context, as well as having the means to implement them, are important characteristics of psychological health.

The case of E and the story of E as a person are embedded in a gendered and cultural context. It is expected that these dimensions will be evident in the actions, projects, and career that she will engage in. Indeed, the counseling itself is a project that is embedded culturally.

Several aspects of E's case stand out as a basis on which to establish a working relationship (a counseling project) with her. It is important to recognize and explore her feelings of confusion. Her goals for counseling provide the basis for articulating the counseling project. Even her ideals, such as wanting to be like Sandra Day O'Connor, provide an initial basis for sharing her enthusiasm. The critical factor, with regard to any additional information the counselor may need, is that E provides it in the form of narratives. Counseling has to give her the opportunity to construct and share a narrative with the counselor. Even the test scores that have been provided can be built into the goals and narratives that she has.

Some of the difficulties E is experiencing appear to be at the action level. E and her counselor may want to look at her project-related actions closely by videotaping their conversations, identifying the thoughts and feelings that guide these conversations, and constructing written or verbal narratives pertinent to these actions (the self-confrontation procedure described earlier). Similarly, this method may be used if members of her family or significant friends with whom she engages in project-related action can be identified and are willing to participate in counseling with her.

The case summary does not include much evidence of emotion. It would be useful in counseling to focus on how emotion figures in her narratives, as well as how she uses it to energize her goals. One of the issues that E may be facing is that of formulating goals. The counselor may help E describe, as narratives, the short-term and focused projects in which she is engaged.

Another area for exploration is how her occupationally related concerns and processes are related to other actions and projects in her life. For example, how do they relate to the family relational project and the identity project mentioned earlier. In exploring this with E, it would also be important to determine who the other participants in these processes are and how their goals interact with E's goals. Constructing a narrative about having an occupation would also be helpful for identifying the goals that E is seeking to fulfill through it, as well as those goals' relation to other projects.

The Case of K

The most significant questions in the case of K are why he is presenting himself for counseling and what he expects from it. These are addressed to a limited extent in the statement, "K admits that he has very little information about careers at this time and expressed an interest in knowing more about technology careers and architecture." K's apparent lack of specificity in articulating the goals for counseling seems to reflect a significant lack of action, projects, and career in some areas of his life. Although K does not manifest psychopathology, the lack of agency and effective functioning in relation to some of the important contexts in which he lives may signal current and future psychological adjustment issues.

One explicit theme is skateboarding and K's desire to be a skateboarder. This provides a link between the past and the future, as he constructs it. Skateboarding is something that K likes, does, and reads about. It is an occupational daydream. He wants to pattern his life after professional skateboarders. Skateboarding can be tentatively proposed as a current project. We may also think of skateboarding as a *career* in K's construction. In this sense, career does not necessarily refer to an occupation. Nevertheless, skateboarding is the major theme that ties many of his actions together. It is interesting to note that the assessment data contain relatively little on his ability or self-efficacy ratings on skateboarding or on the physical ability associated with it.

K's skateboarding project may also provide some information about his current malaise and his reasons for seeking counseling. Notwithstanding his interest in this field, K may be experiencing some incongruence between this project and other projects in which he is engaged. He may, for example, see friends with whom he shared his skateboarding interests move on to college, occupations, and other pursuits. He may be experiencing the tension between a somewhat closed skateboarding subculture and the broader culture.

Belongingness and relationships are important themes that emerge in the case of K. We see it in several aspects; for example, he selected the option of going to college because of his friend's advice. Belonging comes up as an important value-goal in some of the assessment data. It is also interesting to note that the case does not mention relationship-oriented activities. There is a critical statement about his admiration for his cousin, who is "someone to do things with," as well as the cousin's initiation of activities. There is no mention of a close or special friend or of a current group of friends; there is no mention of friends in recollections or in his peak experience. Yet paying for his friend's car is something he would do if he won the lottery. His parents are also mentioned as beneficiaries of his winning the lottery, but they have relatively little explicit place in the rest of the case. As part of his concern with belonging, he may be interpreting the message from his parents that occupational choice is strictly up to him as their lack of concern and involvement. Thus we see belonging as quite important to K but something that he does not appear to be able to realize. The issue of belonging is also in contrast to his valuing of independence, indicating that he may feel that belonging threatens independence or that these cannot coexist.

Gender and cultural issues are embedded in this case. The fact that he is interested in skateboarding is more reflective of male than female gender in North America. Similarly, his declared interest in math, achievement, and making money may be aspects that, for him, provide gender identity and thus are part of his identity project. The fact that he is Japanese-Chinese-American doesn't seem to enter explicitly into the case. The literature indicates that Asian Americans have more specific career goals for their children than Americans of European descent, but this doesn't seem to be so in this case. Depending on where K lives, the issue of belonging (or

lack of it and his need for it) may have something to do with the acceptance of his ethnicity; being of mixed race may be particularly
problematic.

The lack of achievement and general lack of focus, despite reasonably good aptitude scores and self-efficacy estimates, suggest that
the latter may serve K in achieving some goals that are not explicit
in the case, and about which he may be only somewhat aware.

This case provides a particularly strong illustration of the notion
of counseling as a joint counselor-client project. K has not clearly
identified why he is presenting himself for career counseling or what
he expects from it. Other than his interest in skateboarding, this
lack of clarity is reflective of other aspects of his life, particularly
why he is going to college and what he wants to accomplish there.
Relationships also represent a problematic domain for K. Thus the
joint project of counseling, with goals, functional steps, and behavioral components, and based in the counselor-client relationship,
can become the basis for joint projects outside of counseling. For
example, as K and the counselor determine the goals for counseling, so K will learn to negotiate with others goals and steps for common projects.

As part of the negotiation of the goals of counseling, the counselor may wish to explore with K whether he assumes that career
counseling is about determining a suitable occupation for himself.
This may be his implicit assumption and one he attributes to the
counselor as well. Because K is about to begin college, an additional
unstated agenda might be to pick a college major. As action theory
implies, career counseling is not about making a single occupational
choice taken in isolation from the social world in which the individual participates. Rather it is about seeing how goals, steps, and
behavior inform and are informed by actions and projects that, over
time, will result in a long-term career.

The counselor needs to encourage K to talk more about his current life, particularly in terms of what he does. The counselor can
help him develop this talk into narrative themes, which can be used
as the basis for them to identify the projects in which K is currently

engaged, what the goals of those projects are, what meaning K and others make of them, and the thoughts and feelings he has about them. Projects, however limited they may be, are the basis for linking K to the future. Although he is able to frame the future in terms of goals, he has more difficulty with initiating actions. Thus the linking of goals to functional steps and behavioral elements through projects will likely be a helpful approach in counseling K. The counselor might wish to consider using the assessment data as K relates them to his actions and projects rather than to stable dispositions.

The counselor could use the self-confrontation procedure heuristically with K. This could be simply a self-confrontation of the dialogue between the counselor and the client. However, as in the case of E, K's need for belonging and the way in which others are involved in his career decisions warrants, if possible, the involvement of others (for example, his parents or the friend who advised him to attend college) in counseling with K.

Summary

The contextualist explanation proposed in this chapter moves beyond an environmental or structural conceptualization of the career context and beyond conceptualizations that emphasize systems or meanings as the critical contextual perspectives. By basing this explanation on intentional action and emphasizing joint action, we have been able to address the social and dynamic nature of context and retain our concern with the underlying aspects of career such as plans, goals, and agency. All participants in career and career counseling can use intentional concepts without ignoring their social anchoring. Participants can relate to social inhibitors and facilitators of career and counseling and still see these processes as intentional. Our methodology based on the perspectives of manifest action and social meaning, as well as on internal processes such as cognition in individual action, communication in group action, and joint narratives in projects and careers, gives all participants a broad spectrum of involvement. As this explanation uses people's everyday language and constructs, it reduces the gaps among theory, research, and practice. Thus it enables the practitioner to contribute to research and theory building, and it helps researchers and theoreticians include and use the perspective and language of practice. Finally, it has practical relevance for how people lead their lives and how we counsel them about their lives.

References

Averill, J. R., & More, T. A. (1993). Happiness. In M. Lewis & J. M. Haviland (Eds.), *Handbook of emotion* (pp. 617–629). New York: Guilford Press.

Averill, J. R., & Nunley, E. P. (1992). *Voyages of the heart: Living an emotionally creative life*. New York: Free Press.

Baltes, P. B. (1997). On the incomplete architecture of human ontogeny: Selection, optimization, and compensation as foundation of developmental theory. *American Psychologist, 52*, 366–380.

Blustein, D. L. (2001). The interface of work and relationships: Critical knowledge for 21st century psychology. *The Counseling Psychologist, 29*, 179–192.

Blustein, D. L., Fama, L. D., White, S. F., Ketterson, T. U., Schaefer, B. M., Schwam, M. F., Sirin, S. R., & Skau, M. (2001). A qualitative analysis of counseling case material: Listening to our clients. *The Counseling Psychologist, 29*, 240–258.

Boesch, E. E. (1991). *Symbolic action theory and cultural psychology*. New York: Springer-Verlag.

Brandtstädter, J., & Lerner, R. M. (Eds.). (1999). *Action and self-development: Theory and research through the life span*. Thousand Oaks, CA: Sage.

Bronfenbrenner, U. (1979). *The ecology of human development*. Cambridge, MA: Harvard University Press.

Bronfenbrenner, U. (1993). The ecology of cognitive development: Research models and fugitive findings. In R. H. Wozniak & K. Fischer (Eds.), *Scientific environments* (pp. 3–44). Hillsdale, NJ: Erlbaum.

Brown, D. (1995). A values-based model for facilitating career transitions. *Career Development Quarterly, 44*, 4–11.

Brown, D. (1996a). Brown's values-based, holistic model of career and life-role choices and satisfaction. In D. Brown, L. Brooks, & Associates,

Career choice and development (3rd ed., pp. 337–372). San Francisco: Jossey-Bass.

Brown, D. (1996b). Status of career development theories. In D. Brown, L. Brooks, & Associates, *Career choice and development* (3rd ed., pp. 513–525). San Francisco: Jossey-Bass.

Bruner, J. (1986). *Actual minds, possible worlds*. Cambridge, MA: Harvard University Press.

Cahill, L., Babinsky, R., Markowitch, H. J., & McGaugh, J. L. (1995). The amygdala and emotional memory. *Nature, 377*, 295–296.

Capaldi, E. J., & Procter, R. W. (1999). *Contextualism in psychological research? A critical review*. Thousand Oaks, CA: Sage.

Cleveland, J. N., Stockdale, M., & Murphy, K. R. (2000). *Women and men in organizations: Sex and gender issues at work*. Mahwah, NJ: Erlbaum.

Cochran, L. (1990). *The sense of vocation: A study of career and life development*. Albany: State University of New York Press.

Cochran, L. (1998). *Career counseling: A narrative approach*. Newbury Park, CA: Sage.

Collin, A. (1994). Human resource management in context. In I. Beardwell & L. Holden (Eds.), *Human resource management: A contemporary perspective* (pp. 28–66). London: Pitman.

Collin, A. (2000). Epic and novel: The rhetoric of career. In A. Collin & R. A. Young (Eds.), *The future of career* (pp. 163–177). Cambridge, UK: Cambridge University Press.

Collin, A., & Young, R. A. (1992). Constructing career through narrative and context: An interpretive perspective. In R. A. Young & A. Collin (Eds.), *Interpreting career: Hermeneutical studies of lives in context* (pp. 1–12). Westport, CT. Praeger.

Dewey, J. (1969). The logic of verification. In *John Dewey: The early works* (Vol. 3, pp. 83–92). Carbondale, IL: Southern Illinois University Press. (Original work published 1890)

Efran, J. S. (1994). Mystery, abstraction, and narrative psychotherapy. *Journal of Constructivist Psychology, 7*, 219–227.

Egan, G. (1998). *The skilled helper: A problem-management approach to helping* (6th ed.). Pacific Grove, CA: Brooks/Cole.

Epstein, S. (1993). Emotion and self-theory. In M. Lewis & J. M. Haviland (Eds.), *Handbook of emotion* (pp. 313–326). New York: Guilford Press.

Feltham, C., & Dryden, W. (1993). *Dictionary of counselling*. London: Whurr.

Flum, H. (2001). Dialogues and challenges: The interface between work and relationship in transition. *The Counseling Psychologist, 29*, 259–270.

Forgas, J. P., & Bower, G. H. (1987). Mood effects on personal perception judgments. *Journal of Personality and Social Psychology, 51*, 140–148.

Frederickson, B. L. (2001). The role of positive emotions in positive psychology: The broaden-and-build theory of positive emotions. *American Psychologist, 56*, 218–226.

Frijda, N. H. (1986). *The emotions.* Cambridge, UK: Cambridge University Press.

Gillespie, D. (1992). *The mind's we: Contextualism in cognitive psychology.* Carbondale, IL: Southern Illinois University Press.

Gollwitzer, P. M., & Bargh, J. A. (Eds.). (1996). *The psychology of action: Linking cognition and motivation to behavior.* New York: Guilford Press.

Gottfredson, L. S. (1981). Circumscription and compromise: A developmental theory of occupational aspirations. *Journal of Counseling Psychology Monograph, 28*, 545–579.

Grimstad, J. A. (1992). Advancing an ecological perspective of vocational development: The construction of personal work integration. In R. A. Young & A. Collin (Eds.), *Interpreting career: Hermeneutical studies of lives in context* (pp. 79–97). Westport, CT: Praeger.

Hayes, S. C., Hayes, L. J., Reese, H. W., & Sarbin, T. R. (Eds.). (1993). *Varieties of scientific contextualism.* Reno, NV: Context Press.

Hermans, H. J. M. (1992). Telling and retelling one's self-narrative: A contextual approach to life-span development. *Human Development, 35*, 361–375.

Holland, J. L. (1997). *Making vocational choices: A theory of vocational personalities and work environments* (3rd ed.). Odessa, FL: Psychological Assessment Resources.

Höpfl, H., & Atkinson, P. (2000). The future of women's careers. In A. Collin & R. A. Young (Eds.), *The future of career* (pp. 130–143). Cambridge, UK: Cambridge University Press.

Hotchkiss, L., & Borow, H. (1996). Sociological perspective on work and career development. In D. Brown, L. Brooks, & Associates, *Career choice and development* (3rd ed., pp. 281–334). San Francisco: Jossey-Bass.

Isaacson, L. E., & Brown, D. (2000). *Career information, career counseling and career development.* Boston: Allyn & Bacon.

Isen, A. M. (2000). Positive affect and decision making. In M. Lewis & J. M. Haviland-Jones (Eds.), *Handbook of emotions* (2nd ed., pp. 417–435). New York: Guilford Press.

Jones, C. (1996). Careers in project networks: The case of the film industry. In M. B. Arthur & D. M. Rousseau (Eds.), *The boundaryless career: A new employment principle for a new organizational era* (pp. 58–75). New York: Oxford University Press.

Kanter, R. M. (1989). Careers and the wealth of nations: A macroperspective on the structure and implications of career forms. In M. B. Arthur, D. T. Hall, & B. S. Lawrence (Eds.), *Handbook of career theory* (pp. 506–521). Cambridge, UK: Cambridge University Press.

Kidd, J. (1998). Emotion: An absent presence in career theory. *Journal of Vocational Behavior, 52*, 275–288.

Kilduff, M. (2001). Hegemonic masculinity and organizational behavior. In R. T. Golembiewski (Ed.), *Handbook of organizational behavior* (2nd ed., pp. 599–609). New York: Marcel Dekker.

Krumboltz, J. (1998). Serendipity is not serendipitous. *Journal of Counseling Psychology, 45*, 390–392.

Larson, R. W. (2000). Toward a positive psychology of youth development. *American Psychologist, 55*, 17–183.

Lent, R. W., Brown, S. D., & Hackett, G. (2000). Contextual supports and barriers to career choice: A social cognitive analysis. *Journal of Counseling Psychology, 47*, 36–49.

Leong, F. T. L., & Hartung, P. J. (2000). Adapting to the changing multicultural context of career. In A. Collin & R. A. Young (Eds.), *The future of career* (pp. 212–227). Cambridge, UK: Cambridge University Press.

Leong, F. T. L., & Serafica, F. C. (2001). Cross-cultural perspective on Super's career development theory: Career maturity and cultural accommodation. In F. T. L. Leong & A. Barak (Eds.), *Contemporary models in vocational psychology: A volume in honor of Samual H. Osipow* (pp. 167–206). Mahwah, NJ: Erlbaum.

Linde, C. (1993). *Life stories: The creation of coherence.* New York: Oxford University Press.

Little, B. R. (1999). Personal projects and social ecology: Themes and variation across the life span. In J. Brandtstädter & R. M. Lerner,

(Eds.), *Action and self-development: Theory and research through the life span* (pp. 197–222). Thousand Oaks, CA: Sage.

Luzzo, D. A. (Ed.). (2000). *Career counseling of college students: An empirical guide to strategies that work.* Washington, DC: American Psychological Association.

Maranda, M.-F., & Comeau, Y. (2000). Some contributions of sociology to the understanding of career. In A. Collin & R. A. Young (Eds.), *The future of career* (pp. 37–52). Cambridge, UK: Cambridge University Press.

Mayer, J. D., McCormack, L. J., & Strong, S. E. (1995). Mood congruent memory and natural mood. *Personality and Social Psychology Bulletin, 22,* 736–746.

McAdams, D. P. (1995). What do we know when we know a person? *Journal of Personality, 63,* 365–396.

McFarland, C., & Buehler R. (1998). The impact of negative affect on autobiographical memory: The role of self-focused attention to moods. *Journal of Personality and Social Psychology, 75,* 1424–1440.

Mead, G. H. (1934). *Mind, self and society.* Chicago: University of Chicago Press.

Meara, N. M., & Patton, M. J. (1994). Contributions to the working alliance in the practice of career counseling. *Career Development Quarterly, 43,* 161–177.

Miller, J. D., & Stiver, I. P. (1997). *The healing connection: How women form relationships in therapy and life.* Boston: Beacon Press.

New Webster's Dictionary of the English Language (College Ed.). (1975). Chicago: Consolidated Book Publishers.

Niles, S. G., & Hartung, P. J. (2000). Emerging career theories. In D. A. Luzzo (Ed.), *Career counseling of college students: An empirical guide to strategies that work* (pp. 23–42). Washington, DC: American Psychological Association.

O'Brien, K. M., & Fassinger, R. E. (1993). Career orientation and choice of women. *Journal of Counseling Psychology, 40,* 456–469.

Parsons, F. (1909). *Choosing a vocation.* New York: Agathon Press.

Patton, W., & McMahon, M. (1999). *Career development and systems theory: A new relationship.* Pacific Grove, CA: Brooks/Cole.

Pepper, S. C. (1942). *World hypotheses: A study in evidence.* Berkeley: University of California Press.

Phillips, S. D., Christopher-Sisk, E. R., & Gravino, K. L. (2001). Making career decisions in a relational context. *The Counseling Psychologist*, 29, 193–213.

Phillips, S. D., Little, B. R., & Goodine, L. (1996). *Organizational climate and personal projects: Gender differences in the public service*. Ottawa: Canadian Centre for Management Development.

Phillips, S. D., Little, B. R., & Goodine, L. (1997). Reconsidering gender and public administration: Five steps beyond conventional research. *Canadian Public Administration*, 40, 563–581.

Polkinghorne, D. E. (1988). *Narrative knowing and the human sciences*. Albany. State University of New York Press.

Polkinghorne, D. E. (1990). Action theory approaches to career research. In R. A. Young & W. A. Borgen (Eds.), *Methodological approaches to the study of career* (pp. 87–105). New York: Praeger.

Richardson, M. S. (1993). Work in people's lives: A location for counseling psychologists. *Journal of Counseling Psychology*, 40, 425–433.

Richardson, M. S. (2000). A new perspective for counsellors: From career ideologies to empowerment through work and relationship practices. In A. Collin & R. A. Young (Eds.), *The future of career* (pp. 197–211). Cambridge, UK: Cambridge University Press.

Richardson, M. S. (2001). New perspectives for counseling psychologists. *The Counseling Psychologist*, 29, 271–278.

Riger, S. (2000). *Transforming psychology: Gender in theory and practice*. New York: Oxford University Press.

Riverin–Simard, D. (2000). Career development in the changing context of the second part of working life. In A. Collin & R. A. Young (Eds.), *The future of career* (pp. 115–129). Cambridge, UK: Cambridge University Press.

Rokeach, M. (1973). *The nature of human values*. New York: Free Press.

Russell, R. L., & van den Broek, P. (1992). Changing narrative schemas in psychotherapy. *Psychotherapy*, 29, 344–354.

Sarbin, T. R. (1986). *Narrative psychology: The storied nature of human conduct*. New York: Praeger.

Sarbin, T. R. (1992). The narrative as the root metaphor for contextualism. In L. C. Hayes & L. J. Hayes, *Varieties of scientific contextualism* (pp. 51–65). Reno, NV: Context Press.

Savickas, M. (2001). Toward a comprehensive theory of career development: Dispositions, concerns, and narratives. In F. T. L. Leong &

A. Barak (Eds.), *Contemporary models in vocational psychology: A volume in honor of Samual H. Osipow* (pp. 295–320). Mahwah, NJ: Erlbaum.

Schultheiss, D. E. P., Kress, H. M., Manzi, A. J., & Glasscock, J. M. J. (2001). Relational influences in career development: A qualitative inquiry. *The Counseling Psychologist, 29*, 214–239.

Sexton, T. L., & Griffin, B. L. (Eds.). (1997). *Constructivist thinking in counseling practice, research, and training.* New York: Teachers College Press.

Shotter, J. (1993). *Conversational realities: Constructing life through language.* Newbury Park, CA: Sage.

Solomon, R. C. (1993). The philosophy of emotions. In M. Lewis & J. M. Haviland (Eds.), *Handbook of emotion* (pp. 3–15). New York: Guilford Press.

Taylor, C. (1989). *Sources of the self: The making of the modern identity.* Cambridge, MA: Harvard University Press.

Valach, L. (1990). A theory of goal-directed action in career analysis. In R. A. Young & W. A. Borgen (Eds.), *Methodological approaches to the study of career* (pp. 107–126). New York: Praeger.

von Cranach, M., & Harré R. (Eds.). (1982). *The analysis of action: Recent theoretical and empirical advances.* Cambridge, UK: Cambridge University Press.

von Cranach, M., Ochsenbein, G., & Valach, L. (1986). The group as a self-active system: Outline of a theory of group action. *European Journal of Social Psychology, 16*, 193–229.

Vondracek, F. W., Lerner, R. M., & Schulenberg, J. E. (1986). *Career development: A life–span developmental approach.* Hillsdale, NJ: Erlbaum.

Vygotsky, L. S. (1978). *Mind in society.* Cambridge, MA: Harvard University Press.

White, M., & Epston, D. (1990). *Narrative means to therapeutic ends.* New York: W. W. Norton.

Wiese, B. S., Freund, A. M., & Baltes, P. B. (2000). Selection, optimization, and compensation: An action-related approach to work and partnership. *Journal of Vocational Behavior, 57*, 273–300.

Young, R. A., Antal, S., Bassett, M. E., Seigo, N., Post, A., & Valach, L. (1999). The joint actions of adolescents in peer conversations about career. *Journal of Adolescence, 22*, 527–538.

Young, R. A., & Collin, A. (Eds.). (1992). *Interpreting career: Hermeneutical studies of lives in context.* Westport, CT: Praeger.

Young, R. A., Lynam, M. A., Valach, L., Novak, H., Brierton, I., & Christopher, A. (2000). Parent–adolescent health conversations as action: Theoretical and methodological issues. *Psychology and Health, 15*, 853–868.

Young, R. A., Lynam, M. A., Valach, L., Novak, H., Brierton, I., & Christopher, A. (2001). Joint actions of parents and adolescents in health conversations. *Qualitative Health Research, 11*, 40–57.

Young, R. A., Paseluikho, M., & Valach, L. (1997). Emotion in the construction of career in conversations between parents and adolescents. *Journal of Counseling and Development, 76*, 36–44.

Young, R. A., & Valach, L. (1996). Interpretation and action in career counseling. In M. L. Savickas & W. B. Walsh (Eds.), *Handbook of career counseling theory and practice* (pp. 361–376). Palo Alto, CA: Davies–Black.

Young, R. A., & Valach, L. (2000). Reconceptualising career theory and research: An action–theoretical perspective. In A. Collin & R. A. Young (Eds.), *The future of career* (pp. 181–196). Cambridge, UK: Cambridge University Press.

Young, R. A., Valach, L., Ball, J., Paseluikho, Wong, Y. S., DeVries, R. J., MacLean, H., & Turkel, H. (2001). Career development as a family project. *Journal of Counseling Psychology, 48*, 190–202.

Young, R. A., Valach, L., & Collin, A. (1996). A contextual approach to career. In D. Brown, L. Brooks, & Associates, *Career choice and development* (3rd ed., pp. 477–512). San Francisco: Jossey–Bass.

Young, R. A., Valach, L., Dillabough, J., Dover, C., & Matthes, G. (1994). Career research from an action perspective: The self-confrontation procedure. *Career Development Quarterly, 43*, 185–196.

Young, R. A., Valach, L., Paseluikho, M. A., Dover, C., Matthes, G. E, Paproski, D. L., & Sankey, A. M. (1997). The joint action of parents and adolescents in conversation about career. *Career Development Quarterly, 46*, 72–86.

Zunker, V. G. (1998). *Career counseling. Applied concepts of life planning* (5th ed.). Pacific Grove, CA: Brooks/Cole.

PART FOUR

Career Development Theories
Anchored in Learning Theory

7

Social Cognitive Career Theory

Robert W. Lent, Steven D. Brown, Gail Hackett

A number of trends or shifts in direction—some relatively subtle, others more dramatic—have been occurring in theory and research on career development over the past several decades. One of these trends involves an increasing focus on cognitive variables and processes that help to govern career behavior. Observing this trend, Borgen (1991) comments, "The cognitive revolution has quietly overtaken vocational psychology, leaving the field ripe for more explicit integration" (p. 279).

Accompanying this quiet cognitive revolution has been an equally important trend toward viewing people as active agents in, or shapers of, their career development. This emphasis on personal agency (or self-direction) actually has deep roots in the study of career behavior and the practice of career counseling (Borgen, 1991). In a sense, those who study career behavior have been rediscovering what career counselors typically accept as self-evident—that people help construct their own career outcomes; that their beliefs (for example, about themselves, their environments, and possible career paths) play key roles in this process; that we are not merely beneficiaries (or victims) of intrapsychic, temperamental, or situational forces; and that behavior is often flexible and susceptible to change efforts. Indeed, counselors' faith in personal agency is reflected in the very term career *choice*. And their emphasis on self-exploration and related activities would be futile if career development were entirely determined by factors over which clients have no control.

By the same token, counselors, theorists, and researchers are also well aware that career development is not just a cognitive or a volitional enterprise and that there are often potent (external and internal) barriers to choice, change, and growth. For instance, social and economic conditions promote or inhibit particular career paths for particular persons. Affective reactions influence rational thought processes. People differ in their abilities and achievement histories. In short, a complex array of factors such as culture, gender, genetic endowment, sociostructural considerations, and disability or health status operate in tandem with people's cognitions, affecting the nature and range of their career possibilities.

Background of the Theory

This chapter presents an evolving view of career development from a social cognitive perspective—a position that attempts to trace some of the complex connections between persons and their career-related contexts, between cognitive and interpersonal factors, and between self-directed and externally imposed influences on career behavior. Termed *social cognitive career theory* (SCCT), this perspective complements, or builds conceptual linkages with, other theories of career development. Embracing constructivist assumptions about humans' capacity to influence their own development and surroundings, SCCT has been inspired and influenced by a number of key developments in vocational psychology, other psychological and counseling domains, and the cognitive sciences.

Theory Convergence

One source of inspiration has been the recent focus on theoretical convergence and complementarity in vocational psychology (Savickas & Lent, 1994). Although theory and research on career development have expanded at a healthy pace over the past few decades, a number of authors have noted the scientific and practical advantages of considering commonalities among the various career theories and prospects for more integrative frameworks (Borgen, 1991; Hackett, Lent, & Greenhaus, 1991; Osipow, 1990). One viable approach to theory integration is to develop constructs and conceptual scaffolding to bridge some of the differences in competing theories, thereby helping to create a more organized, coherent account of career behavior (Lent & Savickas, 1994).

In this vein, we suggested that it may be useful to build unifying models that, according to Hackett and Lent (1992),

(a) bring together conceptually related constructs (e.g., self-concept, self-efficacy); (b) more fully explain outcomes that are common to a number of career theories (e.g., satisfaction, stability); and (c) account for the relations among seemingly diverse constructs (e.g., self-efficacy, interests, abilities, needs). [p. 443]

Other writers have also noted the need to impose greater conceptual order on the mass of variables and findings that characterize the career literature. Brown (1990), for example, asks, "What are the relationships among values, needs, aptitudes, and interests as they operate in concert to influence occupational choice making?" (p. 346).

SCCT was designed to address such questions, to help construct useful conceptual bridges, to identify major variables that may compose a more comprehensive explanatory system, and to sketch central processes linking these variables together. In particular, SCCT highlights certain experiential and learning or cognitive processes that can help to account for important, if sometimes overlooked, phenomena in other career theories, such as how types develop in Holland's scheme, what factors are responsible for differential role salience in Super's theory, or how people acquire abilities in Dawis and Lofquist's theory. Inasmuch as learning processes cement together the various segments and determinants of career development (Super, 1990), SCCT is intended to offer a potentially unifying framework.

Social Cognitive Roots

SCCT is derived principally from Albert Bandura's general social cognitive theory (Bandura, 1986). Emphasizing the interplay between self-referent thought and social processes in guiding human behavior, SCCT has proven to be immensely heuristic, finding application in a wide range of psychosocial domains such as educational achievement, health behaviors, organizational management, and affective reactions (Bandura, 1986, 1997). In formulating SCCT, we tried to adapt, elaborate, and extend those aspects of Bandura's theory that seemed most relevant to the processes of interest formation, career selection, and performance. We also took a good deal of liberty in suggesting certain theoretical paths and connections that do not follow directly from general social cognitive theory.

SCCT is linked to two branches of career inquiry that have evolved from Bandura's general framework: Krumboltz's social learning theory of career decision making (Krumboltz, 1979; Krumboltz, Mitchell, & Jones, 1976; Mitchell & Krumboltz, 1996) and the application of the self-efficacy construct to women's career development by Hackett and Betz (1981). Conceptually, SCCT is most closely aligned with Hackett and Betz's position, although it also builds on the major conceptual foundation of Krumboltz's theory. Part of SCCT's purpose is to update and extend these earlier branches of inquiry by constructing closer ties to advances in social cognitive theory and its empirical base in both career and noncareer domains.

The similarities and differences with Krumboltz's position, discussed in greater detail elsewhere (Lent & Hackett, 1994), are noteworthy. For example, SCCT shares Krumboltz's emphasis on the learning experiences (direct and vicarious) that shape people's occupational interests, values, and choices. Similarly, SCCT follows Krumboltz's and other theorists' lead in acknowledging the influence of genetic factors, special abilities, and environmental conditions on career decisions. Such conceptual links are essential, given our intent for SCCT to serve as a unifying or bridging framework—and given that it shares with Krumboltz's theory some common theoretical lineage. However, the two positions diverge on a number of key points, for example, in their conceptualization of cognitive processes, in their central constructs, and in the specific outcomes they attempt to explain.

Krumboltz's theory traces its roots to social *learning* theory—an earlier version of Bandura's position—whereas SCCT stems more directly from social *cognitive* theory, reflecting an increased emphasis on cognitive, self-regulatory, and motivational processes that extend beyond basic issues of learning and conditioning. Although both positions acknowledge the impact of reinforcement history on career behavior, SCCT is more concerned with the specific cognitive mediators through which learning experiences guide career behavior; with the manner in which variables such as interests, abilities, and values interrelate; and with the specific theoretical paths by which person and contextual factors influence career outcomes. It also highlights means by which individuals exercise personal agency in their career development.

Finally, SCCT is also linked with, or has been informed by, other cognitively oriented models of career and academic behavior (Barak, 1981; Eccles, 1987; Schunk, 1989); certain theories of work motivation (Locke & Latham, 1990; Vroom, 1964); theory and research on women's and racial-ethnic minority members' career development (Hackett & Lent, 1992); developmental-contextualist views on career behavior (Vondracek, Lerner, & Schulenberg, 1986); and findings from behavior genetics, personality, and social psychology (Ajzen, 1988; Moloney, Bouchard, & Segal, 1991; Watson & Clark, 1984). In order to produce a cohesive framework, we tried to embed these diverse influences within the fabric of general social cognitive theory.

In the following sections, we present an overview of the basic theory, its empirical base, its range of generalizability, and the implications for counseling. Given space limitations, we refer interested readers to other sources for a fuller, more technical elaboration of the theory and its research base (Lent, Brown, & Hackett, 1994, 2000; Swanson & Gore, 2000), as well as discussions of the theory's conceptual underpinnings, relations to established career theories (Lent & Hackett, 1994), and practical applications (Lent & Brown, 1996).

Central Theoretical Concepts and Assumptions

Before we present SCCT's models of interest development, choice, and performance, it is useful to consider some of the theory's underlying assumptions and constructs that extend from social cognitive theory.

Person-Environment Interaction

Each of the major theories of career choice and development acknowledge that vocational outcomes are determined by the transactions occurring between persons and their environments (Osipow, 1990). However, their views on the nature of the person-environment (P-E) interaction differ from those of SCCT in some important ways. First, the foundational career theories tend to view person and environment variables in trait-oriented (Dawis, 1996; Super, Savickas, & Super, 1996) or typological (Holland, 1997) terms, whereas SCCT highlights relatively dynamic and situation-specific features of the self system. Because traits and types involve relatively global, constant, and enduring attributes, theories that rely exclusively on such attributes may not adequately reflect the fluid nature of P-E transactions and, consequently, may underestimate people's capacity to change, develop, and self-regulate. It is noteworthy that proponents of the traditional career theories have made important efforts to reconceptualize them in more dynamic P-E terms (see, for example, Chartrand, 1991; Rounds & Tracey, 1990) and to identify certain variables through which persons may exercise agency (for example, Goodman, 1994; Krumboltz & Nichols, 1990).

A second area of difference involves the way in which SCCT conceptualizes causal influences. Trait- and typology-based theories tend to take what may be described as *partially bidirectional* positions on causality, that is, they conceive of persons and environments as influencing one another, but they view behavior largely as an outcome of the person-environment transaction (B = f [P E]). By contrast, Bandura's position elevates the role of behavior to that of a co-determinant of the causal exchange, arguing that it is primarily through their overt actions that people "influence the situations that, in turn, affect their thoughts, affect, and [subsequent] behavior" (Bandura, 1982, p. 4).

To recognize the mutual, interacting influences among persons, their environments, and behavior, SCCT subscribes to Bandura's *triadic-reciprocal*, or fully bidirectional, model of causality (Bandura, 1986). In this scheme, the following operate as interlocking mechanisms that affect one another bidirectionally:

- *Personal attributes*, such as internal cognitive and affective states, and physical characteristics
- *External environmental factors*
- *Overt behavior* (as distinct from internal and physical qualities of the person)

Within this triadic system, people become both "products and producers of their environment" (Wood & Bandura, 1989, p. 362), with the potential for self-regulation.

Key Theoretical Constructs

In conceptualizing the *personal* determinants of career development within the triadic causal system, SCCT incorporates three central variables from general social cognitive theory: (1) self-efficacy,

(2) outcome expectations, and (3) personal goals. These three variables are seen as basic "building blocks" of career development and represent key mechanisms by which people are able to exercise personal agency. Of the three, self-efficacy has received the most attention in the career literature (Hackett & Lent, 1992; Lent et al., 1994; Locke & Latham, 1990; Swanson & Gore, 2000). *Self-efficacy* refers to people's beliefs about their capabilities "to organize and execute courses of action required to attain designated types of performances" (Bandura, 1986, p. 391).

In the SCCT view, self-efficacy is *not* a unitary, fixed, or decontextualized trait; instead, it involves a dynamic set of self-beliefs that are specific to particular performance domains and that interact in a complex way with other person, behavior, and environmental factors. Self-efficacy beliefs are acquired and modified via four primary sources of information (or types of learning experience): (1) personal performance accomplishments, (2) vicarious learning, (3) social persuasion, and (4) physiological and affective states (Bandura, 1997). Although the specific effects of these sources on self-efficacy depend on several factors, personal attainments are typically seen as the most potent or compelling source of self-efficacy. The experience of success with a given task or performance domain tends to raise self-efficacy, whereas repeated failures lower them.

Outcome expectations are personal beliefs about the consequences or outcomes of performing particular behaviors. Whereas self-efficacy beliefs are concerned with one's capabilities (Can I do this?), outcome expectations involve the imagined consequences of performing given behaviors (If I do this, what will happen?). Outcome expectations include several types of beliefs about response outcomes, such as beliefs about extrinsic reinforcement (receiving tangible rewards for successful performance), self-directed consequences (such as pride in oneself for mastering a challenging task), and outcomes derived from the process of performing a given activity (for instance, absorption in the task itself). A number of theories, both in the vocational realm (Barak, 1981; Vroom, 1964) and in other areas of psychology (for instance,

Ajzen, 1988), accord outcome expectations play a key role in motivating behavior.

Outcome expectations are acquired through learning experiences similar to those that inform self-efficacy. For instance, outcome expectations regarding particular career actions derive from people's appraisal of the outcomes (such as rewards) they received for performing relevant actions in the past; observation of the outcomes produced by other people; attention to self-generated outcomes (such as self-approval) and the reactions of others; and sensitivity to physical cues (such as level of emotional arousal or sense of well-being) during task performance. Outcome expectations are probably also influenced by self-efficacy when outcomes are determined by the quality of one's performance.

Goals may be defined as the determination to engage in a particular activity or to effect a particular future outcome (Bandura, 1986). By setting personal goals, people help to organize, guide, and sustain their own behavior, even through overly long intervals, without external reinforcement. Thus goals constitute a critical mechanism through which people exercise personal agency or self-empowerment. Although environmental events and personal history undoubtedly help shape behavior, behavior is not wholly determined by the vicissitudes of a nonspecific reinforcement history, by genes, or by other nonvolitional factors; it is also motivated, in part, by people's self-directed goals and by the other social cognitive factors with which goals interrelate.

SCCT posits a complex interplay among goals, self-efficacy, and outcome expectations in the self-regulation of behavior (Bandura, 1986). For instance, self-efficacy and outcome expectations affect the goals that one selects and the effort expended in their pursuit. Personal goals, in turn, influence the development of self-efficacy and outcome expectations (for example, goal attainment enhances self-efficacy). As with outcome expectations, goals (defined in various ways) are represented in a variety of other psychological theories, such as the theory of work motivation and performance that Locke and Latham (1990) proposed. The goal construct also plays an important, if generally implicit, role in virtually all theories of career choice and decision making (Lent et al., 1994).

SCCT's Models of Vocational Interests, Choice, and Performance

The SCCT framework organizes career-related interest, choice, and performance into three interlocking models. We present an overview of these models, focusing on the interplay among the central social cognitive variables in guiding career development. We also consider how these variables operate in concert with other important aspects of persons (such as gender and ethnicity), their contexts, and learning experiences.

Before introducing our models, we should highlight a few points. First, although we generally refer to "career development processes," we envision SCCT as subsuming conceptually and developmentally related processes of *academic* interests, choices, and performances. Given the natural overlap between academic and career development processes (Arbona, 2000), as well as concerns over the school-to-work transition of students (Blustein, Juntunen, & Worthington, 2000), we believe it is useful to build stronger bridges between models of academic and career development. Second, in keeping with SCCT's triadic-reciprocal view of person-behavior-situation interaction, we should note that most of the major elements in SCCT are seen as influencing one another bidirectionally over time. (For instance, as we discuss next, self-efficacy promotes interest; in cyclical fashion, interest promotes opportunities for self-efficacy development.) However, our analysis emphasizes directional paths that we posit as having a predominant influence on academic-career interests, choices, and performances.

Interest Development Model

Vocational interests (people's pattern of likes, dislikes, and indifferences regarding various occupations and career-relevant activities) are a standard fixture in career psychology. In particular, interests are assumed to be important determinants of career choice (Betsworth & Fouad, 1997; Hansen, 1984). SCCT's interest model emphasizes both the experiential and cognitive factors that give rise to career-related interests, while tracing the role of interests in helping to motivate choice behavior and skill acquisition.

As children and adolescents, our interpersonal environments expose us to a wide array of activities such as crafts, music, sports, mathematics, and mechanical tasks that have potential relevance to occupational behavior. In addition to direct or vicarious exposure to diverse activities, we are differentially reinforced for pursuing certain activities and for achieving particular levels of performance. It is largely through repeated activity practice, modeling, and feedback from important others that children and adolescents are able, gradually, to develop their skills, adopt personal performance standards, form a sense of their capability at diverse tasks (self-efficacy), and beliefs about what will happen if they perform these tasks (outcome expectations).

Our interest model, depicted in Figure 7.1, holds that self-efficacy and outcome expectations regarding activity involvement exert an important, direct effect on the formation of career interests. Specifically, SCCT asserts that people form enduring interest in an activity when they view themselves as competent at it and when they anticipate that performing it will produce valued outcomes (Bandura, 1986; Lent, Larkin, & Brown, 1989). Conversely, people are likely to fail to develop interests in (or may form aversions to) activities in which their self-efficacy is weak or when they anticipate receiving neutral or negative outcomes.

As Figure 7.1 also shows, emergent interests (along with self-efficacy and outcome expectations) promote particular goals for activity involvement. In other words, as people develop an affinity for an activity at which they feel efficacious and expect positive outcomes, they form goals for sustaining or increasing their involvement in that activity. These goals, in turn, increase the likelihood of engaging in the activity. The attainments accruing from activity performance (such as trophies, grades, or self-satisfaction) then

FIGURE 7.1. Model of How Basic Career Interests Develop Over Time

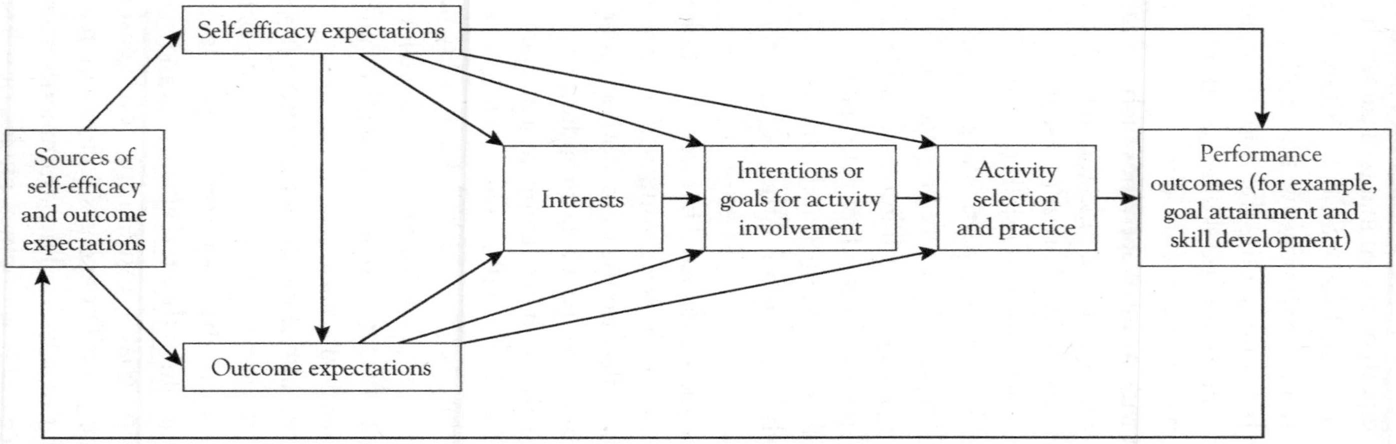

Copyright © 1993 by R. W. Lent, S. D. Brown, and G. Hackett. Reprinted by permission.

form an important feedback loop, helping to solidify or reshape self-efficacy and outcome expectations and, in turn, interests.

SCCT assumes that this basic process is constantly in motion throughout the lifespan and that through this process people come to develop characteristic patterns of career interests. Although occupational interests tend to stabilize by late adolescence or early adulthood (Hansen, 1984), change and growth in interests is theoretically possible at any point in life, particularly when people are presented with environmental conditions or life challenges (such as job restructuring, childbirth, or technical innovations) offering exposure to new activities or encouraging the cultivation of new skills. Of course, occasions for growth in interests may also be self-directed, such as volunteering for new job assignments. Whether new interests emerge depends less on simple exposure and past reinforcement experiences than on how people read their competence (self-efficacy) at the activity and on their prospective expectations about obtaining prized versus nonvalued outcomes.

Aptitudes and Values. Some career theories view interests as an outgrowth of either personal aptitudes and abilities or work values. SCCT acknowledges that abilities and values *are* important parts of the process that gives rise to vocational interests; however, in our scheme, their effects on interests are primarily funneled through self-efficacy and outcome expectations. For instance, we posit that, rather than influence interests directly, abilities inform self-efficacy beliefs, which, in turn, influence outcome expectations and interest. Work values are incorporated within the concept of outcome expectations. Specifically, the latter may be conceptualized as people's preferences for particular work conditions or reinforcers (such as status, money, or autonomy), which is how work values are often defined, together with personal beliefs about the extent to which particular occupations offer these conditions (reinforcers).

Other Person and Contextual Influences. Social cognitive variables do not arise in a vacuum, nor do they function alone in shaping interest or other vocational outcomes. SCCT is concerned with a number of other important person and contextual variables (gender, race-ethnicity, physical health or disability, genetic endowment, and socioeconomic conditions) that are assumed to be intricately related to the social cognitive variables and to the career development process. Figure 7.2 provides an overview of how selected person, contextual, and learning-experiential variables are hypothesized to influence both the social cognitive variables and subsequent career development outcomes. We focus briefly on the complex issues of gender, race-ethnicity, and genetic influences.

Progress in understanding the role of gender, race-ethnicity, and sociostructural factors in career development has been slow (Fitzgerald & Betz, 1994). Historically, the major career development theories tended to deal with such factors in fairly general, descriptive terms, and earlier inquiry on gender and race focused more on documenting group differences on career-related outcomes than on clarifying the specific processes through which gender and race affect career development (Hackett & Lent, 1992). SCCT regards gender and race from a social constructivist position in which these attributes are interwoven features of the person's socially constructed world, not simply inherited biological properties of the person. We believe their relevance to career development stems largely from the reactions they evoke from the social-cultural environment and from their relation to the structure of opportunity within which career behavior transpires.

Instead of focusing only on the study of sex (a biological variable), psychologists are, increasingly, studying gender—a socially constructed concept that includes the psychological, social, and cultural implications of sex (Fassinger, 2000). Similar arguments may be made about conceptualizing ethnicity as the psychological-sociocultural experience of race (Casas, 1984). Viewing gender and ethnicity as socially constructed aspects of people's experience shifts the focus to the social, cultural, and economic conditions that shape the learning opportunities to which particular individuals are exposed, the interpersonal reactions (such as support or

FIGURE 7.2. Model of Person, Contextual, and Experiential Factors Affecting Career-Related Choice Behavior

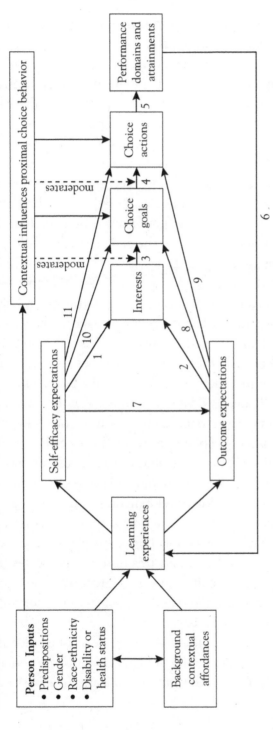

Note: Direct relations between variables are indicated with solid lines; moderator effects (where a given variable strengthens or weakens the relations between two other variables) are shown with dashed lines.

Source: Copyright © 1993 by R. W. Lent, S. D. Brown, and G. Hackett. Reprinted by permission.

indifference) they receive for performing certain activities, and the outcomes they come to anticipate.

The process of gender-role socialization provides a useful example of how gender, context, and cognitions jointly contribute to shaping children's educational and career possibilities. Based on culturally shared expectations about gender-appropriate behavior, parents and teachers tend to treat boys and girls differently in terms of the activities they are encouraged to perform, how well they are expected to do, and the reactions accorded their performance attainments (Arbona, 2000; Eccles, 1994). Thus the beliefs and behaviors of social agents and important others, including peers, have important implications for the acquisition of children's self-efficacy and outcome expectations, as well as for the development of their talents (Bandura, 1997; Lent & Lopez, in press).

For instance, due to biased access to opportunities for observing and practicing particular behaviors, girls are more likely to develop self-efficacy for female-typed activities such as artwork or domestic tasks and to feel less efficacious at activities that are culturally defined as masculine, such as science or athletics (Hackett & Betz, 1981). Externally imposed barriers also become internalized; at an early age, children learn to match their behavior to conceptions of gender appropriateness (Bandura, 1986; Bussey & Bandura, 1999; Gottfredson, 1996). Thus impediments to later career options may stem both from contextually engineered processes, such as differential opportunities for skill development, and from the self-beliefs, performance standards, and outcome expectations that people internalize. Though our example highlights gender-context interactions, we believe that similar psychosocial processes (such as educational access and cultural norms) affect the development of career-related self-efficacy and outcome expectations in children of particular racial-ethnic groups.

In sum, as Figure 7.2 illustrates, the effects of gender and ethnicity on career interest, choice, and performance are conceived as operating largely through the differential learning experiences that shape self-efficacy and outcome expectations. At the same time, as is also depicted in Figure 7.2, gender and cultural factors are intimately linked to the opportunity structure or environmental context within which career goals are framed and implemented. We will consider this important opportunity structure linkage within the context of SCCT's model of career choice behavior in the next section.

Recent research in the area of behavior genetics points to the likely influence of heredity on certain career-related variables such as vocational interests (see Swanson & Gore, 2000). Our framework acknowledges that basic abilities (such as spatial visualization or perceptual speed), affective dispositions, and personality dimensions (such as extraversion) have genetic linkages. However, SCCT also emphasizes the interaction of aptitudes and other heritable factors with environmental and self-directed processes in ways that help to cultivate or limit career options. Figure 7.2 traces the hypothetical path between heritable factors such as primary abilities (included under "person inputs") and career interest and other outcomes. As in its analysis of gender and ethnicity effects, SCCT's conception of inherited qualities draws special attention to the interplay between learning opportunities and person factors.

It is doubtful that either mathematicians or professional basketball players would be able to attain their occupational status based on genetic endowment alone. Environments provide essential ingredients such as supports, barriers, and special resources (for example, books and basketballs) that modulate the expression of inherited qualities. Basic social cognitive and behavior genetic processes (for instance, goal setting, activity practice, selective exposure, and reinforcement) help to transform native aptitudes. Thus, instead of having a preordained, fully determined impact on the careers people might have in the future, the effect of heritable aptitude on career interest and behavior is seen as operating largely through intervening *learning experiences* that both refine abilities and shape self-efficacy and outcome expectations.

Summary. According to SCCT's interest model, interests are a joint function of self-efficacy beliefs and outcome expectations; people express interest in certain career and academic pursuits if they think they can perform well in them and if, at the same time, they think that pursuing these careers will lead to outcomes they desire. Aptitudes and past experiences are related to interests primarily through their impact on persons' developing self-efficacy beliefs and outcome expectations. In other words, having positive experiences in career-related activities and the aptitude to do well in specific careers makes it more likely that people will develop robust efficacy expectations and positive outcomes for these career pursuits. In addition, the model implies that people are unlikely to develop interests in career and academic pursuits for which they are otherwise well-suited if they are not exposed to compelling learning opportunities that promote ability-congruent efficacy beliefs and positive outcome expectations. Thus, for example, women, members of racial-ethnic minority groups, and persons living in poverty may fail to develop interests in particular career options because they may not have been exposed to opportunities and experiences that would lead them to feel efficacious about their abilities to pursue these careers or optimistic about the outcomes they might receive.

Choice Model

SCCT's conception of the career choice process, embedded in Figure 7.2, highlights the diverse person, contextual, and learning influences on choice behavior. It should be noted that Figure 7.2 incorporates the basic interest development model shown earlier, though the goal and action variables now specifically represent career-related goals and the actions required to implement them. The relationship of these two models reflects the developmental continuity between the evolution of basic vocational interests and their eventual translation into career-relevant choices.

Conceptually, the choice process can be divided into three parts:

1. The expression of a primary choice (or goal)

2. Actions, such as enrolling in a particular training program that is designed to implement one's choice

3. Subsequent performance attainments (successes, failures) that form a feedback loop, affecting the shape of future career behavior

The conceptual partition between goals and actions draws on similar distinctions made by earlier models of career decision making (Mitchell & Krumboltz, 1996; Tiedeman & O'Hara, 1963). We believe this partition is important because it highlights the intermediate role of personal agency (via goals) in the choice-making process; emphasizes that choices are dynamic rather than static acts; and illuminates certain variables and decision points at which intervention might profitably be directed.

As hypothesized earlier within the interest development model, self-efficacy and outcome expectations jointly promote particular career-related interests (paths 1 and 2). Interests, in turn, serve as an important influence on goals (intentions or plans to pursue a particular career path; see path 3), and goals stimulate actions designed to implement one's goals (path 4). One's goal-related actions (for instance, enrolling in a calculus class) lead to particular performance experiences (path 5), the outcomes of which (such as receiving a failing grade) help to revise or crystallize self-efficacy and outcome expectations (path 6) and, thereby, help solidify or redirect one's choice behavior.

It should be noted that our choice model shares certain features with prior career choice models. For example, as in Holland's theory (Holland, 1997), SCCT assumes that under optimal conditions people tend to select career options that are congruent with their interests. The notion that persons with, say, artistic interests will tend to gravitate toward artistic work environments is sometimes colloquially referred to as the "birds of a feather hypothesis."

Although sharing this general assumption, SCCT is distinct from, yet complements, Holland's theory in a number of respects. For example, SCCT highlights personal goals as forming an important intermediate link between interests and actions; it also identifies self-efficacy and outcome expectations as shapers of interest patterns and as co-determinants of choice.

This last point deserves clarification. For many persons, career choices are not made under "optimal conditions." Economic need, educational limitations, lack of familial support, or various other considerations may inhibit the pursuit of one's primary interests or preferred career goals (Vroom, 1964; Williamson, 1939). Figure 7.2 shows that career choice goals and actions may be influenced directly by self-efficacy and outcome expectations (see paths 8–11). These supplementary paths help explain the many real-world instances in which people need to compromise their interests in selecting a vocational path. In such instances, goals and actions may be influenced less by interests than by job availability in concert with self-efficacy and outcome expectations (that is, beliefs about whether one can perform the available work and whether the incentives are sufficient).

Contextual Influences.   As implied by the foregoing analysis, there are limits to people's free agency in making career choices. Thus career development theorists need to reckon with both external and internal factors that affect choice behavior. In conceptualizing contextual or environmental influences, we drew on the work of Vondracek, Lerner, and Schulenberg (1986) and Astin (1984). The former called attention to the physical, cultural, material, and social features of the environment and highlighted the concept of "contextual affordances," referring to the resources one perceives as being provided by one's environment. This concept is similar to Astin's notion of the perceived "structure of opportunity." Both concepts' attention to personal *perceptions* of the environment is consistent with the importance that SCCT places on cognitive appraisal processes in guiding behavior. Such a view does not minimize the substantial impact of objective features of the environ-ment, but it does highlight the person's active role in appraising and making meaning out of what the environment provides.

Astin (1984), Mitchell and Krumboltz (1996), and others have identified a number of opportunity structure factors affecting career behavior. For conceptual convenience, we have divided such fac-tors into two subgroups, based on their relative proximity to career choice points:

1. More distal (background) contextual influences (for example, opportunities for skill development, cultural and gender-role socialization processes, range of potential academic-career role models) that help shape social cognitions and interests

2. Proximal influences (for example, emotional and financial support for selecting a particular option, job availability in one's preferred field, sociostructural barriers) that come into play at critical choice junctures

Figure 7.2 outlines the hypothesized connections of each set of contextual factors to various career development outcomes.

Earlier we discussed the more distal role of contextual variables in shaping the acquisition of self-efficacy and outcome expecta-tions. We highlight here two major ways in which contextual fac-tors are assumed to affect the career choice process per se. First, we posit that features of the opportunity structure moderate the rela-tions of interests to goals and goals to choice-related actions (that is, efforts to implement goals). In other words, opportunity structure variables affect people's ability or willingness to transform their career interests into goals and their goals into actions. (These effects are shown by the dotted paths in Figure 7.2.) Persons who experience beneficial environmental conditions (presence of ample support, few barriers) are expected to negotiate these processes more readily than those who experience nonsupportive conditions or obstacles relative to their preferred course of action. Second, cer-tain environmental conditions can exert direct, potent effects on choice formation and implementation (for instance, discrimination in hiring, "glass ceiling" obstacles, or cultural practices wherein career decisions are deferred to one's parents or elders). These direct influences are represented by the solid-line paths from contextual variables to goals and actions in Figure 7.2.

As we will discuss later, the contextual aspects of SCCT's choice model highlight the value of interventions aimed at assisting career clients to negotiate barriers to, and marshal support for, their career choices. Research suggests that familial and other social influences can have an important bearing on career choice (Ferry, Fouad, & Smith, 2000; Lent et al., in press; Tang, Fouad, & Smith, 1999), and that career decision makers perceive barriers and supports to their career aspirations and performances (McWhirter, Torres, & Rasheed, 1998; Richie, Fassinger, Prosser, & Robinson, 1997). Proactive barrier-coping and support-building interventions may, therefore, be particularly helpful for those persons who are most likely to encounter oppressive conditions in educational or work environments (Chartrand & Rose, 1996; Hackett & Byars, 1996).

Summary. SCCT's model of career choice holds that interests are typically related to the choices that people make and to the actions they take to implement their choices. In other words, all else being equal people will choose (develop choice goals for) occupations in which they are interested. The model also states, however, that choices are affected as well by contextual influences and by other person variables. For example, people will be more likely to have to compromise their interests in making career choices if they perceive that their environment is not supportive of their choice or if they perceive significant barriers to entering and prospering in careers that most interest them. When people perceive a need to compromise their interests because of limited opportunities, insurmountable barriers, or a nonsupportive environment, their choices will be made primarily on the basis of job availability, self-efficacy beliefs, and outcome expectations. In other words, when people cannot implement their interests, they will choose less interesting occupational paths that are available to them, that provide adequate outcomes, and in which they feel they can perform adequately.

Performance Model

SCCT's model of performance is concerned with the level (or quality) of people's accomplishments, as well as with the persistence of their behavior in career-related pursuits. As shown in Figure 7.3, our analysis emphasizes the interplay among ability, self-efficacy, outcome expectations, and goals in determining performance outcomes. Ability (as assessed by achievement, aptitude, or past performance indicators) is seen as affecting performance, directly and indirectly, through its impact on self-efficacy and outcome expectations. Self-efficacy and outcome expectations, in turn, affect the level of performance goals that people set for themselves. Stronger self-efficacy beliefs and more favorable outcome expectations promote more ambitious goals, which help people mobilize and sustain their performance behavior.

Consistent with SCCT's triadic-reciprocal view of interaction, Figure 7.3 depicts a feedback loop between performance attainments

FIGURE 7.3. Model of Task Performance

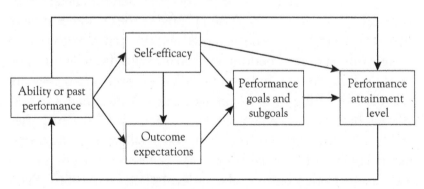

Source: Copyright © 1993 by R. W. Lent, S. D. Brown, and G. Hackett. Reprinted by permission.

and subsequent behavior. Success experiences promote develop-ment of abilities and, in turn, self-efficacy and outcome expecta-tions within a dynamic cycle. As we noted earlier, the refinement of abilities, self-efficacy, outcome expectations, and goals is critically affected by contextual variables (such as teaching quality, socio-economic status, and gender role socialization) that shape the learning experiences and performance conditions to which indi-viduals are exposed.

Role of Self-Efficacy. It is important to emphasize that self-efficacy is seen as a co-determinant of performance, not as a substitute for objectively assessed abilities. What people can accomplish depends, in part, on how they interpret and apply their abilities (Bandura, 1986). Self-efficacy beliefs affect how effectively people deploy their talents, helping to explain why individuals with the same basic capabilities can produce performances of vastly differing quality. Particularly in challenging situations, competent performance requires both basic capabilities and a strong sense of personal effi-cacy. Research confirms that self-efficacy and ability are moderately correlated yet distinct constructs and that they both help to explain performance attainments (Lent et al., 1994).

A practical implication of this model is that people are likely to encounter problems when they either do not possess sufficient abil-ity to succeed at a given course of action or when they greatly mis-construe their self-efficacy. When people seriously underestimate their efficacy (relative to documented ability), they tend to give up more easily, set lower performance goals, suffer from debilitating performance anxiety, and avoid challenges, even when they are capable of meeting those challenges. Large overestimates of self-efficacy, however, embolden people to attempt tasks for which they are ill prepared, increasing the likelihood of failure and discourage-ment. The most beneficial self-efficacy beliefs are those that mod-estly exceed one's current ability level (Bandura, 1986). Such optimistic self-percepts enable people to take on reasonable chal-lenges that promote further skill development.

Finally, we should comment on the nature of goals within SCCT's performance model. Whereas our interest and choice models involved *choice-content goals* (for instance, the type of career field one intends to pursue), the performance model emphasizes *performance goals*, referring to the level of attainment toward which one aspires within a given performance domain. The two goal variants are intimately related yet unique. Choice-content goals orient people toward a particular activity domain (such as an engineering major), whereas the quality of their subsequent attainments depends, in part, on their performance goals (for instance, the grades they strive toward in particular courses). A number of properties of goals help determine their impact on behavior. For instance, goals that are specific, set close in time to actual behavior, and broken into subgoals tend to be more influential than goals that are vague, distal, or global (Bandura, 1986; Locke & Latham, 1990).

Summary. SCCT views occupational and academic performance (and persistence) as being affected in important ways by ability, self-efficacy, outcome expectations, and performance goals. Self-efficacy plays an especially important role in determining how people employ their abilities. Thus people may be at risk for occupational or academic failure or other difficulties when their abilities fail to correspond with the abilities required in an occupation or course of study or when their self-efficacy beliefs substantially underestimate or exaggerate their current performance capabilities. The implications for working with persons with substandard abilities or inaccurate efficacy beliefs are discussed more fully in a subsequent section of this chapter, as are developmentally oriented strategies for promoting accurate and robust efficacy beliefs.

Empirical Support for the Theory

Research on, or relevant to, SCCT has expanded at an impressive rate in recent years. Self-efficacy has been the single most popular topic of inquiry; many studies examine the relation of self-efficacy to such theory-relevant outcomes as vocational interests, academic major choices, and achievement indicators. Other studies have examined gender differences in career-related self-efficacy, the experiential sources of self-efficacy beliefs, experimental and causal modeling tests of hypotheses concerning self-efficacy, self-efficacy in relation to the dilemmas of women managing multiple career-life roles, and development of novel approaches to assessing self-efficacy. More recent studies have been exploring additional SCCT variables, including outcome expectations, goals, and contextual barriers and supports. Of special note, several theory-derived interventions have also been designed and tested.

A full-scale review of SCCT-relevant research is beyond the scope of this chapter. However, we can highlight the findings of existing qualitative reviews and meta-analyses of this literature. Traditional qualitative reviews of research on career self-efficacy (Bandura, 1997; Betz & Hackett, 1986; Hackett, 1995; Hackett & Lent, 1992; Lent & Hackett, 1987; Swanson & Gore, 2000) support the following broad conclusions:

- Domain-specific measures of self-efficacy are predictive of career-related interests, choice, achievement, persistence, indecision, and career exploratory behavior.

- Intervention, experimental, and path analyses support certain hypothesized causal relations between measures of self-efficacy, performance, and interests.

- Gender differences in academic and career self-efficacy help to explain male-female differences in occupational consideration. (We will examine the latter point in more depth in the next section.)

Several meta-analytic investigations have also examined findings relevant to SCCT's major hypotheses (Lent et al., 1994; Multon, Brown, & Lent, 1991; Sadri & Robertson, 1993; Stajkovic & Luthans, 1998). Meta-analysis is a quantitative review method that combines data from a number of independent studies that have addressed the same hypothesis or set of hypotheses. Meta-analysis enables reviewers to calculate a single index of the strength of hypothesized relations across all studies and to test statistically the extent to which studies collectively support or disconfirm theoretical hypotheses. We present an overview of the meta-analytic findings that have directly tested some of the relationships posited by SCCT.

In integrating findings relevant to SCCT's model of interests, Lent and colleagues (1994) observe that both self-efficacy and outcome expectations correlate substantially with occupational interests. The researchers also find support for the hypothesis that the effect of prior ability (or performance) on career-related interests operates indirectly through self-efficacy beliefs. In other words, findings suggest that ability may influence self-efficacy, which, in turn, affects interests (see Figure 7.1). In testing SCCT's choice model, findings have revealed that interests, self-efficacy, and outcome expectations all relate to measures of choice-content goals. The effects of self-efficacy and outcome expectations on choice appear to be largely channeled through interests, though the social cognitive factors also appear to have a small, direct influence on choice (Lent et al., 1994; see Figure 7.2).

SCCT's performance model predictions have been tested in both educational and occupational settings. Multon and colleagues (1991) combine data from studies assessing the relations of self-efficacy beliefs to measures of academic performance, whereas Sadri and Robertson (1993) and Stajkovic and Luthans (1998) include data on both academic and occupational performance. Each of these reviews shows remarkably consistent correlations between self-efficacy and performance; several factors have been shown to affect the strength of this relationship. For example, stronger self-efficacy–performance relations were found in older versus younger students and in low-achieving versus adequately achieving samples (Multon et al., 1991). In addition, as suggested by theory, ability has been found to affect performance both directly and indirectly through its influence on self-efficacy beliefs (Lent et al., 1994; see Figure 7.3).

Finally, Lent and colleagues (1994) explored findings on the hypothesized experiential sources of the social cognitive variables. Personal performance accomplishments, vicarious learning, social persuasion, and physiological arousal were all found to relate significantly to self-efficacy, with the largest relations occurring between performance experience and self-efficacy. Findings have also supported the hypothesized relations between self-efficacy and outcome expectations.

Taken together, the meta-analyses suggest support for SCCT's assumptions that

- Interests are strongly related to one's self-efficacy and outcome expectations.

- Performance accomplishments in a specific endeavor lead to interests in that endeavor to the extent that they foster a growing sense of self-efficacy.

- Self-efficacy and outcome expectations affect career-related choices largely (though not completely) through their influence on interest.

- Past performance affects future performance partly through people's abilities and partly through the self-efficacy percepts they develop, which presumably help them organize their skills and persist despite setbacks.

Generalizability of SCCT

SCCT was designed to aid understanding of the career development of a wide range of students and workers, including persons who are diverse with respect to race-ethnicity, culture, gender, socioeconomic status, age, and disability status. Many of the research and practical applications of the theory have thus far reflected this focus on diversity and individual difference. In this section, we review some of these applications and consider the theory's potential to aid understanding of career development within a changing societal context.

Diversity

In the earliest effort to extend social cognitive theory to career behavior, Hackett and Betz (1981) demonstrated how the construct of self-efficacy might be applied to women's career development. They noted, for example, how gender-role socialization processes tend to provide girls and young women with biased access to the four sources of efficacy information (for example, gender-traditional role models, differential encouragement to pursue culturally prescribed activities), which, in turn, promotes self-efficacy for traditionally female activities but limits self-efficacy in nontraditional domains. Subsequent research has tended to support Hackett and Betz's theoretical analysis. For instance, women tend to report more self-efficacy for performing occupations that are traditionally held by women than for those that are male-dominated (Betz & Hackett, 1981). Such findings suggest that women's career pursuits can be constricted by the self-limiting effects of low self-efficacy. In other words, environment-imposed barriers may become internalized in the form of biased self-efficacy beliefs.

Related research has shown that self-efficacy beliefs mediate gender differences in scientific-technical field interests (for example, Lapan, Boggs, & Morrill, 1989). Studies using general samples of students typically find male-female differences in self-efficacy regarding gender-typed tasks and fields (for example, mathematics), though such differences are less likely to be found in samples of women and men who have had comparable efficacy-building experiences. Occupational sex stereotyping with respect to self-efficacy has also been found to be less pronounced in younger cohorts (see Bandura, 1997; Hackett & Lent, 1992).

The work discussed here highlights several social cognitive mechanisms through which potential career paths can be stymied in women. Apart from the role of self-efficacy beliefs in promoting gender differences in occupational pursuits, "cultural constraints, inequitable incentive systems, and truncated opportunity structures are also influential in shaping women's career development"

(Bandura, 1997, p. 436). Thus larger systemic issues, not just self processes, require attention in the effort to foster women's career options. Although this analysis identifies some daunting obstacles, on a more hopeful note it also implies several developmental routes for redressing or preventing socially imposed limitations on women's career development (for example, via efforts to build self-efficacy and promote support systems relative to non-gender-stereotypical performance domains).

Hackett and Byars (1996) provide a social cognitive analysis of the career development of persons of color, in particular, African American women. They note how culturally based learning experiences corresponding to the sources of efficacy information (for example, social encouragement to pursue certain options, exposure to racism, role modeling) may differentially influence African American women's sense of career self-efficacy, outcome expectations, goals, and subsequent career progress. Hackett and Byars suggest a variety of theory-based methods, including developmental interventions, social advocacy, and collective action, for promoting the career growth of African American women. Related research has found support for applications of SCCT's basic interest and choice models to Hispanic, black, and Asian American student samples (for example, Fouad & Smith, 1996; Gainor & Lent, 1998; Tang, Fouad, & Smith, 1999).

Other applications of SCCT to diverse client populations are also noteworthy. Chartrand and Rose (1996) adapted the theory to a career intervention for adult female prison inmates. Szymanski and Hershenson (1998) considered SCCT's relevance for persons with disabilities, noting that self-efficacy and outcome expectations are particularly useful constructs within a vocational rehabilitation context. Fabian (2000) considered how SCCT could be used to derive career interventions specifically for adults with mental illness. Morrow, Gore, and Campbell (1996) used SCCT as a framework for understanding the career development of lesbian women and gay men, noting how social-contextual influences can affect self-efficacy, outcome expectations, and the process through which interests are translated into choice. SCCT has also been extended to a number of cross-cultural or cross-national applications (for example, de Bruin, 1999; Kantas, 1997; Nota & Soresi, 2000; Van Vianen, 1999). Finally, research on school children (Schunk, 1995; Zimmerman, 1995) and adult workers and managers (Bandura, 1997; Wood & Bandura, 1989) suggests that the SCCT framework is applicable to academic and career development phenomena across the lifespan.

Societal and Economic Shifts

A number of recent or anticipated societal, demographic, and economic mega-trends have the potential to materially affect or reshape the career development climate over the next several decades (Hesketh, 2000; Lent, in press). A few such trends include the increasing representation of workers of color, advances in technology, and corporate contractions wrought by global economic presses. Some economic and technological trends portend far less job security for many workers. Although some writers may see such flux as likely to render existing theories of career development obsolete or irrelevant, we believe that SCCT's emphasis on personal agency, learning experiences, and contextual factors can provide a useful template for career development across generations and despite economic shifts. (Of course, SCCT's temporal validity is ultimately an empirical question that can best be addressed by cross-sectional or longitudinal study.)

We concur with those who argue that the new economy will challenge workers to manage their own careers strategically, with a premium placed on skill updating, goal setting, and networking (Hesketh, 2000; Watts, 1996). Rather than being hapless bystanders to external forces, SCCT views people as capable of self-reflection, self-regulation, and forethought. These capabilities, which can be nurtured by career education and work transition programs, enable people to cultivate new interests and skills, revise plans, anticipate obstacles, and assemble necessary supports. At the same time that workers will need to view their careers as dynamic processes requiring active management, employers will need to be concerned with maintaining a sufficient cadre of workers who can adapt flexibly to changing organizational demands. These presses may, ironically, offer increased rather than lessened opportunities for career development, particularly to the extent that (1) workers take an agentic approach to their career progress and (2) employers and policymakers see the value of promoting workers' career growth and periodic retooling.

In sum, we believe the applications described in this section convey SCCT's potential utility in studying and facilitating the career development of a diverse range of persons and in changing economic times. Although such applications are exciting in their promise, there is also a need for far more research that clarifies how various social cognitive variables (for example, contextual supports and barriers and self-efficacy at managing the multiple demands of career and family roles), interface with culture, ethnicity, socioeconomic status, sexual orientation, and disability or health status to shape the career development trajectories of new cohorts of students and workers. Despite the clear need for additional research, currently available findings may offer valuable implications for career counseling practice—a topic to which we next turn.

SCCT-Derived Interventions

We believe that SCCT holds a number of implications for developmental, preventive, and remedial interventions, that is, for optimizing the development of students' academic and career interests and competencies, for preventing career-related difficulties prior to work entry, and for counseling individuals who manifest problems with career choice or adjustment. Ideas for developmental and preventive applications may be readily derived from hypotheses about how the social cognitive variables such as self-efficacy develop and from SCCT's basic interest, choice, and performance models. In terms of remedial counseling, the theory may be used either to provide an organizing structure for existing career interventions or to develop novel intervention techniques. In this section, we review some of SCCT's basic implications for developmental and remedial interventions (see Lent & Brown, 1996).

Expanding Interests and Facilitating Choice

As implied by SCCT's interest and choice models, self-efficacy beliefs and outcome expectations are central to the cultivation of academic-career interests and to the range of occupational options that people view as viable for themselves. Thus we believe that many individuals prematurely foreclose on potentially rewarding career pursuits either because their environments offer a restricted range of efficacy-building experiences or because they develop inaccurate self-efficacy beliefs or occupational outcome expectations. Methods for fostering reliable self-efficacy and outcome expectations and for maximizing development of abilities may be most useful during the school years, when students' self-percepts and occupational beliefs are likely to be relatively malleable.

SCCT suggests that psychoeducational interventions designed to promote optimum career development (or to prevent future choice or adjustment problems) need to focus not only on students' emergent interests, values, and talents but on the cognitive bases of these characteristics. It is particularly important, from a social cognitive perspective, to ensure that children's and adolescents' self-efficacy beliefs are relatively consonant with their developing abilities and that their career-related outcome expectations are based on accurate information. Thus students' zone of acceptable choice alternatives (Gottfredson, 1996) is not constrained by misperceptions of personal capabilities or work reinforcers (conditions).

In terms of remedial interventions for clients experiencing problems with career choice or change, the SCCT perspective shares a basic goal with most other approaches to career counseling: to help clients choose from an array of occupations that correspond well with important aspects of their work personalities. However, in our view an important aspect of this process, particularly for those evidencing flat interest profiles or feeling stifled by a constricted range of possibilities, is to promote the broadest possible array of occupational options by helping clients to identify and revisit those career paths that they might have already eliminated on the basis of faulty self-efficacy percepts or outcome expectations. We have developed two counseling strategies for this purpose (Brown & Lent, 1996). These strategies require little change in how most counselors, regardless of their theoretical persuasion, go about career counseling because they both represent slight modifications of commonly employed methods.

The first strategy, which employs standardized aptitude, need-value, and interest test data, is derived from well-studied assumptions that occupations generated from need-value and aptitude data represent options that (1) clients will find satisfying (because they correspond with clients' preferences for work conditions and reinforcers), and (2) in which clients will likely perform satisfactorily (because of their correspondence with clients' abilities) (Dawis & Lofquist, 1984). We compare and target for further discussion occupational possibilities that are suggested on the basis of aptitude and need-value data but that are not generated by interest data.

To illustrate, we used this strategy with a thirty-five-year-old woman who sought help in making a career change because of dissatisfaction with her job as a picture editor with a major publisher. From a social cognitive perspective, her testing results were quite dramatic. Her aptitudes and needs data corresponded well with college teaching in a variety of socially oriented fields such as sociology, psychology, and counseling. However, she had responded to the "interest" measure with a large percentage of indifferent responses and, consequently, had a very flat and undifferentiated interest profile.

When these discrepancies between her aptitudes and needs, on the one hand, and her interests, on the other, were discussed with her, she reported that she had earlier considered such occupational possibilities but had failed to consider them seriously because she did not think she had the writing and quantitative skills required for success in such fields. The counselor pointed out that her aptitude data suggested that she *did* have the needed aptitudes, and subsequent discussions with her revealed that her writing skills were well-developed but that she had always disparaged them by comparing her written papers in college to published articles. After a series of additional efficacy-enhancing efforts, she ultimately decided to continue her education in a doctoral program in urban sociology, where she went on to perform quite well.

The second strategy represents a slight modification of standard occupational card sort procedures and can be illustrated with another counseling case. The client was a thirty-year-old woman who was unhappy in her job as an advertising salesperson for a major trade publisher. We had her complete a modified vocational card sort procedure in which she, as is standard practice, was asked initially to sort occupational titles into "might choose," "in question," and "would not choose" categories. We then asked her to sort the occupations in the "in question" and "would not choose" categories further into subcategories reflecting (1) self-efficacy beliefs ("might choose if I thought I had the skills"), (2) outcome expectations ("might choose if I thought they would offer me things that I value"), (3) definite lack of interest ("wouldn't choose under any circumstances"), and (4) "other."

As a result of this two-stage sorting process, she placed several occupations (including social psychology, sociology, and economics) in the "lack of self-efficacy" category. Subsequent discussions with her, as with the first client, revealed that she did not think she had the quantitative aptitude to compete and succeed in such research-oriented social professions. In order for her to gather data on the realism of these self-efficacy beliefs, the counselor asked her to study sources of information on graduate study in these fields. She discovered that her scores on the quantitative section of the Graduate Records Exam (taken several years before) were quite competitive for graduate study in psychology and sociology, though not in economics. She ultimately decided to pursue a career in occupational therapy, which had been suggested by card sort and interest inventory results. However, the modified card sort strategy at least enabled her to generate an expanded range of options, uncontaminated by faulty self-efficacy percepts, from which to choose.

Overcoming Barriers to Choice and Success

A fundamental assumption of SCCT's choice model is that persons will be unable and unwilling to translate their occupational interests into goals and their goals into actions if they perceive insurmountable barriers to career entry or success. Thus we think it is important that counseling for career choice or change focus not only on expanding clients' occupational options but on helping them to (1) carefully consider potential barriers to their career pursuit or success, (2) analyze the likelihood of encountering these barriers, and (3) prepare strategies to prevent or manage likely barriers to occupational attainment and to cultivate social supports in their family or peer environments.

We have found it helpful in our counseling practices to use the decisional balance sheet developed by Janis and Mann (1977) to help our clients identify potential choice barriers (Brown & Lent, 1996). Although this procedure was originally developed to facilitate a thorough consideration of possible consequences to decisional alternatives, it can be modified for use in identifying potential barriers. We ask clients to generate both positive and negative consequences in relation to each career alternative they are seriously considering. We then have them focus specifically on anticipated negative consequences that might prevent them from pursuing particular options. The client is subsequently assisted to estimate the likelihood that each barrier will actually be encountered and to develop strategies to prevent and manage the most likely barriers.

To illustrate, consider again our thirty-five-year-old client. Using the balance sheet procedure, she identified a highly likely and (for her) significant barrier to pursuing an academic career in urban sociology. Specifically, she indicated she was in a longstanding intimate relationship with a man who was self-employed in the local area. Because this area contained only one relevant sociology graduate program, she feared that she might have to move elsewhere, thereby jeopardizing her relationship. At her counselor's encouragement, she discussed this dual-career dilemma with her partner. Together the couple worked out a strategy in which she would apply to graduate programs nationwide but reserve the local program as her first choice. In the event that she was not accepted locally, her partner agreed to move with her, feeling that he could pursue his self-employment in other locations. Although she was ultimately accepted at the local university, prior discussions helped her prepare for an important potential barrier to implementing her preferred career choice.

Developing and Modifying Self-Efficacy Percepts

As our earlier comments suggest, persons with adequate skills but weak self-efficacy beliefs in a particular performance domain may prematurely rule out that domain from further occupational or academic choice consideration. In addition, the basic hypotheses of our performance model and data testing them suggest that self-efficacy beliefs may facilitate attainment in a given academic or career domain as long as an individual possesses at least minimal levels of requisite ability in that domain. Thus procedures designed to boost clients' self-efficacy beliefs may be important treatment ingredients for many persons experiencing career choice or performance difficulties. Such procedures may also constitute a valuable aspect of developmental interventions, ensuring that children's and adolescents' self-efficacy beliefs keep pace with their developing talents. Although efficacy-enhancing procedures may be valuable at all developmental periods, they may be particularly so during (or even prior to) early adolescence—a time when occupational status aspirations become established (Rojewski & Yang, 1997) and ability percepts may, increasingly, affect students' sense of which career options are viable for themselves (Gottfredson, 1996).

SCCT does *not* imply that efficacy-enhancing interventions by themselves will always be effective—or even indicated (Brown, Lent, & Larkin, 1989). For instance, clients entering counseling (or participating in developmental activities) with a constellation of weak efficacy beliefs *and* deficient skills in a particular performance domain will not likely be aided by efforts that attempt only to raise their self-efficacy in that domain. Rather, such persons will need to engage in extensive, remedial skill-building activities or be helped to consider alternative academic or occupational pursuits whose ability requirements are more nearly correspondent with their current skills.

In instances where efficacy-enhancing interventions are appropriate (that is, where persons possess adequate skills but weak efficacy beliefs in a given performance context), theory and research suggest the value of designing procedures that

- Foster personal mastery experiences in areas in which a client's efficacy beliefs seriously undershoot his or her measured abilities (augmented, as needed, by modeling, verbal support, or anxiety-coping strategies
- Promote reconsideration of past performance experiences
- Encourage clients to interpret their past and present successes in a manner that promotes, rather than discounts, perceived competence

In relation to the latter treatment goal, mastery perceptions may be enhanced cognitively in several ways (Brown & Heath, 1984; Brown & Lent, 1996; Goldfried & Robbins, 1982). For example, the counselor can help by keeping the client focused on progress at skill development rather than on ultimate skill attainment. In other words, the client can be reinforced and encouraged to self-reinforce for each successive step at skill acquisition. It is also important to focus on the client's performance attributions, encouraging him or her to ascribe success experiences at skill development to internal, stable factors (such as personal ability) rather than to internal, unstable (such as effort) or external (luck or task simplicity) factors. This can be accomplished by asking clients at each step of the skill acquisition process (or as they review past experiences) for their perceived reasons for task success. Nonadaptive attributions can be challenged, for instance, by having clients generate and evaluate alternative interpretations for their performance successes.

Illustrative Developmental Applications

Negotiating the school-to-work transition process and intervening with students who are at risk for academic failure offer challenging yet socially important forums for SCCT-derived applications. Controversy over the role of schools in preparing workers has stimulated renewed interest among educators, researchers, and policymakers in the school-to-work transition process (Blustein et al., 2000). In particular, concerns have been raised about the adequacy of students' preparation to enter the workforce, ability to translate their educational skills into occupational domains, and subsequent productivity and dependability as workers. Although a variety of solutions, such as job skills training and youth apprenticeship programs, have been offered, such programs have often overlooked the literature on students' developmental needs and on career choice and work adjustment (Lent & Worthington, 1999).

We believe that school-to-work (and career education) programs may be enhanced by incorporating the basic, empirically supported tenets of a variety of career theories. SCCT, for example, would emphasize a variety of intervention elements tailored to students' developmental levels, such as designing skills programs with self-efficacy enhancement (as well as skill development) in mind, attending to the acquisition of accurate outcome expectations, fostering goal-setting skills, and developing multiple facets of self-efficacy in relation to skills (such as communication, conscientiousness, and coping behaviors) that may be required for successful work transition. Also critical, from our perspective, would be efforts to identify barriers to work transition, along with strategies to negotiate them, and to cultivate opportunity structures such as social support. Lent,

Hackett, and Brown (1999) have considered SCCT's implications for understanding and facilitating students' career development across the school years as well as during transition to work per se. Counselors and researchers have begun to use the theory as a template for designing (Prideaux, Patton, & Creed, in press) and evaluating (McWhirter, Rasheed, & Crothers, 2000) career education programs and for intervening with career-undecided students (Luzzo, Hasper, Albert, Bibby, & Martinelli, 1999).

The high dropout rate among disadvantaged, predominantly racial- or ethnic-minority students has prompted compensatory programs aimed at bolstering academic skills (Richardson, Casanova, Placier, & Guilfoyle, 1989). SCCT may offer some useful implications for such programs. For example, students labeled "at risk" for academic failure often lack interest, motivation, and a sense of purpose or life direction. Academic remediation may foster a certain level of perceived efficacy, but sole emphasis on basic, low-level academic skills, as found in most compensatory programs, are unlikely to engender the types of mastery experiences and challenging goals that favor the development of strong efficacy and interests (Bandura, 1986). Further, compensatory programs often do not attend systematically to peer influences on students' achievement motivation (Arbona, 2000). These potentially barrier-producing influences may require intervention in order to jump-start students' motivation regarding academic pursuits and to increase the likelihood of their developing higher-level academic and career aspirations.

Case Studies

In keeping with SCCT's emphasis on theory unification, our work with both K and E brings together a variety of theoretical perspectives using SCCT assumptions and variables as an organizing framework. We also rely on recent empirical research in career psychology and the basic psychological sciences for help in conceptualizing these clients and designing interventions for them.

Overview and General Issues

Before delving into the specifics of our approach with K and E, we offer some general theoretical and empirical observations. First, research on the diagnosis of career problems (for example, Chartrand & Nutter, 1996) and on the critical ingredients of effective career interventions (Brown & Kane, 2000) leads us to anticipate that our work with both K and E may be relatively straightforward. In particular, meta-analytic findings suggest that in the absence of significant affective involvement (such as anxiety, depression, or tendency toward negative affect), most clients benefit maximally from brief, four-to-five-session interventions (Brown & Kane, 2000).

Second, the work of Brown and Krane (2000) suggests that career interventions are most likely to be effective when they include five key ingredients: (1) written exercises, (2) individualized interpretations and feedback, (3) occupational information, (4) modeling, and (5) attention to building social-environmental support for choices. Thus, along with the more specific interventions we would design for K and E, we anticipate assisting both of them to gather occupational information and to develop opportunities for appropriate vicarious experiences. We would also encourage them to keep written records of the information they gather during counseling and to capture their career goals and plans in writing as an aid to further reflection and implementation efforts (Babcock & Kaufmann, 1976; Niles, 1993; Spokane & Rarick, 1998). We would, concurrently, help them interpret the information they gather about self and occupational options, develop realistic career plans, and build social supports for their choices.

Third, we are mindful of data suggesting that clients who enter counseling with career choice concerns do so for at least four reasons (for example, Power, Holland, Daiger, & Takai, 1979). Clients may

1. Seek career choice counseling because they have few options or are not satisfied with the options they have considered
2. Be confused by an excess of options

3. Enter counseling for help with decision making

4. Seek confirmation about a choice they have already made

Although there are no hard data on the strategies that work best for these different client types (primarily because career choice intervention research has typically treated all clients as having the same needs), we would tend to tailor our approach somewhat differently for these four types. From the data presented, we suspect that K may need help in generating and evaluating potentially satisfying career options, whereas E's concern is one of reducing confusion by narrowing the wide range of possibilities that were generated for her by her career class. Of course, we would want to check these hypotheses out directly with our clients.

Finally, as scientifically oriented career counselors, we use SCCT as an integrative framework for drawing together other theoretical viewpoints and hypotheses that have generated support in the career literature. For example, research suggests the importance of helping clients to identify occupational possibilities that are congruent with their interests (Holland, 1997) and that correspond to their values and abilities (Dawis & Lofquist, 1984). Recent research also suggests the utility of considering clients' "core requirements" for occupations (Gati, Garty, & Fassa, 1996). Thus, in addition to more traditional assessment dimensions, we would help both K and E identify what they most want from a career and to analyze occupational possibilities for the degree to which they can satisfy these core requirements. From SCCT's perspective, such an approach can ensure that these clients base their ultimate decisions on relatively complete and accurate outcome expectations.

We next consider in more detail how we would incorporate our theoretical and empirical position into our work with K and E.

The Case of K

K comes to counseling with a set of definite strengths as well as some areas of potential concern. On the positive side, he is very bright, as evidenced by his SAT scores, and has a personality profile that is both very consistent (CR-RC) and somewhat differentiated (46th percentile for male high school students and 40th percentile for male college students; Holland, Powell, & Fritzsche, 1997, Appendix B1). He also has a fairly coherent set of occupational daydreams. Most important, K has developed a strong interest in skateboarding, which is represented among his occupational daydreams and is his first choice of occupations. It is also an activity in which he appears to invest a great deal of time (perhaps to the detriment of his schoolwork), and professional skateboarders represent people whom he admires.

In terms of areas of concern, we note that K has apparently not performed as well in school as his SAT scores would predict (although we have no hard data on this). We would not, however, be overly concerned about this until we had data to suggest that it might interfere with his career choices, successes, or satisfaction.

Two other areas might be of more concern to us. First, although his personality profile is consistent, the CR or RC profile is rare among male college students. RC and CR profiles were obtained, respectively, by only 1.3 percent and 0.3 percent of male college students in the 1994 normative sample of the SDS (Holland et al., 1997, Appendix A21). Thus we are not overly surprised that applying to and completing college may be low priorities for him. Second, and perhaps more important, although K has a somewhat coherent set of occupational daydreams, the high point code of most of these daydreams, as well as his most-liked job as a library assistant (Artistic), is quite inconsistent with the profile (CR-RC) that he obtained on the Self-Directed Search (SDS).

Finally, we should comment on K's tendency to procrastinate. Although it may be tempting to assume that K's pattern of procrastination requires specific intervention or is indicative of deeper affective problems, we would be cautious in making assumptions about his underlying psychological dynamics, based only on the evidence that is presented. It seems to us that K's procrastination occurs when he undertakes tasks for which he has little interest or passion (applying to college) rather than when he is engaged in activities for which he feels excitement (skateboarding). Thus,

before drawing conclusions about whether his pattern of procrastination should receive counseling attention, we need more
specific data about the conditions that do and do not elicit his procrastination. In addition, we would want more direct data on the
degree to which negative affectivity or feelings of dysphoria or anxiety may underlie his career choice uncertainty (the Career Factors
Inventory, Chartrand & Robbins, 1989, may be useful in this regard). We would, therefore, deem it important to collect more data
on K's procrastination and affectivity before deciding whether
these issues will require specific attention or whether our work
with K would conform to the more typical expectation of four-to-
five sessions (Brown & Krane, 2000).

Although we expect that he has sought counseling for help in
generating suitable career possibilities, our first order of business
would be to clarify K's reasons for seeking counseling. We also need
to find out what he would ultimately like to achieve through counseling (that is, his counseling goals). For example, though he
entered counseling seeking options, his goals may also include help
in deciding which option to pursue and developing plans for implementing his desired choice. It is important for us to be clear about
counseling goals so that we (client and counselor) know what we
are working toward and when we are finished; we also want to minimize misunderstandings that could result, either in premature termination or unnecessary additional sessions.

If we are correct in our hypothesis that K is seeking career
options, we would focus on several major tasks. First, we would follow up on K's interest in skateboarding by helping him acquire
information on professional skateboarding and see whether it is
really an occupational option for him. Equally important, we would
encourage him to gather information, using a variety of print, on-
line, and interview sources, on other potential careers in the skateboarding industry, such as manufacturing, Web site or video game
development, teaching, or working in some capacity for skateboarding publications. We would also help him identify, through
the SDS's Occupations Finder, the *Dictionary of Holland Occupa-*

tional Codes (Gottfredson & Holland, 1996), and other on-line and print sources of information, additional occupations with CR or RC occupational codes that he might want to consider further.

As SCCT theorists, we would also be curious about the apparent inconsistency between his occupational daydreams and his personality profile. In particular, we would wonder why his A-theme did not emerge as more significant on his SDS profile; we would hypothesize that his self-efficacy beliefs in artistic activities and occupations are lower than his interests (see, for example, his Educational Self-Efficacy ratings for art subjects). We would collect data on this hypothesis by reviewing his scores on the SDS sections with him (anticipating that his scores on the Competencies and Self-Estimate sections of the SDS would be substantially lower than his scores on the more interest-focused sections).

If our hypothesis is confirmed, we would explore his feelings of efficacy regarding a wider range of artistic activities (such as computer graphics) than are represented on the SDS. To clarify his self-estimates and counteract potentially faulty efficacy expectations, we would also encourage him to collect additional, non-self-report data on his artistic competencies. For example, Brown and Lent (1996) successfully countered a client's faulty self-efficacy beliefs by having her ask significant others to rate her abilities in areas in which she had some self-doubt. This strategy, and others outlined by Brown and Lent (1996), might be useful with K. We might then assist K to further consider his interests in video and film editing, architecture, and other occupational possibilities that make use of his particular blend of interests, aptitudes, and competencies, particularly as they relate to skateboarding and related options.

We would hope that our work with K to this point might enable him to identify a way to follow his passion for skateboarding in the occupational arena or to identify other career possibilities that make use of his talents and interests. Subsequent work with K would include helping him consider how the identified occupational possibilities provide for his major work-related needs, values, and other important occupational requirements so that his outcome expectations for these career paths would be as fully informed and accurate as possible. We would also, as suggested by SCCT, help him to

1. Identify barriers to entering and working in the skateboarding industry and other career paths that he might have identified
2. Develop ways to prevent or manage the identified barriers
3. Consider how he might build choice supports to enable him to pursue his preferred option(s) and overcome barriers that might stand in his way (see Brown & Lent, 1996, for some strategies)

Particularly relevant to his ability to pursue a career in the skateboarding industry might be his parents' expectations (it is possible that they might not be thrilled about or supportive of such a choice) and K's concomitant values for loyalty and responsibility to his family. If confirmed, the conflict elicited by these values and his parents' expectations, which may well reflect important cultural dimensions, could represent significant barriers to his ability to follow his passion. Counseling focused on choice making and choice pursuit may, therefore, need to take into account these cultural considerations and their implications for K's—and his family's—decision making.

The Case of E

E appears to come to counseling with different concerns than K. Whereas K apparently sought counseling because he had yet to identify viable careers, E indicates that her prior career course generated too many options. Further, in this case we are given data on her major goal for counseling, namely, "to narrow her choices to a few viable occupational alternatives." Thus the information provided about E gives us a clearer sense of both the goal toward which we will work and when counseling should terminate.

E's assessment data suggest that she has a consistent personality profile (SE) that is also quite differentiated (at the 71st percentile for female college students) and common for college females (see Holland et al., 1997, Appendixes A21 and B1). Her occupational daydreams are also coherently organized around E and S themes and are, therefore, congruent with her SDS-generated personality profile. Like K, she is also very bright yet presents with a much more differentiated set of Educational Self-Efficacy ratings (ranging from 1 for Art to 10 for History).

Unfortunately, the information that we are provided for a client with a goal of narrowing possibilities is too incomplete to say much in detail about specific counseling strategies. In particular, we lack information on the occupations that were generated through E's career course. This information would form an important starting point for our work with her.

Once we confirm her goals for counseling and discover the choice options that were generated, our general strategy would focus on the outcome expectations that she has for each possibility she is considering and to ensure that these expectations are fully informed by relevant self- and occupational knowledge. Specifically, we would first help her identify and prioritize the core requirements that she has for a career by having her consider and rank order such factors as her basic interests, work-related values, abilities she wants to use in a career, educational goals (that is, the amount of education she is willing to pursue), desired lifestyle, and starting income (see Gati et al., 1996, for a fuller list of possible considerations). We would then help her gather necessary information on each possibility that she is considering and analyze each one in terms of (1) how well it provides for her core requirements, (2) how it is likely to affect her feelings of self-worth and social approval, and (3) the types of barriers and supports she might encounter in pursuing it.

Developing accurate outcome expectations and analyzing for supports and barriers are particularly important from an SCCT perspective. Consideration of core requirements represents one way to foster accurate outcome expectations. Anticipation of how self- and social approval will be affected by the choice of different options offers another important way to clarify outcome expectations; such a strategy has been shown to be an effective component of decision making and is associated with reduced postdecisional regret and increased postdecisional satisfaction and tenure (Janis & Mann, 1977). The overall goal of these strategies is to help E narrow the range of possibilities that she is considering by basing her decisions on relatively complete and accurate expectations of likely outcomes for each choice and on a careful analysis of potential social resources.

Conclusion

We have offered an introduction to the social cognitive models of career-academic interest development, choice, and performance. Our evolving framework builds on earlier efforts to extend the general theory proposed by Bandura (1986) to the understanding of career development. SCCT highlights the interplay of social cognitive variables (such as self-efficacy) with other key person, contextual, and experiential-learning factors, such as gender, culture, support systems, and barriers. It emphasizes the means by which individuals exercise agency in their own career development, as well as those influences that promote or constrain agency. This theory-building effort is aimed, in part, at complementing and helping to bridge certain aspects of existing career theories. In addition to considering the basic theory and its empirical base, we highlighted some ways in which SCCT can be used to inform developmental and remedial career interventions and pondered how it might be employed specifically in the cases of K and E.

References

Ajzen, I. (1988). *Attitudes, personality, and behavior.* Stony Stratford, UK: Open University Press.

Arbona, C. (2000). The development of academic achievement in school aged children: Precursors to career development. In S. D. Brown & R. W. Lent (Eds.), *Handbook of counseling psychology* (3rd ed., pp. 270–309). New York: Wiley.

Astin, H. S. (1984). The meaning of work in women's lives: A socio-psychological model of career choice and work behavior. *Counseling Psychologist, 12,* 117–126.

Babcock, R. J., & Kaufmann, M. A. (1976). Effectiveness of a career course. *Vocational Guidance Quarterly, 24,* 261–266.

Bandura, A. (1982). The self and mechanisms of agency. In J. Suls (Ed.), *Psychological perspectives on the self* (pp. 3–39). Hillsdale, NJ: Erlbaum.

Bandura, A. (1986). *Social foundations of thought and action: A social cognitive theory.* Englewood Cliffs, NJ: Prentice Hall.

Bandura, A. (1997). *Self-efficacy: The exercise of control.* New York: Freeman.

Barak, A. (1981). Vocational interests: A cognitive view. *Journal of Vocational Behavior, 19,* 1–14.

Betsworth, D. G., & Fouad, N. A. (1997). Vocational interests: A look at the past 70 years and a glance at the future. *Career Development Quarterly, 46,* 23–47.

Betz, N. E., & Hackett, G. (1981). The relationship of career-related self-efficacy expectations to perceived career options in college women and men. *Journal of Counseling Psychology, 28,* 399–410.

Betz, N. E., & Hackett, G. (1986). Applications of self-efficacy theory to understanding career choice behavior. *Journal of Social and Clinical Psychology, 4,* 279–289.

Blustein, D. L., Juntunen, C. L., & Worthington, R. L. (2000). The school-to-work transition: Adjustment challenges of the forgotten half. In S. D. Brown & R. W. Lent (Eds.), *Handbook of counseling psychology* (3rd ed., pp. 435–470). New York: Wiley.

Borgen, F. H. (1991). Megatrends and milestones in vocational behavior: A 20-year counseling psychology retrospective. *Journal of Vocational Behavior, 39,* 263–290.

Brown, D. (1990). Summary, comparison, and critique of the major theories. In D. Brown, L. Brooks, & Associates, *Career choice and development* (2nd ed., pp. 338–363). San Francisco: Jossey-Bass.

Brown, S. D., & Heath, L. H. (1984). Coping with critical life events: An integrative cognitive-behavioral model for research and practice. In S. D. Brown & R. W. Lent (Eds.), *Handbook of counseling psychology* (1st ed., pp. 545–578). New York: Wiley.

Brown, S. D., & Lent, R. W. (1996). A social cognitive framework for career choice counseling. *Career Development Quarterly, 44,* 354–366.

Brown, S. D., & Kane, N.E.R. (2000). Four (or five) sessions and a cloud of dust: Old assumptions and new observations about career counseling. In S. D. Brown & R. W. Lent (Eds.), *Handbook of counseling psychology* (3rd. ed., pp. 740–766). New York: Wiley.

Brown, S. D., Lent, R. W., & Larkin, K. C. (1989). Self-efficacy as a moderator of scholastic aptitude-academic performance relationships. *Journal of Vocational Behavior, 35*, 64–75.

Bussey, K., & Bandura, A. (1999). Social cognitive theory of gender development and differentiation. *Psychological Review, 106*, 676–713.

Casas, J. M. (1984). Policy, training, and research in counseling psychology: The racial/ethnic minority perspective. In S. D. Brown & R. W. Lent (Eds.), *Handbook of counseling psychology* (pp. 785–831). New York: Wiley.

Chartrand, J. (1991). The evolution of trait-and-factor career counseling: A person × environment fit approach. *Journal of Counseling and Development, 69*, 518–524.

Chartrand, J. M., Martin, W. F., Robbins, S. B., McAuliffe, G. J., Pickering, J. W., & Calliotte, J. A. (1994). Testing a level versus an interactional view of career indecision. *Journal of Career Assessment, 2*, 55–69.

Chartrand, J. M., & Nutter, K. J. (1996). The Career Factors Inventory: Theory and applications. *Journal of Career Assessment, 4*, 205–218.

Chartrand, J. M., & Robbins, S. B. (1989). *Career Factors Inventory*. Palo Alto, CA: Consulting Psychologists Press.

Chartrand, J. M., & Rose, M. L. (1996). Career interventions for at-risk populations: Incorporating social cognitive influences. *The Career Development Quarterly, 44*, 341–353.

Dawis, R. V. (1996). The theory of work adjustment and person-environment-correspondence counseling. In D. Brown, L. Brooks, & Associates, *Career choice and development* (3rd ed., pp. 75–120). San Francisco: Jossey-Bass.

Dawis, R. V., & Lofquist, L. H. (1984). *A psychological theory of work adjustment: An individual differences model and its applications*. Minneapolis: University of Minnesota Press.

de Bruin, G. P. (1999). Social cognitive career theory as an explanatory model for career counselling in South Africa. In G. B. Stead & M. B. Watson (Eds.), *Career psychology in the South African context*. Pretoria, South Africa: J. L. van Schaik.

Eccles, J. S. (1987). Gender roles and women's achievement-related decisions. *Psychology of Women Quarterly, 11*, 135–172.

Eccles, J. S. (1994). Understanding women's educational and occupational choices: Applying the Eccles et al. model of achievement-related choices. *Psychology of Women Quarterly, 18*, 585–609.

Fabian, E. S. (2000). Social cognitive theory of careers and individuals with serious mental health disorders: Implications for psychiatric rehabilitation programs. *Psychiatric Rehabilitation Journal, 23*, 262–269.

Fassinger, R. E. (2000). Gender and sexuality in human development: Implications for prevention and advocacy in counseling psychology. In S. D. Brown & R. W. Lent (Eds.), *Handbook of counseling psychology* (3rd ed., pp. 346–378). New York: Wiley.

Ferry, T. R., Fouad, N. A., & Smith, P. L. (2000). The role of family context in a social cognitive model for career-related choice behavior: A math and science perspective. *Journal of Vocational Behavior, 57*, 348–364.

Fitzgerald, L. F., & Betz, N. E. (1994). Career development in cultural context: The role of gender, race, class, and sexual orientation. In M. L. Savickas & R. W. Lent (Eds.), *Convergence in career development theories: Implications for science and practice* (pp. 103–117). Palo Alto, CA: Consulting Psychologists Press.

Fouad, N. A., & Smith, P. L. (1996). A test of a social cognitive model for middle school students: Math and science. *Journal of Counseling Psychology, 43*, 338–346.

Gainor, K. A., & Lent, R. W. (1998). Social cognitive expectations and racial identity attitudes in predicting the math choice intentions of Black college students. *Journal of Counseling Psychology, 45*, 403–413.

Gati, I., Garty, Y., & Fassa, N. (1996). Using career-related aspects to assess person-environment fit. *Journal of Counseling Psychology, 43*, 196–206.

Goldfried, M. R., & Robbins, C. (1982). On the facilitation of self-efficacy. *Cognitive Therapy and Research, 6*, 61–380.

Goodman, J. (1994). Career adaptability: A construct whose time has come. *Career Development Quarterly, 43*, 74–84.

Gottfredson, L. S. (1996). Gottfredson's theory of circumscription and compromise. In D. Brown, L. Brooks, & Associates, *Career choice and development* (3rd ed., pp. 179–232). San Francisco: Jossey-Bass.

Gottfredson, G. D., & Holland, J. L. (1996). *Dictionary of Holland occupational codes* (3rd ed.). Odessa, FL: Psychological Assessment Resources.

Hackett, G. (1995). Self-efficacy in career choice and development. In A. Bandura (Ed.), *Self-efficacy in changing societies*. Cambridge: Cambridge University Press.

Hackett, G., & Betz, N. E. (1981). A self-efficacy approach to the career development of women. *Journal of Vocational Behavior, 18*, 326–336.

Hackett, G., & Byars, A. M. (1996). Social cognitive theory and the career development of African American women. *The Career Development Quarterly, 44*, 322–340.

Hackett, G., & Lent, R. W. (1992). Theoretical advances and current inquiry in career psychology. In S. D. Brown & R. W. Lent (Eds.), *Handbook of counseling psychology* (2nd ed., pp. 419–451). New York: Wiley.

Hackett, G., Lent, R. W., and Greenhaus, J. H. (1991). Advances in vocational theory and research: A 20-year retrospective. *Journal of Vocational Behavior, 38*, 3–38.

Hansen, J. C. (1984). The measurement of vocational interests: Issues and future directions. In S. D. Brown & R. W. Lent (Eds.), *Handbook of counseling psychology* (pp. 99–136). New York: Wiley.

Hesketh, B. (2000). Prevention and development in the workplace. In S. D. Brown and R. W. Lent (Eds.), *Handbook of counseling psychology* (3rd ed., pp. 471–498). New York: Wiley.

Holland, J. L. (1997). *Making vocational choices* (3rd ed.). Odessa, FL: Psychological Assessment Resources.

Holland, J. L., Powell, A. B., & Fritzsche, B. A. (1997). *Professional user's guide to the Self-Directed Search*. Odessa, FL: Psychological Assessment Resources.

Janis, I. L., & Mann, L. (1977). *Decision making: A psychological analysis of conflict, choice, and commitment*. New York: Free Press.

Kantas, A. (1997). Self-efficacy perceptions and outcome expectations in the prediction of occupational preferences. *Perceptual and Motor Skills, 84*, 259–266.

Krumboltz, J. D. (1979). A social learning theory of career decision making. In A. M. Mitchell, G. B. Jones, & J. D. Krumboltz (Eds.), *Social learning and career decision making* (pp. 19–49). Cranston, RI: Carroll.

Krumboltz, J. D., Mitchell, A. M., & Jones, G. B. (1976). A social learning theory of career selection. *The Counseling Psychologist, 6,* 71–81.

Krumboltz, J. D., & Nichols, C. W. (1990). Integrating the social learning theory of career decision making (pp. 159–192). In W. B. Walsh & S. H. Osipow (Eds.), *Career counseling: Contemporary topics in vocational psychology.* Hillsdale, NJ: Erlbaum.

Lapan, R. T., Boggs, K. R., & Morrill, W. H. (1989). Self-efficacy as a mediator of Investigative and Realistic general occupational themes on the Strong-Campbell Interest Inventory. *Journal of Counseling Psychology, 36,* 176–182.

Lent, R. W. (in press). Vocational psychology and career counseling: Inventing the future. *Journal of Vocational Behavior.*

Lent, R. W., & Brown, S. D. (Eds.). (1996). Applying social cognitive theory to career counseling [Special section]. *The Career Development Quarterly, 44* (4).

Lent, R. W., Brown, S. D., & Hackett, G. (1994). Toward a unifying social cognitive theory of career and academic interest, choice, and performance [Monograph]. *Journal of Vocational Behavior, 45,* 79–122.

Lent, R. W., Brown, S. D., & Hackett, G. (2000). Contextual supports and barriers to career choice: A social cognitive analysis. *Journal of Counseling Psychology, 47,* 36–49.

Lent, R. W., Brown, S. D., Talleyrand, R., McPartland, E. B., Davis, T., Chopra, S. B., Alexander, M. S., Suthakaran, V., & Chai, C. M. (in press). Career choice barriers, supports, and coping strategies: College students' experiences. *Journal of Vocational Behavior.*

Lent, R. W., & Hackett, G. (1987). Career self-efficacy: Empirical status and future directions [Monograph]. *Journal of Vocational Behavior, 30,* 347–382.

Lent, R. W., & Hackett, G. (1994). Sociocognitive mechanisms of personal agency in career development: Pantheoretical prospects. In M. L. Savickas & R. W. Lent (Eds.), *Convergence in career development theories: Implications for science and practice* (pp. 77–102). Palo Alto, CA: Consulting Psychologists Press.

Lent, R. W., Hackett, G., & Brown, S. D. (1999). A social cognitive view of school-to-work transition. *The Career Development Quarterly, 44,* 297–311.

Lent, R. W., Larkin, K. C., & Brown, S. D. (1989). Relation of self-efficacy to inventoried vocational interests. *Journal of Vocational Behavior, 34,* 279–288.

Lent, R. W., & Lopez, F. G. (in press). Cognitive ties that bind: A tripartite view of efficacy beliefs in growth-promoting relationships. *Journal of Social and Clinical Psychology.*

Lent, R. W., & Savickas, M. L. (1994). Postscript: Is convergence a viable agenda for career psychology? In M. L. Savickas & R. W. Lent (Eds.), *Convergence in career development theories: Implications for science and practice* (pp. 259–271). Palo Alto, CA: Consulting Psychologists Press.

Lent, R. W., & Worthington, R. L. (1999). Applying career development theories to the school-to-work transition process. *Career Development Quarterly, 47,* 291–296.

Locke, E. A., & Latham, G. P. (1990). *A theory of goal setting and task performance.* Englewood Cliffs, NJ: Prentice Hall.

Luzzo, D. A., Hasper, P., Albert, K. A., Bibby, M. A., & Martinelli, E. A. (1999). Effects of self-efficacy-enhancing interventions on the math/science self-efficacy and career interests, goals, and actions of career undecided college students. *Journal of Counseling Psychology, 46,* 233–243.

McWhirter, E. H., Rasheed, S., & Crothers, M. (2000). The effects of high school career education on social-cognitive variables. *Journal of Counseling Psychology, 47,* 330–341.

McWhirter, E. H., Torres, D., & Rasheed, S. (1998). Assessing barriers to women's career adjustment. *Journal of Career Assessment, 6,* 449–479.

Mitchell, L. K., & Krumboltz, J. D. (1996). Krumboltz's learning theory of career choice and counseling. In D. Brown, L. Brooks, & Associates, *Career choice and development* (3rd ed., pp. 233–280). San Francisco: Jossey-Bass.

Moloney, D. P., Bouchard, T. J., Jr., and Segal, N. L. (1991). A genetic and environmental analysis of the vocational interests of monozygotic and dizygotic twins reared apart. *Journal of Vocational Behavior, 39,* 76–109.

Morrow, S. L., Gore, P. A., & Campbell, B. W. (1996). The application of a sociocognitive framework to the career development of lesbian women and gay men. *Journal of Vocational Behavior, 48,* 136–148.

Multon, K. D., Brown, S. D., and Lent, R. W. (1991). Relation of self-efficacy beliefs to academic outcomes: A meta-analytic investigation. *Journal of Counseling Psychology, 38*, 30–38.

Niles, S. (1993). The timing of counselor contact in the use of computer information delivery systems with adult career counseling clients. *Journal of Employment Counseling, 30*, 2–12.

Nota, L., & Soresi, S. (2000). *Autoefficacia nelle scelte: La visione sociocognitiva dell'orientamento (Self-efficacy in choices: A social-cognitive perspective of career development)*. Firenze, Italy: Institute for Training, Education, and Research.

Osipow, S. H. (1990). Convergence in theories of career choice and development: Review and prospect. *Journal of Vocational Behavior, 36*, 122–131.

Power, P. G., Holland, J. L., Daiger, D. C., & Takai, R. T. (1979). The relation of student characteristics to the influence of the Self-Directed Search. *Measurement and Evaluation in Guidance, 12*, 98–107.

Prideaux, L., Patton, W., & Creed, P. (in press). Development and evaluation of a theoretically derived school career program: An Australian endeavor. *International Journal of Vocational Education and Guidance*.

Richardson, V., Casanova, U., Placier, P., & Guilfoyle, K. (1989). *School children at risk*. London: Falmer.

Richie, B. S., Fassinger, R. E., Prosser, J., & Robinson, S. (1997). Persistence, connection, and passion: A qualitative study of the career development of highly achieving African American–Black and White women. *Journal of Counseling Psychology, 44*, 133–148.

Rojewski, J. W., & Yang, B. (1997). Longitudinal analysis of select influences on adolescents' occupational aspirations. *Journal of Vocational Behavior, 51*, 375–410.

Rounds, J. B., & Tracey, T. J. (1990). From trait-and-factor to person-environment fit counseling: Theory and process. In W. B. Walsh & S. H. Osipow (Eds.), *Career counseling: Contemporary topics in vocational psychology* (pp. 1–44). Hillsdale, NJ: Erlbaum.

Sadri, G., & Robertson, I. T. (1993). Self-efficacy and work-related behavior: A review and meta-analysis. *Applied Psychology: An International Review, 42*, 139–152.

Savickas, M. L., & R. W. Lent (Eds.). (1994). *Convergence in career development theories: Implications for science and practice*. Palo Alto, CA: Consulting Psychologists Press.

Schunk, D. H. (1989). Self-efficacy and cognitive skill learning. In C. Ames & R. Ames (Eds.), *Research on motivation in education, Volume 3. Goals and cognitions* (pp. 13–44). San Diego, CA: Academic Press.

Schunk, D. H. (1995). Education and instruction. In J. E. Maddux (Ed.), *Self-efficacy, adaptation, and adjustment: Theory, research, and application*. New York: Plenum.

Spokane, A. R., & Rarick, S. L. (1998, August). *Intervention-process research: The next step in our progress toward a clinical science of career intervention*. In D. A. Luzzo (Chair), *Career counseling, process and outcome*. Symposium conducted at the annual meeting of the American Psychological Association, San Francisco.

Stajkovic, A. D., & Luthans, F. (1998). Self-efficacy and work-related performance: A meta-analysis. *Psychological Bulletin, 124*, 240–261.

Super, D. E. (1990). A life-span, life-space approach to career development. In D. Brown, L. Brooks, & Associates, *Career choice and development* (pp. 197–261). San Francisco: Jossey-Bass.

Super, D. E., Savickas, M. L., & Super, C. M. (1996). The life-span, life-space approach to careers. In D. Brown, L. Brooks, & Associates, *Career choice and development* (3rd ed., pp. 121–178). San Francisco: Jossey-Bass.

Swanson, J. L., & Gore, P. A. (2000). Advances in vocational psychology theory and research. In S. D. Brown & R. W. Lent (Eds.), *Handbook of counseling psychology* (3rd ed., pp. 233–269). New York: Wiley.

Szymanski, E. M., & Hershenson, D. B. (1998). Career development of people with disabilities: An ecological model. In R. M. Parker & E. M. Szymanski (Eds.), *Rehabilitation counseling: Basics and beyond* (3rd ed., pp. 327–378). Austin, TX: Pro-Ed.

Tang, M., Fouad, N. A., & Smith, P. L. (1999). Asian Americans' career choices: A path model to examine factors influencing their career choices. *Journal of Vocational Behavior, 54*, 142–157.

Tiedeman, D. V., & O'Hara, R. P. (1963). *Career development: Choice and adjustment*. New York: College Entrance Examination Board.

Van Vianen, A.E.M. (1999). Managerial self-efficacy, outcome expectations, and work-role salience as determinants of ambition for a managerial position. *Journal of Applied Social Psychology, 29*, 639–665.

Vondracek, F. W., Lerner, R. M., and Schulenberg, J. E. (1986). *Career development: A life-span developmental approach*. Hillsdale, NJ: Erlbaum.

Vroom, V. H. (1964). *Work and motivation*. New York: Wiley.

Watson, D., & Clark, L. A. (1984). Negative affectivity: The disposition to experience aversive emotional states. *Psychological Bulletin, 96,* 465–490.

Watts, A. G. (1996). Toward a policy for lifelong career development: A transatlantic perspective. *Career Development Quarterly, 45,* 41–53.

Williamson, E. G. (1939). *How to counsel students*. New York: McGraw-Hill.

Wood, R., & Bandura, A. (1989). Social cognitive theory of organizational management. *Academy of Management Review, 14,* 361–384.

Zimmerman, B. J. (1995). Self-efficacy and educational development. In A. Bandura (Ed.), *Self-efficacy in changing societies*. Cambridge: Cambridge University Press.

8

A Cognitive Information
Processing Approach to
Career Problem Solving
and Decision Making

Gary W. Peterson, James P. Sampson Jr.,
Janet G. Lenz, Robert C. Reardon

An old adage goes something like this: "Give people a fish and they eat for a day, but teach them how to fish and they eat for a lifetime." In this chapter, that message is applied to career counseling. We show how career counselors can not only help individuals make an appropriate career choice today but, more important, can help them acquire the knowledge, skills, and attitudes that will enable them to make appropriate career choices for a lifetime. The ultimate aim of the theoretical approach presented here is to provide a parsimonious conceptual framework for helping individuals become skillful career problem solvers and decision makers throughout their lives.

We begin this chapter by briefly placing our cognitive information processing (CIP) approach within the context of career theory and practice as well as in cognitive psychology. We then provide information about CIP theory and related research, applications of CIP in practice, and a summary of related research and speculation about future trends; we conclude with two case applications.

Background of the Approach

Perhaps the earliest beginnings of viewing career problem solving from a cognitive theory perspective can be traced to Frank Parsons's work, *Choosing a Vocation* (1909). As was noted in Chapter One, Parsons described three key factors in making career choices: (1) clear self-understanding, (2) knowledge of occupations, and (3) the ability to draw relationships between them. He reasoned that if individuals possess these attributes, not only would they make appropriate choices for themselves but the production function of society would be served by promoting greater efficiency in matching persons to occupations. These three factors are now represented in our CIP theory by the self-knowledge domain, the occupational knowledge domain, and the decision skills domain; they have marked the paths for three distinct lines of inquiry: (1) self-knowledge, (2) occupational knowledge, (3) career decision making.

Self-knowledge: The first line of inquiry relates to helping individuals acquire self-knowledge through the development of measures of traits and factors (Patterson & Darley, 1936; Williamson, 1939). Since the development of earlier instruments such as the Kuder Preference Record (Kuder, 1946) and the Strong Vocational Interest Blank (SVIB; Strong, 1943), more sophisticated measures have been introduced, for example, modern interest inventories such as the Self-Directed Search (SDS; Holland, Powell, & Fritzsche, 1994), the Strong Interest Inventory (SII; Consulting Psychologists Press, 1994), human abilities tests such as the Inventory of Work-Related Abilities (American College Testing, 1998), and values inventories such as the Life Values Inventory (Crace & Brown, 1996) and the Values Scale (Super & Nevill, 1985).

Occupational knowledge: A second line of inquiry targeted the second cornerstone of Parsons's model—occupational knowledge. Occupational classification systems were developed to facilitate the storage and retrieval of information about the nature and characteristics of occupations. Modern classification systems include *Standard Occupational Classification Manual* (U.S. Department of Commerce, 2000), the *Dictionary of Holland Occupational Codes* (Gottfredson & Holland, 1996), and the O*NET (U.S. Department of Labor and the National O*NET Consortium, 1999).

Career decision making: The thought processes by which an individual integrates self-knowledge and occupational knowledge to arrive at an occupational choice may be viewed as a third line of career development inquiry. Parsons identified this as "true reasoning." Early career decision theorists included Janis and Mann (1977), Gelatt (1962, 1989), Katz (1963, 1969), and Miller-Tiedeman (1977), who formulated a career-decision model that may be subsumed under an overarching five-step sequence: (1) define the problem, (2) understand its causes, (3) formulate plausible alternatives, (4) prioritize the alternatives and arrive at a first choice, (5) implement the solution and evaluate the outcomes.

Along with the development of these lines of inquiry, a parallel force in cognitive psychology or cognitive science has emerged that offers an alternative way of thinking about career choice and career development. This paradigm, referred to as *cognitive information processing* (CIP), was initially formulated in the works of Hunt (1971), Newell and Simon (1972), and Lackman, Lackman, and Butterfield (1979). CIP introduces concepts that add an important new perspective to existing theories of career choice and career development and to current practices of career counseling, particularly if career counselors seek to enhance individual career problem-solving skills. With the CIP paradigm, we can now think more comprehensively and systematically about how clients can become independent and responsible career problem solvers and decision makers (Peterson, Sampson, & Reardon, 1991; Reardon, Lenz, Sampson, & Peterson, 2000a).

Cognitive Information Processing Theory

In our most recent book, *Career Development and Planning: A Comprehensive Approach* (Reardon, Lenz, Sampson, & Peterson, 2000a), we introduce, from the field of cognitive psychology, a perspective on career choice and career decision making that seeks to integrate the earlier lines of inquiry in career theory and practice described earlier. The cognitive information processing (CIP) paradigm concerns the actual thought and memory processes involved in solving career problems and making career decisions. In the CIP paradigm we ask, "What can we do as career counselors to enable individuals to acquire self-knowledge, occupational knowledge, and career problem-solving and decision-making skills to become effective and responsible career problem solvers and decision makers?" The paradigm described next seeks to address this question.

Psychological theories may be thought of as comprising four fundamental attributes: (1) definitions, (2) assumptions and propositions, (3) operations, and (4) implications for practice and research (Hall & Lindzey, 1978). Definitions, assumptions, and operations on which the CIP model is based follow; implications for practice are presented in two case studies.

Definitions

The following definitions are central to the CIP paradigm, which may be visualized as ever-broadening concentric circles from the smallest inner circle (a career problem) to the problem space, to career problem solving, to career decision making, to career development, to the largest encompassing outer circle (lifestyle), with each succeeding concept encompassing the previous concept.

> *Career problem:* a *gap* between an existing state of indecision and a more desired state. The gap creates a cognitive dissonance (Festinger, 1964) that becomes the primary motivational source driving the problem-solving process. As career counselors, we hope to help clients progress along a continuum from a state of career indecision, which may entail confusion, anxiety, depression, and an external locus of control toward a more orderly state with attributes such as integration, the ability to plan, hope, self-confidence, and an internal locus of control.

Problem space: all cognitive and affective components contained in working memory as individuals approach a career problem-solving task (Newell & Simon, 1972; Peterson, 1998; Sinnott, 1989). The problem space entails the career problem at hand, in addition to all real-life issues associated with it, such as marital and family relationships, financial, spiritual, and leisure considerations, and prior life experiences, as well as a wide range of emotional states embedded in them.

Career problem solving: a complex set of thought processes involving the acknowledgment of a state of career indecision, an analysis of the causes, the formulation and clarification of alternative courses of action, and the selecting of one of these alternatives to achieve a more integrated state of decidedness. A career problem is solved when a career choice is made from among viable alternatives.

Career decision making: a process that not only encompasses career choice but involves making a commitment to carrying out the actions necessary to implement the choice.

Readiness for career problem solving and decision making: The capability of an individual to make appropriate career choices, taking into account the complexity of family, social, economic, and organizational factors that influence an individual's career development.

Career development: the implementation of a series of career decisions that constitute an integrated career path throughout the lifespan.

Lifestyle: the integration of decisions in the realms of career, personal, and family relationships, spirituality, and leisure that result in a guiding purpose, meaning, and direction in one's life.

One can see from the definitions that the fundamental capability that undergirds successful career and lifestyle adjustment is the ability to acknowledge, define, solve, and act on career problems.

The Nature of Career Problems

Much of what is known about cognition in problem solving has been obtained from research on how individuals solve mathematics problems (Wickelgren, 1974), physics problems (Larkin, McDermott, Simon, & Simon, 1980), and verbal analogies (Sternberg, 1979; Sternberg & Rifkin, 1979). The cognitive processes used to solve these kinds of problems typically appear on standardized tests (Fredrickson, 1982; Sternberg, 1984). In these kinds of problems, the cue is well defined (Reitman, 1965), all required information is provided, and only one solution best satisfies the conditions given in the problem statement.

However, in contrast to structured problems, the solving of career problems is another matter. The cues signaling a career problem are often complex and ill defined, and the reactions to them emotionally laden; these cues may contain either too much or too little information to effectively solve the problem at hand. Furthermore, the options to solve the problem must be created by the problem solver, and there may be no single correct or best option. In fact, with career problems it is more useful to refer to the answer as an *optimal* solution rather than a *correct* solution, because no single alternative may meet all of the conditions in a given circumstance. Some options merely have different sets of advantages and disadvantages regarding their impact on oneself, significant others, cultural group, and society at large. Moreover, even when an individual arrives at an optimal solution based on the information at hand, there is no guarantee that the solution, whether it is a course of study, a college to attend, a job, or occupation, will ensure success and satisfaction. Finally, the solving of one career problem often raises a new set of issues related to implementing and carrying out the solution. For example, an individual who makes a decision to pursue a graduate degree must decide where to attend school, what to specialize in, how to pay for it, whether or not to relocate, whether to attend full-time or part-time, and so on. Thus one can appreciate the breadth and depth of the cognitive processing required to solve career problems and to make appropriate career decisions.

Assumptions and Propositions

Four of the key assumptions regarding the application of CIP theory to career problem solving and decision making are as follows. First, *career problem solving and decision making involve the interaction of both affective and cognitive processes.* Even though CIP emphasizes cognition, we recognize that emotions are an integral part of a complex human task such as career problem solving (Epstein, 1994; Heppner & Krauskopf, 1987; Lazarus, 1982; Saunders, Peterson, Sampson, & Reardon, 2000; Zajonc, 1980). The awareness that a problem exists may be coupled with anxiety, confusion, or depression; the analysis phase may bring curiosity or puzzlement; the development of options may be intriguing or even frightening; the evaluation of the final options may bring about ambivalence; the arrival at a first choice may result in relief; and the carrying out of a solution may be coupled with excitement and anticipation. Thus viewing career problem solving and decision making from a CIP perspective involves recognizing the full range of human emotions as they interact with, enhance, or possibly impair the respective concurrent cognitive processes.

Second, *the capability for career problem solving depends on the availability of cognitive operations as well as knowledge* (Sampson, Peterson, Reardon, & Lenz, 2000a). The essential components of cognition in career problem solving are analogous to the functions of a computer. Data files represent self and occupational knowledge stored in long-term memory (LTM); the programs are cognitive algorithms, also stored in LTM, which transform information into more useful and meaningful forms of information. Executive control operations engage and sequence appropriate lower-order programs to yield a desired outcome. Through these analogous components in humans (databases, information transformation algorithms, and executive control operations), career problems are recognized, defined, and analyzed; alternative solutions are formulated and evaluated; and solution strategies are selected, sequenced, and implemented.

Third, *career development involves continual growth and change in knowledge structures* (Peterson, 1998). Self-knowledge and occupational knowledge consist of networks of memory structures called schemata (the singular is schema) that evolve over the lifespan. Because both the occupational world and individuals are ever-changing, the need to develop and integrate these domains never ceases.

And fourth, *the goal of career counseling is the enhancement of information processing skills*. From a CIP perspective, career counseling involves providing the conditions of learning that enhance the acquisition of self and occupational knowledge, as well as the development of career problem-solving skills that transform information into satisfying and meaningful career decisions. The continued development of these capabilities is necessary for individuals to manage the inevitable occurrences of career problems that arise throughout the course of a lifetime.

Operations

Two fundamental learning processes form the building blocks of CIP are (1) the development of self-knowledge and occupational knowledge structures that form the contents undergirding career problem solving and decision making and (2) the development of information transformation skills that take one from the recognition of a career problem (a gap) to the implementation of a decision to reduce or eliminate it. From an adaptation of the works of Sternberg (1980, 1985), these capabilities may be envisioned as forming a pyramid of information processing domains with three hierarchically arranged levels of processing as displayed in Figure 8.1. Two knowledge domains—self-knowledge and occupational knowledge—lie at the base of the pyramid of information processing domains, with the decision skills placed above it and the executive processing domain at the apex. The characteristics of the pyramid domains are described next, as well as the operations (that is, learning activities) in which career clients engage to facilitate the acquisition of information processing capabilities.

Development of Self-Knowledge. Drawing comparisons between the two knowledge domains at the base can help illuminate their respective structures and functions. Schemata within the self-knowledge domain are structured in long-term memory (LTM)

FIGURE 8.1. Pyramid of Information Processing Domains

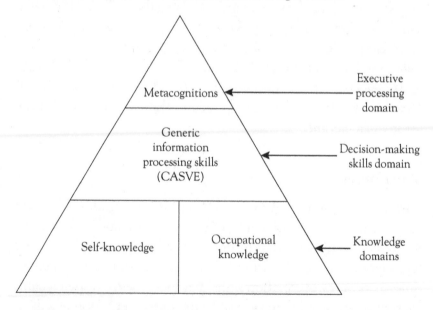

Source: From *Career Development and Services: A Cognitive Approach* by G. W. Peterson, J. P. Sampson, and R. C. Reardon. Copyright © 1991. Reprinted with permission of Brooks/Cole, an imprint of the Wadsworth Group, a division of Thomson Learning. Fax 800-730-2215.

much differently than the schemata of the occupational knowledge domain. The knowledge units of the self-knowledge domain are structured according to episodes (Tulving, 1972, 1984), whereas occupational knowledge is structured according to semantic hierarchies from concrete to ever-more-abstract concepts. The former memory store (episodic memory) consists of networks of events in a temporal-spatial continuum that are not externally verifiable, whereas the latter memory store (semantic memory) consists of schemata in the form of networks of facts, concepts, and relationships among concepts that are verifiable in external reality. The ways in which life episodes are accumulated and integrated in episodic memory constitute a higher-order abstraction—our self-concept. Episodic memory units, integrated and stored in the self-knowledge domain, make our life's experience and behavior comprehensible and predictable, whereas semantic knowledge units in the occupational knowledge domain make the occupational world comprehensible.

The acquisition of self-knowledge involves two fundamental processes: (1) the interpretation of events and (2) the reconstruction of events. Interpretation involves the matching of sensations of present events with episodes already stored in LTM; these episodes contain subjects, actions, objects, outcomes, and affective elements. A match between a present event and an episode stored in LTM strengthens the schemata associated with the present episode. Related episodes are linked across time to form aspects of our self-concept. Thus, according to schema theory (Rummelhart & Ortony, 1976), an individual who has a long history of episodes in which he sees himself as performing in a dominant manner would, as a consequence, likely see himself as possessing a personality trait of dominance. Reconstruction involves interpreting past events to fit present events in one's social context. In perceiving a present event, we draw on existing schemata in the self-knowledge domain to comprehend the situation. In the process, we may reconstruct past events in order to assimilate new data (Neisser, 1981, 1982). Thus each time a present event triggers an association to episodes in the past, we may not only reconstruct our past in a subtle way but shape our self-concept as well. Furthermore, one can see why individuals who are nurtured in consistent, caring environments in which independent thought and actions are encouraged tend to develop strong, stable self-concepts, whereas individuals, who experience capricious, abusive, neglecting, or dependent environments often develop weak, unstable self-concepts.

Development of Occupational Knowledge. The extent of differentiation and complexity of occupational knowledge has a direct bearing on one's capability for identifying appropriate choices at any given point in time (Neimeyer, 1988, 1992; Nevill, Neimeyer, Probert, & Fukuyama, 1986). Structurally, a schema in the occupational knowledge domain may be envisioned as a hierarchy of embedded knowledge (Rummelhart & Ortony, 1976) or as ideational scaffolding (Anderson, 1984; Anderson, Osborn, & Tierney, 1984) in which concepts (for example, "carpenter") are related to superordinate concepts ("construction workers") or to subordinate concepts ("uses hammer; uses saw"). The hierarchical structure of occupational knowledge schemata allows most individuals to organize knowledge about the world of work and, therefore, to think and converse effectively about occupations. When someone uses the word *carpenter* in a sentence ("My father is a carpenter"), a substructure of related concepts becomes accessible in memory without having to actually be said. The extent of these memory substructures depends on a person's degree of familiarity with the concept "carpenter." Without some mechanism for connecting concepts in an orderly and systematic manner, we would be unable to think, communicate, or problem solve. An individual's ability to derive relationships between occupational knowledge and self-knowledge precisely and accurately is related to the breadth, depth, complexity, and organization of schemata within the occupational knowledge domain.

The acquisition of occupational knowledge may be thought of as a constructive process in which an individual continually creates new knowledge units from combining existing knowledge with new information (Mahoney, 1991; Piaget, 1977; Rummelhart & Ortony,

1976). The growth and development of occupational knowledge schemata takes place through two basic processes: (1) *schema specialization* and (2) *schema generalization* (Rummelhart & Ortony, 1976). Schema specialization may be thought of as a top-down process in which an abstract concept such as "teacher" annexes more detailed and subordinate concepts through new learning. For example, an individual may acquire additional occupational knowledge about teachers through reading about and observing their work, thereby learning that teachers prepare performance objectives, assign learning tasks, provide feedback to students, and evaluate and report the results of learning. Schema generalization, however, is a bottom-up process in which concepts such as "elementary teacher," "social worker," and "counselor" are tied together through a higher-order, more abstract concept such as "nurturant occupations." These two processes provide the principal means by which counselors facilitate the acquisition of occupational knowledge.

Development of Decision-Making Skills. Information from the respective knowledge domains at the base of the pyramid is transformed in the decision skills domain from problem recognition to the implementation of a solution. These skills, referred to as generic information processing skills (Peterson & Rumsey, 1981; Peterson & Swain, 1978; Peterson & Watkins, 1979; Warren, 1976), may be configured in the form of a cycle (see Figure 8.2) and are known as the CASVE (communication, analysis, synthesis, valuing, execution) cycle (pronounced *kasah'vy*). They are called generic (Woditsh, 1977) because these are the same skills used in solving a variety of real-life problems in addition to career problems. The phases in this cycle, each involving a different set of skills and subskills, serve as a heuristic in the career decision-making process.

Career decision making involves the following process: (1) communication, (2) analysis, (3) synthesis, (4) valuing, and (5) execution.

1. *Communication.* In the communication (C) phase, information is received by the sense organs and interpreted in the cerebral

FIGURE 8.2. The Five Stages of the CASVE Cycle of Information Processing Skills Used in Career Decision Making

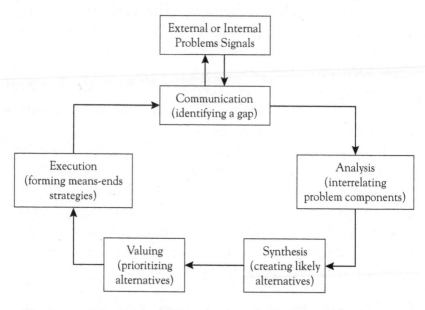

Source: From *Career Development and Services: A Cognitive Approach* by G. W. Peterson, J. P. Sampson, and R. C. Reardon. Copyright © 1991. Reprinted with permission of Brooks/Cole, an imprint of the Wadsworth Group, a division of Thomson Learning. Fax 800-730-2215.

cortex. A problem exists when the brain signals a gap between an existing state and a desired state. The signal may stem from external demands (for example, the need to choose a college major, to secure employment, or to react to input from significant others) or from internal states such as anxiety, depression, confusion, avoidant behavior, or physiological stress reactions. One then queries oneself and the environment to identify the gap between the existing state of indecision and a more desired state of decidedness; such queries serve to frame the problem (Cochran, 1994).

This encoding of internal and external signals and sending out inquiries is the process of communication. This phase involves becoming fully "in touch" with all facets of the problem space (Newell & Simon, 1972; Peterson, 1998; Sinnott, 1989), including information signals from oneself and one's environment. Full identification and description of the gap creates a tension (referred to as cognitive dissonance) that provides a motivational resource for seeking a resolution to the career problem (Festinger, 1964). The two important communication questions for clients at this phase are, "What am I thinking and feeling about my career choice at this moment?" and "What do I hope to attain as a result of career counseling?"

2. *Analysis.* In the analysis (A) phase, causes of the problem are identified and relationships among problem components are placed in a conceptual framework. In this phase, effective problem solvers step back and engage in reflection to understand the dimensions of the problem and its causes. In the pursuit of this understanding, individuals develop a mental model or representation (Cochran, 1994) of the problem and its ostensible causes. Intervening or contributing issues, such as the quality of interpersonal relationships, dual-career coordination, disability accommodation, or the status of the respective components of the pyramid of information processing domains that bear on the career issue are also identified. The analysis question for clients is, "What are the reasons for the gap between my present state of indecision and a more desired state of decidedness?"

3. *Synthesis.* In the synthesis (S) phase, possible courses of action are formulated through two processes: (1) *elaboration* and (2) *crystallization*. Elaboration involves the creative generation of a wide range of possible solutions, even unlikely ones, through techniques such as brainstorming, creating analogies or metaphors, and engaging in mental relaxation to free the mind of reality constraints (Bransford & Stein, 1984). Crystallization is the narrowing of potential options to a manageable set of viable alternatives through the application of relevant personal or provided constructs (Crites, 1969; Neimeyer, 1992). The synthesis question is, "What

are the possible courses of action I could take to reduce or eliminate the gap?"

4. *Valuing.* In valuing (V), each viable course of action is evaluated and prioritized according to one's value system (Super, 1980) to estimate its likelihood of removing the gap and its probable costs and benefits for oneself, significant others, cultural group, and society. In the valuing phase, the use of personal constructs (Kelley, 1955) relevant to the individual becomes vitally important in determining a first choice (Parr & Neimeyer, 1994). The outcome of this phase is not only the designation of a tentative first choice (Gelatt, 1989) but a vision of the future and an internally directed commitment to act on the choice (Cochran, 1994). The valuing question for clients is, "Which alternative is the best course of action for me, and in some cases, my significant others, my cultural group, community, or society?"

5. *Execution.* In the execution (E) phase, a plan or a strategy for implementing the first choice is formulated through a means-ends analysis (Kaufman, 1972; Anderson, 1994). The plan is developed with intermediate steps, milestones, and subgoals to reach a career goal such as to complete a degree, obtain a first job, or pass a proficiency test. Sometimes reality testing (Super, 1957) is called for to try out and experience the first choice directly. We know a decision has been made when a client acts on the plan. The execution question is, "How can I transform my first choice into an action plan and set the plan into motion?"

Upon executing the plan, there is a return to the communication (C) phase to evaluate whether the decision successfully removed the gap. If so, the individual moves on to solve succeeding problems that arise from the implementation of the solution. If not, one recycles through the CASVE cycle with new information about the problem, oneself, and one's options, acquired from the initial pass through the CASVE cycle. This last phase entails reflecting on and reviewing the problem-solving process itself to enhance transfer to the solving of subsequent career problems or even generalization to other real-life problems.

The Executive Processing Domain

There is yet a set of higher-order cognitive functions that is required to monitor, guide, and regulate lower-order functions of the pyramid, namely, the acquisition, storage, and retrieval of information, as well as to execute cognitive strategies to solve a problem (Belmont & Butterfield, 1977). We refer to this domain of regulatory and integrative processes as the executive processing domain. The skills of this domain are referred to as metacognitions (Flavell, 1979; Meichenbaum, 1977). The principal metacognitions comprising the domain include (1) self-talk, (2) self-awareness, and (3) monitoring and controlling.

Self-Talk. To become independent and responsible problem solvers, individuals must also become their own best friends as problem solvers. Individuals who use and believe in positive self-talk such as, "I can learn to be a good career problem solver" or "I know I can trust that my career decision will be the right one for me," will approach the task of career problem solving and decision making much differently than individuals who uses negative self-talk such as, "I've tried to find a good occupation many times before, but I can't ever arrive at good decisions," or "People, like counselors or teachers, are better suited to solve my career problems than me." Negative self-talk is often associated with chronic indecisiveness (Hartman, Fuqua, & Blum, 1985), whereas positive self-talk not only creates positive expectations (Bandura, 1977, 1982) but reinforces effective problem-solving behavior as well.

Self-Awareness. One of the characteristics of competent performance is the capability of maintaining an awareness of oneself as a performer of the task (Brown, 1981; Kahnaman, 1973; Peterson & Swain, 1978). Self-awareness enables a problem solver to recognize such executive processes as the existence of debilitating negative self-talk, the need for more self or occupational information, one's place in the problem-solving process, or the concurrent affective states that accelerate, retard, or confound the process (Piaget, 1973; Zajonc, 1980). The capacity for self-awareness keeps problem solvers centered on the task at hand and provides a buffer against extraneous influences that may interrupt or alter the process.

Monitor and Control. The regulation, coordination, and integration of lower-order processing are additional vital functions of the executive processing domain (Atkinson & Shiffrin, 1968; Shiffrin & Schneider, 1977). Through monitoring, good problem solvers sense when a sufficient amount of information has been acquired in each phase in the cycle so as to move on to the next phase. The control function then moves one forward to the next phase when a phase is sufficiently completed or back to a preceding phase for more thorough consideration when necessary (Bransford & Stein, 1984; Peterson et al., 1991). Thus monitoring and controlling serve as "quality control" mechanisms to ensure a complete, orderly, and timely progression through the CASVE cycle.

Cultural Considerations in the Use of CIP

Although we tend to think of CIP as a culture-free paradigm, in practice, we have become aware of important differences in how clients from various ethnic and racial backgrounds engage the respective domains of the pyramid and the phases of the CASVE cycle in career problem solving and decision making. Unfortunately, because of space limitations, we cannot explore this topic as fully as we would like. Nevertheless, to gain a sense of how human diversity is managed in the CIP framework, examples of cultural considerations are presented next, according to the domains of the pyramid.

The Acquisition of Self-Knowledge. The principal concern in the development and refinement of self-knowledge structures lies in the use of normed tests and inventories in the assessment of personality constructs and abilities. Scores from such instruments are often used in career counseling to examine existing self-perceptions of important personality dimensions critically involved in the formulation and identification of potential career opportunities. However, the validity of such measures may be called into question when the life's experiences that shape the development of self-knowledge schemata, the semantic interpretation of words contained in the measures or the opportunity to master certain cognitive skills differ appreciably from the dominant culture. Thus counselors may wish to emphasize the use of reality testing to explore interests and abilities when the language and culture of clients differ appreciably from population samples used to norm the instruments.

The Acquisition of Occupational Knowledge. Cultural and intergenerational issues in the acquisition of occupational knowledge relate to (1) the breadth of experience and opportunity to learn about the complexities of the world of work and the possibilities it holds, (2) the meanings and attitudes attached to the knowledge acquired, and (3) the processes through which occupational knowledge is assimilated and stored. If individuals are exposed early in life to restricted environments in which family members and adult role models perform work, it is likely their first-hand knowledge of the world of work may also be narrow. In CIP terms, the occupational knowledge schemata may lack differentiation and complexity (Neimeyer, 1988). Furthermore, if occupational knowledge is assimilated and associated with negative or demeaning attitudes and stereotypical thinking, the world of work will not be seen as a place where one's creative potential can be actualized but as a threatening, oppressive place with little reward, financially or socially. Finally, members of certain cultural groups may acquire occupational knowledge more effectively through a social construction process rather than through an individual construction process (Lyddon, 1995). Thus learning about occupations within closely connected family and community groups may be more meaningful and relevant than in learning individually from print or other media typically available in career centers (Fouad & Arbona, 1994).

The Acquisition of Career Decision-Making Skills. Important cultural issues are present in each phase of the CASVE cycle. In the communication phase, members of minority groups must become aware of and explore the wide range of affective components in the problem space that result from perceived institutional and cultural bias, racism, and oppression in education and the workplace. At the analysis phase, members of minority groups may externalize the career problem: "I'm undecided and don't know what to do, but because of society's racism and oppression, it really doesn't matter what I do." In synthesis, members of cultural or ethnic groups may be drawn either to occupations with which they are familiar or to "glamour occupations" in which there may be limited chances for success. In the valuing process, a prominent consideration involves the relative balance in importance between one's own beliefs and the influence of significant others or the cultural group in making a career choice (Fouad & Arbona, 1994). Finally, at the execution phase, a common issue is the confronting and overcoming of resistances and constraints of cultural or racial bias and prejudice in the workplace as one reality-tests an occupational choice. At each phase in the CASVE cycle, cultural issues, if they are present, must be identified and resolved for effective career problem solving and decision making to take place.

The Executive Processing Domain. Cultural issues in this domain involve the nature of metacognitions, especially self-talk, that are instrumental in regulating lower-order cognitive processes in the pyramid. Ultimately, self-defeating or negative self-talk severely limits or distorts the formulation and consideration of career options and opportunities, which may, in turn, lead to inappropriate actions or inaction. Such phrases as, "I can't because I'm. . . . " or "Yes, but members of my group. . . . " alert a counselor to dysfunction in the executive processing domain. Members of disadvantaged groups need to be cognizant of any self-imposed metacognitive constraints that inhibit progress through the phases of the CASVE cycle. Cognitive restructuring, as well as systemic interventions such as advocacy, networking with active minority support organizations, and securing legal advice, may help empower individuals to develop and apply newly acquired positive self-statements and feelings of self-confidence in career problem solving and decision making.

We now move toward the application and practice of CIP in career counseling. Clients come for career counseling in different states of preparedness for problem solving and decision making (Voight & Peterson, 2000). Some are in a high state of preparedness and require little assistance to solve a career problem, whereas others are in a highly confused and anxious state and require considerable assistance from a skillful career counselor. A model of readiness for career counseling is presented next that enables career counselors to assess a client's needs for kinds of assistance to successfully engage and complete the career problem-solving and decision-making process.

Applications to Practice

This section begins by describing the use of a two-dimensional model for assessing clients' readiness to engage in career problem solving and decision making. The Career Thoughts Inventory, an instrument based on CIP theory, is discussed as a tool for readiness assessment. The CIP model for readiness assessment is then related to determining levels of service and the selection of career interventions. Finally, the CIP seven-step service delivery sequence is presented.

A Two-Dimensional Model of Readiness for Career Problem Solving and Decision Making

At the communication phase of the CASVE cycle, when individuals become aware of a career problem and seek assistance, they vary in terms of a state of readiness to solve problems and make decisions. *Readiness* is defined as "the *capability* of an individual to make appropriate career choices taking into account the *complexity* of family, social, economic, and organizational factors that influence an individual's career development" (Sampson, Peterson, Reardon, & Lenz, 2000a, p. 156). *Capability* is concerned with internal factors, whereas *complexity* is concerned with external factors that influence career problem solving and decision making.

The Capability Dimension. *Capability* is defined as "the cognitive and affective capacity of an individual to engage in effective career problem solving and decision making" (Sampson et al., 2000a, p. 157). Persons in a high state of readiness have the cognitive capacity and positive affective states required to effectively engage the problem-solving task, whereas persons in a lower state of readiness may be inhibited by dysfunctional thoughts and negative emotions, making them less ready. The capability of persons to successfully engage in career problem solving and career decision making is influenced by their

- Willingness to honestly explore knowledge of self (for example, values, interests, and skills) that leads to a clearer sense of identity (self-knowledge domain)
- Motivation to learn about the world of work (occupational knowledge domain)
- Willingness to learn about and engage in career problem solving and decision making, including the capacity for thinking clearly about a career problem, confidence in the ability to make decisions, the commitment to follow through with a plan of action, and the acceptance of personal responsibility for decision making (decision-making skills domain)
- Awareness of how negative thoughts and feelings can limit the ability to solve problems and make decisions, the willingness to seek assistance with career choice when needed, and the capacity to monitor and regulate lower-order problem-solving and decision-making processes (executive processing domain).

The Complexity Dimension. Complexity alludes to the extent of issues interrelated with the career problem within the problem space and is defined as "contextual factors, originating in the family, society, employing organizations, or the economy, that make it more or less difficult to process information necessary to solve career problems and make career decisions" (Sampson et al., 2000a, p. 158). Persons having a higher state of readiness have fewer family, social, economic, and organizational factors to deal with in career choice. Persons having a lower state of readiness may be coping with one seriously debilitating factor, such as blatant discrimination, or they may be coping with a series of contextual factors that, taken as a group, make career choice more difficult, such as being a single parent who is working for an employer who is downsizing during a recession. Furthermore, the emotional states that can result from experiencing these factors, such as anxiety, depression, and anger, can make it difficult or impossible to process the information necessary for effective career problem solving (Hill & Peterson, 2001; Saunders, Peterson, Sampson, & Reardon, 2000). Because of the complexity of issues in the problem space and the capability to manage them, not all clients are prepared to immediately engage the career problem-solving process. Some clients may require intensive personal assistance from a counselor to manage factors in the problem space that impede learning *before* they are able to progress effectively through the CASVE cycle. However, other clients categorized as possessing low readiness may, due to extenuating life circumstances (for example, the need for employment to meet basic life needs), proceed with career problem solving while receiving ongoing support for other personal issues. Thus the assessment of readiness for career problem solving is a key feature in the use of CIP in career counseling.

The assessment of readiness may be accomplished through the integration of information gathered from self-report measures and interviews. A useful readiness measure, based on CIP theory, is the Career Thoughts Inventory (CTI; Sampson et al., 1996a). The CTI is a forty-eight-item self-report instrument that assesses the level of a client's dysfunctional thinking through three principal construct scales: Decision Making Confusion (DMC), Commitment Anxiety (CA), and External Conflict (EC). Scale scores enable career counselors to identify specific blocks that impede the processing of information within the domains of the pyramid and the respective phases of the CASVE cycle. The DMC scale reveals dysfunction in the communication, analysis, and synthesis phases, which entail the derivation of career alternatives; the CA scale alludes to the transition from arriving at a solution to the career problem in the valuing phase to a commitment to action in the execution phase; and the EC scale addresses the valuing phase in which clients weigh the importance of their views in relation to the views of significant others.

On the basis of CTI scores and interview data, a client is assigned to one of three levels of readiness: high, moderate, or low (Sampson et al., 2000). Individuals with elevated scores on most CTI dimensions, suggesting both high complexity and low capability, would be seen as possessing a low state of readiness. Individuals with CTI scores in the average range, suggesting moderate complexity and capability, would be considered in a moderate state of readiness. Individuals with low CTI scores and high levels of capability would be viewed as having a high state of readiness for career problem solving and decision making.

Making Decisions About Career Interventions

From a CIP perspective, the cost-effectiveness of career services depends on the level of practitioner support meeting, but not exceeding, the needs of the person being served. Therefore, persons collaboratively judged by the counselor and the client to have *high* career decision-making readiness may be most cost-effectively served by self-help services. Persons initially assessed to have *moderate* career decision-making readiness may be most cost-effectively served by brief staff-assisted services; individuals with *low* readiness may best be served by individual case-managed services. Figure 8.3 shows the relationship between CIP readiness constructs (capability and complexity) and levels of career service delivery (self-help, brief staff-assisted, and individual case-managed).

FIGURE 8.3. Two-Dimensional Model of Readiness for Career Decision Making

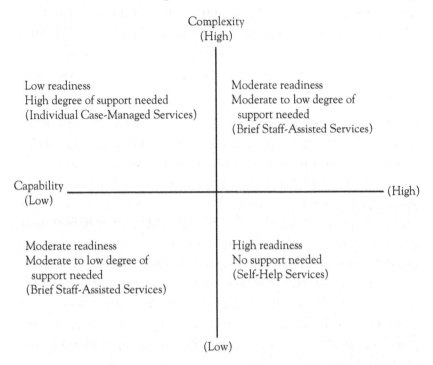

Complexity
(High)

Low readiness
High degree of support needed
(Individual Case-Managed Services)

Moderate readiness
Moderate to low degree of
    support needed
(Brief Staff-Assisted Services)

Capability _____ (High)
(Low)

Moderate readiness
Moderate to low degree of
    support needed
(Brief Staff-Assisted Services)

High readiness
No support needed
(Self-Help Services)

(Low)

Source: Reprinted from *The Career Development Quarterly, 49,* 2000, p. 161. Copyright © National Career Development Association. Reprinted with permission from NCDA.

Self-Help Services. Self-help career services involve the self-guided use of career resources in a librarylike or Internet-based remote setting, where the resources have been designed for autonomous use by individuals with a *high* readiness for career choice. The successful use of self-help interventions depends on the provision of an effective safety net that identifies persons who are not making good use of self-help career resources and then providing a higher, more appropriate level of service such as brief, periodic checks with users to ask, "Are you finding the information you need?" (Sampson, 1999a; 1999b; Sampson & Reardon, 1998). In self-help services, individuals with high readiness for career choice are provided minimal or no assistance from staff. Guiding and monitoring the selection, location, sequencing, and use of resources is the responsibility of the individual, with support provided within the nature of the resources being used. Resource guides that recommend specific assessments, information sources, and instruction for common career concerns can be used to help individuals locate and use the resources they need.

Brief Staff-Assisted Services. Brief staff-assisted career services involve the practitioner-guided use of resources in a librarylike classroom or group setting for clients with *moderate* readiness for career choice. In brief staff-assisted career services, persons with moderate readiness for career choice are provided minimal assistance from staff. Practitioners are responsible for collaboratively guiding and monitoring the selection, location, sequencing, and use of resources with the client. An individual learning plan is used to document the goals, resources selected, and potential outcomes for the client. Examples of brief staff-assisted career services include (1) self-directed career decision making, (2) career courses with large group interaction, (3) short-term group counseling, and (4) workshops.

Individual Case-Managed Services. Individual case-managed career services involve the practitioner-guided use of career resources in an individual office, classroom, or group setting for clients with *low* readiness for career choice. In individual case-managed services, low-readiness individuals are provided substantial assistance from practitioners. Similar to brief staff-assisted services, practitioners are responsible for collaboratively guiding and monitoring the selection, location, sequencing, and use of resources as stated on the individual learning plan. Examples of individual case-managed services include (1) individual counseling, (2) career courses with small group interaction, and (3) long-term group counseling. The variation among self-help, brief staff-assisted, and individual case-managed services is further described in Sampson, Peterson, Reardon, and Lenz (2000a).

Seven-Step Service Delivery Sequence

The CIP approach can be delivered in self-help, brief staff-assisted, and individual case-managed interventions through a seven-step sequence (see Figure 8.4). This sequence is meant to serve as heuristic for progressing systematically through the CASVE cycle.

Step 1: Initial Interview. In this step, a practitioner with appropriate training and experience gains qualitative information about the context and nature of the career problem and the problem space.

FIGURE 8.4. Seven-Step Service Delivery Sequence

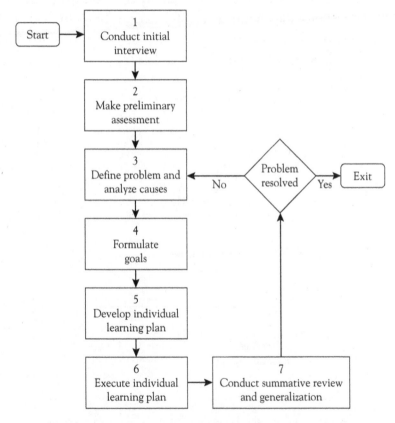

Source: From *Career Development and Services: A Cognitive Approach* by G. W. Peterson, J. P. Sampson, and R. C. Reardon. Copyright © 1991. Reprinted with permission of Brooks/Cole, an imprint of the Wadsworth Group, a division of Thomson Learning. Fax 800-730-2215.

Beginning in the initial interview and continuing through the seven steps, the counselor (1) attends to both the emotional and cognitive components of the client's problem; (2) develops a relationship with the client using appropriate communication and counseling skills such as empathy, clarification, summarization, and open-ended questions; (3) uses appropriate self-disclosure to enhance the counseling relationship and to model risk taking and insight; and (4) uses immediacy to enhance the counseling relationship and identify any problems that need attention. During the initial interview, client versions of the pyramid and the CASVE cycle (shown in Figures 8.5 and 8.6) are used to (1) clarify client needs, (2) provide a schema for problem solving and decision making, and (3) provide clients with information they can read after their session, which reinforces concepts discussed in counseling (Sampson, Peterson, Lenz, & Reardon, 1992).

FIGURE 8.5. What's Involved in Career Choice?

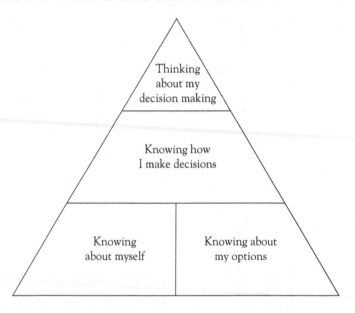

Source: Reprinted from *The Career Development Quarterly, 41,* 1992, p. 70. Copyright © National Career Development Association. Reprinted with permission from NCDA.

Step 2: Preliminary Assessment. Preliminary assessment entails determining an individual's readiness for career problem solving and decision making (Crites, 1974; Fredrickson, 1982; Super, 1983). The CTI (Sampson et al., 1996a) described earlier is one of several readiness screening measures that can be used at this point in service delivery. The CTI includes items relating to self-knowledge, occupational knowledge, the CASVE cycle, and executive processing (Peterson et al., 1991; Peterson, Sampson, Reardon, & Lenz, 1996). When discussing CTI results with the client, the terms *negative career thinking* or *negative career thoughts* are used in place of *dysfunctional career thinking* or *dysfunctional career thoughts* to avoid inappropriately labeling the client. Based on information gained from the initial interview and any readiness assessment measure, the outcome of the preliminary assessment process is a determination of the client's level of readiness for career counseling and decision making—low, moderate, or high.

FIGURE 8.6. Guide to Good Decision Making: The CASVE Cycle (Client Version)

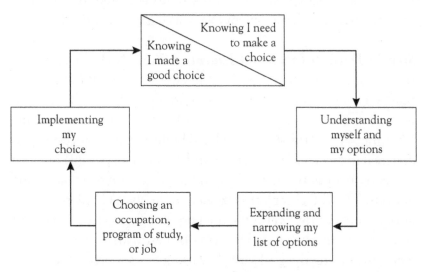

Source: From *The Career Development Quarterly, 41,* 1992, p. 70. Copyright © National Career Development Association. Reprinted with permission from NCDA.

Step 3: Define Problem and Analyze Causes. The counselor and client come to a preliminary understanding of the problem (Krumboltz & Baker, 1973; Yost & Corbishley, 1987), defined in terms of a gap between an existing state of career indecision and a desired state of career decidedness (Cochran, 1994). The counselor provides a summary statement that describes the nature of the gap and potential causes for the gap, followed by client input regarding the accuracy of the statement.

Step 4: Formulate Goals. The counselor and client collaboratively develop a set of attainable goals (Blustein, 1992; Brown & Brooks, 1991; Crites, 1981; Yost & Corbishley, 1987) to remove the gap. Goals, stated in behavioral terms, are written on an Individual Learning Plan (ILP), which is described more fully in the following section. The counselor's willingness to collaborate with the client in setting goals provides an important message that the client is in control of the process and is capable of contributing positively to the counseling process. The agreement on a set of concrete goals also sets forth a set of expectations for both the client and the counselor and enhances the development of a working therapeutic alliance.

Step 5: Develop Individual Learning Plan (ILP). The practitioner collaborates with the client in developing an ILP that identifies a sequence of resources and activities to help the client attain his or her goals for career problem solving and decision making. Creating the ILP involves a modified brainstorming process that is designed to first maximize a creative elaboration of possible resource and activity options, then select and sequence the most promising options. The ILP completion sequence involves (1) identifying a resource or activity, (2) noting the purpose of using the resource or completing the activity, (3) noting the estimated time commitment, (4) noting the goal served by using the resource or completing the activity, and (5) selecting a priority sequence for using all resources and completing all activities.

ILPs can be effective tools for planning the completion of a potentially complex series of service delivery activities and resources. Taking the time to explain the resources, activities, and corresponding purposes communicates to clients that they are valued, capable collaborators in the career-intervention process. (Sample ILPs are provided in Tables 8.1 and 8.2 that follow the cases of K and E.)

Step 6: Execute Individual Learning Plan. The client carries out the ILP with the practitioner providing encouragement, information, clarification, reinforcement, and planning for future experiences. During this step, the client versions of the pyramid and the CASVE cycle (shown in Figures 8.5 and 8.6) and the ILP are used to monitor progress in problem solving and decision making (Sampson, Peterson, Lenz, & Reardon, 1992). In cases where dysfunctional career thinking has been identified as limiting career problem solving and decision making, clients can use the *Career Thoughts Inventory Workbook* (Sampson et al., 1996b), which describes a four-step procedure for cognitive restructuring: identifying, challenging, and altering any dysfunctional career thoughts and then taking concrete action to make career decisions.

Step 7: Summative Review and Generalization. When the client has completed the ILP, the client discusses with the counselor his or her progress toward reaching the counseling goals established in Step 4. During summative review and generalization, the client versions of the pyramid and the CASVE cycle (shown in Figures 8.5 and 8.6) are used to (1) review and reflect on the progress in resolving the gap that motivated the client to seek counseling, (2) review follow-through actions in the execution phase of the CASVE cycle, and (3) generalize problem-solving knowledge and skills learned in counseling to other future career problems or to current and future personal and family problems (Sampson, Peterson, Lenz, & Reardon, 1992).

Present Status and Future Directions of the CIP Approach

The CIP approach has been operationalized in a variety of strategies and resources for service delivery and has been applied to varied settings and in several case studies. Strategies for service delivery using the CIP approach include

Readiness assessment (Sampson, Peterson, Reardon, & Lenz, 2000a, 2000b)

Intervention planning (Peterson, Sampson, & Reardon, 1991; Peterson, Sampson, Reardon, & Lenz, 1996; Sampson, Peterson, Reardon, & Lenz, 2000a)

Career assessment (Peterson, Sampson, & Reardon, 1991; Peterson, 1998; Reardon, Sampson, & Lenz, 2000)

Counseling (Peterson, Lumsden, Sampson, Reardon, & Lenz, in press; Peterson, Sampson, & Reardon, 1991; Peterson, Sampson, Reardon, & Lenz, 1996; Reardon & Lenz, 1998)

Information use (Peterson, Sampson, & Reardon, 1991)

Computer-assisted career guidance (Sampson, Peterson, & Reardon, 1989)

Employment problem solving and decision making (Sampson, Lenz, Reardon, & Peterson, 1999)

Career resource room design (Peterson, Sampson, & Reardon, 1991; Sampson, 1999b)

Staff training (Lenz, 2000; Saunders, Reardon, & Lenz, 1999)

Program development and evaluation (Lenz, Reardon, Peterson, & Sampson, in press; Peterson, Sampson, Lenz, & Reardon, 1999; Peterson, Sampson, & Reardon, 1991; Vernick, Garis, & Reardon, 2000)

International collaboration in theory application (Sampson, Watts, Palmer, & Hughes, 2000).

Resources to apply CIP theory to practice include

A readiness assessment instrument, the CTI (Sampson, Peterson, Lenz, Reardon, & Saunders, 1996a, 1998)

A workbook for cognitive restructuring of negative career thoughts (CTI Workbook; Sampson et al., 1996b)

A career assessment card sort (Peterson, 1998)

Instruction for credit courses (Reardon, Lenz, Sampson, & Peterson, 2000a, 2000b)

Counseling handouts and exercises (Sampson, Peterson, Lenz, & Reardon, 1992)

Settings in which the CIP approach has been applied include

Higher education (Reardon & Wright, 1999)

Community services (Lenz, 1998)

One-stop career centers (Sampson & Reardon, 1998)

Middle schools and secondary schools (Peterson, Sampson, & Reardon, 1991; Peterson, Long, & Billups, 1998)

Correctional institutions (Railey & Peterson, 2000)

Case studies are also available that describe how the CIP approach is used in practice (Peterson, Sampson, & Reardon, 1991; Peterson, Sampson, Reardon, & Lenz, 1996; Sampson, Peterson, Lenz, Reardon, & Saunders, 1996c; Reardon & Wright, 1999; Watson & Lenz, in press). A comprehensive listing of research studies involving the CTI was compiled by Vernick (2001). These studies have examined CTI constructs in relation to a variety of variables, including depression, anxiety, anger, neuroticism, and decision-making confidence. Updated information, including bibliographies on the CIP approach (Reardon, 1998; Sampson, Peterson, Reardon, & Lenz, 2001a), research studies, and current CIP strategies, resources, and settings (Sampson, Peterson, Reardon, & Lenz, 2001b) may be found at http://www.career.fsu.edu/techcenter/designing_career_services/index.html.

Future directions for the continued development and applications of CIP include investigating how occupational knowledge, self-knowledge, and career problem-solving and decision-making skills can be acquired in a variety of learning contexts (for example, one-on-one, classroom, media, or on-line); investigating cross-cultural factors in the acquisition of career problem-solving and decision-making skills; and investigating processes of transfer and generalization of career problem-solving skills to other contexts, future career decisions, or to other kinds of human problems.

Case Studies

The sections that follow describe two case studies using essential elements of the CIP approach, including readiness assessment and the seven-step service delivery sequence. Selected data from each client's case notes have been integrated into the case application; additional information from a hypothetical CTI has been added to each case.

The Case of K

Initial Interview. K was seen at a college career center during his visit to campus as part of the spring-semester new-student orientation. His parents had accompanied him but attended a special parents' session on campus while he met with Eva Jackson, one of the center's career advisers. K brought with him the results of various academic and career assessments that he had completed while in high school. As part of his opening comments, K stated: "I'm not sure why I'm here, but it seems like it might be a good idea since I need to figure out what classes I'm going to take and I haven't selected a major yet." K's internal cues suggested that he was feeling fairly anxious about starting college when his career plans were so unclear. He said, "I'm worried about wasting time and money, and I'm afraid I might drop out or fail if I don't have a goal to keep me motivated." He seems to feel some pressure to complete college, as indicated by his comment that "he will be sorry later in his life if he does not go at this time."

Preliminary Assessment. Given the lack of specificity in K's opening remarks and her concern regarding K's readiness to engage in the career counseling process, Eva asked K to complete the CTI as part of the preliminary assessment process. K's hypothetical CTI results were used to assess his level of readiness and to develop a plan for providing him with assistance. K's CTI results would likely indicate elevated scores on the DMC and CA scales because he has not faced major decisions in his past and has tended to go with the flow, leaning heavily on the advice of others. In addition, K had done limited exploration of the options he is presently considering. From a "capability" perspective, K's general confusion and anxiety over committing to a choice may make it hard for him to progress through the problem-solving and decision-making process. In his conversation with Eva, he had a tendency to move from one topic to the next very quickly without any closure to the issue he raised, suggesting that he may need more intensive one-on-one help to keep him focused and ensure that he effectively engages each aspect of the pyramid and the CASVE cycle. Eva noted to herself the need to attend carefully to K's decision-making style, recognizing that K may have some difficulty with a linear approach to decision making, given the presence of Artistic personality characteristics, as indicated by his SDS results.

With regard to "complexity," K appears to have some factors in his life situation that have the potential to negatively affect his ability to engage the career decision-making process. One key issue may have to do with the influences of family and culture. Although K stated that his parents are leaving his occupational choice "strictly up to him," there is some indication of their influence on his choices, as indicated by their interest in K attending college. It may be important to explore how the work histories of his parents have influenced his career thinking to this point. Eva may also want to discuss with K any cultural traditions in his family that may have affected his thinking about career choices.

K's father works in what can be considered a high-prestige, high-achievement occupation. As the firstborn male child in a Japanese-Chinese-American family, K may feel some pressure to follow in this tradition, especially given his strong math skills. K's "free spirit" lifestyle seems somewhat contradictory to his high values of financial prosperity and achievement. K stated that he values the fact that his parents have not put a lot of pressure on him and have let him "do his own thing" but feels some desire to have them be proud about what he ends up doing. He noted that he doesn't get much encouragement from them when he jokes about becoming a professional skateboarder!

In examining K's SDS results, Eva began by asking him to further discuss each of his daydreams, including how each option listed fit with his skills, interests, and values. With respect to the self-knowledge area of the pyramid, Eva wanted to see how K views each of these options in relation to his self-concept. Eva explored his ideas about working with computers and his interest in learning more about this field. K stated that he really had not looked very closely at the SDS Occupations Finder. Eva noted the closeness of K's summary scores and pointed out that there are several code combinations he could use in looking at options. Eva helped K further define his daydreams using the SDS Occupations Finder and the *Dictionary of Holland Occupational Codes* (DHOC; Gottfredson & Holland, 1996) and showed him how the daydream codes could be used to generate a Daydreams Summary Code (Reardon & Lenz, 1998).

In both the SDS daydreams and the VI, K seemed to place a great deal of emphasis on making money. Eva discussed with him his concept of "a lot of money" and what amount that actually represents for him. A key aspect of reviewing K's SDS results would be to look at his items on the individual scales (Reardon & Lenz, 1998). It would be important to know which scales contributed to his top three high point codes and how the high point scores on the scales that deal with interests (Activities and Occupations) differ from the high point scores on the scales that deal with abilities (Competencies and Self-Estimates). Given the likelihood that K has experienced some negative thinking relative to his career plans, Eva discussed with him how his career thoughts may have influenced his responses on the SDS. Having K talk through his responses on individual scales provided a window into how his thinking affected his view of himself and his options, as reflected in his SDS results. It would be useful to compare K's educational self-efficacy ratings with his ratings on the SDS Self-Estimates section to look for any patterns. Using the client version of the pyramid, Eva helped K see how this information related to the self and occupational knowledge domains. It is likely that K's score on the Conventional scale has been heavily influenced by his work history, which has included a number of C-type jobs. A comparison of K's high point code on the Occupations scale in relation to the high point code for his daydreams summary could yield some valuable information.

No data were provided on K's SDS Enterprising scores. This would be important to know, given K's interest in making money and the fact that several of his occupational daydreams include or could potentially include an E. For instance, K's interest in "something with computers and a lot of money" could include the following options: computer systems hardware engineer (RIE), scientific programmer (IRE), and Internet consultant (IER). Looking at the SDS total scores provides only a partial window into a person's personality types and how that has been influenced by his or her life experience to date.

Define Problem and Analyze Causes. From a CIP perspective, K's "gap" could be described as a need to determine his course of study in college and to clarify his occupational goals. He thought the assessment activities he had completed earlier accurately reflect him (Self-Knowledge), but he was not sure how to relate the information to a specific course of study and was reluctant to choose an occupation because he knows very little about what's out there. He acknowledged that after completing the assessment activities he had not done much with them but had simply stuck them in a drawer. He said he likes to daydream about what he might do in the future but hasn't done anything specific to further research those options or determine which one might be his first choice (Occupational Knowledge). K said he has a tendency to put off decisions until it gets to "crunch time." In addition, K acknowledged that there might be occupations he knows very little about or doesn't even know exist (Synthesis). K said he felt like he had some time to explore options before committing to a choice. This is consistent with the philosophy of the college where he was enrolling, which recommends a plan of general studies for the first two years. K's reflections on his thoughts about his career choices, as well as his comments during the counseling sessions, pointed to the difficulties he was having in understanding how to go about making a career decision and the anxiety he was feeling over committing to a choice.

Formulate Goals. Eva talked with K about what he hoped would happen as a result of his visit to the career center. Given K's tendency to go with the flow sometimes or be influenced by others, Eva encouraged him to set some specific goals for his career counseling experience. She introduced the idea of an individual learning plan (ILP) as a means for keeping track of this information. K appreciated the fact that she was not "telling him what he needed to do" but was letting him take the lead on what happened next. This also played into K's value of independence, being able to "do things your own way." K said that one goal he had was to identify some majors at the college that relate to his interests and learn more about the coursework required (see Table 8.1). Another goal was to "learn more about occupations that I'm considering." K said, "I don't feel

TABLE 8.1. K's Individual Learning Plan

Goal(s): #1 _Identify majors related to my interests_

#2 _Learn more about occupations I'm considering_

#3 _Have a clearer idea about occupations that might fit me_

Activity	Purpose/Outcome	Estimated Time Commitment	Goal #	Priority
Review SDS Occupations Finder	to identify other occupations I might want to consider	20 min	2,3	1
Use Internet-based computer system	learn more about options in the computer & architecture fields	1 - 2 hrs.	2	2
Complete sections of the Guide to Good Dec-Making exercise	to organize info about myself & my options; help me evaluate & prioritize options	ongoing	1,3	6
Visit Internet sites related to prof. skateboarding, incl. chatrooms	learn more about work options I'm considering; conduct info interview	1 hr.	2	4
Meet w/ advisors in selected departments	learn more about specific majors + course requirements	30 min. 1 hr.	1	3
Read CTI workbook sections	see how my thinking influences my career decision making	1 - 3 hrs.	3	5
Get experience in my career interest areas by exploring internship options	help me confirm & try out my tentative choices	30 min - 1 hr.	2	7
Follow-up 4 Career Advisor	to review above activities & determine next steps	1 hr.	1,3	8

This plan can be modified by either party based upon new information learned in the activities of the action plan. The purpose of the plan is to work toward a mutually agreed upon career goal. Activities may be added or subtracted as needed.

_K_	5/25/01	_Eva Jackson_	5/25/01
Student/Client/Customer	Date	Staff Member	Date

like I have to know my ultimate goal at this point but I would like to have a clearer idea about several occupations that might fit me." Eva wrote these on the ILP and asked K to verify that he was comfortable with the plan so far. Eva also revisited K's CTI results and suggested that his responses may help explain why he has difficulty with career decisions. He agreed that his thoughts and feelings caused him to avoid dealing with making future plans and was willing to work on these during his appointments with Eva. He said he felt like that was a good place to start and acknowledged that this was a process that would take some time.

Develop ILP. Eva, recognizing that K often seems influenced by others, encouraged him to share ideas about what he would like to do next. He acknowledged that he needed to know more about some of the options (Occupational Knowledge) he was considering. He said that he really didn't have much confidence in how he makes decisions, acknowledging that in the past his process for making decisions has been pretty haphazard and that the decision about his field of study and future occupation probably required more thought. Eva and K brainstormed a series of activities for his ILP that would help him use his current self-knowledge (Analysis), relate this knowledge to options, expand his knowledge about options (Synthesis-Elaboration), reduce those options to a manageable number (Synthesis-Crystallization), prioritize his options (Valuing), and help K monitor his decision-making process (Executive Processing).

K agreed that he could use the computer at home for several of the activities on his ILP but also said that probably having a set time when he planned to visit the career center to use resources would also be helpful in keeping him on-track. His librarian assistant job brings him to campus two days a week in the morning, so he agreed to visit the career center on one of those days after he leaves work. Both K and Eva agreed that he would probably be happier just coming into the career center on his own schedule to do library research. However, given his tendency to procrastinate, he agreed to meet with Eva once a week to report on his progress, help him stay motivated, and monitor his thinking, especially when he finds himself losing motivation or becoming overwhelmed.

During their second meeting, Eva shared with K a resource called the Guide to Good Decision Making—an exercise that could be used to help him keep track of the information he would be collecting through this process. Eva also introduced K to the *CTI Workbook* as an activity to help him challenge some of the thinking that may be interfering with his career problem solving and decision making. K liked the fact that he could use the workbook at his own pace whenever he felt like it. Finally, they also discussed the idea of K's doing an internship over the summer to give him some experience with occupations related to his career interests (Execution).

Execute ILP. Over the next several weeks, K spent time both at home and in the career resource center using print and Internet resources to learn more about options he was considering. He found the Internet-based guidance system useful for researching computer and architecture occupations but felt it didn't adequately cover some of the more creative options he was considering. He talked with Eva about this, and she encouraged him to pursue additional Internet research to find contacts in the field. Eva showed him a directory of professional associations that included listings related to his interests. He was excited to know that such groups existed, and he jotted down their Web sites to use in further exploring options related to video game software design and skateboard manufacturing. She also showed him how to use the center's Web-based networking program to find persons working in some of the fields in which he has an interest.

Using contacts from the career center's faculty-staff resource directory, he made appointments with selected advisers to learn more about specific majors he was considering. He learned about a combined degree program that involved computer graphics and information studies. He also visited with advisers in the film and communications schools. While using the career center's occupational information files, K learned about the field of video game design. In a follow-up session with Eva, he excitedly discussed the idea of designing video games that would involve the sport of skateboarding. He saw this as a way of using his creative side (A), his scientific side (I), and his interest in hands-on work (R). Eva affirmed the fact that this seemed like a great way to combine his interests and skills. On his Guide to Good Decision Making Exercise, K had described the costs and benefits of this option. He noted that he liked the way it combined his skills and interests but was concerned that it is a competitive field, that only a few people are really successful, and that those are the ones who make a lot of money.

He had also weighed the pros and cons of being an architect. He liked the creative aspect of the field and the income potential, but he was concerned about having to spend "too much time stuck in an office" and being bound by too many rules. Through his leisure reading, he had learned about persons who are involved in designing courses used in professional skateboarding but worried that this type of focus might be too narrow and limit his options. During his research on computer occupations, he learned about organizations that have a really flexible work environment, for example, casual dress, varied work hours, and leisure activities onsite. He liked the idea of a work setting that is somewhat relaxed yet provides enough structure to keep him on-task. These comments fit with K's self-knowledge that identifies Independence as an important value but recognizes that "he does better when others set the agenda for him."

In his fourth session with Eva, K shared his experience using the *CTI Workbook* and said, "I can see how my thinking tends to get me in trouble!" K said that while he had gotten better with regard to how he thinks about this whole process of choosing a career, he still had a tendency to daydream and procrastinate. Eva reinforced the good work he had done so far and reassured him that it was natural to do both of those things.

Summative Review and Generalization. K stayed in touch with Eva throughout the spring semester. He missed a few appointments but sent Eva an occasional e-mail to let her know he was making progress. He had identified additional computer courses that he planned to take over the summer, along with continuing his basic studies requirements. K planned to attend a skateboarding tournament over the summer. He found out through the career center's internship office that one of the major sponsors for skateboard tournaments offers an internship for persons with coursework in computer science. K was excited to learn that he could apply directly to the company on-line. He used the career center's Web site resources for help in developing a résumé (Execution), which he brought in to Eva for a critique. K has not entirely ruled out architecture as an option and is including coursework that would meet the prerequisite requirements for this field. K said he was glad he had sought help at the career center. He appreciated the fact that the process Eva used gave him the freedom to use his own style in helping resolve his career problems while providing some structure to help him see what areas he needed to focus on and strategies for getting the information he needed. K expressed confidence in being able to use what he had learned through this process for future career decisions.

The Case of E

Initial Interview. E was referred to the career center by the group leader for her career exploration class. She was encouraged to continue working with the center in light of the fact that she had made very little progress with respect to her career choices after completing activities for the career class. E indicated that she was frustrated about this whole process of choosing an occupation. She indicated that she had so many interests that it was hard to settle on one choice and that was partly the reason she had chosen to double major. E had used the career center to complete assignments for the career class but had become overwhelmed by all the information that was available. She brought with her the SDS results from her career planning class and a copy of her transcript.

Preliminary Assessment. As part of a comprehensive screening process in the CIP approach, E would also be asked to complete the CTI. Hypothesizing about E's CTI scores, we would suspect that she would have moderately elevated levels of DMC and CA and a lower level of EC. The elevated level of CA would not be surprising, given E's good academic record and lack of knowledge about specific occupations. A concern is that, despite having the opportunity to complete a number of self-assessments as part of the career class and completing several occupational research activities, E has been unable to translate her self-knowledge into a manageable list of occupational alternatives. From a CIP perspective, she is unable to make the transition from the Synthesis phase to Valuing. A positive sign is that E's top two scores on the SDS are consistent with her occupational daydreams, which have a summary of ESA, as well as the important values she wants to satisfy in her job role, concern for others, and financial prosperity. It would also be important to review E's scores on each of the SDS scales to see how the high point code for each might have differed.

E's Artistic and Investigative scores were not provided. The relative closeness of these two types to her top three scores would be important to examine, given the presence of Artistic and Investigative codes in her daydream codes and the fact that she could be classified as an undecided multipotential individual. E may lack differentiation in her SDS profile, which further illustrates why she is feeling overwhelmed with options. One difficulty for E is that her Holland code results presented her with many more options, and she lacked an effective schema for narrowing (Synthesis-Crystallization) down those options.

The career adviser discussed with E her choice of history (SEI) and religion (SAE) as majors. E said that her main reasons for choosing these was she thought they would be good preparation for law school. She acknowledged that although she enjoyed some of the classes, she worried about what she would do with these majors if she didn't go to law school. She said she knew a lot about being a lawyer because of her family, but she was less informed about her other alternatives. In addition, her prior work experiences had not given her an opportunity to investigate options that she was presently considering.

E's readiness to engage the career problem-solving and decision-making process was to some degree hampered by her negative thinking. Her anxiety over selecting one option from her many areas of interest and her frustration over not having made a decision made it difficult to further clarify her self-knowledge and option knowledge. At the time of her visit to the career center, E seemed to be low on the capability dimension of the readiness model (see Figure 8.3). In contrast, E does not seem to be affected by issues associated with the complexity dimension. She comes from a supportive, intact family that appears to be providing adequate financial support. She has no physical limitations and has had opportunities to work, take responsibility, and develop useful skills that might serve her in future occupations. Given E's low capability and low complexity, the career adviser concluded that E possessed a moderate level of readiness for career decision making and could be helped through brief staff-assisted services.

Define Problem and Analyze Causes. From a CIP perspective, E's gap was the lack of a specific occupational goal (Occupational Knowledge), as well as a tendency toward negative thinking (Executive Processing) that essentially shut down her ability to effectively process information and make a career decision. Although E had used a decision-making strategy to identify a course of study, she had been unable to apply this same strategy to the choice of an occupation. E's negative thinking caused her to overgeneralize and be fairly rigid in her thinking about options. Her role models were primarily in the legal field, and it was hard for her to imagine what it might be like to work in a different field. From a Valuing perspective, it is likely that E was having a difficult time reconciling her "concern for others" with her desire for "financial prosperity." The career adviser talked with E about what she meant by "too many options" and what would be a reasonable number of options to consider. E indicated that she was very motivated to work on figuring out her career goals. She wanted to have the decision made by the end of her sophomore year so she could focus on getting some experience in the field and begin to explore plans for graduate study if she chose a field that required an advanced degree.

Formulate Goals. E said she wanted to have a clearer picture of her occupational goals and wanted to have more confidence in her choice of an occupation. E said that she had done some reading about occupations as part of her career exploration class but liked it more when she could actually talk to people who were working in a field in which she had an interest. This statement is consistent with the Social and Enterprising aspects of E's Holland code, which suggests that getting information through contact with others may fit well with her personality characteristics. E stated that she knew "plenty of lawyers she could talk to" but was interested in using the career center's networking database to find persons working in other fields that she had listed on her SDS.

E acknowledged that sometimes she gets so overwhelmed with trying to make a choice that she just wants to forget about it. That statement led the career adviser to discuss some of the CTI items that E had marked "Strongly Agree," especially those dealing with CA and the Valuing phase of the pyramid. The career adviser introduced E to the *CTI Workbook* and explained that E could learn more about how her thinking influences her choices and how her thinking might be making it difficult for her to commit to a choice. E agreed that she has a tendency to "sabotage herself" and was willing to work on this issue as part of the process. With these goals in mind, E and her career adviser developed a plan of action to address her career concerns.

TABLE 8.2. E's Individual Learning Plan

Goal(s): #1 Narrow down my list of occupations to no more than 3
#2 Feel less overwhelmed by the process of choosing an occupation
#3 Have a plan for how to enter my 1st choice of experience

Activity	Purpose/Outcome	Estimated Time Commitment	Goal #	Priority
Select 3-5 occupations for further research.	to have a manageable list to use in getting more information	15-20 min	1	1
Talk with someone in my fields of interest	Get more first hand information about what work is like	30 min - 1 hr.	1	5
Participate in classes relates to speech, public speaking	to gain skills related to my career interests	1-3 hrs.	3	6
Use the CTI workbook	to help me feel less anxious about my choice & develop a strategy	ongoing	2,3	4
Discuss with academic advisor English as a possible minor	Broaden my background gain additional skills for my resume	30 min	3	2
Use selected Career Center Library Resources	to further clarify & evaluate my initial choices	ongoing	1,2	3
Follow-up w/ Career Advisor	to discuss progress & identify future activities	20 min	1,2,3	7

This plan can be modified by either party based upon new information learned in the activities of the action plan. The purpose of the plan is to work toward a mutually agreed upon career goal. Activities may be added or subtracted as needed.

"E"   5/25/01   Amy   5/25/01
Student/Client/Customer   Date   Staff Member   Date

Develop ILP. E's career adviser, mindful of the fact that E has not been very successful in using occupational information in the past to narrow her choices, talked with her about how she might like to approach learning about the options she's considering. To avoid becoming overwhelmed with options, E's career adviser asked her to pick three to five that she was most interested in learning more about. E said that she really needed to look more closely at Writer and Teacher but also wanted to consider several new occupations that had been generated by her SDS results (both her Summary code and her Aspirations Summary code), including Volunteer Services Director and Association Executive.

The career adviser discussed E's comments about her English classes, particularly "I'm not always able to share my opinions verbally." E agreed that this was a problem, especially given her interest in Social and Enterprising occupations, where verbal skills are likely to be important. She indicated that her public speaking was something she would like to work on and improve. She agreed to use the university's Web site to look into campus activities and classes that might give her more experience with this skill to help her determine whether it is one she wants to use in her future work. E's career adviser also shared with her a local community referral directory that gave the lists of Toastmaster Clubs in the area.

Given E's strong interest in English classes, the career adviser discussed whether E wanted to investigate this major as a possible minor area, especially given the fact that E had listed Writer as one of her aspirations. E agreed that she had missed taking English classes since starting her major coursework and was glad to know that this might be a possibility. Because of her strong academic background, she had tested out of several general studies requirements, so she had some flexibility in her schedule.

E's career adviser included the *CTI Workbook* on her ILP. They reviewed the different sections and spent some time discussing how the reframing section could be used to help E begin to work on her CTI items that were answered "Strongly Agree" or "Agree." The career adviser showed E how her responses were connected to various sections of the pyramid, and this helped illustrate the difficulty that E was having in the Valuing phase of the CASVE cycle. E's career adviser helped her see how the search for the "perfect occupation" could make it hard for her to commit to a choice. E's career adviser shared the example of how a well-known lawyer had become one of the country's best-selling authors. This example helped E see how it is possible for one's career path to combine many aspects of one's interests, values, and skills.

Execute ILP. E visited the career center library on several occasions to research three specific options identified through her earlier assessments (Synthesis). As one activity to help her gain more confidence with public speaking, E signed up for a summer school class through the College of Communication called Introduction to Public Speaking. E participated in a "Women and the Law" symposium sponsored by the university's College of Law. She learned more about how women cope with the stress of work and having a family life. One of the panel members included a female faculty member who had previously been a corporate attorney. E was excited to see how this might be an option for combining her interest in law with her interest in teaching. E used the career center's networking database to schedule an information interview over the semester break with an alumna who was currently working as a publications specialist with a large publishing firm. E met with an academic adviser in the English Department who helped her identify a series of classes consistent with E's interests that would meet the minor requirements. E was excited about getting back into this area and felt good about the fact that many of the courses would help her develop skills that could be relevant to several of the occupations she was considering.

Summative Review and Generalization. As a result of the activities on E's ILP, she was able to further differentiate her choices and tentatively commit to a first choice. She had used the Guide to Good Decision Making Exercise to clarify her options and arrive at a ranking of those options. The *CTI Workbook* had helped reduce her either-or thinking and her tendency to allow negative thinking to sabotage her decision making. She had grown more comfortable with the ambiguity of the world of work and acknowledged that it was OK to change her mind. E agreed that pursuing her first choice did not eliminate some of the other alternatives she was considering. She recognized how she might combine several of her interests, skills, and values in one or more of the alternatives on her final list. E visited the center as a later date and updated the career adviser on her plans to attend law school (Execution). The career adviser mentioned the center's upcoming Graduate and Law School Expo and suggested E might attend to gather additional information as part of her effort to target schools. E stated:

> Though it might seem like I'm simply going the law school route because of my family history, I feel like I have learned through this process how to make an informed choice based on my own knowledge and decision-making process. I am more relaxed about my future, can envision using my law degree in many settings, and don't feel like I have to have all of my future plans completely decided to move forward with the next steps.

References

American College Testing. (1998). *Career planning survey technical manual*. Iowa City, IA: Author.

Anderson, J. R. (1994). Problem solving and learning. *American Psychologist, 48*, 35–44.

Anderson, R. C. (1984). Some reflections on the acquisition of knowledge. *Educational Researcher, 13*(11), 5–10.

Anderson, R. C., Osborn, J., & Tierney, R. S. (1984). *Learning to read in American schools*. Hillsdale, NJ: Erlbaum.

Atkinson, R. C., & Shiffrin, R. M. (1968). Human memory: A proposed system and its control processes. In K. W. Spence & J. I. Spence

(Eds.), *The psychology of learning and motivation: Advances in research and theory, Vol. 2.* New York: Dell.

Bandura, A. (1977). Self-efficacy: Toward a unifying theory of behavior change. *Psychological Review, 84,* 191–215.

Bandura, A. (1982). Self-efficacy mechanism in human agency. *American Psychologist, 37,* 122–147.

Belmont, J., & Butterfield, E. (1977). The instructional approach to developmental cognitive research. In R. Keil & J. Hagen (Eds.), *Perspectives on the development of memory and cognition.* Hillsdale, NJ: Erlbaum.

Blustein, D. L. (1992). Applying current theory and research in career exploration to practice. *The Career Development Quarterly, 41,* 174–184.

Bransford, J. D., & Stein, B. S. (1984). *The ideal problem solver.* New York: W. H. Freeman.

Brown, A. L. (1981). Metacognition: The development of selective attention strategies for learning from texts. In M. L. Kamil (Ed.), *Directions in reading: Research and instruction* (pp. 21–43). Washington, DC: National Reading Conference.

Brown, D., & Brooks, L. (1991). *Career counseling techniques.* Boston: Allyn & Bacon.

Cochran, L. (1994). What is a career problem? *The Career Development Quarterly, 42,* 204–215.

Consulting Psychologists Press. (1994). *Strong Interest Inventory.* Palo Alto, CA: Author.

Crace, R. K., & Brown, D. (1996). *Life Values Inventory.* Chapel Hill, NC: Life Values Resources.

Crites, J. O. (1969). *Vocational psychology.* New York: McGraw-Hill.

Crites, J. O. (1974). A reappraisal of vocational appraisal. *The Vocational Guidance Quarterly, 22,* 272–279.

Crites, J. O. (1981). *Career counseling: Models, methods, and materials.* New York: McGraw-Hill.

Epstein, S. (1994). Integration of the cognitive and the psychodynamic unconscious. *American Psychologist, 49,* 709–724.

Festinger L. (1964). Motivations leading to social behavior. In R. C. Teevan & R. C. Burney, (Eds.), *Theories of motivation in personality and social psychology* (pp. 138–161). New York: Van Nostrand.

Flavell, J. H. (1979). Metacognition and cognitive monitoring: A new idea of cognitive-developmental inquiry. *American Psychologist, 34,* 906–911.

Fouad, N. S., & Arbona, C. (1994). Career in a cultural context. *The Career Development Quarterly, 43,* 96–194.

Fredrickson, R. H. (1982). *Career information.* Englewood Cliffs, NJ: Prentice Hall.

Gelatt, H. B. (1962). Decision-making: A conceptual frame of reference for counseling. *Journal of Counseling Psychology, 9*(3), 240–245.

Gelatt, H. B. (1989). Positive uncertainty: A new decision making framework for counseling. *Journal of Counseling Psychology, 36*(2), 252–256.

Gottfredson, G. D., & Holland, J. L. (1996). *Dictionary of Holland occupational codes* (3rd ed.). Odessa, FL: Psychological Assessment Resources.

Hall, C. S., & Lindzey, G. (1978). *Theories of personality* (3rd ed.). New York: Wiley.

Hartman, B. W., Fuqua, D. R., & Blum, C. R. (1985). A path-analytic model of career indecision. *The Vocational Guidance Quarterly, 33,* 231–246.

Heppner, P. P., & Krauskopf, C. J. (1987). An information processing approach to problem solving. *The Counseling Psychologist, 15,* 371–447.

Hill, S., & Peterson, G. W. (2001). *The impact of decision-making confusion on the processing of occupational information.* Paper presented at the annual meeting of the American Educational Research Association, Seattle.

Holland, J. L., Powell, A. B., & Fritzsche, B. A. (1994). *The Self-Directed Search professional user's guide.* Odessa, FL: Psychological Assessment Resources.

Hunt, E. B. (1971). What kind of computer is man? *Cognitive Psychology, 2,* 57–98.

Janis, I. L., & Mann, L. (1977). *Decision making: A psychological analysis of conflict, choice, and commitment.* New York: Free Press.

Kahnaman, D. (1973). *Attention and effort.* Englewood Cliffs, NJ: Prentice Hall.

Katz, M. R. (1963). *Decisions and values: A rationale for secondary school guidance.* New York: College Entrance Examination Board.

Katz, M. R. (1969, Summer). Can computers make guidance decisions for students? *The College Board Review, 72*, 13–17.

Kaufman, R. (1972). *Educational system planning*. Englewood Cliffs, NJ: Prentice Hall.

Kelly, G. A. (1955). *The psychology of personal constructs: Vols. 1–2*. New York: W. W. Norton.

Krumboltz, J. D., & Baker, R. D. (1973). Behavioral counseling for behavioral decisions. In H. Borrow (Ed.), *Career guidance for a new age* (pp. 235–283). Boston: Houghton Mifflin.

Kuder, F. (1946). *Manual to the Kuder Preference Record*. Chicago: Science Research Associates.

Lackman, R., Lackman, J. L., & Butterfield, E. C. (1979). *Cognitive psychology and information processing*. Hillsdale, NJ: Erlbaum.

Larkin, J., McDermott, J., Simon, D. P., & Simon, H. A. (1980, June). Expert and novice performance in solving physics problems. *Science, 208*, 1335–1345.

Lazarus, R. S. (1982). Thoughts on the relations between emotion and cognition. *American Psychologist, 37*, 1019–1024.

Lenz, J. G. (1998). A career center's community connection. *Australian Journal of Career Development, 7*, 3–4.

Lenz, J. G. (2000). *Paraprofessionals in career services: The Florida State University model* (Tech. Rep. No. 27). Tallahassee, FL: Florida State University, Center for the Study of Technology in Counseling and Career Development.

Lenz, J. G., Reardon, R. C., Peterson, G. W., & Sampson, J. P., Jr. (in press). Applying cognitive information processing (CIP) theory to career program design and development. In W. Patton & M. McMahon (Eds.), *Career development programs: Preparation for lifelong career decision-making*. Camberwell, VIC: ACER Press.

Lyddon, W. L. (1995). Cognitive therapy and theories of knowing: A social constructivist view. *Journal of Counseling and Development, 73*, 579–585.

Mahoney, M. S. (1991). *Human change process*. New York: Basic Books.

Meichenbaum, D. (1977). *Cognitive-behavior modification*. New York: Plenum.

Miller-Tiedeman, A. L. (1977). Structuring responsibility in adolescents: Actualizing "I" power through curriculum. In G. D. Miller (Ed.),

Developmental theory and its application in guidance programs: Systematic efforts to promote personal growth. Minneapolis: Minnesota Department of Education.

Neimeyer, G. J. (1988). Cognitive integration and differentiation in vocational behavior. *The Counseling Psychologist, 16*, 440–475.

Neimeyer, G. J. (1992). Personal constructs and vocational structure: A critique of poor status. In R. A. Neimeyer & G. J. Neimeyer (Eds.), *Advances in personal construct psychology*, (pp. 91–120). Greenwich, CT: JAI Press.

Neisser, U. (1981). John Dean's memory: A case study. *Cognition, 9*, 1–22.

Neisser, U. (1982). Snapshots or benchmarks? In U. Neisser (Ed.), *Memory observed: Remembering in natural contexts* (pp. 3–19). San Francisco: W. H. Freeman.

Nevill, D. D., Neimeyer, G. J., Probert, B., & Fukuyama, M. A. (1986). Cognitive structures in vocational information processing and decision making. *Journal of Vocational Behavior, 28*, 110–122.

Newell, A., & Simon, H. (1972). *Human problem solving*. Englewood Cliffs, NJ: Prentice Hall.

Parr, J., & Neimeyer, G. J. (1994). Effects of gender, construct type, occupational information, and career relevance on vocational differentiation. *Journal of Counseling Psychology, 41*, 27–33.

Parsons, F. (1909). *Choosing a vocation*. Boston: Houghton Mifflin.

Patterson, D. G., & Darley, J. G. (1936). *Men, women, and jobs*. Minneapolis: Minnesota Press.

Peterson, G. W. (1998). Using a vocational card sort as an assessment of occupational knowledge. *Journal of Career Assessment, 6*, 49–67.

Peterson, G. W., Long, K. L., & Billups, A. (1999). The effect of three career interventions on educational choices of eighth grade students. *Professional School Counseling 3(1)*, 34–42.

Peterson, G. W., Lumsden, J. A., Sampson, J. P., Jr., Reardon, R. C., & Lenz, J. G. (in press). Using cognitive information processing in counseling with adults. In S. Niles (Ed.), *Adult career development* (3rd ed.). Columbus, OH: National Career Development Association.

Peterson, G. W., & Rumsey, M. G. (1981). *A methodology for measuring officer job competence*. Paper presented at the annual convention of the American Psychological Association, Los Angeles.

Peterson, G. W., Sampson, J. P., Jr., Lenz, J. G., & Reardon, R. C. (1999, May). *Three contexts of career problem solving and decision making*.

Paper presented at the annual meeting of the Society for Vocational Psychology. Milwaukee.

Peterson, G. W., Sampson, J. P., Jr., & Reardon, R. C. (1991). *Career development and services: A cognitive approach.* Pacific Grove, CA: Brooks/Cole.

Peterson, G. W., Sampson, J. P., Jr., Reardon, R. C., & Lenz, J. G. (1996). Becoming career problem solvers and decision makers: A cognitive information processing approach. In D. Brown & L. Brooks (Eds.), *Career choice and development* (3rd. ed., pp. 423–475). San Francisco: Jossey-Bass.

Peterson, G. W., & Swain, W. (1978, October). Critical appreciation: An essential element in educating for competence. *Liberal Education, 64,* 293–301.

Peterson, G. W., & Watkins, K. (1979). *Identification and assessment of competence* (Final report, Florida Competency-based Articulation Project). Tallahassee, FL. (ERIC Document Reproduction Service No. ED 169 839)

Piaget, J. (1973). The affective unconscious and the cognitive unconscious. *Journal of the American Psychoanalytic Association, 21,* 249–261.

Piaget, J. (1977). *The development of thought: Equilibration of cognitive structures.* New York: Viking Press.

Railey, M. G., & Peterson, G. W. (2000). The assessment of dysfunctional career thoughts and interest structure among female inmates and probationers. *Journal of Career Assessment, 8(2),* 119–129.

Reardon, R. C. (1998). *Bibliographic references: Curricular-career information service.* Tallahassee: The Career Center, Florida State University.

Reardon, R., & Lenz, J. (1998). *The Self-Directed Search and related Holland career materials: A practitioner's guide.* Odessa, FL: Psychological Assessment Resources.

Reardon, R. C., Lenz, J. G., Sampson, J. P., Jr., & Peterson, G. W. (2000a). *Career development and planning: A comprehensive approach.* Pacific Grove, CA: Brooks/Cole.

Reardon, R. C., Lenz, J. G., Sampson, J. P., Jr., & Peterson, G. W. (2000b). *Student handbook for career development and planning: A comprehensive approach.* Pacific Grove, CA: Brooks/Cole.

Reardon, R. C., Sampson, J. P., Jr., & Lenz, J. G. (2000). Career assessment in a time of changing roles, relationships, and contexts. *Journal of Career Assessment, 8,* 351–359.

Reardon, R. C., & Wright, L. K. (1999). The case of Mandy: Applying Holland's theory and cognitive information processing theory. *The Career Development Quarterly, 47*, 195–203.

Reitman, W. R. (1965). *Cognition and thought: An information-processing approach*. New York: Wiley.

Rummelhart, D. E., & Ortony, A. (1976). Representation of knowledge in memory. In R. C. Anderson, R. J. Spiro, & W. E. Montague (Eds.), *Schooling and the acquisition of knowledge* (pp. 99–135). Hillsdale, NJ: Erlbaum.

Sampson, J. P., Jr. (1999a). Integrating Internet-based distance guidance with services provided in career centers. *The Career Development Quarterly, 47*, 243–254.

Sampson, J. P., Jr. (1999b). Elements of an effective career resource room. Tallahassee, FL: Florida State University, Center for the Study of Technology in Counseling and Career Development [On-line]. Available: http://www.career.fsu.edu/techcenter/CareerResourceRoom.html

Sampson, J. P., Jr., Lenz, J. G., Reardon, R. C., & Peterson, G. W. (1999). A cognitive information processing approach to employment problem solving and decision making. *The Career Development Quarterly, 48*, 3–18.

Sampson, J. P., Jr., Peterson, G. W., Lenz, J. G., & Reardon, R. C. (1992). A cognitive approach to career services: Translating concepts into practice. *The Career Development Quarterly, 41*, 67–74.

Sampson, J. P., Jr., Peterson, G. W., Lenz, J. G., Reardon, R. C., & Saunders, D. E. (1996a). *Career Thoughts Inventory*. Odessa, FL: Psychological Assessment Resources.

Sampson, J. P., Jr., Peterson, G. W., Lenz, J. G., Reardon, R. C., & Saunders, D. E. (1996b). *Career Thoughts Inventory workbook*. Odessa, FL: Psychological Assessment Resources.

Sampson, J. P., Jr., Peterson, G. W., Lenz, J. G., Reardon, R. C., & Saunders, D. E. (1996c). *Career Thoughts Inventory: Professional manual*. Odessa, FL: Psychological Assessment Resources.

Sampson, J. P., Jr., Peterson, G. W., Lenz, J. G., Reardon, R. C., & Saunders, D. E. (1998). The design and use of a measure of dysfunctional career thoughts among adults, college students, and high school students: The Career Thoughts Inventory. *Journal of Career Assessment, 6*, 115–134.

Sampson, J. P., Jr., Peterson, G. W., & Reardon, R. C. (1989). Counselor intervention strategies for computer-assisted career guidance: An information processing approach. *Journal of Career Development*, 16, 139–154.

Sampson, J. P., Jr., Peterson, G. W., Reardon, R. C., & Lenz, J. G. (2000a). Using readiness assessment to improve career services: A cognitive information processing approach. *The Career Development Quarterly*, 49, 146–174.

Sampson, J. P., Jr., Peterson, G. W., Reardon, R. C., & Lenz, J. G. (2000b). The viability of readiness assessment in contributing to improved career services: A response to Jepsen (2000). *The Career Development Quarterly*, 49, 179–185.

Sampson, J. P., Jr., Peterson, G. W., Reardon, R. C., & Lenz, J. G. (2001a). *Bibliography: A cognitive information processing approach to career development and services.* Tallahassee, FL: Florida State University, Center for the Study of Technology in Counseling and Career Development [Online]. Available: http://www.career.fsu.edu/techcenter/CIPBIBnew.html

Sampson, J. P., Jr., Peterson, G. W., Reardon, R. C., & Lenz, J. G. (2001b). *Key elements of the CIP approach to designing career services.* Unpublished manuscript, Florida State University, Center for the Study of Technology in Counseling and Career Development, Tallahassee [On-line]. Available: http://www.career.fsu.edu/techcenter/keyelements.html

Sampson, J. P., Jr., & Reardon, R. C. (1998). Maximizing staff resources in meeting the needs of job seekers in one-stop centers. *Journal of Employment Counseling*, 35, 50–68.

Sampson, J. P., Jr., Watts, A. G., Palmer, M., & Hughes, D. (2000). International collaboration in translating career theory to practice. *The Career Development Quarterly*, 40, 332–339. Also in 2000, *Journal of Employment Counseling*, 37(2).

Saunders, D. E., Peterson, G. W., Sampson, J. P., Jr., & Reardon, R. C. (2000). The relation of depression and dysfunctional career thinking to career indecision. *Journal of Vocational Behavior*, 56, 288–298.

Saunders, D. E., Reardon, R. C., & Lenz, J. G. (1999). Specialty training for career counselors: 25 years at Florida State University. *Career Planning and Adult Development Journal*, 15(2), 23–33.

Shiffrin, R. M., & Schneider, W. (1977). Controlled and automatic human information processing: Vol. II. Perceptual learning, automatic attending, and a general theory. *Psychological Review*, 84(2), 127–190.

Sinnott, J. D. (1989). A model for the solution of ill-structured problems: Implications for everyday and abstract problem solving. In J. D. Sinnott (Ed.), *Everyday problem solving*. New York: Praeger.

Sternberg, R. J. (1979). The nature of mental abilities. *American Psychologist, 34*, 214–230.

Sternberg, R. J. (1980). Sketch of a componential subtheory of human intelligence. *Behavioral and Brain Sciences, 3*, 573–584.

Sternberg, R. J. (1984). Testing intelligence without IQ tests. *Phi Delta Kappan, 65*(10), 694–698.

Sternberg, R. J. (1985). Instrumental and componential approaches to the nature of training on intelligence. In S. Chapman, J. Segal, & R. Glaser (Eds.), *Thinking and learning skills: Research and open questions*. Hillsdale, NJ: Erlbaum.

Sternberg, R. J., & Rifkin, B. (1979). The development of analogical reasoning processes. *Journal of Experimental Child Psychology, 27*, 195–232.

Strong, E. K., Jr. (1943). *Strong Vocational Interest Blank (SVIB)*. Palo Alto, CA: Stanford University Press.

Super, D. E. (1957). *The psychology of careers*. New York: Harper & Row.

Super, D. E. (1980). A life span, life space approach to career development. *Journal of Vocational Behavior, 16*, 282–298.

Super, D. L. (1983). Assessment in career guidance: Toward truly developmental counseling. *The Personnel and Guidance Journal, 61*, 555–562.

Super, D. E., & Nevill, D. D. (1985). *The Values Scale*. Palo Alto, CA: Consulting Psychologists Press.

Tulving, E. (1972). Episodic and semantic memory. In E. Tulving & W. Donaldson (Eds.), *Organization of memory*. London: Oxford University Press.

Tulving, E. (1984). Precis on elements of episodic memory. *The Behavioral and Brain Sciences, 7*, 223–268.

U.S. Department of Commerce. (2000). *Standard occupational classification manual*. Springfield, VA: Technology Administration, National Technical Information Service.

U.S. Department of Labor and the National O*Net Consortium. (1999). O*Net. Washington, DC: Author.

Vernick, S. H. (2001). *The Career Thoughts Inventory (CTI) in research and practice*. Unpublished manuscript, Florida State University, Center for the Study of Technology in Counseling and Career Development, Tallahassee [On-line]. Available: http://www.career.fsu.edu/techcenter/designing_career_services/career_thoughts_inventory/index.html

Vernick, S. H., Garis, J., & Reardon, R. C. (2000). Integrating service, teaching, and research in a comprehensive university career center. *Career Planning and Adult Development Journal, 16(1)*, 7–24.

Voight, L., & Peterson, G. W. (August, 2000). *Parental attachment and ego identity as antecedents of career identity*. Paper presented at the annual conference of the American Psychological Association, Washington, DC.

Warren, J. R. (1976). Describing college graduates in 87 phrases or less. *Findings: Educational Testing Service, 3(2)*, 5–8.

Watson, J., & Lenz, J. G. (in press). The case of Raven. In S. G. Niles, J. Goodman, & M. Pope, (Eds.), *The Career counseling casebook: A resource for counselors, students, and practitioners*. Columbus, OH: National Career Development Association.

Wickelgren, W. A. (1974). *How to solve problems: Elements of theory of problems and problem solving*. San Francisco: W. H. Freeman.

Williamson, E. G. (1939). *How to counsel students*. New York: McGraw-Hill.

Woditsh, G. A. (1977). *Developing generic skills: A model for competency-based education*. Bowling Green, OH: CUE Project, Bowling Green State University.

Yost, E. B., & Corbishley, M. A. (1987). *Career counseling: A psychological approach*. San Francisco: Jossey-Bass.

Zajonc, E. (1980). Feeling and thinking: Preferences need no inferences. *American Psychologist, 35*, 151–175.

PART FIVE

Trait-Factor Theories and Summation

9

Holland's Theory of Personalities in Work Environments

Arnold R. Spokane, Erik J. Luchetta,
Matthew H. Richwine

> We have come to realize that the old arguments about whether heredity or environment—nature or nurture—is the cause of human individuality are irrelevant. A human individual represents an interaction of unique genetic endowment with a unique course of development. It is a complex, non-additive process.
>
> Leona Tyler, 1995, p. 2

Most social scientists would agree that major features of the physical and social environment affect the behavior of inhabitants. These environmental characteristics mediate not only the behavior of individuals but the behavior of subcultures and societies over long time periods (Diamond, 1999). That the larger physical world affects behavior has been obvious for some time to environmental psychologists (Altman, 1975; Garling, 1998; Proshansky, Ittelson, & Rivlin, 1976), colleagues in environmental health (Moeller, 1997), geography (Diamond, 1999), architecture (Gallagher, 1999; Hall, 1966; Nasar, 2000; Sommer, 1969), urban planning (Duany & Plater-Zyberk, 1992), and engineering (Zmeureanu & Marceau, 1999). The reader would readily acknowledge that behavior in a bustling urban neighborhood differs substantially from that on a sun-drenched beach or in a serene mountain setting. When we study an individual, we also study the context in which that individual lives and interacts.

Much of psychology's theory and systems research in the study of human environments traces to Kurt Lewin (1936), whose topological model of behavior broke new ground for psychologists. Roger Barker, Lewin's primary student, demonstrated that in large environments, as well as in smaller, more encapsulated, environments such as schools (Barker & Gump, 1964), behavior and social roles differ, depending on essential characteristics of the environment (for example, big school versus small school). This general area of inquiry has been called ecological psychology. Interest in ecological psychology or person-environment interaction has increased with advances in environmental measurement (Szapocznik et al., in progress) and research methodology (Edwards & Rothbard, 1999), as well as with renewed appreciation for the richness of person-environment transactions (Tyler, 1995).

In a more-or-less parallel universe, the longstanding tradition of individual differences (Dawis, 1992; Lubinski, 2000; Lubinski & Dawis, 1995), bolstered by behavioral genetics (Betsworth et al., 1994; Gottfredson, 1999; Plomin and DeFreis, 1998), assures us that stable dispositions such as values, interests, personality, and the behavioral repertoires associated with these dispositions can be readily identified and studied. Indeed, such dispositions may dictate which environments individuals select, thereby multiplying their effects. Individual diversity, in this view, dictates the lion's share of human behavior. As Rene Dawis (1992) reminds us, we have a rich and enduring individual differences tradition on which we can build future research. Broader definitions of the nature of interests (Savickas, 1999; Silva, 1999; Hogan & Blake, 1999) are examples of recent developments in the area of individual differences and vocational behavior.

In vocational psychology, as in other areas of social science, it is a continuing struggle to study human interactions at the level of complexity warranted by the phenomena under study and at a level of parsimony necessary to be able to understand the findings. Whether we choose to emphasize those aspects of behavior that are stable or those that are fluid, we cannot escape the simultaneous study of individual and environmental contributors to behavior in our theory and research. Person-environment interaction is a fundamental concept in the study of human behavior (Stokols, 1995; Tinsley, 2000; Tyler, 1995; Walsh, Craik, & Price, 2000). As the quote from Leona Tyler's insightful and perhaps final writing effort (Tyler, 1995) reflects, then, person-environment interaction involves the interplay of a diverse but limited set of stable personalities with the nature and demands of the environments they inhabit.

The principal proponent of the person-environment interaction position in vocational psychology has been, and continues to be, John L. Holland. Holland's unflagging devotion to creativity, integrity, empirical evidence, and practical application in revising his theory accounts for its unprecedented influence. Holland was awarded the American Psychological Association's prestigious Award for Distinguished Contributions to Professional Knowledge in 1995 in recognition of his sustained work in vocational psychology.

Background of Holland's Theory

Since its emergence more than forty years ago, Holland's theory has become a major force in applied psychology. The first presentation of the theory in 1959 emphasized the "searching" aspects of person-environment fit: "The person making a vocational choice in a sense searches for situations which satisfy his hierarchy of adjustive orientations" (Holland, 1959, p. 35). In this early version, the importance of resemblance to all six of the types was evident. There was also an emphasis on the acquisition and processing of environmental information. "Persons with more information about occupational environments make more adequate choices than do persons with less information" (pp. 40–41). And there was strong focus as well on development through external influences such as parents and teachers. A precursor article on the Vocational Preference Inventory (VPI) in 1958 (Holland, 1958) describes the core of the theory—the projection of one's personality onto the world of work:

The choice of an occupation is an expressive act which reflects the person's motivation, knowledge, personality, and ability. Occupations represent a way of life, an environment rather than a set of isolated work functions or skills. To work as a carpenter means not only to have a certain status, community role, and a special pattern of living. In this sense, the choice of an occupational title represents several kinds of information: the S's motivation, his knowledge of the occupation in question, his insight and understanding of himself, and his abilities. In short, item responses *may be thought of as limited but useful expressive or projective protocols.* [Holland, 1958, p. 336; italics added]

A remarkable series of research articles followed while Holland was at the National Merit Scholarship Corporation documenting the characteristics of the types, their preferred activities, self-descriptions, and competencies. These studies, which were summarized in Holland (1997), reveal that the six types, when calculated using one of the several inventories available to measure them, show a reliable pattern of characteristics consistent with theoretical predictions. For example, Realistic types are hard-headed and conforming; they prefer industrial arts and agriculture as major fields and surveyor and mechanic as occupational choices, whereas Artistic types are imaginative, nonconforming, and emotional, prefer art and music as major fields and artist and writer as occupational choices (Holland, 1997).

In addition to the studies exploring the nature of the types, Holland collaborated with Alexander Astin (Astin & Holland, 1961) to study the nature of college environments. The Environmental Assessment Technique (EAT) involved a census of the type of majors, courses, and students at a particular university as a means of characterizing the educational environment that resulted. The initial work, especially that in college environments, was summarized in an important American College Testing monograph by W. Bruce Walsh (1973), a student of Holland's at the University of Iowa.

The 1970s were characterized by an intense period of measurement research and development. The Self-Directed Search (SDS) emerged; there were revisions of the VPI; the Holland themes were added to the Strong-Campbell Interest Inventory (Campbell &

Holland, 1972), and Bolles (1998) introduced the theory to the lay public. Throughout this period, Holland was director of the Center for Social Organization of Schools at Johns Hopkins University. During this same period, the work on the classification of higher education environments gave way to classification of work environments, and intense attention turned to gender questions in interest measurement.

A significant advance in our understanding of the nature of interests was occasioned by the discovery of the structure that is revealed in Holland's hexagon (Holland, Whitney, Cole, & Richards, 1973; see Figure 9.1), the full heuristic impact of which is only now being appreciated (Rounds, 1995; Day & Rounds, 1998).

Two changes occurred during the 1980s. Gary Gottfredson initiated a complex reanalysis of occupational description data that resulted in the *Dictionary of Holland Occupational Codes* (Gottfredson & Holland, 1996; Gottfredson, Holland, & Ogawa, 1982). This reanalysis stimulated a revision of the Occupations Finder using job activities. Whereas in the theory initially, environments were defined by the number of individuals of a certain type inhabiting that environment (for example, a social environment consisted of

FIGURE 9.1. The Holland Hexagon

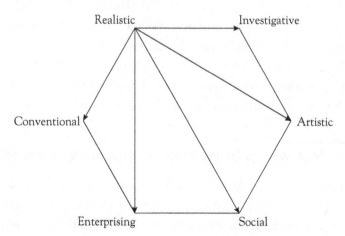

Note: R-person in an R-environment = 4; in a C- or an I-environment = 3; in an E- or an A-environment = 2; and in an S-environment = 1.

individuals with similar social codes and who solved problems by interacting socially), environments were now defined not only by the census of their inhabitants but by an analysis of data (level of data, people, items from job analysis data) concerning what those individuals actually did in their environments. This change was aptly described as a shift from "incumbent-based" to "public-record-based" environmental measurement (Gottfredson & Richards, 1999). A second change in the 1980s was a shift in emphasis from theory construction to vocational intervention (Holland, Magoon, & Spokane, 1981). This change paralleled the success of the SDS (Holland, Fritsche, & Powell, 1994) and the change of hands to its present publisher, Psychological Assessment Resources—an innovative and consumer-driven publisher devoted to enhancing and expanding the intervention capabilities of the SDS.

The 1990s showed a renewed interest in the theory and its revision, as well as in the question of convergence among career theories (Savickas & Lent, 1994)—a surprisingly vigorous research program on the underlying structure of vocational interests with an increasing emphasis on the cultural validity of the theory (Day & Rounds, 1998) and an equally vigorous debate on the complex nature of interests (Hogan & Blake, 1999; Savickas & Spokane, 1999). Recent research reviews examined the large, accumulated research literature on person-environment congruence in Holland's theory (Devinat, 1999; Spokane, Meir, & Catalano, 2000; Tinsley, 2000), increasingly with an interest in the cultural context of the theory (Spokane, Fouad, & Swanson, 2001). That work continues unabated on the theory, instruments, and research paradigms popularized by Holland is a tribute to the theory's enormous heuristic value.

A Practical Model of Person-Environment Interaction

Holland's theory describes the nature or disposition of the individual worker. He uses six basic personality-interest types and classifies the composition of the work environments in which those individuals function, according to a parallel set of constructs. The interaction of certain types (and subtype combinations) with specific environments predicts and explains the behavior and interactions that occur in those environments (satisfaction, stability, performance, and so on). This model of person-environment fit implies some change and adjustment in people and in the environments in which they work (Holland, 1997; Spokane et al., 2001). The individual is viewed as a relatively stable entity (Costa, McCrae, & Holland, 1984; Tyler, 1995) who moves in and out of environments rationally when the perceived fit is no longer optimal.

The organizing system described in this chapter has been applied to the construction and interpretation of interest inventories, to the organization and classification of occupational information in libraries, to the construction of self-help materials, books, and computer programs, and especially to research on nearly every aspect of vocational and counseling psychology.

Formal Statement of the Theory

The following statements from Holland's book (1997) provide an overview of the model:

1. In our culture, most persons can be categorized as one of six types: Realistic, Investigative, Artistic, Social, Enterprising, or Conventional.
2. There are six model environments: Realistic, Investigative, Artistic, Social, Enterprising, or Conventional.
3. People search for environments that will let them exercise their skills and abilities, express their attitudes and values, and take on agreeable problems and roles.
4. Behavior is determined by an interaction between personality and environment. [Holland, 1997, p. 4]

Holland Personality Types

An interest type is a theoretical organizer for understanding how individuals differ in their personality, interests, and behaviors. Types originate in heredity and in direct activities that yield interests and competencies; they culminate in a disposition or propensity to act in certain predictable ways (repertoires). Types are measured using interest items but are expressions of personality (Holland, 1997).

The six Holland personality types and their characteristics, drawn from repeated empirical investigations of the correlates of the types, are presented in Table 9.1. Work environments, according to the theory, are characterized by the same six types. *The theory implies that many people resemble more than one, and in most cases all, of the types to a degree.* An individual's personality is a composite of all of the types; each individual has a unique combination. These types reliably show characteristic repertoires of behavior and patterns of likes and dislikes, hold specific values, and endorse unique self-descriptions (Holland, 1997).

Subtypes. An individual may resemble one, two, or all six of the Holland types. The pattern of scores and resemblance is called a subtype. For example, a computer programmer might have a full code of IRCA. Typically, however, the highest three letters of the type code (IRC; called the three-letter code or summary code) are used in assessment and intervention. The diagnostic signs describe the relationships among types within a subtype or the relationship between the subtype of an individual and the subtype of the environment that individual inhabits.

The Hexagon and Diagnostic Signs. A detailed theoretical-empirical calculus, or diagnostic system, has been logically derived from the theory using the hexagon and is periodically undergoing empirical test. An understanding of the indicators in this system (congruence, consistency, differentiation, and identity) is essential to a complete understanding of Holland's organizing system.

Congruence. Congruence taps the degree of fit between an individual's personality and the type of work environment in which he or she currently resides or anticipates entering. An example of a highly (though not completely) congruent person would be an individual who had a three-letter code on the SDS of SEI and is considering a

TABLE 9.1. Descriptors Associated with the Six Holland Types

	Realistic	Investigative	Artistic	Social	Enterprising	Conventional
TRAITS Self-Ratings	Hardheaded	Analytical	Aloof	Capable	Aggressive	Content
	Mechanical	Intellectual	Artistic	Enthusiastic	Dominant	Not Artistic
	Scientific	Curious	Broad Interests	Friendly	Enterprising	Not Idealistic
	Quiet	Mechanical	Careless	Good Leader	Extroverted	Normal
	Reserved	Scholarly	Disorderly	Kind	Good Leader	Practical-minded
	Unassuming	Scientific	Dreamy	Persuasive	Not Quiet	Shrewd
	Highly Trained	Broad Interests	Idealistic	Not Scientific	Not Scientific	Speculative
	Low Self-	Precise	Imaginative	Sincere	Persuasive	Conforming
	Understanding	Thorough	Intellectual	Trusting	Pleasure-seeking	Conventional
			Introspective	Understanding	Popular	Not Original
			Intuitive	Generous	Power-seeking	Conscientious
			Not Conforming	Receptive	Practical-minded	Rebellious
			Original	Sociable	Shrewd	Neat
			Radical	Warm	Sociable	
			Rebellious		Speculative	
			Sensitive		Striving	
			Sophisticated		Versatile	
			Unconventional		Confident	
			Unusual		Energetic	
			Verbal			
			Witty			
			Complicated			
			Power-seeking			
Stereotypes of Types	Skilled	Scientific	Creative	Important	Ambitious	Precise
	Mechanically Inclined	Intelligent	Imaginative	Influential	Aggressive	Mathematical
	Trained	Studious	Talented	Helpful	Leaders	Methodical
	Builders	Scholarly	Expressive	Devoted	Shrewd	Meticulous
	Practical	Brilliant	Sensitive	Patient	Busy	Unimaginative
	Well Paid	Inventive	Interesting	Understanding	Responsible	Invaluable
		Introverted	Unconventional	Friendly	Status Seeking	Dull
		Respected	Temperamental		Dynamic	

TABLE 9.1. Descriptors Associated with the Six Holland Types, Cont'd.

	Realistic	Investigative	Artistic	Social	Enterprising	Conventional
Inventory and Scales	Mechanical Dogmatic	Open Academic Type Analytical Curious Mechanical Scholarly Scientific Broad Interests	Open Nonconforming Feminine Introverted Original Expressive Nonconformist Type	Extroverted Sociable Enthusiastic Liking to Help Others Feminine Dependent Understanding of Others Cooperative Interest in Religion Collegiate Type	Extroverted Sociable Dominant Enthusiastic Adventurous Dependent (Group) Leadership Sociability Self-confidence (Social) Popularity Collegiate Type	Conservative Dogmatic Vocational Type
VALUES	Institutional Restraint Christian Conservative Docility Freedom True Friendship (–) Ambitious Self-controlled Forgiving (–)	Self-Determination Theoretical Adolescent Revolt Wisdom Family Security (–) True Friendship (–) Intellectual Logical Ambitious Cheerful (–)	Self-expression World of Beauty Equality Imaginative Courageous Obedient (–) Capable (–) Responsible (–) Clean (–) Logical (–)	Service to Others Social Friendly Interest Equality Mature Love (–) Exciting Life (–) Helpful Forgiving Capable (–) Logical (–) Intellectual (–)	Control of Others Economic/Political Dominant/Striving Freedom World of Beauty (–) Ambitious Forgiving (–) Helpful (–)	Institutional Restraint Christian Conservative Economic/Political Docility Comfortable Life Self-respect (–) World of Beauty (–) True Friendship (–) Ambitious Polite Obedient Imaginative (–) Forgiving (–)

	Mechanics	Science	Arts	Human Relations	Leadership	Business
Life Goals	Inventing Apparatus or Equipment Becoming Outstanding Athlete	Inventing Valuable Product Theoretical Contribution to Science Technical Contribution to Science	Becoming Famous in Performing Arts Publishing Stories Original Painting Instrumental Musician or Singer Musical Composition Played or Published	Helping Others in Difficulty Making Sacrifices for Others Competent Teacher or Therapist Being Religious Person Being Good Parent Leader in Church Contributing to Human Welfare	Being Well Dressed Being Community Leader Influential in Public Affairs Expert in Finance and Commerce	Expert in Finance and Commerce Producing a Lot of Work
APTITUDES AND COMPETENCIES	Technical Competencies Mechanical Ability	Intelligence Mechanical Comprehension Arithmetic Ability Scientific Competencies Math Ability Research Ability Scientific Ability	Musical Talent (Seashore) Art Judgment (Meier) Spatial Visual (MPFB) Art Competencies Foreign Language Competencies Artistic Ability	Interpersonal Problem Solving Assessment Social and Educational Competencies Leadership and Sales Competencies Interpersonal Competency	Leaderless Group Discussion Leadership and Sales Competencies Social and Educational Competencies Business and Clerical Competencies Interpersonal Competency	Clerical Aptitudes (Minn Clerical) Business and Clerical Competencies Clerical Ability
Greatest Ability Lies in Area of	Mechanics	Science	Arts	Human Relations	Leadership	Business
IDENTIFICATIONS	Thomas Edison Admiral Byrd	Madame Curie Charles Darwin	T. S. Eliot Pablo Picasso	Jane Addams Albert Schweitzer	Henry Ford Andrew Carnegie	Bernard Baruch John D. Rockefeller

career as a hospital administrator (classified as SER). Congruence has been calculated using first-letter codes, three-letter codes, and six-letter codes but requires the use of one of several mathematical indexes (Brown & Gore, 1994; Camp & Chartrand, 1992) of the degree of fit between the code of the person and the code of the environment.

Consistency. Consistency is a measure of the internal coherence of an individual's type scores. Consistency is calculated by examining the position of the first two letters of the three-letter code on the hexagon. The closer the position, the more consistent the code and individual. Types that are adjacent to each other on the perimeter of the hexagon (for example, Realistic and Investigative) are more common and, therefore, harmonious than types that are opposite each other on the perimeter of the hexagon (for example, Enterprising and Investigative). An individual with an I-E type might experience a chronic discomfort or "dis-ease" between Enterprising and Investigative interests, which are not often found together and require nearly mutually exclusive repertoires of behavior.

Differentiation. Differentiation is a measure of the crystallization of interests and provides information about the relative definition of types in an individual's profile. Typically, differentiation is defined as the highest minus the lowest score among the six types or among the three scores making up the three-letter code. The highest differentiation possible would be a high level of resemblance to one type alone, whereas the lowest would be a perfectly flat profile with identical scores on all six types. As Holland indicates: "My purpose was to create a concept that would capture what clinicians mean by a well-defined profile" (Holland, 1997, p. 26).

Identity. Identity is an indicator of the degree of clarity of the "picture of one's goals, interests and talents" (Holland, 1997, p. 5). Identity is related to differentiation and consistency in defining the strength of personalities and environments. Measurement of identity is done with the Vocational Identity (VI) scale from My Vocational Situation (Holland, Gottfredson, & Power, 1980). A comprehensive review of the psychometrics and uses of the VI are contained in Holland, Johnston, & Asama (1993).

The relationships among these four diagnostic-theoretical indicators (congruence, consistency, differentiation, identity) and their use as interpretive ideas, as well as organizing or theoretical constructs, is described in detail in Table 9.2. Here again, we are just beginning to understand how and why some individuals develop a sharp spike in one type, whereas others develop strong interests in three or four types. All things being equal, however, an individual with high identity who is congruent, consistent, and differentiated should be more predictable and better adjusted than one who is incongruent, inconsistent, and undifferentiated. "For example, a conventional-enterprising person whose personality pattern is consistent and differentiated and who enters a conventional-enterprising environment with a high degree of differentiation will probably do competent work, be satisfied and personally effective, and engage in appropriate social and educational behavior" (Holland, 1997, p. 40).

Application of the Holland Organizing Schema to Occupational Environments. Occupational environments are classified in a manner similar to the classification of personality types. A census can be conducted of the percentage of employees of a given type in an organization (Holland, 1997), thus characterizing its "personality pattern." Consistency and differentiation can be calculated by examining the three-letter code that results from the census. Identity of a work setting is calculated by estimating the number of different occupations present. A large number of different occupations would result in a diffuse identity, whereas a small number of occupations would result in a focused identity (Holland, 1997). For example, a small or medium-sized accounting firm might consist of eight to ten accountants whose codes would cluster around C (CIS, CES, and so on), and five or six accounting clerks whose codes would also cluster around C (CIS, CIE, and so on), and perhaps several secretaries whose codes would also cluster around C (CSA).

TABLE 9.2. Summary of Interpretive Ideas and Indices.

Question	Diagnostic Construct	Basic Interpretive Ideas — Indices or Information	Source
Degree of Fit Between:	Congruency		
Current Aspiration or Occupation and SDS Code?		Zener-Schnuelle Index (7-Step—No Calculation Necessary; Use Simple Table)	SDS Manual, Tables 16 or 18, p. 43
Current Occupation and Alternative Occupation?		Iachan Agreement Index (28 Steps—Simple Arithmetic Calculation)	SDS Manual Supplement; See Table 6 for How to Calculate and Table 5 for Norms
Any Pair of Occupations, Aspirations, People?			
Interest Personality Interests. Traits. Life Goals. Values.	Personality Type and SDS Profile	Descriptions of the Types	SDS Manual Supplement; See Tables 1 and 28 or Holland (1985a)
		Secondary Interpretive Ideas	
Persistence, Tenure, or Stability of Vocational Aspiration, Choice, or Career	Coherence of Vocational Aspirations	Summary Code of Aspirations (Weighted or Unweighted)	SDS Manual Supplement (pp. 8–11)
		Summary Code of Work History	SDS Manual Supplement (Same as Above)
	Consistency of Two-Letter Code or Entire Profile	Hexagonal Model (Adjacent Types = Very Consistent, Every Other Type = Moderately Consistent, Opposite Types = Inconsistent)	SDS Manual, p. 4 or Holland (1985), pp. 26–28
	Differentiation of Entire Profile	Highest Summary Score Minus Lowest Summary Score	SDS Manual, Tables B-1, B-2, pp. 65–66 for Norms
		Iachan Differentiation Index	SDS Manual Supplement. See Table 8 for How to Calculate and Table 7 for Norms
		Visual Inspection: Does the Profile of Summary Scales Have High Peaks and Low Valleys or Is It Relatively Flat?	
	Common or Rare One-, Two-, or Three-Letter Code	Common Codes Associated with Stability; Rare Codes with Change	SDS Manual, Tables B-14 to B-19, pp. 71–75

Clearly, this accounting environment would be highly differentiated, with reasonable consistency and a clear identity. One might
expect the behavior and interactions to be relatively homogeneous,
stable, and predictable. Contrast this accounting environment with
a moderate-sized automobile dealership that contains enterprising
sales personnel, mechanics, and secretaries with different skills,
repertoires of behaviors, and ways of solving problems.

   Work environments can be classified more formally using the
Position Classification Inventory (PCI; Gottfredson & Holland,
1991)—an eighty-four-item assessment of the job requirements,
skills, perspectives, values, personal characteristics, talents, and key
behaviors performed in a particular job. The PCI yields nine variables. Differentiation and consistency are also calculable from the
PCI. The PCI grid or profile for counselor, based on twenty-two
counselors in a variety of settings, is depicted in Figure 9.2. Although

FIGURE 9.2. PCI Profile Grid for a Counselor

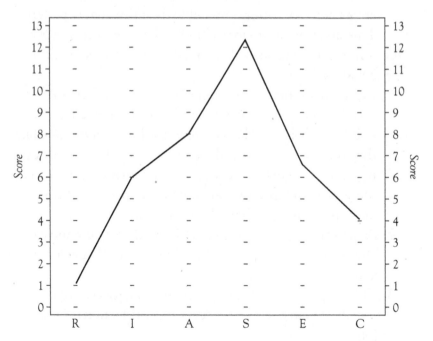

Note: N = 22; differentiation = 2.84.

their dominant profile is SAE, there is a distribution of subtypes within the group (SAE = 7, SAI = 4, SIA = 4, SEA = 3, SEC = 2, SCI = 2, SAC = 1, ASI = 1). Such a distribution is common when examining work environments and suggests that although many individuals resemble the dominant subtype (in this case SAE), some individuals will resemble variations of the code, and some will be incongruent.

People Interacting with Work Environments

The remaining theoretical propositions cover the interactions of persons and environments. These propositions are critical theoretically and practically but in spite of their importance have received only scant attention in the research literature (see Spokane, 1985; Spokane et al., 2001, for reviews).

5. People find environments reinforcing and satisfying when environmental patterns resemble their personality patterns. This situation makes for stability of behavior because persons receive a good deal of selective reinforcement of their behavior.

6. Incongruent interactions stimulate change in human behavior; conversely, congruent interactions encourage stability of behavior. Persons tend to change or become like the dominant persons in the environment. This tendency is greater, the greater the degree of congruence is between the person and the environment. Those persons who are most incongruous will be changed least.

7. A person resolves incongruence by seeking a new and congruent environment or by changing personal behavior and perceptions.

8. The reciprocal interactions of person and successive jobs usually lead to a series of success and satisfaction cycles. [pp. 53–54]

The Family of Inventories and Diagnostic Measures Associated with the Holland Model

Among its most valuable contributions, Holland's theory has generated a substantial array of practical devices for assessing persons and environments, which are described next.

The Self-Directed Search. The Self-Directed Search (SDS; Holland, Fritzsche, & Powell, 1994), one of the most widely used interest inventories, consists of an Assessment Booklet, an Occupations Finder, and an Interpretive Guide titled "You and Your Career." Unlike its competition, the SDS was designed to be self-administered and self-scored. No sophisticated computer or mail in scoring is required. Originally published in 1971, the SDS has been revised several times, most recently in 1994 (Form R). Nearly a dozen studies examine the functional utility, or outcomes, accomplished when the SDS is properly used in a self-directing manner. The companion materials include the following:

- Technical Manual (Holland, Fritzsche, &Powell, 1994)
- Professional Users Guide (Holland, Powell, & Fritzsche, 1994)
- SDS Form E (Easy language) and SDS CP (Career Planning [Corporate] Version)
- SDS Career Explorer (Holland & Powell, 1994)
- Educational Opportunities Finder (Rosen, Holmberg, & Holland, 1994)
- Alphabetized Occupations Finder
- Leisure Activities Finder (Holmberg, Rosen, & Holland, 1990)

Foreign language editions are available for some versions.

Figure 9.3 presents a description of the steps involved in using SDS (Form R). Included are directions for using the assessment

FIGURE 9.3. Steps in Using the SDS

Step 1

Using the assessment booklet, a person

• Lists occupational aspirations
• Indicates preferred activities in the six areas
• Reports competencies in the six areas
• Indicates occupational preferences in the six areas
• Rates abilities in the six areas
• Scores the responses he or she has given and calculates six summary scores
• Obtains a three-letter summary code from the three highest summary scores

R = Realistic
I = Investigative
A = Artistic
S = Social
E = Enterprising
C = Conventional

Step 2

Using the Occupations Finder, a person locates among the 1,335 occupations those with codes that resemble his or her summary code.

Step 3

The person compares the code for his or her current vocational aspiration with the summary code to determine the degree of agreement.

Step 4

The person is encouraged to take "Some Next Steps" to enhance the quality of his or her career decision making.

booklet to derive a code and then using the finder as an exploration experience.

The Vocational Preference Inventory. The Vocational Preference Inventory (VPI; Holland, 1985)—the first of the Holland inventories—has undergone six revisions since its introduction in 1953. The 1985 (7th) edition contains 160 occupational titles as items and yields the six type scales and five supplemental scales (Self-Control, Masculinity, Status, Infrequency, Acquiescence). Although data on construct validity for the VPI seems substantial, little in the way of internal consistency information was reported in the manual, which is in need of revision and is much less comprehensive than the SDS manuals.

My Vocational Situation and the VI Scale. The VI (see Holland, Gottfredson, & Power, 1980) is an eighteen-item true-false scale that taps the respondent's possession of a clear and stable picture of his or her goals, interests, and talents (Holland et al., 1993). A comprehensive review of existing studies on the VI is provided, along with its correlates and properties as a scale. The VI appears to have uses as a screening instrument in colleges and universities, as a pretreatment diagnostic test, and as a measure for evaluating the effectiveness of treatments (Holland et al., 1993).

The Position Classification Inventory. The Position Classification Inventory (PCI; Gottfredson & Holland, 1991) is an eighty-four-item inventory containing six thirteen-item scales corresponding to the six Holland work-environment types. The PCI is the only psychometric device for classifying work environments using the Holland system. Earlier systems by Astin and others required taking a census of inhabitant types or majors in an environment as a measure of the nature of that environment. The manual (Gottfredson & Holland, 1991) is clear, practical, and concise. Correlations between supervisor and employee ratings of the same jobs using the

PCI were very substantial, ranging from .59 to .79. Alpha coefficients were adequate-to-high across scales. In general, this inventory provides a useful, independent rating of the environment for use in research and counseling and has been much underused. Users should note, however, that this system of classifying environments relies on individuals' judgments of the nature of that environment, not on an actual census of Holland types inhabiting that environment.

The Career Attitudes and Strategies Inventory. The Career Attitudes and Strategies Inventory (CASI; Holland & Gottfredson, 1994) is the newest measure in the Holland system and is a 130-item four-position scale with nine subscales (Job Satisfaction, Work Involvement, Skill Development, Dominant Style, Career Worries, Interpersonal Abuse, Family Commitment, Risk-Taking Style, and Geographical Barriers).

Cronbach alphas for the nine subscales range from .76 to .92 in the final version; test-retest reliabilities range from .66 to .94. Normative data for 763 respondents were used to calculate T scores for the profile sheet. Correlations with the Hoppock Job Satisfaction scale and a measure of positive dispositional affect generally showed relationships in predicted directions.

Other Inventories and Measures. Although space does not permit their description, the Holland types can also be assessed using the new Strong Interest Inventory (SII; Harmon, Hansen, Borgen, & Hammer, 1994), the new Armed Services Vocational Aptitude Battery workbook—a clever and colorful intervention for students (Department of Defense, 1993), the Vocational Exploration and Insight Kit (VEIK; Holland et al., 1992), and other Vocational Card Sorts as well as the Bolles Party Game (Bolles, 1998), to name a few.

Several of these devices are now available in computer-driven format and, in the case of the SDS, in on-line format [http://www.self-directed-search.com]. Such formats provide appropriate access for individuals seeking assistance on their own (see Figure 9.4).

Welcome to the Self-Directed Search® by Dr. John L. Holland

Discover the careers that best match your interests.

Whether you are looking for a college major, beginning a job search, or thinking about a career change, the SDS will provide valuable career information. For information about the major career groups, click on the images at the bottom of your screen.

- The SDS takes 15 minutes and costs only $8.95.
- Your 8-16 page personalized report will appear on your screen.
- This printable assessment report provides a list of the occupations and fields of study that most closely match your interests.

➤ **Take the SDS Now**

➤ **More about the SDS**

➤ **Sample Report**

➤ FAQs

➤ **Payment Information**

➤ **Find a Career Counselor**

➤ **About the Publisher**

➤ Home

Empirical Research on Holland's Theory

The body of evidence testing Holland's theory is now so large that only a selective review is possible in the limited space allocated here. We urge the reader to consult the numerous independent reviews (Spokane et al., 2001; Tinsley, 2000; Walsh, Craik, & Price, 1992) or, better still, to consult the original material before passing judgment on the weight of this evidence. Although the empirical evidence documenting the six Holland types is large and supportive, the evidence on the environmental types is more scant (Gottfredson & Richards, 1999).

There remain several scientific controversies, as reflected in the research literature, that occupy most of the scholarly attention devoted to the theory. Four of these controversies are still actively pursued:

Is there a consistent relationship between congruence and vocational outcomes?

Are interests and personality unique constructs?

What is the underlying structural organization (shape) of interests?

Are the theory and its constructs, measures, and interventions valid outside of Western cultures and subcultures?

Whatever one's theoretical inclination or conclusions on these issues, the scientific process and argumentation about these crucial issues underscores the theory's enormous heuristic value and is a tribute to the serious regard accorded the theory by scholars.

Research on the Six Holland Types

A detailed review of studies of the six types can be found in Holland (1997). In general, studies support the existence of a limited set of vocational personality types and a unique pattern of competencies, identifications, values, and so on. This literature is now voluminous, numbering in the hundreds of studies. Recently, however, Leong, Hartung, Goh, and Gaylor (2001) found birth order to correlate with Holland type and occupational interests in a sample of medical students. First-born students were lower in Realistic and Artistic than their second-born counterparts, and "only" children were higher on Investigative. Later-born children scored higher on music, athletics, and nature. This study sheds some light on the developmental origins of the types.

Parallel or Commensurate Work Environments. Holland postulates a parallel set of six work environments and combinations or subtypes of those six environments with the same names and definitions as the person types (Realistic, Investigative, Artistic, Social, Enterprising, Conventional). Work on the environments has been slower but even more interesting than that conducted on persons. The early work on environments, led by Alexander Astin, was rigorous, complex, and longitudinal (Astin, 1999; Spokane, 1985). Although there have been few studies recently, and the person studies have eclipsed the environment studies, the importance of the environmental studies to the ecological base of Holland's theory is paramount (Chartrand, Strong, & Weitzman, 1997; Chartrand & Walsh, 1999; Hesketh, 2000).

Three studies (Smart, 1997; Smart & Feldman, 1998; Thompson & Smart, 1999) illustrate the complex manner in which academic environments exert their influence on students with regard to self-perceived growth and student competencies. Faculty, according to Smart and his colleagues, actively create environments consistent with Holland's theory and then require, reinforce, and reward students differentially according to their patterns of behavior.

Two novel studies redirect our attention to the complex social processes and interactions that transpire in work environments (Wampold et al., 1995; Wampold, Mondin, & Ahn, 1999). The first of these studies (Wampold et al., 1995) tested chemistry laboratory groups and found that Holland Social types demonstrated high levels of social, as opposed to problem-focused, coping skills. In spite of the limited social skills of the individuals in the groups (largely IR types), the groups adapted and adjusted to individual member differences. In the second study (Wampold et al., 1999) conducted in natural work settings, individuals of Social and Investigative Holland types demonstrated behavior consistent with theoretical predictions.

Relationship Between Congruence and Vocational Outcomes. It is no surprise that a large number of studies have examined the degree of fit (interaction) between individuals of different Holland types and subtypes in different work environments. The research paradigm that has evolved in this area includes taking a measure of the individual and a classification of the environment, then calculating congruence or fit between the two, using one of several indices (Spokane, 1985). Congruence is then related to a variety of outcome measures. Studies of person-environment congruence in Holland's theory are now in their third generation. First-generation studies used simple first-letter Holland codes largely in educational environments. Second-generation studies employed more complex congruence indices, using three or more of the types in the code and analytic methods employing moderator variables. Third-generation studies have examined mathematical indices of fit and employed fluid or adaptive models and presumptions examining changes in congruence over time.

Three recent and contrasting reviews of research on congruence (Furnham, 2001; Spokane et al., 2001; Tinsley, 2000) illustrate, with some clarity, both the shortcomings and the contributions of the congruence research paradigm in vocational psychology. The first of these reviews (Tinsley, 2000) offers ten principles on congruence drawn from reviews of the research literature:

1. P-E fit models are ubiquitous in vocational psychology.

2. The P-E fit models works.

3. Sampling inadequacies have influenced P-E fit results.

4. Commensurate measurement is essential when testing P-E fit models.

5. Fit indices are unfit.

6. Present status models may work as well as P-E fit models.

7. Hexagonal congruence and satisfaction do not correlate significantly.

8. Measures of Holland's model lack commensurability.

9. Most hexagonal congruence indices are invalid.

10. Holland's hexagonal model lacks validity.

Tinsley offers a number of suggestions for improving theory and research on P-E fit, including broadening theories, using more repeated measures designs, and adding polynomial regression and hit-rate analyses as analytic strategies. Tinsley's critical treatise argues strongly for the commensurate measurement of persons and environments, as well as design and analysis strategies appropriate to the complexity of the issues under study (Tinsley, 2000).

A second comprehensive review (Spokane et al., 2001) reasons that correlational studies, although crucial at the early stages of congruence research, do not reflect the complexity of P-E theory as well as do longitudinal, interactional, and experimental studies. Conclusions based on correlational studies must, therefore, be inconclusive by definition. This review concludes that congruence is a sufficient but not necessary condition for vocational satisfaction and identifies six benchmark studies of congruence with appropriate research designs that incorporate

- Experimental and social process elements (Helms, 1996)
- Longitudinal analyses (Elton & Smart, 1988)
- Multidimensional congruence (Melamed, Meir, & Samson, 1995)
- Moderator variables (Meir, Keinan, & Segal, 1986)
- Qualitative data (Blustein et al., 1997)

Finally, (Furnham, 2001) focuses on the cross-cultural validity of Holland's theory and a reconsideration of the concept of congruence and fit and improvements in research methodology and consideration of alternative approaches to studying person-environment interaction.

Congruence Indices. An unusually rich set of methods has evolved for calculating the agreement or fit between person and environment type codes (Camp & Chartrand, 1992; Gore, 1995; Young, Tokar, & Subich, 1998). Further, the evidence suggests that the method selected can influence the degree of fit found (Spokane, 1985). One particularly thoughtful analysis of the congruence literature (Assouline & Meir, 1987) conducted a meta-analysis of the congruence literature and compared indexes graphically (see Figure 9.5). Assouline and Meir's findings show that the indices of congruence are not interchangeable.

Three recent studies of the congruence indices (Camp & Chartrand, 1992; Brown & Gore, 1994; Young et al., 1998) compared multiple indices in an attempt to clarify differences among them. Camp and Chartrand (1992) studied 157 undergraduates using thirteen congruence indices and six outcome measures; similarly to Assouline & Meir (1987), they found that the magnitude of the congruence correlation was often dependent on the index used. Some of the indices yielded quite different findings on the same data. Camp and Chartrand reasoned that indices that do not incorporate either the circumplex or the order presumptions of the model should not be used in congruence studies. This study warrants replication, however, as the sample was entirely female and the measure used was the CAI—one that is almost never used in congruence studies. The subjects were all psychology majors, which should have yielded an adequate array of types. However, the high correlation between aptitude and congruence indicates that the subjects may have been quite homogeneous. The "Monte Carlo" method (using the same data but with multiple indices for comparing utility) was a notable advance.

FIGURE 9.3. Meta-Analysis on Congruence

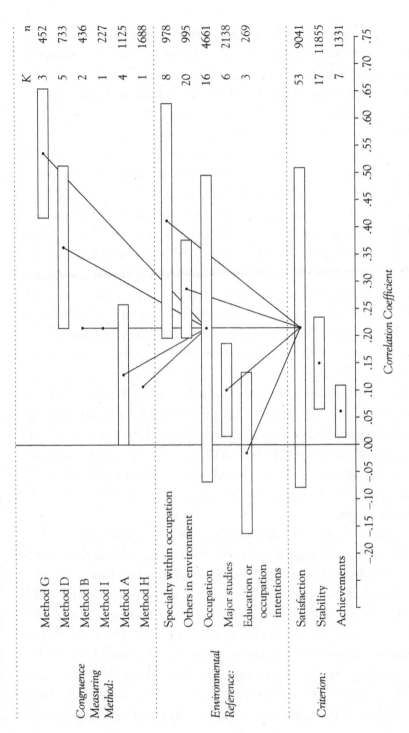

Note: Mean Congruence-criterion correlations with confidence intervals (95 percent) following meta-analysis. *k* = number of studies; *n* = number of subjects.

Brown and Gore (1994), in another Monte Carlo study, compared ten indices and created a new index (c), with a symmetrical underlying distribution (as opposed to positively skewed distributions underlying most other indices). This study used simulated data and explored not only the sensitivity of the index and its ability to distinguish codes with the same three letters in different order but showed that indices with normal curves underlying them were more useful in congruence studies. This research clarified the reasons for different findings with different indices, created a new index with a symmetrical underlying distribution, and spawned an extremely useful new computer program for calculating congruence (Gore, 1995).

Finally, Young and colleagues (1998) compared eleven indices of congruence and found weak relationships between congruence and job satisfaction using all eleven congruence indices with 483 employed adults in 170 occupations. The researchers found little moderating effect for sex and a weak moderating effect for different Holland types, with Investigative being the strongest relationship with job satisfaction ($r = .21$). This study is not in accord with other, more recent studies and deserves close scrutiny. Tinsley (2000) argues, however, that absent true commensurate measurement (of environments and persons), indices of fit will be no better than a "present status" model in which dimensions of persons, environments, and interactions are entered simultaneously (Edwards, 1991). Clearly, this criticism of the index paradigms is worthy of careful consideration.

The extensive research literature on person-environment fit in Holland's theory suggests several conclusions. Although all of the outcomes have shown contradictory findings at one time or another, the correlational studies of congruence are particularly susceptible to methodological artifact and conflicting findings. Nonetheless there is a consistent but modest (ranging from $r = .15$ to $r = .54$) relationship between person-environment fit and job satisfaction. This relationship, though slight, appears to be moderated by type and by the importance with which an individual views group interactions. Further, evidence continues to mount that individuals will move toward congruent occupational choices when opportunities arise to do so (Spokane, 1985; Oleski & Subich, 1996). Because Holland researchers have generally not corrected studies for the attenuating effects of range restriction (especially on job satisfaction) and unreliability of measures, these findings may constitute an underestimate of the congruence effect. Experimental and social process studies, as well as methodologically sound longitudinal analyses, offer more compelling tests of the model and generally appear to be more supportive of the fluid propositions in Holland's theory (Spokane et al., 2001).

Findings on the relationship of consistency and differentiation with career outcomes have been less favorable to the theory, though the methodology and quality of these studies has been spotty. Further, only one or two studies have adequately examined the compound effects of all of the diagnostic signs on career outcomes.

Interests and Personality as Unique Constructs   Relations between interests and personality are a topic of intense, ongoing debate (Costa, McCrea, & Holland, 1984; De Fruyt & Mervielde, 1997, 1999; Gottfredson, Jones, & Holland, 1993; Hogan & Blake, 1999; Schinka, Dye, & Curtiss, 1997; Tokar & Fischer, 1998; Tokar & Swanson, 1995; Tokar, Vaux, & Swanson, 1995). The issue, stated simply, is the possibility that measures of interests and measures of personality differ only with respect to item content employed. The implication of this position is that when we are measuring interests, we are tapping the same underlying construct as when we are measuring personality; interests and personality are simply two duplicative aspects (for example, arms or legs) of the same individual and therefore largely similar, despite one being the left (arm, personality) and the other being the right (leg, interests). Depending on the perspective from which one views the individual (from a personality perspective or from an interest perspective), one is simply examining the same individual's makeup from a different direction. Holland types, then, would be broad personality-based dispositions reflecting the full range of behavior, attitudes, and so on rather than defined more narrowly as interests that are simply patterns of item responses on interest inventories (Spokane & Decker, 1999).

The empirical evidence bearing on this problem is growing, but much remains to be learned. In a particularly provocative article, Borgen (1986) argues that when using the NEO-PIR (Costa & McCrae, 1992), interests and personality were not highly correlated until neuroticism is removed as a confounder. Stated another way, when working within the normal range of personality (absent significant pathology), interests and personality overlap substantially for both men and women ($r = .48$). As the magnitude of this correlation approaches 1.0, the two constructs in question (interest and personality) could be considered to be identical. Correlations of near .50 suggest moderate levels of overlap. Similarly, even when neuroticism is not controlled for (Schinka, Dye, & Curtiss, 1997; Tokar & Fischer, 1998; Tokar & Swanson, 1995), correlations between Holland types and Extraversion and Openness scales of the NEO-PIR are substantial. Replications with European samples yielded similar findings (De Fruyt & Merivelde, 1997, 1999).

Gottfredson, Jones, and Holland (1993) examined the relationship between Holland's types and personality dimensions on the NEO-PIR (Costa & McCrae, 1992) in 725 military recruits. Correlations between VPI scales and NEO types were modest but in expected directions (for example, Aesthetics $r = .45$ with Artistic type). Similarly, Gottfredson and Jones (1993) conducted a reanalysis of indices of profile elevation and differentiation relating them to several personal and psychological variables. Elevation appeared to be associated with Openness to Experience, Status, and Involvement for men and women, and with Extraversion for men. Elevation was also strongly associated with Acquiescence and negatively correlated with Control and Masculinity. Although no measure of depression was available in this reanalysis, the possibility of a relationship between depression and profile elevation has been discussed for years.

Similarly, Strack (1994) found correlations ranging from $-.34$ to .46 between SDS type scores and Millon Personality Styles, with

the styles being most similar along dimensions of (1) social domi-
nance-submissiveness and (2) emotionality-restraint. Reasoning in
a related study that a measure of private self-consciousness should
relate to an Artistic personality and, to a lesser degree to an Investigative or Social type, Carson and Mowesian (1993a) extracted
samples of each of the six Holland types from existing SII files and
sent the subjects a mailing. A private self-consciousness scale, a self-
monitoring scale, and demographic questions were included. Re-
turns from 139 (35 percent) of the sample revealed a very clear
pattern of predicted correlations between private self-consciousness
and Investigative and Artistic type for men and Artistic type for
women. The study also replicated previous findings on the relation
between self-monitoring and the Enterprising and Social types.
Finally, Holland, Johnston, and Asama (1994) found that Openness to Experience was correlated .62 with Investigative for men
and .43 for women and .50 and .44 with Artistic for men and
women. Extraversion was correlated .40 and .51, with Enterprising
for men and women and .31 and .39 for Social.

Thus interests and personality overlap to a considerable degree
when pathology is minimal (Borgen, 1986); psychopathology, as
opposed to personality, has a minimal impact of vocational outcomes,
except in the extreme. As Holland has repeatedly alleged, then,
"interest inventories are personality inventories" (Holland, 1997,
p. 8). Yet even at the .50 to .60 range, the relationship between the
two domains suggests that each is measuring at least some unique
component of the individual's makeup. Hogan and Blake (1999), in
a particularly insightful contribution, suggest that personality assessment "reflects the individual viewed from the perspective of an observer" (that is, reputation or perspective external to the individual),
whereas interest "reflects the perspective of the actor" (that is, identity or internal perspective). This possibility, which should be examined empirically, explains both the overlap and the uniqueness of
personality and interests. If this perspective proves accurate, the relationship between the two domains could be richly explored both
theoretically and practically. For the moment, however, interests

should be considered complex measures that reflect personality, as well as preferences, motivation, values, self-efficacy, style, and so on. (Savickas, 1999; Silva, 2001; Hogan & Blake, 1999).

Underlying Structure of Vocational Interests. In a controversy related to personality and interests, the question of the underlying theoretical structure of variables such as interests and personality is crucial to the theory and to measurement in vocational behavior. To illustrate the importance of the structure issue, consider the implications of a hypothetical finding that the underlying structure of interests is substantially different for men than women (or for some cultures when compared with others). If such differences exist, then different inventories and possibly different theoretical models as well might be necessary for each group. Answers to these questions depend, in large measure, on delineating the underlying structures of interests for use in such comparisons.

Holland's discovery in 1973 (Holland et al., 1973; see Figure 9.1) that a regular statistical structure could be found to underlie interest inventories was a breakthrough of major proportions. This structure permitted an exact diagnostic calculus and confirmed theoretical statements about the organization of interests. This work went more or less unchallenged until a recent special issue of the *Journal of Vocational Behavior* on the hexagonal structure of Holland's theory. In an unusually synchronous series of articles, James Rounds and Terrence Tracey (Day & Rounds, 1998; Rounds & Tracey, 1993, 1996; Ryan, Tracey, & Rounds, 1996; Tracey, 1997; Tracey & Rounds, 1992, 1993, 1995, 1996) reanalyzed correlation matrices (structural meta-analysis) from previous studies of the structure of occupational interests. This work, though highly technical, is fundamental to our understanding of the nature and organization of occupational interests. The question being addressed is how regular and symmetrical are the relationships among the types, the degree to which the relationships are similar across diverse cultural groups, and whether the configurations that result are two-dimensional (hierarchy, hexagon, or circumplex), three-dimensional (sphere), or hierarchical (Gati, 1991).

These studies by Rounds and Tracey, along with others in the last five years by Hansen, Collins, Swanson, and Fouad (1993), Khan, Alvi, and Kirkwood (1990), Prediger, Swaney, and Mau (1993), Care (1996), and Boyle and Farris (1992), confirm the existence of and efficiency of a circular structure with occupations ordered in the manner Holland and colleagues (1993) described. The structure appears in studies of women and men and has regular distances between and among types that are characteristic of a circumplex. It is possible that a three-dimensional sphere (Tracey & Rounds, 1996) may provide a reasonable approximation of the structure of interests and would be useful if clients and professionals could understand and use the spherical structure. There is some question about the shape of the circumplex across cultures; apparently, metanalysis does not reveal the circumplex structure in non-Western cultures. Although there may be problems in sampling, cross-cultural measurement, and translation, this finding, if replicated, would be of concern to all of us.

Validity of the Theory. Are the theory—its constructs, measures, and interventions—valid outside of Western cultures and subcultures? Social science models and theories, because of their context-sensitivity, are particularly sensitive to cultural bias. Thus we should not presume a theory to be culturally valid or useful until research results support that assumption. Conversely, we should not conclude that a theory is invalid unless evidence concerning its invalidity is presented. Unfortunately, cross-cultural validity is much more difficult to establish than is generally presumed (Spokane, 1986). Although the SDS, the VPI, and the SII have each been translated into multiple languages (Shaowen & Yaoxian, 1999), and cross-cultural studies are available, these studies are not without problems. Samples are rarely comparable across cultures, measures may not translate well, and even the basic constructs and assumptions of the theory may translate poorly for test (Spokane, 1986). Thus our conclusions about cultural compatibility should be carefully ascertained. Nonetheless, there is no more crucial goal for vocational psychology than to contribute to the understanding of cultural differences and to determine the extent to which there may be cultural "universals" or commonalities on which we can construct more comprehensive theories. This section on cultural utility and validity emphasizes studies published since the previous chapter (Spokane, 1996) and leads, naturally, to the discussion of the two cases, one of which has cross-cultural implications (the case of K); the other has gender issues (the case of E).

Four studies (Farh, Leong, & Law, 1998; Leong, Austin, Sekaran, & Komarraju, 1998; Leung & Hou, 2001; Soh & Leong, 2001) have examined the cross-cultural validity of Holland's theory in Hong Kong, India, and Singapore). Farh and colleagues (1998) examined 1,813 male and female freshmen in science, engineering, and business management. Holland codes were derived from self-reported preferences for occupations and the UNIACT inventory using a combination of English and Chinese items. A linear model supported a circular but not a hexagonal model of interests. Further, students who preferred occupations of a particular Holland type generally had interest scores consistent with that choice (that is, congruent). Evidence supporting the Artistic and Social types was weaker, which might be expected from the nature of the sample under study (science, engineering, and technology majors). Similarly, Soh and Leong (2001) used the UNIACT to examine the structural equivalence of samples in Singapore and the United States. They concluded that similar structural and criterion validity were found and that there was cultural equivalence for the S and E types and possibly for I types but not for the A and R types. Although we applaud the conduct of such difficult cross-cultural research, we urge caution in the interpretation of the findings because of the use of (1) a restricted sample of types (the UNIACT is one of the weakest indicators of Holland types [Savickas, Taber, & Spokane, submitted]), (2) self-reports rather than actual occupation among adults, and (3) correlational methodology (Spokane, 1986; Spokane et al., 2001).

In a third study of 456 female and 321 male Chinese high school students in Hong Kong, Leung and Hou (2001) administered the SDS (language unspecified). The College Majors Finder was used to classify students' preferred majors. Hit rates for male students were lower than those for comparable U.S. students but similar for female students (Leung & Hou, 2001). The authors conclude that the SDS could be used to differentiate science- and arts-track students. Hit rates (congruence) were comparable to those found in U.S. samples. Leung and Hou, however, were careful to note that the classifications and the instruments were developed in the United States.

Finally, Leong and colleagues (1998) used a modified English version of the VPI, which employs a five-position Likert scale ("do not understand," "does not exist in India," "too low in status") rather than the usual three-position scale, as well as a measure of job satisfaction, to examine congruence, consistency, and differentiation. Congruence was minimally related to occupational satisfaction in females ($r = .20$) and to job satisfaction among males ($r = .14$). The authors addressed directly the issue of equivalence of measurement by asking subjects to indicate when they did not understand the meaning of an item (occupational title). Twenty-four percent (14 of 160) of items had 5 percent or more of subjects indicating that they did not understand the item.

Day and Rounds (1998) examined the underlying structure of interests comparing African American, Mexican American, Asian American, Native American, and Caucasian American groups ($n = 49,450$), using three-way individual difference scaling. They concluded that "10 groups' responses reflected a remarkably similar underlying structure, consistent with conventional interpretations of vocational interpretations of vocational interest patterns" (p. 728). The authors note the problems of differences in sampling. The discussion in this well-written article suggests that there may well be universals in the underlying structure of vocational interests and personality (Day & Rounds, 1998). Similarly, Davison-Aviles and

Spokane (1999), in one of the few studies incorporating both an English and a Spanish-language version of the SDS, compared Hispanic, African American, and white middle school students with a finding that there may be differences in the outcomes of such studies when linguistically appropriate inventories are employed.

In sum, the increase in the number of studies of the cross-cultural utility and validity of Holland's theory could culminate in a body of evidence from which to draw firm conclusions about the theory's applicability across cultural and subcultural boundaries. Given the youthful state of research in this area and the array of methodological and conceptual issues that need to be addressed, however, definitive conclusions may be some years away.

Among the serious problems to be addressed are (1) the use of linguistically appropriate and previously validated instruments and measures, (2) comparability of sampling with respect to SES, age, employment status, gender, Holland type, and so on, and (3) consideration of fundamental cultural variables in studies. As three recent studies on culture and career illustrate (Juntunen et al., 2001; Gomez et al., 2001; Pearson & Bieschke, 2001), we may need to pursue more information about career development in a variety of specific cultures and subcultures before any universal variables or generalizations can be made.

With these caveats in mind, vocational interests and their underlying regular structures may be one possible universal. In addition, the cultural dimension of individuality versus collectivity appears to be one variable that is relevant to the career development of most cultural groups (Spokane, Fouad, & Swanson, 2001). Despite the numerous translations of the Holland instruments, cross-cultural work has been slow to accumulate. More work in this area is sorely needed.

Summary of Empirical Research. The Holland theory is unique in employing a comprehensive and integrated assessment system based on empirical research. The system has been subjected to more tests and analyses than any other model of career development. A surprising amount (though certainly not all) of this research has been supportive of the existence of a limited set of types, the underlying circular (or hexagonal) structure of those types, the validity of the instruments to measure types (though not to the same degree for the instruments designed to measure environments), and, to a lesser extent, the interactive proposition of the theory. The cross-cultural validity and utility of the model and the interventions that logically derive from it remain to be demonstrated (though absent a sufficient body of rigorous empirical evidence, we should no more assume that the model is culturally nonviable than we should assume that it is). In addition, Holland's devotion to practical application has resulted in the evaluation of the functional utility of several of the assessment devices generated by the model and the resulting adoption of the model in schools, colleges, industry, and private practices. The combination of empirical support and practical application accounts for the theory's popularity among the public, as well as among professionals. The practical nature of the theory is illustrated in the case studies—one of which has cultural implications.

A Culture-Centered, Person-Environment Approach to the Cases of K and E

The cases of K and E provide a good opportunity to illustrate the subtleties of Holland's theory and to underscore the importance of addressing intervention issues in the formulation of a career theory. Before responding to the cases, however, we want to discuss a few assumptions and observations about the career development process consistent with the Holland theory.

First, and perhaps most important, the core process in the Holland model is the projection of the respondent's personality onto occupational titles. The effectiveness (completeness) of that projection process depends on a number of internal and external factors, the most crucial of which is the clarity of that individual's personality at the moment in which the projection process is being studied—thus the prominent role of identity in the most recent revision of the theory (Holland, 1997). Culture, gender role, cognitions such as self-efficacy or agency (Lent, Brown, & Hackett, 1994), and other aspects of personality could reasonably be expected to influence the projection process and the feedback the individual receives during that process. Once initiated, the projection process continues to clarify and affirm (or disaffirm) an individual's career and life decisions. Although the projection and feedback process is somewhat unique for each individual, it is clear that groupings of individuals (called types) will respond similarly in their reaction to occupations. These types help us to understand both the repertoire of behaviors the individual is likely to display and the assets that individual might possess. We are not talking simply about clients here but about the general population as it is involved in vocational selection.

A second, equally important aspect of the vocational choice and implementation process concerns the individual's ability to act in a constructive manner to execute a chosen option in the face of environmental uncertainties, barriers, and opportunities. Thus it may not be sufficient to be clear about one's type and to have located a reasonably fitting choice. Mobilizing the behaviors and attitudes required to implement that choice is also necessary and is affected by internal and external factors. Each of the types also has a characteristic repertoire of behaviors that it is likely to employ in work situations (Holland, 1997). When under stress, each type may show a somewhat different reaction. For example, Realistic types could be expected to be prone to physical acting out, Investigative types to denial and rationalization, Artistic types to "crazy" experiences, Social types to depression, Enterprising types to manipulation, and Conventional types to obsessive details. Further, culture-centered career intervention may be possible if we can ascertain the degree to which an individual is acculturated within a group that values collectivity and shared values, as opposed to individual achievement, as a norm for success (Juntenen et al., 2001; Gomez et al., 2001; Spokane et al., 2001). Finally, to the extent that a cultural or subcultural group is in a dominant or subordinate position (has majority or minority status) may dictate the degree of structure necessary to achieve a successful outcome (Spokane et al., 2001).

The selection of therapeutic interventions in the career arena may also differ, depending on the nature of the problems being presented. We prefer the term *career intervention* to the term *career counseling* because of its breadth and inclusiveness with respect to what can be conducted, as compared with the more narrow term *career counseling*, which implies a one-on-one or group interaction. Counseling psychologists are trained, specifically, to handle a blend of career and mental health concerns and are challenged, increasingly, to do so as the profession expands from college-based to adult client populations.

In both of these cases, we have been asked to indicate what additional background or assessment data our particular approach might require, what culture, gender, and mental health interventions we might see, and how we would proceed to intervene in these cases. The information presented includes limited biographical and educational data, limited occupational history data (one client is seventeen, the other twenty), self-efficacy data, partial SDS data, values data, and responses to several open-ended questions around lifestyle issues.

Although we have been asked to indicate how we would proceed with career counseling in these two cases, the selection of therapeutic interventions in the career arena may depend on the nature of the problems being presented. We prefer the term *career intervention* to the term *career counseling* because of its breadth and inclusiveness with respect to what can be conducted, compared with the more narrow term *career counseling*, which implies a one-on-one or group interaction. Counseling psychologists are trained to handle a blend of career and mental health concerns and are challenged, increasingly, to do so, as the profession expands from college-based to adult-client populations. The focus of an intervention may be on career material exclusively, or the focus may shift from a narrow, closely directed emphasis in career or personal areas to a broad and more diffuse emphasis on general lifestyle concerns. Lifestyle issues are prominent in both cases, consistent with the youthful age of the clients (see Spokane, 1991). In addition, both E and K are first-born children (Leong et al., 2001)—a characteristic that could have implications for their careers and the degree of pressure that each feels from family.

Contemporary career intervention can contain a blend of the curative elements that have been found to lead to successful outcomes (Brown, Ryan, & Krane, 2000; Holland, Magoon, & Spokane, 1981; Spokane, 1991; Spokane et al., 2001). These curative elements or therapeutic ingredients generally fall in four general categories:

1. *Cognitive rehearsal of vocational aspirations*, including written and oral exercises designed to stimulate the client's envisioning of future possibilities and scenarios

2. *Information about self and the world of work*, provided by individualized feedback from assessment devices, and exploratory activities

3. *Social support*, provided by a therapeutic relationship with a counselor, or from group members, family members, teachers, coaches, or clergy, which effectively aids in restoring the client's morale

4. *A framework for understanding how to make and implement a career selection*, which could be a theoretical structure such as Holland's (or other theorists) or an elicited one derived from the individual's experience

5. *A mobilization for constructive behavior*, which may require effective management of optimum levels of anxiety (neither too high nor too low) and modeling on the part of the counselor

These therapeutic elements can be embedded in an array of intervention strategies (Spokane, 1991), including individual and group counseling, workshops, structured groups, classes, and self-guided activities.

The Case of K

A culture-centered intervention consistent with Holland's theory would begin with a discussion of K's strengths and assets, lifestyle considerations, culture and gender issues, and social constraints and barriers. Such information can be garnered indirectly through a few open-ended leads: "Can you tell me about your family background" or "How do your culture and or religion affect your choices?" We would also supplement this information with several additional sources in consultation with K—perhaps with a decisional diagnostic inventory such as the Career Attitudes and Strategies Inventory (CASI; Holland & Gottfredson, 1994), the Career Factors Inventory (CFI; Chartrand, Robbins, Morrill, & Boggs (1990), or the Career Beliefs Inventory (CBI; Krumboltz, 1991). A decision status inventory would provide additional insight into the genesis and nature of indecision in both of these cases, especially on the degree of anxiety present.

Next, we would use not only a homogeneous inventory such as the SDS but a criterion-based inventory such as the SII or the Campbell Interest and Skills Inventory. This information permits a thorough examination of contradictions between expressed and measured interests (Spokane & Decker, 1999), as well as motivational insights (Silva, in press). In both of these cases, ability appears to be substantial, but some assessment of specific abilities (for example, mechanical aptitude) might be useful in K's case, as well as a thoughtful examination of his relationship with his family, their views about acceptable careers, and the extent of pressure or influence being applied.

In particular, we would explore the apparent contradiction between K's stated values of belonging and financial prosperity with his repertoire of self-defeating behaviors (for example, skateboarding as only stated interest). The addition of one or more criterion-based inventories such as the SII, CISS, or Kuder would help us evaluate the apparent contradictions between K's Artistic daydreams and his CRI Holland code. This would clarify the "leading edge" of his interests (Spokane & Decker, 1999). A Card Sort

would aid in unearthing the underlying positive and negative constructs through which K is evaluating his future possibilities.

Generally, Holland scholars recommend breaking ties using
norm tables. If we do this in K's case, his code becomes CRA (A is
less common in a male code type and therefore is more influential),
which we would consider to be an infrequent (0.0 percent of HS
norm sample), largely inconsistent, and only modestly differentiated code type. According to Holland's "rule of 8," scores on the
SDS that are fewer than 8 points apart are essentially tied in any
case. We would also want to see K's full SDS to examine competencies and self-estimates in relation to his reported educational
self-efficacy scores. Because the scores are tied, ARC, RAC, CAR,
or ACR code types are also exploratory possibilities.

Although it is tempting to focus on the somewhat hostile and
oppositional tone of K's responses, given his age and developmental
stage we would initiate instead a systematic set of exploratory experiences in fields compatible with any of the codes listed in the Holland Dictionary (for example, CRA; Computer-Typesetter-Keyliner
[print & Pub.] [906.683.014] Photo Checker and Assembler [photo-
finishing] [976.687.014]; RCA; Glass Blower, laboratory apparatus
[glass products, instr. & apar.] [772.281.010] Airbrush Artist [prof &
kindred] [970.281.010] Photographic Retoucher [photofinishing]
[970.281.018] Manugrapher [fabrication] [970.681.022] Inker and
Opaquer [motion picture] [970.681.018]).

The fact that only five occupational possibilities could be found
in K's code combination is testimony to the rarity of the code type
and the unusual nature of K's interests. To avoid future problems,
K might be encouraged to appreciate the complexity and uniqueness of his code, especially the combination of A and CR interests.
Artistic types typically resent close supervision, need independence, and may express unusual interests and behaviors—the genesis of their creativity. Although it is tempting to pathologize this
young man's presentation, Holland, who continues to emphasize
more positive approaches to intervention (see the case analysis in
Spokane, 1986), would undoubtedly prefer to view K's predica-

ment through a preventative-developmental lens. Interests—their strength, pattern, and underlying structure—probably all do clarify with time, as developmental theorists have alleged (see Savickas, 1999). Thus we need to find ways to channel K's energy into positive and constructive behaviors that will lead to a successful career outcome.

K's assets include a certain degree of physical courage and willingness to undertake unusual activities. His math self-efficacy is a potentially important asset as well. Exploratory experiences in K's case should consist of written materials but also of on-site explorations with individuals employed in compatible occupations. Strategies should probably include group work or classes, given his valuation of "belonging," and attention should be paid to whether this "belonging" may also indicate a collective cultural orientation. Working as part of a creative team may allow K to combine both his artistic interests and his need for belonging. Counseling and exploratory activities and strategies should include as many creative interactions as possible to hold K's interest; computer-driven assessments and explorations may be very appropriate for K. Perhaps the most difficult issue that K faces is the decision about further education. Here again, systematic exploration would be crucial. Resolution of family pressures and influences would also be helpful.

The Case of E

E's Holland code, although still undifferentiated, is at least consistent and more frequently occurring (20 percent of the college sample). Although her SDS summary code is SEC, her daydreams reflect more E and A than does her Holland code. An interesting note: the occupational code for Lawyer in the Holland dictionary is ESA; on the SII, the code for Lawyer-female is ASE. This inconsistency illustrates the danger in using only one interest inventory.

Additional supporting information about lifestyle considerations, culture, and gender issues may help to clarify any inconsistency between the careers of her father and her mother, as they affect E's choice. E's occupational daydreams are very high in occupational prestige (see Gottfredson, this volume) but generally congruent with her summary code, as are the jobs in her vocational history. Prestige may be even more critical as a determinant of E's choice than are interests. This may be problematic if she aspires to a legal career but is uncomfortable with the lifestyle implications. I would clearly explore how E feels about the fact that her occupational daydreams include lawyer and judge—and both her parents are attorneys. This issue deserves considerable attention. Clearly, E is much further along in her choice than is K. A comprehensive battery of interest and decisional status inventories may provide E with reassurance of her preliminary choices or serve to redirect them somewhat. Further exploration with her mother's law partner would be in order, as would advance preparation for LSAT and law school admissions if that is an option for E.

Summary

We have tried to present a clear, practically oriented and balanced overview of the Holland theory and the instruments and interventions that derive logically from the theory. It is tempting to oversimplify the model, and we urge the reader to consider the theory in the full complexity with which it was crafted. As Tyler's quote at the beginning of this chapter implies, it is a mistake to oversimplify the processes we see in our clients and equally mistaken to oversimplify the theoretical models in this volume. In the end, each student must derive a composite (integrative, eclectic, transtheoretical) model that suits his or her theoretical beliefs and style of practice.

References

Altman, I. (1975). *The environment and social behavior.* Pacific Grove, CA: Brooks/Cole.

Assouline, M., & Meir, E. I. (1987). Meta-analysis of the relationship between congruence and well-being measures. *Journal of Vocational Behavior, 31,* 319–332.

Astin, A. W. (1999). The early years of Holland's research: Some personal reflections. *Journal of Vocational Behavior, 55*, 155–160.

Astin, A. W., & Holland, J. L. (1961). The environmental assessment technique: A way to measure college environments. *Journal of Educational Psychology, 52*, 308–316.

Barker, R. G., & Gump, P. (1964). *Big school small school.* Stanford, CA: Stanford University Press.

Betsworth, D. G., Bouchard, T. J., Cooper, C. R., Grotevant, H. D., Hansen, J.I.C., Scarr, S., & Weinberg, R. A. (1994). Genetic and environmental influences on vocational interests assessed using adoptive and biological families and twins reared apart and together. *Journal of Vocational Behavior, 44*, 263–278.

Blustein, D. L., Phillips, S. D., Jobin-Davis, K., Finkelberg, S. L., & Roarke, A. E. (1997). A theory-building investigation of the school-to-work transition. *The Counseling Psychologist, 25*, 364–402.

Bolles, R. N. (1998). *What color is your parachute?* Berkeley, CA: Ten Speed Press.

Borgen, F. H. (1986). New approaches to the assessment of interests. In W. B. Walsh & S. H. Osipow (Eds.), *Advances in vocational psychology. Vol. I: The assessment of interests* (pp. 83–125). Hillsdale, NJ: Erlbaum.

Boyle, G. J., & Farris, S. (1992). LISREL analyses of the RIASEC model: Confirmatory and cogeneric factor analyses of Holland's Self-Directed Search. *Personality and Individual Differences, 13*(10), 1077–1084.

Brown, S. D., & Gore, P. A. (1994). An evaluation of interest congruence indices: Distribution characteristics and measurement properties. *Journal of Vocational Behavior, 45*, 310–327.

Brown, S. D., Ryan, & Krane, N. E. (2000). Four (or five) sessions and a cloud of dust: Old assumptions and new observations about career counseling. In S. D. Brown & R. W. Lent (Eds.), *Handbook of counseling psychology* (3rd ed.). New York: Wiley.

Camp, C. C., & Chartrand, J. M. (1992). A comparison and evaluation of interest congruence indices. *Journal of Vocational Behavior, 41*, 162–182.

Campbell, D. P., & Holland, J. L. (1972). A merger in vocational interest research: Applying Holland's theory to Strong's data. *Journal of Vocational Behavior, 2*, 353–376.

Care, E. (1996). The structure of interests related to college course destinations. *Journal of Career Assessment, 4*, 77–89.

Carson, A. D., & Mowesian, R. (1993a). Self-monitoring and private self-consciousness: Relations to Holland's vocational personality types. *Journal of Vocational Behavior, 42*, 212–222.

Carson, A. D., & Mowesian, R. (1993b). Moderators of the prediction of job satisfaction from congruence: A test of Holland's theory. *Journal of Career Assessment, 1*, 130–144.

Chartrand, J. M., Robbins, S. B., Morrill, W. H., & Boggs, K. (1990). Development and validation of the Career Factors Inventory. *Journal of Counseling Psychology, 37*, 491–501.

Chartrand, J. M., Strong, S. R., & Weitzman, L. M. (1997). The interactional perspective in vocational psychology. In W. B. Walsh & S. H. Osipow (Eds.), *Handbook of vocational psychology: Theory, research, and practice.* Hillsdale, NJ: Erlbaum.

Chartrand, J., & Walsh, W. B. (1999). What should we expect from congruence? *Journal of Vocational Behavior, 55*, 136–146.

Costa, P. T., Jr., & McCrae, R. R. (1992). *Manual for the NEO-PIR.* Odessa, FL: Psychological Assessment Resources.

Costa, P. T., Jr., McCrae, R. R., & Holland, J. L. (1984). Personality and vocational interests in adulthood. *Journal of Applied Psychology, 69*, 390–400.

Davison-Aviles, R., & Spokane, A. R. (1999). *Journal of Multicultural Counseling and Development.*

Dawis, R. V. (1992). The individual differences tradition in counseling psychology. *Journal of Counseling Psychology, 39*, 7–19.

Day, S. X., & Rounds, J. (1998). Universality of vocational interest structures among racial and ethnic minorities. *American Psychologist, 53*, 728–736.

De Fruyt, F., & Mervielde, I. (1997). The five-factor model of personality and Holland's RIASEC interest types. *Personality and Individual Differences, 23*, 87–103.

De Fruyt, F., & Mervielde, I. (1999). RIASEC types and big five traits as predictors of employment status and nature of employment. *Personnel Psychology, 52*, 701–727.

Department of Defense (1993). *Armed Services Vocational Aptitude Battery.* Washington, DC: Author.

Devinat, A. (1999). L'adequation personne-environnement et la satisfaction au travail: Une meta-analyse. *Science et Comportement, 28*, 77–101.

Diamond, J. (1999). *Guns, germs, & steel*. New York: W. W. Norton.

Duany, A., & Plater-Zyberk, E. (1992). The second coming of the American small town. *Wilson Quarterly, 16*, 19–48.

Edwards, J. R. (1991). Person-job fit. A conceptual integration, literature review, and methodological critique. In C. Cooper & I. Robertson (Eds.), *International review of industrial and organizational psychology* (Vol. 6, pp. 283–357). New York: Wiley.

Edwards, J. R., & Rothbard, N. P. (1999). Work and family stress and well-being: An examination of person-environment fit in work and family domains. *Organizational Behavior and Human Decision Processes, 77*, 85–129.

Elton, C. F., & Smart, J. C. (1988). Extrinsic job satisfaction and person-environment congruence. *Journal of Vocational Behavior, 32*, 226–238.

Farh, J., Leong, F.T.L., & Law, K. S. (1998). Cross-cultural validity of Holland's model in Hong Kong. *Journal of Vocational Behavior, 52*, 425–440.

Furnham, A. (2001). Vocational preference and P-O fit: Reflections on Holland's theory of vocational choice. *Applied Psychology: An International Review Special Issue: P–O Fit, 50*, 5–29.

Gallagher, W. (1999). How places affect people. *Architectural Record, 187*, 74.

Garling, T. (1998). Introduction: Conceptualizations of human environments. *Journal of Environmental Psychology, 18*, 69–73.

Gati, I. (1991). The structure of vocational interests. *Psychological Bulletin, 109*, 309–324.

Gomez, M. J., Fassinger, R. E., Prosser, J., Cooke, K., Meija, B., & Luna, J. (2001). Voces abriendo caminos (voices forging paths): A qualitative study of the career development of notable Latinas. *Journal of Counseling Psychology, 48*, 286–300.

Gore, P. (1995). Congruence software for windows. Chicago: Loyola University: Author.

Gottfredson, G. D., & Holland, J. L. (1990). A longitudinal test of the influence of congruence: Job satisfaction, competency utilization, and counterproductive behavior. *Journal of Counseling Psychology, 37*, 389–398.

Gottfredson, G. D., & Holland, J. L. (1991). *The Position Classification Inventory: Professional manual*. Odessa, FL: Psychological Assessment Resources.

Gottfredson, G. D., & Holland, J. L. (1996). *Dictionary of Holland occupational codes* (2nd ed.). Odessa, FL: Psychological Assessment Resources.

Gottfredson, G. D., Holland, J. L., & Ogawa, D. K. (1982). *Dictionary of Holland occupational codes*. Palo Alto, CA: Consulting Psychologists Press.

Gottfredson, G. D., & Jones, E. M. (1993). Psychological meaning of profile elevation in the Vocational Preference Inventory. *Journal of Career Assessment, 1*, 35–49.

Gottfredson, G. D., Jones, E. M., & Holland, J. L. (1993). Personality and vocational interests: The relation of Holland's six interest dimensions to five robust dimensions of personality. *Journal of Counseling Psychology, 40*, 518–524.

Gottfredson, L. S. (1999). The nature and nurture of vocational interests. In M. L. Savickas & A. R. Spokane (Eds.), *Vocational interests: Their meaning, measurement, and counseling use* (pp. 57–85). Palo Alto, CA: Davies-Black.

Gottfredson, L. S., & Richards, J. M. (1999). The meaning and measurement of environments in Holland's theory. *Journal of Vocational Behavior, 55*, 57–73.

Hall, E. T. (1966). *The hidden dimension*. New York: Doubleday.

Hansen, J. C., Collins, R. C., Swanson, J. L., & Fouad, N. A. (1993). Gender differences in the structure of interests. *Journal of Vocational Behavior, 42*, 200–211.

Harmon, L. W., Hansen, J. C., Borgen, F. H., & Hammer, A. L. (1994). *Strong Interest Inventory: Applications and technical guide*. Palo Alto, CA: Consulting Psychologists Press.

Helms, S. (1996). Some experimental tests of Holland's congruency hypotheses: The reactions of high school students to occupational simulations. *Journal of Career Assessment, 4*, 253–268.

Hesketh, B. (2000). The next millennium of "fit" research: Comments on "The congruence myth: An analysis of the efficacy of the person-environment fit model" by H.E.A. Tinsley. *Journal of Vocational Behavior, 56*, 190–196.

Hogan, R., & Blake, R. (1999). John Holland's vocational typology and personality theory. *Journal of Vocational Behavior, 55*, 41–56.

Holland, J. L. (1958). A personality inventory employing occupational titles. *Journal of Applied Psychology, 42*, 336–342.

Holland, J. L. (1959). A theory of vocational choice. *Journal of Counseling Psychology*, 6, 35–45.

Holland, J. L. (1985). *Manual for the Vocational Preference Inventory*. Odessa, FL: Psychological Assessment Resources.

Holland, J. L. (1992). *Vocational exploration and insight kit*. Odessa, FL: Psychological Assessment Resources.

Holland, J. L. (1997). *Making vocational choices: A theory of vocational personalities and work environments* (3rd ed.). Odessa FL: Psychological Assessment Resources.

Holland and Associates. (1980). *Counselor's guide to the Vocational Exploration and Insight Kit (VEIK)*. Palo Alto, CA: Consulting Psychologists Press.

Holland, J. L., Fritszche, B. A., & Powell, A. B. (1994). *Technical manual for the Self-Directed Search*. Odessa, FL: Psychological Assessment Resources.

Holland, J. L., & Gottfredson, G. D. (1994). *CASI: Career Attitudes and Strategies Inventory: An inventory for understanding adult careers*. Odessa, FL: Psychological Assessment Resources.

Holland, J. L., Gottfredson, D. C., & Power, P. G. (1980). Some diagnostic scales for research in decision making and personality: Identity, information, and barriers. *Journal of Personality and Social Psychology*, 39, 1191–1200.

Holland, J. L., Johnston, J. A., & Asama, N. F. (1993). The Vocational Identity Scale: A diagnostic and treatment tool. *Journal of Career Assessment*, 1, 1–12.

Holland, J. L., Magoon, T. M., & Spokane, A. R. (1981). Counseling psychology: Career interventions, research, and theory. *Annual Review of Psychology*, 32, 279–305.

Holland, J. L., & Powell, A. B. (1994). *SDS career explorer*. Odessa, FL: Psychological Assessment Resources.

Holland, J. L., Powell, A. B., & Fritzsche, B. A. (1994). *Professional user's guide of the Self-Directed Search*. Odessa, FL: Psychological Assessment Resources.

Holland, J. L., Whitney, D. R., Cole, N. S., & Richards, J. M., Jr. (1973). An empirical occupational classification derived from a theory of personality and intended for practice and research (ACT Research Report No. 29). Iowa City, IA: American College Testing Program.

Holmberg, K., Rosen, D., & Holland, J. L. (1990). *The Leisure Activities Finder*. Odessa, FL: Psychological Assessment Resources.

Juntanen, C. L., Barraclough, D. J., Broneck, C. L., Seibel, G. A., Winrow, S. A., & Morin, P. M. (2001). American Indian perspectives on the career journey. *Journal of Counseling Psychology, 48,* 274–285.

Khan, S. B., Alvi, S. A., & Kirkwood, K. J. (1990). Validity of Holland's model: A confirmatory factor analysis. *Canadian Journal of Counseling, 24,* 178–185.

Krumboltz, J. D. (1991). *Manual for the Career Beliefs Inventory*. Palo Alto, CA: Consulting Psychologists Press.

Lent, R. W., Brown, S. D., & Hackett, G. (1994). Toward a unifying social cognitive theory of career and academic interest, choice, and performance [Monograph]. *Journal of Vocational Behavior, 45,* 79–122.

Leong, F.T.L., Austin, J. T., Sekaran, U., & Komarraju, M. (1998). An evaluation of the cross-cultural validity of Holland's theory: Career choices of workers in India. *Journal of Vocational Behavior, 52,* 441–455.

Leong, F.T.L., Hartung, P. J., Goh, D., & Gaylor, M. (2001). Appraising birth order in career assessment: Linkages to Holland's and Super's models. *Journal of Career Assessment, 9,* 25–39.

Leung, S. A., & Hou, Z. (2001). Concurrent validity of the 1994 Self-Directed Search for Chinese high school students in Hong Kong. *Journal of Career Assessment, 9,* 283–296.

Lewin, K. (1936). *Principles of topological psychology*. New York: McGraw-Hill.

Liu, S., & Gong, Y. (1999). Construction and standardization of the Vocational Interest Inventory. *Chinese Journal of Clinical Psychology, 7,* 77–80.

Lubinski, D., & Dawis, R. V. (1995). *Assessing individual differences in human behavior: New concepts, methods, and findings*. Palo Alto, CA: Davies-Black.

Meir, E. I., Keinan, G., & Segal, Z. (1986). Group importance as a mediator between personality-environment congruence and satisfaction. *Journal of Vocational Behavior, 28,* 60–69.

Meir, E. I., & Melamed, S. (1986). The accumulation of person-environment congruences and well-being. *Journal of Occupational Behaviour, 7,* 315–323.

Melamed, S., Meir, E. I., & Samson, A. (1995). The benefits of personality-leisure congruence: Evidence and implications. *Journal of Leisure Research, 27*, 25–40.

Moeller, D. W. (1997). *Environmental health* (Rev. ed.). Cambridge, MA: Harvard University Press.

Niles, S. G. (1993). The relationship between Holland types preferences for career counseling. *Journal of Career Development, 19*, 209–220.

Oleski, D., & Subich, L. M. (1996). Congruence and career change in employed adults. *Journal of Vocational Behavior, 49*, 221–229.

Pearson, S. M., & Bieshke, K. J. (2001). Succeeding against the odds: An examination of familial influences on the career development of professional African American women. *Journal of Counseling Psychology, 48*, 301–309.

Plomin, R., & DeFreis, J. C. (1998). *American Psychologist.*

Prediger, D., Swaney, K., & Mau, W. C. (1993). Extending Holland's hexagon: Procedures, counseling applications, and research. *Journal of Counseling and Development, 71*, 422–428.

Proshansky, H. M., Ittelson, W. H., & Rivlin, L. G. (Eds.). (1976). *Environmental psychology: People and their physical settings.* New York: Holt, Rinehart & Winston.

Rosen, D., Holmberg, K., & Holland, J. L. (1994). *The Educational Opportunities Finder.* Odessa, FL: Psychological Assessment Resources.

Rounds, J. B. (1995). Vocational interests: Evaluating structural hypotheses. In D. Lubinski, R. V. Dawis (Eds.), *Assessing individual differences in human behavior: New concepts, methods, and findings* (pp. 177–232). Palo Alto, CA: Davies-Black.

Rounds, J., & Tracey, T. J. (1993). Prediger's dimensional representation of Holland's RIASEC circumplex. *Journal of Applied Psychology, 78*, 875–890.

Rounds, J., & Tracey, T. J. (1996). Cross-cultural structural equivalence of RIASEC models and measures. *Journal of Counseling Psychology, 43*, 310–329.

Ryan, J. M., Tracey, T.J.G., & Rounds, J. (1996). Generalizeability of Holland's structure of vocational interests across ethnicity, gender, and socioeconomic status. *Journal of Counseling Psychology, 43*, 330–337.

Savickas, M. L. (1999). The psychology of interests. In M. L. Savickas & A. R. Spokane (Eds.), *Vocational interests: Their meaning, measurement, and counseling use* (pp. 19–56). Palo Alto, CA: Davies-Black.

Savickas, M. L., & Lent, R. W. (Eds.). (1994). *Convergence in career development theories: Implications for science and practice.* Palo Alto, CA: Consulting Psychologists Press.

Savickas, M. L., & Spokane, A. R. (Eds.). *Vocational interests: Their meaning, measurement, and counseling use.* Palo Alto, CA: Davies-Black.

Savickas, M. L., Taber, B. J., & Spokane, A. R. Manuscript submitted for publication. Convergent and discriminant validity of five interest inventories.

Schinka, J. A., Dye, D. A., & Curtiss, G. (1997). Correspondence between five-factor and RIASEC models of personality. *Journal of Personality Assessment, 68,* 355–368.

Shaowen, L., & Yaoxian, G. (1999). Construction and standardization of the Vocational Interest Inventory. *Chinese Journal of Clinical Psychology, 7,* 77–80.

Silva, P. J. (in press). Interest and interests: The psychology of constructive capriciousness. *Review of General Psychology.*

Smart, J. C. (1997). Academic subenvironments and differential patterns of self-perceived growth during college: A test of Holland's theory. *Journal of College Student Development, 38,* 68–77.

Smart, J. C., & Feldman, K. F. (1998). Accentuation effects of dissimilar academic environments: An application and exploration of Holland's theory. *Research in Higher Education, 39,* 385–418.

Soh, S., & Leong, F.T.L. (2001). Cross-cultural validation of Holland's theory in Singapore: Beyond structural validity of RIASEC. *Journal of Career Assessment, 9,* 115–133.

Sommer, R. (1969). *Personal space.* New York: Prentice Hall.

Spokane, A. R. (1985). A review of research on person-environment congruence in Holland's theory of careers [Monograph]. *Journal of Vocational Behavior, 26,* 306–343.

Spokane, A. R. (1986). Comments on professors Tanaka and Ogawa's paper. *Hiroshima Forum on Psychology, 11.*

Spokane, A. R. (1991). *Career intervention.* Englewood Cliffs, NJ: Prentice Hall.

Spokane, A. R. (1996). Holland's theory. In D. Brown & L. Brooks (Eds.), *Career choice and development* (3rd ed., pp. 33–74). San Francisco: Jossey-Bass.

Spokane, A. R., & Decker, A. R. (1999). Expressed and measured interests reconsidered. In M. L. Savickas and A. R. Spokane (Eds.),

Vocational interests: Their meaning, measurement, and counseling use (pp. 211–233). Palo Alto, CA: Davies-Black.

Spokane, A. R., Fouad, N. A., & Swanson, J. E. (2001). *Culture-centered career intervention*. Paper presented at a symposium on career intervention (S. Whiston, Chair). San Francisco: American Psychological Association.

Spokane, A. R., Meir, E. I., & Catalano, M. (2000). Person-environment congruence and Holland's theory: A review and reconsideration. *Journal of Vocational Behavior, 14,* 47–33.

Strack, S. (1994). Relating Millon's basic personality styles and Holland's occupational types. *Journal of Vocational Behavior, 45,* 41–54.

Thompson, M. D., & Smart, J. C. (1999). Student competencies emphasized by faculty in disparate academic environments. *Journal of College Student Development, 40,* 365–376.

Tinsley, H.E.A. (2000). The myth of congruence. *Journal of Vocational Behavior, 40,* 109–110.

Tokar, D. M., & Fischer, A. R. (1998). More on RIASEC and the five-factor model of personality: Direct assessment of Prediger's (1982) and Hogan's (1983) dimensions. *Journal of Vocational Behavior, 52,* 246–259.

Tokar, D. M., & Swanson, J. L. (1995). Evaluation of the correspondence between Holland's vocational personality typology and the five-factor model of personality. *Journal of Vocational Behavior, 46,* 89–108.

Tokar, D. M., Vaux, A., & Swanson, J. L. (1995). Dimensions relating Holland's vocational personality typology and the five-factor model. *Journal of Career Assessment, 3,* 57–74.

Tracey, T.J.G. (1997). The structure of interests and self-efficacy expectations: An expanded examination of the spherical model of interests. *Journal of Counseling Psychology, 44,* 32–43.

Tracey, T. J., & Rounds, J. (1992). Evaluating the RIASEC circumplex using high-point codes. *Journal of Vocational Behavior, 41,* 295–311.

Tracey, T. J., & Rounds, J. (1993). Evaluating Holland's and Gati's vocational-interest models: A structural meta-analysis. *Psychological Bulletin, 113,* 229–246.

Tracey, T.J.G., & Rounds, J. R. (1995). The arbitrary nature of Holland's RISEC types: A concentric circles structure. *Journal of Counseling Psychology, 42,* 431–439.

Tracey, T.J.G., & Rounds, J. R. (1996). The spherical representation of vocational interests. *Journal of Vocational Behavior, 48,* 3–41.

Tyler, L. E. (1995). The challenge of diversity. In D. Lubinsky & R. Dawis (Eds.), *Assessing individual differences in human behavior: New concepts, methods, and findings* (pp. 1–13). Palo Alto, CA: Davies-Black.

Walsh, W. B. (1973). *Theories of person-environment interaction: Implications for the college student.* Iowa City, IA: American College Testing Program.

Walsh, W. B., Craik, K. H., & Price, R. H. (2000). *Person-environment psychology: New directions and perspectives* (2nd ed.). Mahwah, NJ: Erlbaum.

Wampold, B. E., Ankarlo, G., Mondin, G., Trinidad-Carillo, M., Baumler, B., & Prater, K. (1995). Social skills and social environments produced by different Holland types: A social perspective on person-environment fit models. *Journal of Counseling Psychology, 42,* 365–379.

Wampold, B. E., Mondin, G., & Ahn, H. (1999). Preference for people and tasks. *Journal of Counseling Psychology, 46,* 35–41.

Ward, C. C., & Tracey, T.J.G. (2000). The structure of interests in children. Unpublished manuscript, University of Illinois, Urbana-Champaign.

Young, G., Tokar, D. M., & Subich, L. M. (1998). Congruence revisited: Do 11 indices differentially predict job satisfaction and is the relation moderated by person and situation variables? *Journal of Vocational Behavior, 52,* 208–233.

Zmeureanu, R.P.E., & Marceau, M. (1999). Evaluating energy impact on people's behavior in a house: A case study. *Journal of Architectural Engineering,* 99–102.

10

Person-Environment-
Correspondence Theory

Rene V. Dawis

Person-environment-correspondence (PEC) theory is the generalized version of the theory of work adjustment (TWA; Dawis & Lofquist, 1984), which is described in detail in the third edition of this volume (Brown & Brooks, 1994). TWA evolved over some forty-odd years, beginning in the late 1950s, as the theoretical framework for the Work Adjustment Project. This project had been organized to conduct research on factors affecting the work adjustment of vocational rehabilitation clients. As TWA evolved, it became clear that (1) TWA could be generalized to other environments besides work and to other populations besides rehabilitation clients, and (2) TWA and its subsequent generalized form (PEC theory) were themselves specific cases of a more generic type of theory in psychology: person-environment (P-E) theory. The second observation requires some preliminary comments about psychological theory; then PEC theory can be presented.

Psychological Theory

Psychological theory is unique among the sciences because it deals with so-called subjective reality. All other sciences deal with objective reality, that is, the observer is separate (apart and distinct) from what is being observed. Not so in psychology. In psychology, sometimes the observation itself is to be observed, and we have the enigma of the observer observing the observation. Also in psychology, the nature of the observer may influence the observation or the recording of the observation or both. Psychological data often depend on who is doing the observing and how the observing is being done.

Subjective reality lies in the awareness of the person. In the last analysis, what we call reality resides in the person alone and is known only to the person. Subjective reality consists of an "inner world" that is accessible only to the person and an "outer world" that is accessible also to other persons and forms the foundation for objective reality. A person can reach consensus with other persons about things and events in the outer world, hence consensus is the basis for objective reality. But because only one person can directly observe it, there is no similar basis for consensus about a person's inner world. Much of psychology is about this inner world, but psychology deals with the outer world as well.

This "two-world view" is unique to psychology among all the sciences, and it complicates the rigorous application of scientific methodology. One way psychologists have approached this problem is through P-E theory. In P-E theory, the two-world view is reduced to a two-entity encounter—the interaction between person and environment—hence, person-environment (P-E) theory.

Person-Environment Theory

Generic P-E theory assumes two entities in interaction: person (P) and environment (E). P-E theory may appear to focus on P, but in P-E theory P cannot be understood without E. E may be defined narrowly or broadly; it may be limited to people (other persons) only; it may be the physical environment only; it may be short term or long term. Furthermore, the interaction between P and E may be momentary or sustained. Indeed, one immediately recognizable difference among specific P-E theories is the designation of the E to which the theories apply (for example, to the work environment versus the school environment or within the work environment or to the job environment versus the career environment).

Interaction means that P and E *act on* and *react to* the other (each is both active and reactive). Both P and E have characteristics that are influential in the interaction. The interaction occurs in a certain way and has certain results or consequences for each. P-E theory, therefore, tries to answer three basic questions:

What characteristics of each are important to the interaction?

How does the interaction take place?

What are the consequences of the interaction for each?

The particulars of the answers to these three basic questions are what differentiate one P-E theory from another.

Person-Environment-Correspondence Theory

Person-environment-correspondence (PEC) theory starts with the basic P-E-theory assumption of P interacting with E. P and E are both active and reactive. To start with, E is typically a social E, that is, an E composed of other Ps. PEC theory can be adapted to deal with a nonsocial E or a strictly physical E, but the discussion that follows assumes a social E—the type that P most frequently encounters.

According to PEC theory, the P-E interaction comes about in the first instance because both P and E have *requirements* that have to be filled, and each expects the interaction to result in filling at least some of these requirements. Furthermore, P and E are able to interact because each has *capabilities* to bring to bear in the interaction. Using their capabilities, P and E attempt to fill their own respective requirements, which they perceive can only happen by filling the requirements (or at least some requirements) of the other, which is why the interaction takes place. Success (or failure) in filling requirements results in satisfaction or dissatisfaction for either P or E, or for both. Satisfaction brings about *maintenance* behavior, whereas dissatisfaction brings about *adjustment* behavior. Adjustment is pursued until satisfaction is achieved or until P (or E) gives up on the interaction. In PEC theory, therefore, requirements and capabilities are the basic characteristics of both P and E, and satisfaction (of both P and E) is the desired outcome of the P-E interaction. (The preceding presumes choice on the part of P and E. In real life, however, some Ps are in their Es involuntarily, and some Es include Ps that have been forced upon them. Otherwise, everything else holds.)

As a psychological theory, PEC theory focuses on P, but P can only be understood as P-in-an-E; E is essential, even if the focus is on P. That said, we begin by explicating the variables PEC theory uses to describe P.

Against the backdrop of its genetic makeup, P's requirements crystallize as *needs* and P's capabilities as *skills*. P acquires needs and skills through experience (long-term learning) and through training (short-term learning), that is, through interaction with E (or, more correctly, with many Es). P's set of needs and skills enlarges during the growing years and becomes relatively stable with the long-term adoption of a particular lifestyle (which typically occurs during adulthood). The stable set of needs and skills becomes characteristic of P. However, needs and skills can erode and may even drop out of the set; new needs and skills may be added. Thus, even while seeming to be stable, P may actually be changing.

Needs and Skills

Need is usually defined in terms of a deficit of some kind. For example, a water deficit in the body becomes a thirst need. The most basic human needs, such as hunger and thirst, are those involved in survival and are often termed *physiological* or *biological* needs. Through the process of conditioning, humans acquire other needs that have to do with their well-being (beyond just surviving), such as the needs for recognition and for comfort. These well-being needs are often termed *psychological* needs.

Given a "deficit," the "something" that fills it is technically termed a *reinforcer* because it reinforces or strengthens the behaviors that result in filling the need. The two terms, *need* and *reinforcer*, can sometimes be circular in definition, such as when a need has to be inferred from the effectiveness of a reinforcer, especially a conditioned reinforcer. A need, then, may also be viewed as a requirement for a reinforcer (a thirst need requires water; a recognition need requires attention and praise). Because there are many reinforcers (especially conditioned reinforcers), some reinforcers come to be preferred over others. If such preferences become stable, needs may also be described as preferences (to varying degrees) for reinforcers. This view of needs as reinforcer preferences is used in the measurement of needs via questionnaire—the most common way needs are measured.

Needs measured by questionnaire are typically scaled on a dimension of "importance," that is, in terms of how important a particular reinforcer is to P. Importance has an affective component: the greater the importance assigned to a reinforcer, the more affect or emotion is presumed to be associated with it. Some needs become more important to P than others, which is to say their reinforcers become more important to P than other reinforcers. Different needs may be the more important for different Ps or for the same P at different times. In time, certain needs (usually the most important and the least important) become more stable than the rest—so much so that they become characteristic of P.

As a theoretical aside, there is a disagreement among behavior theorists between those who think "reinforcer class" is the more important construct (following the lead of Tolman, 1932) and those who think "reinforcement schedule" is more important (following the lead of Skinner, 1938). PEC theory is on the side of the reinforcer class theorists because we believe that a "reinforcer class" includes "reinforcement schedule" as a primary characteristic of the class.

In PEC theory, P attempts to fill its needs by obtaining the required reinforcers. P's needs are filled from E for the most part, which implies that E has some kind of capability to fill needs, which might be termed *reinforcement capability*. In addition, some of P's needs are filled from within P. For example, the reinforcers' "water," attention and praise, come from E, but a feeling of accomplishment may depend on both E and P. This implies that P has some *self-reinforcement capability*.

Skill may be defined in terms of behavior sequences emitted in response to a task. Skill varies on a number of dimensions: (1) repeatability of the behavior sequence, (2) economy of effort (energy expenditure), (3) speed of performance (economy of time), and (4) difficulty of the task. The last dimension—difficulty—is the dimension used most often in scaling skill performance. The higher the level of difficulty of the task that P is able to perform, the more proficient P is in that skill. And the skills that P exercises more frequently—usually the ones at which P is more proficient—become more stable and more characteristic of P.

In PEC theory, a task is a *response requirement*, that is, a requirement for a desired response. P responds to a task by using its skills. Task and skill (like need and reinforcer) can sometimes be circular in definition; thus, a typing task requires typing skill, and typing skill is defined by a typing task. In other instances, a task may require more than one skill, and a skill may be used in filling more than one task.

Tasks ordinarily originate with E, but P may also be the source of some tasks ("self-imposed tasks"). Tasks vary from simple to complex, requiring P to respond using skills ranging from simple to complex as well. Complex skills are essentially combinations of simpler skills. In response to the same complex task, however, different Ps may use different combinations of simpler skills.

Because a task is a requirement, it may be considered a kind of need. This suggests that needs can be of two kinds: (1) reinforcer (or reinforcement) requirements (the kind for which the term *need* is most commonly used) and (2) response requirements, that is, the needs for responses that are desired. In a parallel fashion, skills can also be of two kinds: response capabilities (the kind ordinarily associated with the term *skill*) and reinforcement capabilities, as discussed previously.

Evolution theory would suggest that needs and skills must be related somehow because without the appropriate skills, P cannot fill its needs. For example, the carnivore has to develop (evolve) the appropriate predatory skills (stealth, speed, strength) in order to satisfy its need for meat.

Having the appropriate skills, however, does not automatically mean that the task will be completed or the need will be filled. Having skills is not the same as using them. P has to be motivated to use the skills. But then, using the skills, even the appropriate skills, does not automatically mean either that P will complete the task or fill the need. P must be enabled by E to succeed in completing the task or filling the need; that is, E must be supportive of P if P's (motivated) use of (appropriate) skills is to succeed.

Satisfaction

When one's needs are filled, we say that P is *satisfied* (from the Latin, *satis*, meaning "enough," and *facere*, meaning "to make." The mirror-image term is *satisfactory* (with the same Latin derivation). Something is satisfactory only because someone is (or has been) satisfied.

Satisfaction is seen in PEC theory as the objective of P-E interaction, that is, its desired outcome. Satisfaction, in PEC theory, is an affect—a feeling that is produced when one perceives a need to be filled. The goal of both P and E in their interaction is to achieve satisfaction. *Achieving satisfaction is the motivational force that powers the P-E interaction.*

P and E interact because their respective satisfactions depend on satisfying the other; in simple terms, each has something the other wants. So P sets out to satisfy E, and E tries to satisfy P; each attempts to fill the needs of the other (or at least the needs each believes the other wants filled). In PEC theory, then, satisfaction is the dependent variable, and P-E interaction is the independent variable responsible for producing it.

Satisfaction may fluctuate. P's satisfaction can change with changes in E or P, with changes in P's needs or skills (more precisely, the effectiveness of skills), or both. Whatever changes there may be, P tries to achieve a certain level of satisfaction and maintain it.

There are a number of problems with the construct, satisfaction. For one, satisfaction depends on perception. Satisfaction occurs only when P perceives a need as being filled. This brings up a problem that complicates all theoretical reckoning in psychology: the problem of the "perceived" versus the "actual." Thus, for example, P may be dissatisfied, even if E is actually filling P's needs. Conversely, P may be satisfied, even if E is actually not filling P's needs. Satisfaction or dissatisfaction in these instances appears to be based on "faulty" perception. But how do we determine when perception is faulty?

Another problem is posed by the fact that the satisfaction of one need may be separate from the satisfaction of other needs. In other words, there may be as many satisfactions as there are needs. Furthermore, these single-need satisfactions may be distinct from overall satisfaction, which may be based on the satisfaction of some, most, or all needs—or even of just one extremely important need.

The relation of overall satisfaction to single-need satisfaction is an unresolved problem in PEC theory. There is a choice between overall satisfaction as "global" (separate from single-need satisfaction) or as "total score" (the sum of single-need satisfactions). For the latter, there is the further choice between compensatory and noncompensatory models. *Compensatory* is when surplus for one need can compensate for lack in another, whereas in *noncompensatory*, all needs have to be minimally satisfied; surpluses do not count.

PEC theory sees these choices (global versus total score, compensatory versus noncompensatory) as a matter of individual differences. This creates problems in assessing satisfaction for a group of Ps, although less so for a single P (say, in a counseling setting, where we can ascertain which model a particular client holds). The solution for research purposes has been to make one approach fit all situations. But even if there were good reasons to use one approach, the question would still be which to use.

Individual Differences

Ps differ. On any given PEC variable—need, skill, or satisfaction—different Ps will differ in their status (score) on the variable being assessed. Being high on one variable does not necessarily mean being high on another. One P may be high on a few needs, another P on many needs, yet another on all needs; and this variation will be true of skills and satisfactions as well. Because of individual differences, each P has to be viewed individually, with its own pattern of highs, lows, and mediums, as well as on needs, skills, and satisfactions. Each P's pattern will be different from those of other Ps. To paraphrase an old saying, some Ps may be the same on many variables, and many Ps may be the same on some variables, but no Ps are the same on all variables.

Environmental Differences

Just as Ps differ, so do Es. Any P will experience many Es in its lifetime—even several Es simultaneously (depending on the definition of E). P's satisfaction will differ with different Es. P's satisfaction with a particular E may change over time. P's overall satisfaction at one time will depend on the accumulation of satisfactions from the several Es with which P is interacting at that time. Some Es may be more salient for P's satisfaction than other Es. Different Es may be salient for P's satisfaction at different times. There may even be times when one particular E is the only salient E for P.

Correspondence

Correspond originally meant "mutual response" (co-respond). Correspondence is used in PEC theory to denote the mutual responsiveness of P and E. This mutual responding is what goes on in P-E interaction. Both P and E have certain needs they expect the other to fill, and both "respond" (do something to fill the other's needs) because doing so will be instrumental in filling their own needs. Each is able to respond because each has skills. PEC theory assumes that certain skills are more appropriate for responding to certain needs, but which skills are appropriate for which needs is deemed an empirical question.

When both P and E respond satisfactorily to the other's needs, that is, each is satisfied with the other's response, we infer *P-E correspondence*. Otherwise, we have *discorrespondence*, which is when either P or E (or both) is not satisfied or is dissatisfied with the response of the other. (To simplify matters, *dissatisfied* will be used as including *not satisfied*). Thus mutually responding to each other's needs is what *correspondence* means when the term is used as a dependent variable in PEC theory. Its indicators are P's satisfaction with E and E's satisfaction with P. The way we know that the needs P expects E to fill are indeed filled—that E has responded satisfactorily—is through P's satisfaction. The converse is true: we know that P has responded satisfactorily when E is satisfied, that is, P's satisfactoriness is equivalent to E's satisfaction. Thus when the focus is on P, we say that the indicators of "correspondence" are P's satisfaction and satisfactoriness.

Correspondence is also used as an independent variable in PEC theory. In this usage, *correspondence* means the agreement or fit between P and E. To assess this agreement, P and E are viewed as commensurate constructs; hence, each can be described using the same terms as those used to describe the other. In PEC theory, *E is described in P terms but as the complement of P*. Thus, when P is described in need terms, E is described in terms of the needs that E can fill (that is, in terms of the reinforcers that E can provide for P). When P is described in skill terms, E is described in terms of the skills appropriate to fill E's response requirements (that is, in terms of the P skills that E's needs require). Thus, in PEC theory, the way to characterize any particular E would be to specify the distinctive reinforcers (for P) it provides and the skills (of P) it requires. The focus of PEC theory is on P, even in the description of E.

This use of commensurate P and E variables enables a direct one-to-one assessment of P-E correspondence, first, by examining the difference on each commensurate variable and, second, by examining overall correspondence as aggregated across all variables or all variables of one class. (We should note that in mathematics, there are four ways of assessing correspondence: one-to-one, one-to-many, many-to-one, and many-to-many. We chose to begin with the simplest way.)

As an independent variable, P-E correspondence has at least two outcome (or dependent) variables: P satisfaction and E satisfaction (or P satisfaction and P satisfactoriness, when the focus is on P. Note that these two variables serve as independent variables when P-E correspondence is used as a dependent variable). P-E correspondence can serve as the independent variable to several other outcome variables, such as (for work environments) productivity, profit, morale, mental health, turnover or retention rates, and accident or safety records.

To summarize: *correspondence* has two meanings in PEC theory: (1) a process meaning, that is, the mutual responsiveness of P and E, indicated by each other's satisfaction and satisfactoriness (correspondence as a dependent variable), and (2) a content meaning, that is, the one-to-one match-up of the commensurate characteristics of P and E (correspondence as an independent variable). This second meaning of P-E correspondence is the operational definition that will be used in the propositions of PEC theory given in the next major section.

Adjustment

According to PEC theory, when there is correspondence, both P and E strive to maintain it by continuing to do what they have been doing. When there is discorrespondence, whoever is dissatisfied (either P or E or both) attempts to restore correspondence by doing "something else," that is, by "adjusting." Hence *adjustment* is defined in PEC theory as the attempt to restore P-E correspondence; *maintenance* and *adjustment* are the two major modes of behavior. P and E are in one or the other mode at any given time in the P-E interaction.

Adjustment entails change, if discorrespondence is to be replaced by correspondence. The change may occur (or be effected) in either P or E or both. The change may be in requirements (needs) or in capabilities (skills) or in both. To focus on P for the moment: P's adjustment may take one or some combination of four basic forms, depending on what change takes place and where change takes place, as follows:

When P is dissatisfied with E,

1. P may get E to change the kind or number of reinforcers that P is receiving from E to fill P's needs.
2. P may change the kind or number of needs (reinforcer requirements) that it (P) has.

When P is unsatisfactory and E is dissatisfied with P, which then affects P's satisfaction,

3. P may use more skills, use them at higher (more effective) levels, or acquire new skills to fill E's response requirements (E's needs).
4. P may get E to change the kinds or levels of response requirements (E needs) that P has to fill.

There are therefore four points at which intervention may be introduced for P's adjustment to take place: the reinforcers provided (see 1) and response requirements (see 4) of E, and the needs (see 2) and skills (see 3) of P. In other words, P's adjustment can be accomplished by effecting change in E (termed *active adjustment*) or change in P (termed *reactive adjustment*), and the change can be in skills or in needs.

What applies to P can be applied to E in symmetric fashion. When E is dissatisfied, E can adjust by getting P to effect changes in its needs or skills (active adjustment by E) or by E effecting change in its own needs or skills (reactive adjustment by E).

There is one more—and last—way by which P and E can adjust: P can change E (move to a new E) or E can change (expel or replace) P. In other words, P or E can terminate the interaction when either one gives up on adjusting or is compelled (by other forces) to end attempts at adjusting.

Structure Versus Style

Thus far, we have discussed two classes of variables for P and E: needs and skills. These variables refer to the dispositional (or "trait") content of a person's behavior and collectively contribute to what is termed *structure*, implying stability of the needs and skills for a given P or E. *Structure* is stable status; hence it can be used in description and prediction.

When P and E are behaving, whether in maintenance or adjustment mode, they may be described on temporal (time-linked), process dimensions that are separate from and independent of structure. These temporal, process variables taken collectively are termed *style*. Four general style variables (for either behavior mode) are

1. *Celerity*, or quickness of responding, from slow to fast
2. *Pace*, or intensity of responding, from low to high
3. *Rhythm*, or pattern of responding: steady, cyclical or erratic
4. *Endurance*, or duration of responding, from short to long

These four general style variables were "borrowed" from four variables commonly used to characterize behavior in the laboratory: (1) response latency, (2) response intensity, (3) response pattern, and (4) response duration. These four "lab" variables correspond respectively to the four "real-world"-style variables described earlier. Over time, when much of P's behavior becomes more stable and more characteristic, we say that P has developed a style. We can then more easily describe P's behavior in terms of trait-like style variables. (The same might be said of E.)

When in the adjustment mode, other style variables may be used to describe behavior. Adjustment does not automatically take place when there is discorrespondence. P might tolerate some degree of discorrespondence (even if manifested as some degree of dissatisfaction) before attempting to adjust. When adjusting, P might effect change in either E or P. How long P perseveres in adjustment behavior before giving up is a final consideration. Thus PEC theory posits four adjustment style variables:

1. *Flexibility*, or tolerance for discorrespondence, from low to high

2. *Activeness*, or adjusting by effecting change in the other (active adjustment)

3. *Reactiveness*, or adjusting by effecting change in self (reactive adjustment)

4. *Perseverance*, or duration of adjustment behavior, from short to long

As with the four general style variables listed earlier, the levels on these four adjustment style variables may vary in the early going. With time, they may become more stable, such that they become characteristic of P. (The same may occur for E.)

Thus PEC theory uses four general style variables to describe the maintenance behavior and eight style variables to describe the adjustment behavior of P (or of E). Endurance and perseverance may appear to be the same variable in the adjustment mode. However, for some Ps, level of endurance in the maintenance mode may differ from level of perseverance in the adjustment mode, so it is worthwhile to keep these variables separate.

Personality

Taken together, the structure and style variables may be used to produce an overall description of P, which PEC theory terms the *personality* of P. For lack of a comparable term, we might call the structure and style of E the *environment personality* ("environmentality" won't do!). For precision, one might say "P-personality" and "E-personality," but for the most part in this chapter, unless otherwise indicated, the term *personality* will refer to P-personality.

PEC theory draws a distinction between *personality* and *self*. To begin with, P can be seen from either P's point of view or E's point of view. In PEC theory, personality is P seen from E's point of view, that is, P seen from an external point of view. Personality may be a consensus view or an average view but, however viewed, it is the view from the outside, that is, from E's vantage point. It is the view of P as seen by other persons who constitute E. As such, personality might be considered a social construct (dependent on people), and, in principle, it can be measured objectively (independently of P and the observer). As mentioned earlier, personality is described in PEC theory in terms of the structure and style variables discussed previously, measured objectively.

In contrast, *self*, in PEC theory, is P seen from P's point of view. The awareness of self is P's awareness alone; no one else has immediate access to self. Self may be inferred from P's behavior and background (including the biological, especially the genetic), but the only direct channel to self from the outside is through P's self-disclosure. In other words, the only direct way to find out about self is through what P tells us: the self-disclosed or self-reported self. But even the self-disclosed self is not necessarily a faithful rendering of the true or actual self because such disclosure is affected by P's ability to self-disclose and P's motivation to self-disclose, among other factors.

In PEC theory, self is also described in terms of the structure and style variables previously discussed, as these are disclosed by P. In this case, self is P as revealed by P. Incidentally, the various "self" constructs proposed in psychology (self-concept, self-esteem, self-efficacy, self-monitoring) are all premised on self-disclosure, in principle. Although it may be possible, as mentioned earlier, to describe self from data other than self-disclosure, the final validation of "self" constructs cannot avoid having to use the channel of self-disclosure.

Other Person Variables

There are two important classes of person variables that are used in other theories but not in PEC theory: (1) *interests* and (2) *personality traits*. Interests are usually defined as preferences (liking or disliking) for activities (for example, occupational, leisure). Other definitions add preferences for people, social situations, points of view (social values), and so on. These differences in preference objects notwithstanding, the defining dimension of interests is "liking or disliking," which is used in its operational definition.

In recent times, interest measurement has settled on Holland's model as definitive of interest content (at least, vocational interest content). Holland (1997) posits six types of interest: Realistic, Investigative, Artistic, Social, Enterprising, and Conventional.

Personality traits—variables measured by personality inventories and personality tests—typically refer to stable or enduring behavioral dispositions that are characteristic of particular persons. The traits are typically described via several items, and the respondent, in effect, describes self through these items (for example, by the number of items endorsed). Many of these so-called traits have to do with at least five basic dimensions (Digman, 1990): (1) extraversion, (2) agreeableness, (3) conscientiousness, (4) emotional stability, and (5) openness.

PEC theory does not deal with interests and personality traits. Interests may look similar to needs, but they are two different kinds of constructs. Some personality traits appear similar to skills or to style dimensions, but they are, again, different kinds of constructs.

One untested hypothesis is that interests and personality traits are higher-order constructs, with their roots in the basic constructs of requirement and capability. Interests may be seen as a form of requirement, but from the viewpoint of attention rather than need. Personality traits may be seen as a form of capability, but from the viewpoint of tendency rather than skill. More theoretical development in PEC theory is required to incorporate these two important classes of person variables.

Measurement of PEC Variables

A theory cannot be applied in practice or research if its variables cannot be measured. The variables of PEC theory can be measured in a number of ways, not just the way they were measured in the Work Adjustment Project and not just by using the Minnesota instruments (even if, modesty aside, these instruments are as good as any. For detail on the Minnesota instruments, see Dawis & Lofquist, 1984, and the *Minnesota Studies in Vocational Rehabilitation* series). The discussion that follows will elaborate on these points and, for convenience, will focus on P measurement.

Skills

We begin with skills because the technology of skill measurement dates back to the beginnings of scientific psychology. The measurement of human skills, especially cognitive skills, was scientific psychology's first problem. It gave rise to both psychophysics and psychometrics, and to psychological testing as well. Even today, much of psychology is engaged in the assessment and measurement of human capabilities, that is, human skills.

With the technology of skill measurement, we can in principle develop a measure of practically any human skill. However, the problem is that there are many human skills, almost too many to measure (not to mention the fact that new human skills are evolving all the time). Therefore, the assessment of all the skills a person has is not practicable.

Fortunately, there is a way to "summarize" or "compress" scores on many variables. Factor theory (factor analysis theory) allows us to mathematically identify a small set of dimensions (factors) that can be used to reconstitute each of a larger set of variables. Each variable in the larger set is described as a weighted linear composite of the factors. Thus a score on any variable in the larger set can be reproduced from scores on the factors. Using factor analysis, the U.S. Employment Service, for example, was able to reproduce scores on more than seventy skill measures from just ten factors, leading to the development of the General Aptitude Test Battery (GATB; U.S. Department of Labor, 1970). As the result of further development (test validation studies), the GATB can now be used, not just to describe P's skills but to predict P's potential (aptitude) for many different occupations, which can be differentiated by their configuration of skill requirements.

In PEC theory, these skill factors are seen as dimensions underlying all human skills, extant and still to come. These dimensions are termed *abilities*, following conventional usage (Carroll, 1993). Thus *abilities* are defined in PEC theory as reference dimensions for the description of skills. They are usually measured by ability tests and typically grouped together in an ability test battery.

Studies in ability testing have shown that there are at least three types of abilities: (1) perceptual (including acuity and speed of perception; perception of detail, form, depth, and motion in the several sense modalities), (2) cognitive (including speed and fluency of comprehension, memory, reasoning, and judgment in verbal, numerical, and spatial modalities), and (3) motor or psychomotor (including speed, fluency, dexterity, strength, and coordination in small- or large-muscle modalities). There might be a fourth type, not well studied, called affective abilities, which include emotional control, empathy, emotional mimicry (as in acting), emotional production on demand, and so on. The first three types of abilities appear to underlie response skills, whereas affective abilities might underlie reinforcement skills.

Another way to categorize abilities is in terms of (1) input, (2) central processing, and (3) output. All behavior (for example, skills) consists of input, central processing, and output components.

These components, when found to occur commonly, are what PEC theorists mean by the term *abilities*.

Ability measurement is more advantageous than skill measurement in terms of time, effort, cost, and ease of record keeping, as well as the amount of information that is implicit. For example, in career counseling, the use of ability measurement enables the assessment of a client's potential for skills that the client does not have, not just the ones the client has. One does not have to be a captive of the skills one has; with ability measurement, one can explore one's potential for skills that one does not have, and then develop them!

Needs

Needs are P's requirements; therefore, the most direct way to measure needs would be to ask P about them. There are several ways to ask about P's needs, one of which is to use a standardized self-report questionnaire. Most such questionnaires in current use are cast in a rating format, to take advantage of the well-developed technology of rating (see, for example, Guilford, 1954, or Landy & Farr, 1980). This technology can be used to maximize the accuracy of self-disclosure (validity) and to minimize the errors that can distort self-disclosure (reliability).

Each need can be measured by one question (item) or several items. Item scores can be aggregated to yield need scale scores. Aggregation can be done by using any of a number of methods, known as scaling methods (Dawis, 2000). Most of the published need scales are of the self-report–questionnaire variety.

Needs are requirements for reinforcers, which have two sources: E and P (the environment and the self). Because P is a social being, one class of environmental reinforcers exerts a particularly strong influence on P: social reinforcers. Thus reinforcers can be classified into three groups according to source: (1) environmental, (2) social, and (3) self.

In principle, each reinforcer would define a need and, therefore, would require its own need scale. Given this, the number of needs (and need scales) would be large, because the number of known reinforcers is large and growing. The situation with needs is the same as the situation with skills, and PEC theory's answer is the same: use factor theory to identify a smaller number of dimensions (factors) that can then be used to describe a large number of needs. TWA research has identified six such dimensions, which TWA-PEC theory terms *values*—a term chosen to underscore the fact that "importance" is the underlying dimension in the measurement of needs (in the same way that "difficulty" is the underlying dimension in the measurement of skills). To parallel the definition of abilities, *values* are defined in PEC theory as reference dimensions for the description of needs.

The six values (need reference dimensions) identified in TWA research are

1. *Achievement*—the importance of using one's abilities and having a feeling of accomplishment
2. *Altruism*—the importance of harmony with, and being of service to, others
3. *Autonomy*—the importance of being independent and having a sense of control
4. *Comfort*—the importance of feeling comfortable and not being stressed
5. *Safety*—the importance of stability, order, and predictability
6. *Status*—the importance of recognition and being in a dominant position

This list of six values is by no means exhaustive. Just as happened in the case of abilities, the list of values will grow as more needs come under study.

As one can see from the preceding discussion, need measurement as currently practiced has focused almost exclusively on P's reinforcer needs. P's response needs have rarely been studied. However, E's response needs—tasks for P—have been studied much more than E's reinforcer needs. Redressing this imbalance is an urgent research task.

Personality Structure

In the development and application of PEC theory, the emphasis has shifted from skills and needs to abilities and values. Personality structure is described more parsimoniously in terms of abilities and values than in terms of skills and needs. (Nonetheless, description in terms of the latter may be necessary when the skills and needs involved are not well described when using known abilities and values.) Also, because of their derivation as reference dimensions, abilities and values are much more stable than skills and needs. P's skills and needs may change without any change showing up in P's abilities and values. This robustness of abilities and values makes it more compelling to use them as the variables with which to describe personality structure.

Personality Style

The measurement of personality style has not progressed as much as the measurement of personality structure (abilities and values, skills and needs). Some style dimensions (for example, flexibility, perseverance, activeness, reactiveness) may be indirectly measured by scales in existing self-report personality inventories. However, such scales were developed with other intentions in mind, not as measures of PEC theory's personality style, and so they usually wind up as unsatisfactory substitutes.

Attempts have been made to develop self-report scales according to PEC theory, but these scales (in Ph.D. dissertations) have not been developed further for use in professional practice. Probably as good a method as any now available is that old reliable—an improvised self-rating on a 10-point scale, with the ends of the scale anchored by descriptive phrases. Another alternative might be to estimate P's standing on such 10-point scales from other data (for example, biographical data, interest, and personality inventory data). Also the 10-point scale might be anchored to the general population and might stand for particular percentiles (for example, top 1 percent, top 10 percent, top 15 percent, top 25 percent, upper 50 percent, lower 50 percent, lower 40 percent, lower 30 percent, lower 20 percent, lowermost 10 percent, representing 10, 9, 8, 7, 6, 5, 4, 3, 2, 1, respectively, on the rating scale.)

Personality Profile

A good way to view the total personality, given the measurements just discussed, would be to display the various scores as profiles (usually, one profile for each kind of variable). The advantage of a profile of scores is that it displays many features not readily seen from just a collection of scores. For example, one can see the overall elevation of scores (the mean of the profile) and the dispersion of scores around the mean (whether there are outstanding highs or lows or whether the scores are bunched up around the mean). Using the same set of variables, profiles can be correlated with other profiles (for example, a person's profile with an occupation's profile, a person's profile with another person's profile, and so on).

E Measurement

This section would be incomplete without a word about E measurement. As might be recalled from the previous discussion, in PEC theory E measurement parallels P measurement, but with a difference. Whereas the focus of ability measurement for P is on the abilities P has, the corresponding focus for E is on E's ability requirements (E's response needs). Whereas the focus of need measurement for P is on values (P's reinforcer requirements), the corresponding focus for E is on the reinforcers E provides (E's reinforcement capabilities). These complementary emphases make it possible to operationalize "P-E correspondence." The Minnesota Occupational Classification System

(Dawis et al., 1987) illustrates how E measurement may be accomplished according to PEC theory. (Note that PEC theory postulates the symmetry of P and E, which implies that E can also be measured on abilities and values, and P also on ability requirements and reinforcers provided; in practice, however, they are not.)

Propositions of PEC Theory

PEC theory may be stated in a number of propositions adopted from TWA (Dawis & Lofquist, 1984), which are stated with P as the point of reference. A parallel set of propositions can be stated with E as the point of reference, but these will not be given here.

The formal propositions of PEC theory are given next in both prose form and symbolic form:

Proposition I: P's correspondence with E is indicated by P's satisfactoriness and satisfaction.

I. SS,SN $\rightarrow$ pCe or pCe = f(SS,SN)

Proposition II: P's satisfactoriness is a function of the correspondence of P's abilities to E's ability requirements, provided that E's reinforcers correspond to P's values.

II. SS = f(aCr | sCv $\rightarrow$ max)

Corollary IIA: Knowledge of P's satisfactoriness and abilities permits inference of E's ability requirements.

IIA. (SS,a) $\rightarrow$ r

Corollary IIB: Knowledge of P's satisfactoriness and E's ability requirements permits inference of P's abilities.

IIB. (SS,r) $\rightarrow$ a

Proposition III: P's satisfaction is a function of the correspondence of E's reinforcers to P's values, provided that P's abilities correspond to E's ability requirements.

III. $SN = f(sCv \mid aCr \rightarrow max)$

Corollary IIIA. Knowledge of P's satisfaction and E's reinforcers permits inference of P's values.

IIIA. $(SN,s) \rightarrow v$

Corollary IIIB. Knowledge of P's satisfaction and P's values permits inference of E's reinforcers.

IIIB. $(SN,v) \rightarrow s$

Proposition IV: P's satisfaction moderates the relationship between P's satisfactoriness and P's ability-requirement correspondence.

IV. $SS = f(aCr \mid SN) = f(aCr, aCr \times SN)$

Proposition V: P's satisfactoriness moderates the relationship between P's satisfaction and P's reinforcer-value correspondence.

V. $SN = f(sCv \mid SS) = f(sCv, sCv \times SS)$

Proposition VI: The probability of P's being forced out of E is inversely related to P's satisfactoriness.

VI. $P(FO) = f(1/SS)$ or $P(FO) = f(SS)$

Proposition VII: The probability of P's leaving E is inversely related to P's satisfaction.

VII. $P(LE) = f(1/SN)$ or $P(LE) = f(SN)$

Proposition VIII: P's tenure in E is a joint function of P's satisfactoriness and satisfaction.

VIII. $TE = f(SS,SN)$

Corollary VIIIA: P's tenure in E is a joint function of P's ability-requirement correspondence and P's reinforcer-value correspondence.

Corollary VIIIA. $TE = f(aCr,sCv)$

Corollary VIIIB: P's tenure in E is a function of the correspon_ dence of P's structure with E's structure.

VIIIB. TE = f(pstCest)

Proposition IX: P-E correspondence increases as a function of P's tenure.

IX. pCe = f(TE)

Proposition X: The correspondence of P's style to E's style moderates the prediction of P's correspondence with E from the correspon- dence of P's structure to E's structure.

X. pCe = f(pstCest | psyCesy) = f(pstCest, pstCest × psyCesy)

Proposition XI: E's flexibility moderates the relationship between P's satisfactoriness and P's ability-requirement correspondence.

XI. SS = f(aCr | FLe) = f(aCr, aCr × FLe)

Proposition XII: P's flexibility moderates the relationship between P's satisfaction and P's reinforcer-value correspondence.

XII. SN = f(sCv | FLp) = f(sCv, sCv × FLp)

Proposition XIII: The probability that E will go into adjustment mode is inversely related to P's satisfactoriness.

XIII. P(AMe) = f(1/SS) or P(AMe) = f(SS)

Corollary XIIIA: Knowledge of E's adjustment-mode probability associated with P's satisfactoriness permits the determination of E's flexibility.

XIIIA. (P[AMe] | SS) → FLe

Proposition XIV: The probability that P will go into adjustment mode is inversely related to P's satisfaction.

XIV. P(AMp) = f(1/SN) or P(AMp) = f(SN)

Corollary XIVA: Knowledge of P's adjustment-mode probability associated with P's satisfaction permits the determination of P's flexibility.

XIVA. $(P[AMp] | SN) \rightarrow FLp$

Proposition XV: The probability of P's being forced out of E is inversely related to E's perseverance.

XV. $P(FO) = f(1/PEe)$ or $P(FO) = f(PEe)$

Proposition XVI: The probability of P's leaving E is inversely related to P's perseverance.

XVI. $P(LE) = f(1/PEp)$ or $P(LE) = f(PEp)$

Proposition XVII: P's tenure in E is a joint function of P's satisfactoriness and satisfaction, and P's and E's perseverance.

XVII. $TE = f(SS, SN, PEp, PEe)$

The reader is reminded that the seventeen propositions are stated from P's point of view and that parallel propositions can be stated from E's point of view, although they are not given here. In addition, there are other propositions of PEC theory for which research has not been conducted; these are stated in Lofquist and Dawis (1991).

Explanation of the PEC Propositions

There are two focal points for the seventeen propositions: (1) P's satisfactoriness and (2) P's satisfaction. P's satisfactoriness, it should be remembered, is E's satisfaction with P. Thus the two focal points are actually P's satisfaction and E's satisfaction (with P).

P's satisfaction depends primarily on the correspondence of E's reinforcers with P's values (P's reinforcer-value correspondence, for short). But it also depends on P's satisfactoriness and P's flexibility. P's satisfaction cannot be predicted from reinforcer-value correspondence if P is unsatisfactory (that is, E is dissatisfied with P). Also, the more flexible P is, the easier it is for E to satisfy P (the more relaxed the reinforcer-value-correspondence fit required by P).

In contrast, P's satisfactoriness depends primarily on the correspondence of P's abilities with E's ability requirements (P's ability-requirement correspondence, for short), moderated by P's satisfaction and E's flexibility. If P is dissatisfied, P's satisfactoriness cannot be predicted from P's ability-requirement correspondence. And if E is flexible, E will tolerate a more relaxed ability-requirement-correspondence fit for P.

P's tenure in E depends on P's satisfactoriness and satisfaction, which depend in turn on P's ability-requirement correspondence and reinforcer-value correspondence, respectively. Thus we can predict P's probable tenure in a potential E if we can estimate P's probable ability-requirement correspondence and reinforcer-value correspondence for that potential E.

When using PEC theory in a career counseling setting, given that a client's abilities and values can be assessed, one has to find out what a potential career occupation's ability requirements and reinforcers are in order to predict the client's probable satisfactoriness and satisfaction—and therefore probable tenure—in that occupation. However, most occupational information is not given in these terms (that is, ability requirements and reinforcers), so it becomes the counselor's job to estimate the "terms." (This assumes that the client does not know how to estimate them. If the client does estimate them, the counselor's own estimates can serve as a "validation" for the client's estimations.)

In career choice, the client's abilities and values may be used as the initial "criteria" for choosing an occupation or for choosing from among several occupations. Each occupation being considered can be rated as to its degree of "fit" to the client's abilities and values. Such assessment will be equivalent to predicting satisfactoriness and satisfaction for the client in each occupation being considered.

Closeness of "fit"—P-E correspondence—is, of course, only one element going into a career choice; though important, it may not even be definitive. Accessibility of training institutions, training time required, cost of training and availability of other income sources while training, family requirements, and future job prospects are among the other conditions that have to be considered. One or more of these conditions may outweigh PEC correspondence in a choice decision at a given time.

The PEC theory just stated appears best adopted to a work setting, which is not surprising, being derived as it is from TWA. However, a careful reading will show that PEC theory can be applied to any environment, such as school, home, or even to social relationships, in which one or more persons serve as "environment" to the index person. What would be different from TWA would be the requirements and capabilities that are salient for each E. The set of salient requirements and capabilities would, in effect, distinguish the E in question. In principle, all P variables (all P values and all P abilities) would apply, although they would be weighted differently for different Es. It is in this sense that PEC theory is a generalization of TWA.

Validity of the PEC Theory

Dawis and Lofquist (1984) have summarized the research that has been done to validate the propositions of PEC theory as applied to the work environment, and the interested reader is referred to that book for details.

Research Backing for the Propositions

In brief, there is good support for the first nine propositions of PEC theory (on which the Work Adjustment Project concentrated its efforts), but only a little research has been done to back up the last eight propositions, mostly in unpublished doctoral dissertations. Since the mid-1980s, most of our efforts shifted from theory testing to using PEC theory in the real world. PEC theory was, and still is, used as the guiding framework for a Vocational Assessment Clinic that provides career counseling to nonstudent adults and for a Vocational Assessment Program that provides information in PEC-theory terms to assist vocational rehabilitation clients of the Minnesota State Rehabilitation Service.

Individual Differences

In recent years, U.S. society has become more and more conscious of its diverse composition, in part because it is becoming more and more diverse, as the year 2000 census has shown. Furthermore, diversity is at the root of several contemporary controversies and differences of opinion about social policy and social practice. What has PEC theory to say about diversity?

To begin with, diversity is about individual differences; they are a fact of nature. Individuals differ within any group: gender groups, age groups, socioeconomic class groups, ethnic groups—even within the family. The psychology of individual differences is the branch of psychology that has long studied this phenomenon (Dawis, 1992). PEC theory is grounded on the psychology of individual differences.

Two important questions arise: (1) How much do individuals really differ? and (2) Do these differences make a difference?

The psychology of individual differences has produced many findings that bear on these two questions (see Lubinski, 2000, for an updated review). The following statements summarize some of the basic findings of this field:

- Individuals in any group will differ in the magnitude of any characteristic they possess.

- The range of these differences is typically large, expressed statistically as five to six standard deviations or more.

- When groups differ, they are often characterized by the differences in their mean values.

- Groups may also differ in variability within the group. Unfortunately, within-group variability (standard deviation) almost always goes unreported.

- Most mean differences between groups are small, rarely exceeding one-half of a standard deviation, especially when the groups being compared are similar in age and gender composition. This is to be compared with the large within-group differences.

- Many characteristics are correlated. For such characteristics, prediction from one to another is easy and precise.

- However, many characteristics are uncorrelated or only slightly correlated; for these characteristics, prediction from one to another is poor to nil.

- Some characteristics are prized by society, especially "social outcome" variables such as success in school or work. These variables may be predicted from combinations of other individual-differences variables.

- Prediction of social outcome variables from person variables is rarely high, often moderate to low, usually less than 0.50 correlation.

Researchers in the field of the psychology of individual differences have studied differences between groups intensively, especially differences between the genders, among age groups, among racial or ethnic groups, and among socioeconomic groups. Most of the differences reported between groups are mean differences—an important detail often glossed over—and most of these mean differences are small, less than half a standard deviation. A few reported mean differences of up to one standard deviation have been the object of much controversy (for example, in the IQ difference between black and white groups, in gender differences in spatial ability, favoring males, and in the ability to perceive detail, favoring females). Because of sampling problems and, in many cases, problematic data-gathering and recording techniques, most of these reported group mean differences are unreliable (that is, they have large error terms). The heated controversies of the day are based on bad data!

But even if two groups did differ in means by as much as one standard deviation, such a difference pales in comparison with the within-group variability of five or six standard deviations. Thus a person in the "inferior" group who scores one standard deviation above its mean would still be at the mean in the "superior" group, that is, better than 50 percent of the superior group; and a person in the inferior group scoring three standard deviations above its mean will be two standard deviations above the mean in the superior group—better than 98 percent of the superior group.

The point is this: Group membership per se is a poor indicator of a person's standing, if only because the error term is so large—equivalent to one standard deviation. Group membership cannot substitute for individual assessment. Furthermore, characterizing all members of a group by the group's mean is indefensible, if not malicious. Thus the psychology of individual differences shows why each person has to be treated as an individual, not as a member of a group. This conclusion alone should have dissipated the controversies surrounding diversity.

Another important finding of the psychology of individual differences is that many human traits do not correlate highly with one another. (If they did, then only one trait would be needed to describe humans. This is essentially what is wrong with the "IQ" concept.) When two traits do not correlate highly, a person's standing on one trait does not allow accurate prediction or estimation of that person's standing on the other trait because the standard error of estimate will be large.

The number of human traits that do not correlate highly with one another is large (Dawis, in press) and growing larger as research on personality proceeds. Relying on the information provided by one or even a few traits will produce a very restricted and biased picture of a person. The psychology of individual differences shows why a person must be assessed on many traits, not just on a single trait, no matter how important it may be.

Thus the psychology of individual differences exposes the fallacy of stereotypes, whether based on group membership or on characterization by a single trait. But humans have only stereotypes to go on in the absence of more information. Therefore, one way to combat stereotypes and stereotyping is to disseminate more information about group variability and about other traits.

PEC theory goes even farther than the psychology of individual differences. PEC theory postulates that there are E differences as well as P differences. When P and E interact, we have a multiplicative situation. P × E is much more than P + E, much more than P differences and E differences combined.

Cultural Validity

The theoretical structure of PEC theory and its constructs can apply to any culture. People in any culture will have needs and skills, abilities and values, satisfaction and satisfactoriness, maintenance and adjustment. But there will be cultural differences. Even when it is valid and possible to use the same instruments with different cultural groups, one should expect differences in their means and, to a much lesser extent, in their variabilities. Intercorrelation among variables should be the least different among cultural groups, as studies in individual differences have shown.

However, most frequently it is the instruments that do not apply in theory transfer. It is a very difficult undertaking to demonstrate measurement equivalence across cultural groups. Language differences will be a major stumbling block; translation of an instrument into another language has always been fraught with problems. Even when the same language is spoken, there may be cultural differences in meaning for certain words and phrases. Thus the problem of cultural validity may lie not so much in the theory as in the instruments used to operationalize the theory. This is a sort of chicken-and-egg problem because a theory cannot be validated for another culture without the use of instruments. (PEC theory has not been validated for any culture other than the contemporary, English-speaking, Anglo-American culture.)

Intergenerational Validity

The problem of intergenerational validity is similar in many respects to that of cultural validity. The theory may be valid, but the instruments may not be. To validate the theory will require generation-equivalent measures. Even if language were not a problem, the question of measurement equivalence will be. It might be possible to select items with equivalent psychometric characteristics across generation groups, but this would require an extremely large item pool to begin with. But then such instruments would bias the test of the theory because equivalence has been built in. Thus we have another chicken-egg problem.

The question of theory validation is a tricky one. In principle, it is possible through item selection to select items that favor the theory, using a back-solution or post hoc strategy. If on cross-validation the items hold up, the theory is favored. If they don't, the fault is in the item selection. With either outcome, the theory "wins"—but this is circular reasoning.

As stated in the measurement section, PEC theory can be operationalized with instruments other than those used in the Work Adjustment Project. Indeed, testing PEC theory will be more credible if other instruments are used. At our present state of instrumentation technology, theory testing is at best a fuzzy procedure with fuzzy results. Most instruments are constructed according to the dictates of some theory, and then we turn around and test the theory with those same instruments. Until our instruments are much more "theory-free" (as, for example, I believe ability tests are), all our theory testing will be not much more than going around in circles.

Application of PEC Theory to Two Cases

In discussing the application of PEC theory to the two cases, counseling process issues will be set aside and the focus will be on counseling content. The basic counseling strategy to be followed consists of these ten points:

1. Ascertain the client's (P's) requirements (needs, values), capabilities (skills, abilities), and personality style characteristics.

2. Ascertain the various Es with which P is interacting and which of these Es are most salient.

3. Ascertain the response requirements, reinforcement capabilities, and style characteristics of each E (time permitting) or each salient E (if time is limited).

4. Ascertain P's perception of PEC (P-E correspondence) for each E and compare it with the counselor's perception; explore the significant differences, if any.

5. Ascertain P's motivation for counseling, that is, P's career development stage, whether exploration (still looking) or pre-establishment (deciding on one from among a few).

6. If in exploration, help P develop a long list (not so much many as wide-ranging), then a short list (one or two, no more than three or four), of potential career occupations to consider.

7. Ascertain the response requirements, reinforcement capabilities, and style characteristics of each E on the short list.

8. Ascertain P's perception of PEC for each potential career E.

9. If in pre-establishment, discuss the implications of degree of PEC with the target career E or Es, that is, predicted satisfactoriness and satisfaction.

10. Discuss the implications of other factors (for example, family responsibilities, cost of training in time and money, other financial considerations, willingness to relocate, alternative career pathways, future job prospects).

These ten points are not necessarily discrete or set in this particular sequence. Some may occur simultaneously, or there may be some jumping back and forth, but generally the first points occur early and the last points occur late in the counseling.

The Case of K

K's capabilities are given as high verbal and quantitative abilities, as well as specific motor skills (skateboarding, drums). His values shift with different Es: high Autonomy, Achievement, and Status for E-job and E-school but not for E-home; high Altruism and Safety for E-home but not for E-other-than-home. K is low on Celerity and tends toward Reactiveness. It would be helpful to have more assessment data (for example, from a multiple-ability battery, other value measures, style estimates), but at this point it is not yet necessary (see point 1).

Because of the apparent value conflict between home and the outside, I would explore the different Es in depth with K to get a detailed picture of their response requirements and reinforcement capabilities. Because K tends to be Reactive, his expressed values might reflect what he feels he is expected to say, not his own values (if he has a consistent set). I would explore whether this apparent value conflict is mirrored in other home-versus-outside conflicts for K (that is, a conflict of cultures; see points 2, 3, and 4).

K's parents appear to be assimilated into the wider culture (for example, allowing K to decide for himself) but may still behave according to their birth cultures (Japanese, Chinese). (Incidentally, a Japanese-Chinese marriage is, I believe, very rare. The two cultures have many contrasts, so I would spend some time exploring and understanding K's home E, where there is potential for cultural conflict.)

K appears to be still in the exploratory stage, so at this point I would help him develop a "long list" of occupations in technology, architecture, and other areas suggested by vocational interest inventories, providing him with or guiding him to occupational information literature. If K does his homework, I would then help him develop his "short list," taking into account other factors such as feasibility of training, expense, parental expectations, and job prospects (see points 5, 6, 7, 8, 9, and 10).

If K does not do his homework, this might mean that he is not yet "ready" for career choice and decision. I would summarize his "long list" with him and advise him to keep thinking about the different possibilities and then return for further career counseling after his sophomore year. His strong interest in skateboarding might still be a hangover from high school. I would check it out thoroughly as a career interest. (Would K consider skateboarding as a career? How good is he? Has he participated in any contests, won any prizes? How good does he think he is? See points 5, 6, 7, and 8.)

Finally, the data do not indicate the presence of any significant mental health problem.

The Case of E

"E" will now refer to the client, not to environment, as it does in PEC theory.

E appears to be at a later career development stage than K, that is, in a pre-establishment stage. Or at least she is looking for "a few viable occupational alternatives" to make educational planning easier (more comfortable).

If E were not in a hurry, it may be useful to ascertain her values via more than one medium—for example, by discussing the reinforcement capabilities of the various environments she is currently experiencing and, through her comments, developing a clearer idea of what she requires of an occupational environment.

From the data on hand, it appears that Altruism is a very strong value for E, so much so that it poses that inevitable potential conflict: "helping others" in a career versus "helping others" in one's own family.

E's ability level is high enough for her to pursue most any professional-level occupation. One way to narrow down her occupational choices would be to use empirically keyed interest scales, such as are found in the Strong Interest Inventory or the Kuder

Occupational Interest Survey. These scales would compare her interests with those of incumbents of the various professions at the interest-item level—a much finer-grained examination than is possible with the more popular Holland scales. Unfortunately, this same fine-grained comparison of P-E correspondence is not available at the need level; otherwise, that would have been the way from the vantage point of PEC theory to help narrow down E's occupational choice alternatives.

One obvious choice suggested by the data and especially by her family background is a career in the law. The counselor's job, then, would be to explore with E all the available fields of law to find the ones that will allow E's desired balance between career and family. This approach might be indicated if E were in a hurry to reach a decision.

As with K, I see no significant mental health problem in E.

References

Brown, D., Brooks, L., and Associates (1994). *Career choice and development* (3rd ed.). San Francisco: Jossey-Bass.

Carroll, J. B. (1993). *Human cognitive abilities*. Cambridge: Cambridge University Press.

Dawis, R. V. (1992). The individual differences tradition in counseling psychology. *Journal of Counseling Psychology, 39*, 7–19.

Dawis, R. V. (2000). Scale construction and psychometric considerations. In H.E.A. Tinsley & S. D. Brown (Eds.), *Handbook of applied multivariate statistics and mathematical modeling* (pp. 65–94). New York: Academic Press.

Dawis, R. V. (in press). Vocational interests, values, and preferences, Psychology of. In N. J. Smelser & P. B. Baltes (Eds.), *International encyclopedia of the social & behavioral sciences*. Oxford, England: Pergamon/ Elsevier Science.

Dawis, R. V., Dohm, T. E., Lofquist, L. H., Chartrand, J. M., & Due, A. M. (1987). *Minnesota occupational classification system III*. Minneapolis: Vocational Psychology Research, Department of Psychology, University of Minnesota.

Dawis, R. V., & Lofquist, L. H. (1984). *A psychological theory of work adjustment*. Minneapolis: University of Minnesota Press.

Digman, J. M. (1990). Personality structure: Emergence of the five-factor model. *Annual Review of Psychology, 41*, 417–440.

Guilford, J. P. (1954). *Psychometric methods* (2nd ed.). New York: McGraw Hill.

Holland, J. L. (1997). *Making vocational choices* (3rd ed.). Englewood Cliffs, NJ: Prentice Hall.

Landy, F. J., & Farr, J. L. (1980). Performance rating. *Psychological Bulletin, 87*, 72–107.

Lofquist, L. H., & Dawis, R. V. (1991). *Essentials of person-environment-correspondence counseling*. Minneapolis: University of Minnesota Press.

Lubinski, D. (2000). Scientific and social significance of assessing individual differences: "Sinking shafts at a few critical points." *Annual Review of Psychology, 51*, 405–444.

Minnesota Studies in Vocational Rehabilitation series (Vols. 1–30). Minneapolis: Industrial Relations Center, University of Minnesota.

Skinner, B. F. (1938). *The behavior of organisms*. New York: Appleton-Century-Crofts.

Tolman, E. C. (1932). *Purposive behavior in animals and men*. New York: Appleton-Century-Crofts.

U.S. Department of Labor (1970). *Manual for the general aptitude test battery*. Washington, DC: U.S. Government Printing Office.

11

The Role of Work Values and Cultural Values in Occupational Choice, Satisfaction, and Success

A Theoretical Statement

Duane Brown

Career development theorists have all but ignored the career development of ethnic and cultural minorities (Brooks, 1990; Cheatham, 1990; Isaacson & D. Brown, 2000; Osipow & Littlejohn, 1995). One result of this neglect is that current career development theories provide little in the way of theoretical guidelines for practice or research (Betz & Fitzgerald, 1995; Leong, 1995a). However, Leong (1995b) assembled a group of scholars who reviewed the empirical literature regarding the career development of ethnic and racial minorities and made suggestions for the revision of some of the major theories of occupational choice and career development (Arbona, 1995; M. Brown, 1995; Johnson, Swartz, & Martin, 1995; Leong & Serifica, 1995). Although the suggestions generated by this group may be helpful to career counselors and researchers, the major theories have not been revised and no new theories have been advanced.

Much of the theoretical portion of this chapter appeared in the *Journal of Counseling and Development*; used by permission of the American Counseling Association.

The primary objective of this chapter is to partially address the neglect of cultural issues by career development theorists. Here I set forth a theory of occupational choice, success, and satisfaction that will be applicable to cultural and ethnic minorities as well as to white European Americans. The approach used in the development of the propositions set forth in this chapter is not unlike the one employed by Super (1953) and by Holland (1959), in that the research and theoretical positions of others serve as the primary foundation for the ideas that are advanced. I hope that the proposals presented here will be provocative enough to generate empirical tests of their value.

Assumptions of the Theory

All theories are based on certain assumptions, and the theory presented here is no exception. The basic assumptions here are as follows:

1. Many occupational choices (perhaps most) are uninformed, that is, they are the result of chance or external variables and circumstances that have little to do with the nature of occupations or the individuals' self-evaluations (D. Brown & Minor, 1992; NCDA, 1999; Hoyt & Lester, 1995).

2. An informed occupational decision is one in which individuals engage in a conscientious process of exploring their personal characteristics, the rewards that may accrue if various occupations are chosen, and the environmental variable that may influence the outcomes of their decisions. The result of this process is the formulation of expectations about the outcomes of the choices being considered. *Outcomes* are defined here as the accumulation of positive outcomes and avoidance of negative outcomes. *Expectancies* (Vroom, 1964) are beliefs that choices can be realized and involve estimates of abilities, as well as the potential impact of factors such as discrimination and short- and long-term occupational trends on the chances of implementing the choices being considered.

3. The values system, which is made up of the cultural and work values of individuals, is the primary basis of perception, cognition, and affect.

4. The assignment of positive and negative properties to occupations is done primarily on the basis of an individual's values (Rokeach, 1973).

5. All decisions regarding occupations are made under conditions of uncertainty because decision makers do not have access to complete information about their abilities, external conditions that may influence the outcome of their decisions, or the outcomes that will actually accrue as a result of a particular occupational decision (Vroom, 1964; Wright, 1984). Historic patterns of discrimination, as well as current discriminatory attitudes and behavior, add to the uncertainty experienced in the choice making of women (Melamed, 1995, 1996) and minorities (Leong, 1995b).

6. Most existing theories of occupational choice are based on a white, Eurocentric perspective and thus have limited utility for many minorities (Leong, 1995a). Continuing to apply existing theories without modification to take into consideration the unique worldviews of minority groups is at best insensitive and inappropriate. For example, Soh and Leong (2001) asked whether people in different cultures with the same Holland code might have differing perceptions of occupations. Their research supports the idea that at least some Holland types may have culturally specific perceptions and thus should be approached differentially by career counselors.

Building Blocks of the Theory

Any theorist is faced with the task of identifying and defining the constructs that influence the phenomena addressed by the theory. I have chosen values as the cornerstone of this theory, partly because work values have been identified as critical variables in the career development process (for example, Fouad, 1995; Super & Sverko, 1995). It has also been suggested that cultural values, particularly social relationship values, play an important role in the career development process (Hartung, et al., 1998; Ibrahim, Ohnishi, & Wilson, 1994). I believe that a number of cultural values play important roles in the career development and occupational choice-making process.

In a sense, values are similar to Bandura's concept of outcome expectations (Bandura, 1986). However, a human value is a much more robust construct than outcome expectations, which is defined as the anticipated result of taking a course of action such as choosing an occupation. Values, like outcome expectations, are instrumental in the goal-setting process. Values and outcome expectations are cognitive structures that have behavioral and affective dimensions (Rokeach, 1973). However, it is at this point that the similarity between the two constructs ends. Values are core beliefs that individuals experience as standards that guide how they "should" function. The idea that values are experienced as standards can be used to explain successful and unsuccessful interpersonal relationships on and off the job.

Because values focus partially on desired end states, they can be used to explain why people who choose some occupations are unhappy with their choices, even when they perform the tasks associated with those jobs in exemplary fashion. Similarly, values can be used to explain motivational processes. Every teacher has wondered why many students with high academic aptitudes do not do well in the classroom. Bandura (1986) suggests that individuals exhibit the behaviors they have acquired more often when they believe those behaviors will be rewarded. He also suggests that people develop evaluative reactions to their own behavior, and they exhibit behaviors they find satisfying and reject those they deem inappropriate. In these statements, Bandura comes close to defining values as Rotter (1954) viewed them, with the exception already noted.

Individuals experience their values in terms of "oughts" that identify both the processes and objectives to be pursued. Although much behavior is acquired through our routine interactions as children and adults, values focus the learning process and play the central role in the acquisition of occupational behavior. Moreover, values can be used to explain the complex human interactions that occur in the workplace because they are the basis for the evaluation of others. The idea that values serve as standards sets them apart from both interests and outcome expectations.

Values develop so that individuals can meet their needs in socially acceptable ways (Rokeach, 1973), and thus they are shaped by the cultural context of the individual. The result is that cultural groups develop unique cultural values, although the values systems of people within a cultural group are by no means homogeneous. Values, unlike outcome expectations, may operate out of awareness or may be brought into awareness through a process of crystallization and prioritization (D. Brown, 1996a). Values are crystallized when individuals can identify them and tell how they influence their behavior. They are prioritized when individuals can rank order them in terms of their relative importance. Finally, values provide the basis for rationalizing one's behavior (Rokeach, 1973). It is relatively easy for a CEO to justify laying off several thousand people in the name of increasing shareholders' equity if the CEO has highly prioritized financial prosperity, regardless of the cost in human misery.

The values system contains all the values held by individuals, including their cultural values and work values. Cultural values have been identified through research as being those typically held by certain cultural groups (Carter, 1991). They include values regarding

- Human nature (human beings are good, bad, or neither)
- Person-nature relationship (nature dominates people; people dominate nature; living in harmony with nature is important)
- Time orientation (past, past-future, present, or circular, that is, oriented to changes that recur in nature, as opposed to time as measured by watches and calendars)
- Activity ([being] spontaneous self-expression is important; [being-in-becoming] controlled self-expression is important; [doing] action-oriented self-expression is important)

- Self-control (it is either highly or moderately important to control one's thoughts and emotions)
- Social relationships ([individual] the individual is most important social unit; [collective] it is important to put the group's concerns ahead of the concerns of the individual) (Kluckhorn & Strodtbeck, 1961).

Finally, although research has indicated that some cultural values seem to be more prevalent in certain cultural groups than others, Carter (1991) concludes that *there is considerable diversity within the values systems of people from the same cultural groups and extensive overlap in the cultural values held by people from different cultural groups*. Counselors should keep Carter's conclusions in mind when considering the points raised in this chapter.

Work values are the values that individuals believe should be satisfied as a result of their participation in the work role (a desired end state) and lead them to set directional goals: "I ought to move in this direction by acting in a certain way." Values also play the central role in the decision-making process because they are the basis of goal setting. Goals, if properly constructed, move the individual toward desired end states (for example, being accepted by others). Financial prosperity, altruism, achievement, and responsibility are examples of work values.

In addition to work values, individuals develop a number of other values that they expect to be satisfied in life roles other than work, such as in the family (D. Brown, 1996a). The major underlying assumption of the theory being advanced in this chapter is that cultural and work values are the primary variables that influence the occupational choice-making process, the occupation chosen, and the resulting satisfaction with and success in the occupation chosen. However, other life-role values also influence many aspects of the career development process.

Values change in two basic ways (Rokeach, 1973). The most obvious of these is through contemplation. Individuals often employ their cognitive ability to consider their core beliefs about religion, relationships, and the importance of work. The contemplative process is often initiated after observing models perceived to be similar to themselves, which results in the consideration of new beliefs. The process may also begin as a result of day-to-day experiences or because of more dramatic events. Many people report life-changing experiences after experiencing a near-fatal accident or the loss of a loved one. Ultimately, these new beliefs are put into practice where they are confirmed or disconfirmed by external and internal feedback. Of these sources of feedback, internal feedback (intrapersonal) is the most powerful source of information for an individual with an individualism social value. External feedback from esteemed others such as parents, elders, and godparents is the most important source of feedback for people who hold a collective social value.

The second stimulus for changes in values is conflict. Acculturation in all likelihood occurs primarily because of conflict. Acculturation is the process by which people new to a culture adopt the values of the dominant culture because of the continuing conflict between their beliefs and the people around them. Consider the newly arrived Mexican American student who is thrust into a school based on Eurocentric values, is exposed daily to the values of the dominant culture via the media, and interacts with peers who hold Eurocentric values. Unless the family continues to teach and reinforce the values of the student's native culture, acculturative pressure builds because of the ongoing conflict the individual experiences. Groups such as gangs and cults exert tremendous pressure on new members to reject their values and adopt the values of the group. The pressure to conform to the values in the workplace is more subtle than those exerted by gangs and cults, but it is nonetheless an important force in either reinforcing values or causing conflicts that result in the individuals either leaving the organization or altering their values system, most typically by reprioritizing their values rather than adopting entirely different values.

A second source of conflict occurs when the highly prioritized values conflict. Intrapersonal conflict occurs when values such as

Belonging, which may require a fair amount of conformity to satisfy, and Independence are both considered important by the individual (Brown, 1996a). These conflicts may be resolved by reprioritizing values or by the adoption of life roles that allow the satisfaction of both values.

Although values are primary factors in choosing, deriving satisfaction from, and advancing in a career, a number of other variables interact with values to influence occupational choice and the outcomes of the choice. In some instances, these factors constrain both the occupational choice-making process and the choices made. In other instances, these factors have the opposite effect and make the process easier and expand the number of occupational options available to the decision maker. For example, contextual variables such as socioeconomic status (SES) (for example, Hotchkiss & Borow, 1996; Sinha, 1990), family or group influence (for example, Leong & Serifica, 1995; Johnson, Swartz, & Martin, 1995), and history of discrimination (for example, Leong & Serifica, 1995; Melamed, 1996; Robinson & Ginter, 1999) influence both the decision-making process and the career chosen. Gender (for example, M. Brown, 1995; Gottfredson, 1996; Melamed, 1995) also plays a major role in the occupations chosen, as do aptitudes (for example, Blau & Duncan, 1967; Jencks, Crouse, & Mueser, 1983; Phillips & Imhoff, 1997). Other variables that may constrain the occupational choice-making process, as well as the choice itself, include the mental health of the decision makers (Casserly, 1982; Pietromonaco & Rock, 1987), the information available to them, and self-efficacy as it relates to occupational options chosen (Lent, Brown, & Hackett, 1996).

Propositions: Factors That Influence the Choice-Making Process

In this section, eight propositions about the role of values and other variables mentioned earlier are advanced. In some instances, subpropositions will be set forth as well. When empirical support is available to support propositions and subpropositions, it will be presented.

Proposition 1

Highly prioritized work values are the most important determinants of career choice for people with an individualism social value (that is, the individual is the most important unit) if their work values are crystallized and prioritized. Such individuals feel unconstrained to act on their work values if there is at least one occupational option available that will satisfy the values held, values-based information about occupational options is available, the difficulty level of implementing the options is approximately the same, and the financial resources available are sufficient to support the implementation of the preferred option.

Proposition 1A. Factors that limit the number of occupational options considered for people with an individualism social value are low SES, minority status, mental health problems, physical disabilities, gender (Gottfredson, 1996), low scholastic aptitude, perception that they will be discriminated against in an occupation, and lack of values-based information. Women, minorities, people from lower SES levels, and people with mental or physical limitations with an individualism social value will choose occupations consistent with their work values, but they are likely to choose from a more restricted range of occupations than white, European American males.

Proposition 1B. Self-efficacy will become a constraining factor in the occupational decision-making process of individuals who value individualism when the options being considered require widely divergent skills and abilities.

There is considerable evidence to support the proposition that work values influence the occupational decision-making process (for example, Ben-Shem & Avi-Itzhak, 1991; Judge & Bretz, 1992; Knoop,

1991; Ravlin & Meglino, 1987). Although these and other research-ers did not identify the *social values* (whether the individuals main-tained a social value or not) of the people studied, they were for the most part European Americans who typically value individualism (Carter, 1991).

To this point, no research has been produced that examines the occupational decision-making process in the absence of occupa-tional alternatives that will satisfy the values of the decision maker, and thus this aspect of Proposition 1 is unsupported. Research by Judge and Bretz (1992) has shown that the availability of values-based information is influential in the occupational choice process. In their research, *values-based* information was defined as informa-tion that clearly demonstrates which values would be reinforced in the workplace. In addition, Feather (1988) studied the occupational choice-making process of college students. He found that *self-efficacy* became an issue in the process of choosing an occupation when one of the options being considered required more rigorous (numerous skills and abilities were required) preparation than the others.

There is support for the idea that self-efficacy plays an important role in shaping the list of occupations that are considered when occu-pational decision making takes place (see Betz, 2000). However, recent research on social cognitive career theory (Lent at al., 1996) explored the relationship between outcome expectations and self-efficacy in predicting what Gore and Leuwerke (2000) term *occupa-tional considerations*. Gore and Leuwerke asked a gender-balanced sample of college students to rate (1) their occupational self-efficacy beliefs regarding eighty-four occupational titles, (2) their occupa-tional outcome expectations regarding the same eighty-four occu-pations, and (3) the extent to which they might consider each of the eighty-four occupations. Outcome expectations accounted for 30 percent of the common variance associated with occupational con-siderations, and self-efficacy beliefs accounted for 24 percent of the common variance. The hierarchical regression with occupational considerations as the dependent variable yielded beta weights for the two variables of .42 and .32, respectively. The study is cited as supporting the proposition that work values are the most important factor in occupational choice because the material contained in the occupational outcome expectations questionnaire was derived from the major work values found on the Minnesota Importance Questionnaire (Rounds et al., 1981).

Several research studies support the idea that expectations regarding occupational attainment are positively correlated with SES (for example, Gibbs, 1985; Gregory, Wells, & Leake, 1986). The results of these studies have documented the importance of SES as a predictor of occupational attainment (Hotchkiss & Borow, 1996; Ponterotto & Casas, 1991). Impoverished people tend to have "lower aspirations" than individuals who are higher on the economic ladder, regardless of their race or ethnicity, perhaps because they believe their fate is controlled by external factors (Sinha, 1990).

Generally speaking, members of ethnic minority groups and women are over-represented in lower-paying occupations when compared to European American males (for example, Arbona, 1995; M. Brown, 1995; Melamed, 1996; Ong, 1990; Saunders, 1995). There are numerous reasons for this disparity, but discrimination undoubtedly plays a major role in the difference (Arbona, 1995; Arce, Murgia, & Frisbie, 1987; Cox & Harquail, 1991; Jeanquarte-Barone & Sekaran, 1996; Leong & Serifica, 1995; Phillips & Imhoff, 1997; Montalvo, 1991; Powell & Butterfield, 1997). Melamed (1995) concluded that discrimination accounted for between 55 and 62 percent of the variance in the differential career success of men and women in a British sample. Because of the widespread prevalence of discrimination in the United States (Robinson & Ginter, 1999), it seems likely that ethnic minorities vicariously or directly have experienced some degree of discrimination that influences their decision-making processes. It is likely that the same may be true for women as well. Morrow, Gore, and Campbell (1996) suggest that this same supposition might also apply to gay men and lesbian women. This is an area that warrants considerable investigation.

Gender is a constraining factor in the occupational decision-making process for a reason other than discrimination. Harpaz and

Fu (1997) found that women in Israel, Germany, the United States, and Japan assigned lower importance to the centrality of work in their lives than men. The researchers suggest that this is the result of women's orientation to other life roles, primarily concern regarding participation in the family role. Others (for example, Gati, Osipow, & Givon, 1995; Larsen et al., 1994; Phillips & Imhoff, 1997) have made similar observations. Although there is evidence that the constraints regarding occupational participation related to family issues are lessening (Phillips & Imhoff, 1997), it seems unlikely that this factor will be eliminated in the near future.

Feather (1992) suggests that mood is a major determinant of motivation in the occupational decision-making process and research (Casserly, 1982; Pietromonaco & Rock, 1987) generally supports the contention that mental health problems do, in fact, influence motivation to make decisions. Therefore, it seems likely that the mental health of the individual will be a major factor in the occupational choice-making process and limit the options considered.

Proposition 2

Individuals who hold collective social values and come from families or groups who hold the same social value will either defer to the wishes of the group or family members or be heavily influenced by them in the occupational decision-making process. The result will be that the occupations chosen will correlate less with the individual's work values than is the case with individuals who value individualism and make their own occupational choices.

Proposition 2A. Gender will be a major factor in the occupations entered by individuals who hold a collective social value because of sex-stereotyped perceptions of occupations by decision makers. The result will be that occupational choices are more likely to be stereotypical male and female; women with a collective social value will enter a more restricted range of occupations than men with a collective social value.

Proposition 2B. Perceptions that discrimination may occur if an occupation chosen will be a deterrent to choosing that occupation for decision makers who hold a collective social value.

Proposition 2C. Perceptions that the resources are unavailable to implement an occupational choice will be a major limiting factor in the occupational decision-making process of individuals who hold a collective social value.

Proposition 2D. The outcome of the occupational decision-making process for people who hold a collective social value will be less influenced by the availability of the values-based occupational information than it will be by the work values of their family or group.

Young (1994), after studying the role of parents in the occupational-decision making process of a primarily European American group, observed, "There seems to be a cultural belief in North America that the choice of one's occupation is an individual right, much like the choice of one's spouse" (p. 197). Unfortunately, the assumption of independence in the occupational decision-making process may have been misapplied to some minority clients in a culturally oppressive manner by unwitting career counselors. For example, the construct of career indecisiveness (Goodstein, 1972; Newman, Fuqua, & Seaworth, 1989) is based on the assumption that the decision maker should be able to make an independent decision. Leong (1991) found that Asian American college students were more likely to prefer a dependent decision-making style than their European American counterparts. Although Leong (1991) used "cultural group membership" instead of "internalized culture" to identify cultural background, his results support Proposition 2 to some degree. Asian American, Hispanic American, Native American Indian, and other decision makers who hold a collective social value may have a very different view of the decision-making process than European

Americans. A collective social value is often manifested in a strong respect and obedience for one's parents and the traditions of the family or group (Lee, 1991). When collective social relationships is a highly prioritized value for both the decision maker and the decision maker's family, the values of family members, depending on the structure (for example, patriarchal) of the family, are likely to be the primary determinants of occupational choices (Sue & Sue, 1990; Yagi & Oh, 1995). The rationale for Proposition 2D was drawn from this line of thinking. However, the factors that influence the occupational decision making of people with a collective social value have not been studied directly.

Respect for the traditions of the family or group may also be instrumental in the decision-making process for some Native American Indians (Herring, 1996) but in a somewhat different way. In this context, "the family" refers to biological as well as tribal relations that come to bear on decision makers (Martin, 1995; Thomason, 1995). Some American Indian families practice noninterference in the decision-making process, but their emphasis on cooperation and collateral relationships, as well as respect for the traditions of the tribe, are likely to be powerful influences on the decision-making process (Herring, 1996; Martin, 1995). Therefore, subtle, as well as more overt, expectations of the family or tribe may be important forces in the occupational decision-making process. Unfortunately, at this time there is only observational support for this supposition (for example, Herring, 1996; Thomason, 1995).

Proposition 3

When taken individually, cultural values regarding activity (doing, being, being-in-becoming) will not constrain the occupational decision-making process. However, people who value individualism and have both a future and a past-future time value and a doing activity value are more likely to make decisions at important transition points (such as graduation from high school) and act on those choices than people who hold either a collective or individualism social value and a being or being-in-becoming activity value.

Currently, there is no empirical support for Proposition 3. It was derived from the descriptions of the values orientations of cultural groups advanced by Kluckhorn and Strodtbeck (1961). For example, they found that people with a doing value emphasized action-oriented activities that can be measured by an external criterion such as an achievement. People with a future orientation emphasize looking ahead and planning for change to occur. Individuals who value individualism, doing, and a future time orientation should be advantaged in the occupational choice-making process. Clearly, research is needed if Proposition 3 is to be supported.

Proposition 4

Because of differing values systems, males and females and people from differing cultural groups will enter occupations at varying rates.

Earlier in this article, research findings were presented that support the proposition that values vary among and within cultural groups (Carter, 1991). Similarly, differences between the values structures of males and females generally and within cultural groups have also been well documented (Bartol, Anderson, & Schneider, 1981; Bassoff & Ortiz, 1984; Beutell & Brenner, 1986; de Vaus & McCallister, 1991; Stimpson, Jenson, & Neff, 1992; Vacha-Haasa et al., 1994; Wagoner & Bridwell, 1989). However, the literature regarding occupational values of cultural groups is mixed, probably because "level of acculturation" is not typically an independent variable in the studies that have been conducted. For example,

Lebo, Harrington, and Tillman (1995) studied the work values of high school students from six countries and concluded that the values of the groups studied were more similar than different. Because all students studied were from countries with Eurocentric cultural orientations, this finding is not surprising.

Leong and Tata (1990) examined the occupational values of Chinese American students at various levels of acculturation. They found significant differences in the work values of males and females. However, students at various levels of acculturation varied only on the value of self-realization, which the researchers observed is a value more likely to be a part of European American culture than Chinese American culture. In an investigation that compared Asian American students to European American students, Leong (1991) found that Asian American students placed greater emphasis on extrinsic values (for example, making money) than did European American students. Vondracek and colleagues (1990) investigated samples of students from Japan and the United States and found differences in the work values of the groups studied. Elizur, Borg, Hunt, and Beck (1991) studied samples from eight countries (four from Europe and four from Asia) and found significant differences among their subsamples, which they characterized as "minor variations." The sample (college-educated men) and methodology (a gross ranking without consideration of cultural values or acculturation) used by Elizur and colleagues (1991) may have masked some of the differences that were present.

As noted earlier, empirical data support the idea that women and most minorities are over-represented in lower-paying occupations (in proportion to their numbers in the population) when compared to European American males (Phillips & Imhoff, 1997). For example, Swinton (1992) reports that African Americans are over-represented in social and low-level occupations. Moreover, Aguirre (1990) notes that women are decidedly over-represented in certain occupations, including clerical, social service, and service jobs, and under-represented in the crafts and scientific occupations. However, Hsia (1988) reports that Asian Americans are over-represented in professional, technical, and service occupations and under-represented in sales, manufacturing, and laborer job classifications.

Occupational segregation can be accounted for to some degree by the twin processes of enculturation (Arbona, 1995; Fouad, 1995; Gottfredson, 1996) and discrimination in the workplace (Hotchkiss & Borow, 1996; Melamed, 1995; Phillips & Imhoff, 1997). Other factors such as luck (Brown & Minor, 1992) and SES also play a role in occupational segregation. However, it may well be that the initial occupational choice is the major factor in occupational success (Phillips & Imhoff, 1997). Fortunately, this is one factor that counselors, particularly school and college counselors can affect; facilitating occupational choice is generally considered a major role of both groups.

Proposition 5

The process of choosing an occupation involves a series of "estimates." These include estimates of (1) one's abilities and values, (2) the skills and abilities that will be required to be successful in an occupation, and (3) the work values that the occupational alternatives being considered will satisfy. For people who value individualism, the ability to accurately make these estimates will be a critical factor in their success in their occupations and their satisfaction with them. For individuals who hold a collateral social value, the estimates made by decision makers will be the key factors in their success and occupational satisfaction.

Proposition 5A. Individuals who hold an individualism social value and who come from backgrounds where little emphasis is placed on feedback about individual strengths and weaknesses and personal traits and who make their own occupational decisions will make more errors in the process, as defined by mismatches between their values and those values satisfied by the job. The result will be lowered job satisfaction, lower levels of success, and shorter job tenure. In the case of people with a collateral social value, satisfaction, success, and tenure will be based on the ability of the decision maker to make these estimates.

There is evidence that African American adolescents may not be as proficient at making estimates of their abilities and other traits as are European American adolescents (D. Brown, Fulkerson, Vedder, & Ware, 1983; Westbrook, Buck, Wynne, & Stanford, 1994), although the reason for these differences is not clear. It may well be that the results are more attributable to SES than ethnicity because the researchers did not control for income level. As noted earlier, low SES appears to be related to lowered aspirations. It may also be related to the tendency to underestimate their ability to act on their values and an overall malaise because poor people may have the perception that they have little control over their lives (Graves, 1967; Sinha, 1990). This is an area that deserves additional study.

The importance of having occupational information is attested to in most authoritative texts on career development (for example, Isaacson & D. Brown, 2000). People who choose occupations rely on accurate information as the basis of their estimates about both the abilities needed to perform the tasks required in an occupation and the extent to which the occupation will satisfy their values. Values-based information, unlike more statistically oriented information, allows decision makers to ascertain not only what workers do but how they feel about what they do (Brown, 1996a).

Some minority groups and people living in rural settings may be particularly disadvantaged in the occupational choice-making process because of the dearth of all types of occupational information. Martin (1995) drew on the research of McDiarmid and Kleinfeld (1986) to support his case that American Indians may have less information about jobs. He pointed out that many American Indians live in rural areas and have limited contacts with individuals who are knowledgeable about the world of work; their work values and interests are abridged as a result. Brown and Minor (1992) report that a higher proportion of African Americans, Asian Americans, and Hispanics felt that they needed assistance in finding information about jobs than did white European Americans. Newly immigrated Hispanics and Asian Americans may need help finding values-based information more often than their white counterparts due to their English proficiency. It seems likely that any group with limited proficiency with English will have limited amounts of occupational information and that the information they have may not be as accurate as that available to their counterparts who have greater language skills.

Proposition 6

Occupational success will be related to job-related skills acquired in formal and informal educational settings, job-related aptitudes and skills, SES, participation in the work role, and the extent to which discrimination is experienced, regardless of the social relationship value held.

Proposition 6A. Because success in the occupational role requires an awareness of future events and the ability to accommodate the dynamic changes that occur in the workplace, success in the occupational role will be related to time and activity values with individuals who have future or past-future paired with a doing activity value being the most successful, those with a present time value and being activity value second most successful, and those with a circular time value and a being-in-becoming activity value being least successful.

The roles of scholastic aptitude (Melamed, 1996), family SES (Blau & Duncan, 1967), and discrimination (Leong & Serifca, 1995; Melamed, 1995, 1996) have been presented elsewhere and will not be discussed here. However, research has shown that the extent to which workers, particularly women, participate in the work role is directly related to their success (Tharenou & Conroy, 1994). Research has also shown the positive impact of educational participation on occupational success (Blau & Duncan; Tharenou & Conroy, 1994). Finally, the role of special aptitudes in occupational success has been well documented (for example, Ghiselli, 1973).

The importance of time perspective in the career development process seems to have appeared first in 1957 (Super et al., 1957) in a discussion of the determinants of vocational maturity. In 1981, Super set forth an interactive model of career maturity that suggested that time perspective develops as a result of early information about careers, interaction with key figures in the environment, and the interests of the individual. In this 1981 statement, a variety of factors, including time perspective, were merged to form what Super termed *planfulness*—a critical component of career maturity. In 1991, Savickas echoed Super's suggestion that the time perspective held by individuals is an important ingredient in the career-planning process. Savickas, drawing on the earlier work of Hughes (1958), suggested that not everyone has internalized the idea of having a career. For this to happen, individuals must be able to draw on the past and project the future. People with a circular or present time orientation may be lacking an essential construct: a detailed vision of the future.

Research regarding career maturity has not been highly supportive of the construct (Super, 1990), perhaps because of problems with instrumentation. However, the importance of time orientation per se in occupational success has not been tested directly. The groups that research has shown are most likely to have either circular or present time orientations (American Indians, Hispanics, and African Americans; Carter, 1991) are under-represented in all of the best-paying occupations and over-represented in the lowest-paying occupations (U.S. Department of Labor, 1995; Johnson, Swartz, & Martin, 1995). Conversely, Asian Americans, who are more likely to have a past-future orientation (Carter, 1991; Sue &

Sue, 1990), are over-represented in these same occupations, as are European Americans (U.S. Department of Labor, 1995). However, it would be impossible to attribute these data solely to the idea that these groups have a particular time orientation, given the historic patterns of discrimination against minorities and other factors that may influence success in an occupation.

Research on children by Burd, Dodd, and Grassi (1981) and adolescents by Anderson, Burd, Dodd, and Kekler (1980) reveals that American Indian students are less able to make accurate estimates of the amount of time it would take to complete a task than other public school children. Success in the preparation for and performance of the duties involved in most occupations requires individuals to make accurate estimates of the amount of time it will take to complete them. Although many factors influence occupational achievement, the findings in these studies suggest that researchers and career counselors may need to concern themselves with this time orientation, as Super (1981) and Savickas (1991) suggest.

Proposition 7

Occupational tenure will be partially the result of the match between the cultural and work values of the worker, supervisors, and colleagues.

Currently, there is no support for Proposition 7. Sanderson (1993) indicates that "a major characteristic of a good work environment is one where employees understand each other's unique cultural characteristics" (p. 5). However, it is likely that few workplaces meet this criterion currently. More research is needed regarding how cultural values and the characteristics of the workplace interact. To this point, no research has surfaced that examines the specific hypotheses advanced in Proposition 7.

Proposition 8

The primary bases for job satisfaction for people with an individualism social value, in order of importance, will be (1) the congruence between the values reinforced on the job and individuals'
work values, (2) conflicts that occur between the occupational role
and other life roles, and (3) the approval of the work roles by others such as parents, spouses, and friends. Job satisfaction for people
with a collective social value will be, in order of importance, (1) the
extent to which the work role is approved by significant others such
as parents, spouses, and friends, (2) conflicts between the occupational role and other life roles, and (3) the congruence between the
values reinforced by the job and individuals' work values.

The support for Proposition 8 is indirect at this time. For example, Nevis (1983) found that workers on the Chinese mainland put
group goals ahead of their personal goals, which is consistent with
their collective social value (M. Ho, 1987). Because of the role that
satisfying goals plays in occupational satisfaction (D. Brown, 1996a),
it seems likely that achieving the goals of the primary group will be
a major factor in the occupational satisfaction of individuals with a
social value.

Researchers have not looked at the relationship between individuals' cultural values and values held by people in their workplaces
as a factor in occupational outcomes. Posner (1992) and Meglino,
Ravlin, and Adkins (1989) did find that job satisfaction was related
to congruence between individuals' work values and those held by
people in the workplace. The latter study looked specifically at the
relationship between individuals' work values, the work values held
by supervisors, and job satisfaction. Their findings support the part
of Proposition 8 that suggests that congruence between workers' and
supervisors' values is related to job satisfaction.

In a related study, Yu and Wu (1985) investigated the impact of unemployment and stress among unemployed Chinese Americans. The inability of the unemployed workers to provide support for aging relatives was a primary source of dissatisfaction among those studied. This result supports the proposition that individuals with a collective social value are oriented to their families and provides indirect support for the idea that the family may influence job satisfaction to a greater degree for people who hold a collective social value than for people who value individualism. Direct tests of this hypothesis are needed before conclusions can be drawn, however.

Research on the Theory

Dorval (1999) explored the importance of relational values in women's career roles. She administered the Life Values Inventory to a sample of ninety-eight female students drawn from four different faculties (thirty-one from engineering, seventeen from science except biology, eighteen from social work, and thirty-two from nursing) at the University of Calgary. Not surprisingly, concern for others was the most important work value held by women in traditional majors (nursing and social work), followed by achievement, responsibility, and financial prosperity. Achievement, responsibility, independence, and financial prosperity were the most highly ranked work values for women in nontraditional majors. Although this research supports the idea that occupations are chosen on the basis of work values, it failed to support the classification system developed by D. Brown (1996b) suggesting that creativity would be one of the work values of engineers, social workers, and nurses and that scientific understanding would be important to people in engineering and the sciences. This study is currently being replicated in Australia with a broader sample and, if the results support Dorval's findings, revisions of the classification system will be needed.

Jepsen (1998) conducted a study that directly tested the major hypothesis of this theory, namely, that work values are an important determinant of occupational choice. A personal data form, the Career Decisions Report, the six General Occupational Theme scales, and twelve selected occupational scales from the Strong-Campbell Interest Inventory, the values section of SIGI, and the Occupations Values Rating were used to collect data from seventy-two college freshmen women at the University of Iowa. Judges were used to identify expressed work values that surfaced in the written responses to the Career Decision Report; the Occupations Values Ratings was used to ascertain the importance of working in an occupation that offered them an opportunity to satisfy their values.

Among Jepsen's findings were

- SIGI value weights were for the most part unrelated to the interest measures.
- SIGI value weights were not associated with Holland types in the manner Holland (1997) theorized.
- Students in the study seemed to rank occupations using both interests and values.
- Students in the study almost universally included their work values in their discussions of the occupations they had ranked first or second.

Jepsen concluded that work values seem to function as hypothesized in an earlier version of this theory (Brown & Crace, 1996a), which, it should be added, pertained to people with an individualism social value.

Recommendations for Research

Several suggestions for needed research have been advanced throughout this article, and they will not be reiterated at this time. However, one general recommendation should be noted. The role of cultural values in occupational choice, occupational satisfaction, and occupational success is relatively unexplored. Future research on the role of values in occupational choice should explore how cultural values interact with work values to influence both occupational choice and outcomes.

Second, sociodemographic variables such as race and ethnicity should not be used as proxies for internal culture by either researchers or practitioners (D. Ho, 1995). As was noted at the outset, research has clearly demonstrated within-group differences for all cultural groups, as well as overlap across groups (Carter, 1991). Therefore, counselors who rely on external variables as indicators of values are likely to err (D. Ho, 1995). This, of course, raises the issue of how best to assess cultural values. Leong and Gim-Chung (1995) identified the Suin-Lew Asian Self-Identity Acculturation scale as one means of measuring acculturation for Asian Americans. Martin (1995) suggests that, for American Indians, information such as family structure, clients' perceptions of their acculturation, involvement in traditional ceremonies, and clients' work values may provide useful information about acculturation. Results of the Life Values Inventory (Crace & D. Brown, 1996), particularly scores on the Loyalty to Family or Group versus Independence and Humility scales, may also provide some useful information regarding important cultural values. The language spoken at home by bilingual individuals is also an indicator of the degree to which members of racial and ethnic minorities adhere to their cultural traditions (LaFromboise, Trimble, & Mohatt, 1990). These are but a few of the defensible approaches that can be used to assess cultural values.

Intergenerational Differences

Empirical evidence suggests that there has been a shift in the values of college students in the past forty to fifty years (Babbitt & Burbach, 1990; Conger, 1988; Green & Astin, 1985). The shift is away from an orientation to the welfare of others and a concern for society in general to an orientation to self-fulfillment and financial prosperity. Not unexpectedly, the negativity of college students' judgments of selfishness and misrepresentations for financial gain have decreased over this same period (Bovasso & Jacobs, 1991). The implications of this shift for career counselors are not great in the sense that college students will still tend to choose careers consistent with their values, but the implication for employers and personnel officers in particular are more dramatic. Greater efforts will be needed to inculcate a positive attitude toward cooperation in work groups, honesty, and the workplace in general, given the results of the studies cited.

Summary of the Theory

Because the occupational choice-making process of cultural minorities has gone largely unaddressed, it seemed necessary to advance a theory that attempts to explain both the occupational choice-making and adaptation process of all groups. Cultural and work values were advanced as the primary factors in occupational choice and the outcomes of those choices. Gender, SES, history of discrimination, scholastic aptitude, special aptitudes, self-efficacy, and other variables were also included as salient variables in the theory. What is needed at this point is research that focuses on the role of values generally and cultural values specifically and on the occupational decision-making processes, the choices made, and the outcome of those choices.

Recommendation for Practice and Reaction to the Cases

It is not my intent to address the nuances of practice issues for the myriad of individuals with varying cultural values. However, issues related to career counseling and assessment of ethnic minorities can be found in a number of sources (Arbona, 1995; Bowman, 1995; Fouad, 1994, 1995; Hartung et al., 1998; Leong & Gim-Chung, 1995; Leong & Leung, 1994; Thomason, 1995). Many aspects of these discussions are related to matching assessments and interventions to the cultural values of clients. Also it is beyond the scope of this article to discuss specific techniques and interventions for various groups. However, the following is offered as a guiding principle when working with clients. Once the cultural values and other information such as language proficiency are determined, assessment strategies and interventions should be designed that are in accord with the values and the language proficiency of the individual. In this assessment, special attention should be given to social values, time orientation, and activity values. Finally, career counselors need to be aware that the values in the workplace are primarily Eurocentric and that people with different values systems may be disadvantaged in these settings.

Career counselors need to be prepared to

- Help their clients become familiar with the values-laden expectations in the workplace

- Identify ways that their values may diminish their success in the Eurocentric workplace

- Encourage clients to maintain their cultural values while adapting to the Eurocentric workplace in some instances

- Become advocates for change in the workplace so that people who hold values that may not be those of the dominant culture can be successful

Specific recommendations regarding the selecting of counseling techniques and the design of interventions can be found in Srebalus and Brown (2001).

Not unexpectedly, given the foregoing discussion, several basic assumptions guide my career counseling activities (Brown, 1996; Brown & Crace, 1996a). These are discussed in the sections that follow.

Assumption 1

The decision maker is the person who will make the decision and may not be the individual who will implement the choice.

Gati and Saka (20001) describe the ideal career decision maker as one who (1) is aware of the need to make a career decision, (2) is motivated to make the decision, and (3) is able to choose a career commensurate with his or her personal resources. This is not my description of the perfect career decision maker because it applies only to clients who have an independent social value. Moreover, the idea of the independent decision maker undoubtedly works best for young decision makers, when both the decision maker and her or his family both value individualism. Therefore, I do not assume that the client will be an independent decision maker. Dependent decision-making styles characterize the approaches used by people in many cultures, and a career counselor must anticipate that some clients will look to parents, godparents, and others to have a major role in the choice of a career. In this discussion, the term *decision maker* does not necessarily refer to what we have traditionally seen as "the client."

Assumption 2

As would be expected from Assumption 1, I do not assume that the identified client is the only person who should be included in the decision-making process. Parents or members of the extended family should be included in the process of career counseling if the identified client is a dependent decision maker and if that dependency results from a collective social value.

Assumption 3

The choice of an occupation is part of a broader decision; the choice of a lifestyle and the process should be embedded in this context of lifestyle design.

Assumption 4

For independent decision makers, my first concern is to promote crystallization and then the prioritization of values, as they are often uncrystallized and unprioritized. My role with dependent decision makers is to make both the identified client and the decision maker aware of the implications of a career choice, both in terms of the values of both parties and the ramifications of the choice for lifestyle. Although the Life Values Inventory is highly useful when identifying some of the work and cultural values of a client, it does not measure activity or time orientation values. Therefore, an in-depth exploration (clinical, if you prefer) of the client's most highly prized beliefs is typically necessary to complete the process. This in-volves (1) determining who the decision maker(s) will be, (2) con-firming the social value, and (3) determining time orientation and activity values of the decision maker.

Decision makers have varying ideas about the urgency of the need to make a career decision and the influences that should come to bear on the decision. Savikas (1991) indicates, "Everyone has a career, but not everyone knows that he or she has a career" (p. 237). To rephrase this statement for students: "Every student can have a career in the future, but not every student is aware of the possibility that they can shape their careers in the future." Savickas goes on to indicate that some clients focus on the past, in that they expect their careers to be replays of the things that have happened to them or their families. Other clients orient their career decision making to the future because they are concerned about survival, according to Savickas. To these categories, I would add a group that never engages in career planning. They are content to let things happen, trusting luck or a calling from a higher power or the environment to select their career.

It goes without saying that if individuals focus on the past or the present, career counseling or other career development interven-tions are not considered as options (Savickas, 1991). Therefore, ca-reer counselors will probably need to recruit individuals who do not possess a future or past-future orientation rather than wait for them to appear of their own accord. Once they come into the process, work on their time orientation becomes a part of the career coun-seling process. Savikas identifies the Circles Test (Cottle, 1967), futures autobiographies (Maw, 1982), Future Plans Questionnaire (Pearlson & Raynor, 1982), and life lines, starting with birth and going to death, forecasting events such as things that may happen in schools, and rationale explanations regarding the importance of a future orientation in career planning as helpful strategies in this area. To this list, I would add guided fantasies (Brown & Brooks, 1991) that contrast different futures and alternative careers games that contrast futures in various careers.

Identifying the client's activity orientation will have to be done clinically, perhaps using open-ended leads such as "When I am confronted with a problem or dilemma, I. . . ." or "If I had to classify my approach to making decisions, I would say. . . ."

Assumption 5

In the case of minority clients who have adopted an independent decision-making style and come from families who believe that the locus of the decision should be in the family or group, I must become an interpreter of cultural values and their impact on perceptions regarding career decisions. This must be done in a fashion that will not cause family members or the client to lose face if it is to be successful. Indigenous helpers may be employed in this process if it is deemed appropriate.

Assumption 6

Career counseling techniques must be adapted to the cultural values of the client and others involved in the decision-making process. For example, techniques that require high levels of self-disclosure of thoughts and feelings should be avoided when the decision makers have a highly developed self-control value. In addition, using strategies that might cause parents or members of the extended family to lose face, such as disputing or confronting, should be avoided. It may be wisest in cross-cultural career counseling to assume that Native Americans and Asian Americans have a high concern for self-control and then temper judgment based on the clients' propensity to self-disclose feelings, thoughts, and information about themselves and their families.

Assumption 7

When cultural values conflict with the expectations in the workplace, two approaches may be employed. First, the idea of acceptability of adopting a "bicultural" identity should be explored, that is, adopting the values required for success in the workplace while retaining traditional values in other life roles. The second approach involves advocating for the client in the workplace to enhance the possibility that people with different values systems are accepted.

Assumption 8

Conflicting values must be identified and reconciled. The values systems of clients often include conflicting values that may immobilize them in the occupational decision-making process. For example, young clients who come from families with collective social values and frequently associate with adolescents with Eurocentric values may begin to adopt an individualism social value because of acculturation. Eurocentric clients with an individualism social value may also value belonging—a value that often requires conformity to group norms. Work values can also conflict. Many career counselors find that their financial prosperity value and their concern for others value conflict because many of the jobs available to career counselors offer modest financial rewards. If these conflicts exist, they must be identified and reconciled.

Assumption 9

There must be an ongoing search for mental health problems that will limit functioning in careers, either on a short-term or long-term basis. An example of a problem that may limit an individual on a short-term basis if it is treated is aviophobia. People who are afraid to fly are obviously constrained, but because the problem is rather easily treated with existing interventions, it need not be a long-term barrier to career choice or advancement in a career. Bipolar disorders and schizophrenia are long-term inhibitors of career-related behaviors.

The Case of K

No additional formal assessment data are needed in the case of K. For most Asian clients, I would want more data about the extent to which acculturation has taken place, but there are several indicators that K and his parents have adopted cultural values that are more in keeping with white, Western, European views than the traditional views of either Japan or China. One indicator is that the only language spoken in the household is English; another is that K's friends are mostly white students. A third indicator of acculturation is that his parents have placed the responsibility for the career decision on K—a position that K prefers; he intends to make his own decision. On the basis of these indicators, I would not expect to include the family directly in the career counseling process. The level of acculturation also increases my confidence in the results of the instruments that were administered.

There are some interesting aspects of K's case that warrant in-depth examination. One is that Independence and Belonging are often contradictory values. People who hold an Independence value have as one of their core beliefs that it is important to make your own decisions and do things your own way. This belief is affirmed by many of K's statements and the results of the Life Values Inventory. However, acting on the Belonging value (the belief that it is important to be accepted and included by others) often requires a fair amount of conformity to the wishes of others. Clearly, K expects to satisfy his Belonging value in his relationships with family members and significant others while he satisfies his other highly prioritized values in his work and leisure roles. I doubt that the apparent conflict between Independence and Belonging will pose a barrier in the decision-making process, but I need to be aware that this is a possibility.

There is other evidence that K does not act independently, in spite of his Independence value. The main example of this was his decision to go to college, which was greatly influenced by the urgings of a friend. His parents want K to go to college, but they are not pushing the issue, perhaps because they are aware that his expectations of completing college are not high. It is also worth noting that K attended an alternative high school that had no counseling program. The result is that he did not have the typical career and educational planning sessions provided to many high school students. Without parental support or educational and career guidance, the idea of attending college may not have occurred to K until a friend brought it up. Therefore, I suspect that K's decision making was influenced more by lack of information than by his inability to make decisions, but I need to explore both possibilities in detail.

Although K's SAT scores suggest that many careers are open to him, other indicators may be used to narrow his choices. He describes himself as unimaginative, which is consistent with his primary Holland types (Conventional and Realistic) and the fact that Creativity is not one of his highly prioritized values. In fact, K mentions his desire to satisfy his Creativity values only in relationship to his leisure role. This suggests that he needs to thoroughly explore one of his occupational daydreams—architecture—to determine the role that imagination plays in it. K's work values are Financial Prosperity, Achievement, and Independence. Many jobs would allow him to satisfy these values, some of which are linked to mathematics. Mathematics is one of K's strengths, according to his test scores and his self-perceptions, and thus it makes sense for him to explore occupations that have an applied mathematics base, such as accounting and engineering, both of which would allow him to satisfy his work values. It would also be important for K to explore his fantasy choices, including film editing.

The Case of E

Rarely do career counselors encounter a client with a profile as consistent as E's. Her self-efficacy ratings are almost entirely congruent with what would be predicted on the basis of her Holland type. For example, her self-efficacy ratings in the sciences are low, which is what one would expect of an individual whose Holland code can be viewed as any combination of SEC. Her work values—Responsibility, Concern for Others, and Financial Prosperity—are for the most part consistent with her personality type. One of her occupational daydreams—writer—is a bit inconsistent with her personality type and values, but the others are generally in keeping with her values.

There is one interesting aspect of E's profile that bears investigation early in the process of career counseling. She claims to be an independent decision maker and espouses the idea that she want to establish a lifestyle based on her own accomplishments, although she admits that she hopes to marry and have children. However, Independence is absent from her list of highly prioritized values. Moreover, it did not surface as a highly prioritized value in any of her life roles. There are two possibilities. One is that being Independent is contrary to E's perception of herself and perhaps of women in general and thus is uncrystallized at this time. There is a hint of this in that she does not list Loyalty to Family or Group as one of the values she hopes to satisfy in the family and in the role of significant other. The other possibility is that E is consciously or unconsciously planning her lifestyle with the expectation that she will marry and perhaps place greater emphasis on the family role than the work role, as her mother has done. Both alternatives should be explored. My suggestion to E is that, in either case, she should prepare for a career that best satisfies her work values and allows her to develop a lifestyle that will satisfy all her highly prioritized values.

There seems to be little doubt that E should explore careers in the legal profession, given her background and interests. This search should probably focus on those aspects of the legal profession that would allow her to have her Concern for Others value satisfied, such as family law. Managerial careers, particularly in charitable and "help-giving" businesses and public health, should probably be explored as well because of the salience of E's Concern for Others value. E's primary reason for seeking career counseling was to narrow her choices and make certain that she had chosen an appropriate major. The addition of some business electives might be recommended if she decides to pursue a managerial career.

Summary

The model described at the outset of this section and applied in the cases of K and E can be seen in Exhibit 11.1.

EXHIBIT 11.1.   A Values-Based Career Counseling Model

Stage 1
IDENTIFY THE DECISION-MAKER
∇

Independent Decision-Maker   ↔   Collaborative or Dependent

Proceed with Individual   Decision-Maker—Involve
                                                 Family or Other Participants
                                                 (decision-making system)

Stage 2
⇐ RELATIONSHIP BUILDING ⇒

Use Culturally Appropriate Techniques
Based on Self-Control Value

For example, traditional techniques such as questioning, reflection, confronta-
tions for clients with a moderate concern for self-control. Focus on behavior
for clients with high degree of concern for self-control; deference to family
members and other who may lose face if contradicted by authority figure.

Stage 3
ASSESSMENT AND GOAL SETTING

(1) Conflicts in decision-making (for example, conflicting values for clients
with individualism social values; conflicts within the decision-making system,
and so on; (2) Premature elimination of career options because of gender,
racial, or other stereotypes; (3) Fear of discrimination; (4) Lack of values-
based occupational information; (5) Work values not crystallized or prioritized; (6) Values-based conflicts within/among life roles; (7) Present or circular
time orientation that limits planning; (8) Unable to reconcile cultural values
and traditions and workplace values and expectations; (9) Psychological problem that precludes immediate decision making and/or limits occupational
choices in the long-term; (10) Immediate need to meet basic needs prior to
long-term planning, and/or (11) Physical limitations that eliminate options.

Stage 4
⇐ PROBLEM-SOLVING ⇒

Interventions matched to the cultural values of the decision-maker or
decision-making system and the problems that have been identified in the assessment stage.

Stage 5
TERMINATION

References

Aguirre, A. (1990). Poverty in the United States: Race, ethnic and gender differences. In S. Chan & J. Currie (Eds.), *Income and status differences between white and minority Americans: A persistent inequality* (pp. 101–121). Lampeter, Dyfed, Wales: Edwin Mellen Press.

Anderson, B., Burd, L., Dodd, J., & Kekler, K. (1980). A comparative study in time estimating. *Journal of American Indian Education, 19*, 1–4.

Arbona, C. (1995). Theory and research on racial and ethnic minorities: Hispanic Americans. In F.T.L. Leong (Ed.), *Career development and vocational behavior of ethnic and racial minorities* (pp. 37–66). Mahwah, NJ: Erlbaum.

Arce, C. E., Murgia, E., & Frisbie, W. P. (1987). Phenotype and life chances among Chicanos. *Hispanic Journal of Behavioral Sciences, 9*, 19–32.

Babbitt, C. E., & Burbach, H. J. (1990). A comparison of the self-orientation among college students across the 1960s, 1970s and 1980s. *Youth and Society, 21*, 472–483.

Bandura, A. (1986). *Social foundations of thought and action: A social cognitive theory.* Englewood Cliffs, NJ: Prentice Hall.

Bartol, K. M., Anderson, C. R., & Schneider, C. E. (1981). Sex and ethnic effects on motivation to manage among college students. *Journal of Applied Psychology, 66*, 40–44.

Bassoff, B. Z., & Ortiz, E. T. (1984). Teen women: Disparity between cognitive values and anticipated life events. *Child Welfare, 63*, 125–138.

Ben-Shem, I., & Avi-Itzhak, T. E. (1991). On work values and career choices in freshman students: The case of helping vs. other professions. *Journal of Vocational Behavior, 39*, 369–379.

Betz, N. E., & Fitzgerald, L. F. (1995). Career assessment and intervention with ethnic and racial minorities. In F.T.L. Leong (Ed.), *Career development and vocational behavior of racial and ethnic minorities* (pp. 263–280). Mahwah, NJ: Erlbaum.

Beutell, N. J., & Brenner, O. C. (1986). Sex differences in work values. *Journal of Vocational Behavior, 28*, 187–192.

Blau, P. M., & Duncan, O. D. (1967). *The American occupational structure.* New York: Wiley.

Bovasso, G., & Jacobs, J. (1991). Changes in moral values over three decades, 1958–1998. *Youth and Society, 22*, 468–472.

Bowman, S. L. (1995). Career intervention strategies and assessment issue for African Americans. In F.T.L. Leong (Ed.), *Career development and vocational behavior of racial and ethnic minorities* (pp. 137–164). Mahwah, NJ: Erlbaum.

Brenner, O. C., Blazini, A. P., & Greenhaus, J. H. (1988). An examination of race and sex differences in manager work values. *Journal of Vocational Behavior, 32*, 336–344.

Brooks, L. (1990). Recent developments in theory building. In D. Brown & L. Brooks (Eds.), *Career choice and development* (pp. 364–394). San Francisco: Jossey-Bass.

Brown, D. (1996a). Brown's values-based, holistic model of career and life-role choices and satisfaction. In D. Brown, L. Brooks, and Associates. *Career choice and development* (pp. 337–372). San Francisco: Jossey-Bass.

Brown, D. (1996b). *Occupations locator—OOH*. Chapel Hill, NC: Life Values Resources.

Brown, D., & Brooks, L. (1991). *Career counseling techniques*. Boston: Allyn & Bacon.

Brown, D., & Crace, R. K. (1996a). Values in life role choices and outcomes: A conceptual model. *Career Development Quarterly, 44*, 211–223.

Brown, D., & Crace, R. K. (1996b). *Manual and user's guide for the Life Values Inventory*. Chapel Hill, NC: Life Values Resources.

Brown, D., Fulkerson, K. F., Vedder, M., & Ware, W. B. (1983). Self-estimate ability in Black and white 8th, 10th, and 12th grade males and females. *Career Development Quarterly, 32*, 21–28.

Brown, D., & Minor, C. W. (1992). *Career needs in a diverse workforce: Implications of the NCDA Gallup Survey*. Alexandria, VA: NCDA.

Brown, M. T. (1995). The career development of African Americans: Theoretical and empirical issues. In F.T.L. Leong (Ed.), *Career development and vocational behavior of racial and ethnic minorities* (pp. 7–30). Mahwah, NJ: Erlbaum.

Burd, L., Dodd, J. M., Grassi, P. (1981). A comparison of reservation Native Americans and other public school children's time estimation skills. *Child Study Journal, 4*, 147–152.

Campbell, D. P. (1992). *Campbell Interest and Skills Survey*. Minneapolis: NCS.

Carter, R. T. (1991). Cultural values: A review of empirical research and implications for counseling. *Journal of Counseling and Development, 70,* 164–173.

Casserly, M. (1982). Effects of differentially structured career counseling on the decision quality of subjects with varying cognitive styles. Unpublished doctoral dissertation, University of Maryland.

Cheatham, H. E. (1990). Africentricity and the career development of African Americans. *Career Development Quarterly, 38,* 334–346.

Conger, J. J. (1988). Hostages of fortune: Youth values, and the public interest. *American Psychologist, 43,* 291–300.

Cottle, T. (1967). The circle test: An investigation of the perceptions of temporal relatedness and dominance. *Journal of Projective Techniques and Personality Assessment, 31,* 58–71.

Cox, T. H., & Harquail, C. V. (1991). Career paths and career success in early career stages of male and female MBAs. *Journal of Vocational Behavior, 39,* 54–75.

Crace, R. K., & Brown, D. (1996). *Life Values Inventory.* Chapel Hill, NC: Life Values Resources.

Denton, N., & Massey, D. S. (1989). Racial identity among Caribbean Hispanics: The effect of double minority status on residential status. *American Sociological Review, 54,* 790–808.

de Vaus, D., & McCallister, I. (1991). Gender and work orientation. *Work and Occupations, 18,* 72–93.

Dorval, C. E. (1999). *Relational values in women's career role.* Unpublished master's thesis, University of Calgary, Calgary, Alberta, Canada.

Elizur, D., Borg, I., Hunt, R., & Beck, I. M. (1991). The structure of work values. *Journal of Organizational Behavior, 12,* 21–38.

Feather, N. T. (1988). Values systems across cultures: Australia and China. *International Journal of Psychology, 21,* 697–715.

Feather, N. T. (1992). Values, valences, expectations, and actions. *Educational Psychology, 80,* 381–391.

Fouad, N. A. (1994). Career assessment with Latinos/Hispanics. *Journal of Career Assessment, 2,* 226–239.

Fouad, N. A. (1995). Career behavior of Hispanics: Assessment and intervention. In F.T.L. Leong (Ed.), *Career development and vocational behavior of racial and ethnic minorities* (pp. 165–192). Mahwah, NJ: Erlbaum.

Gati, I., Osipow, S. H., & Givon, M. (1995). Gender differences in career decision-making: The content and structure of preferences. *Journal of Counseling Psychology, 42*, 204–216.

Gati, I., & Saka, N. (2001). High school students' career related decision-making difficulties. *Journal of Counseling and Development, 79*, 331–340.

Ghiselli, H. H. (1973). The validity of aptitude tests in personnel selection. *Personnel Psychology, 26*, 461–477.

Gibbs, J. T. (1985). City girls: Psychosocial adjustment of urban adolescent Black females. *Sage: A Scholarly Journal of Black Women, 2*, 28–36.

Goodstein, L. (1972). Behavioral views of counseling. In B. Stefflre & W. H. Grant (Eds.), *Theories of counseling* (2nd ed., pp. 243–286). New York: McGraw-Hill.

Gore, P. A., Jr., & Leuwerke, W. C. (2000). Predicting occupational considerations: A comparison of self-efficacy beliefs, outcomes expectations, and person-environment congruence. *Journal of Career Assessment, 8*, 237–250.

Gottfredson, L. S. (1996). Gottfredson's theory of circumscription. In D. Brown, L. Brooks, and Associates. *Career choice and development* (3rd ed., pp. 121–178). San Francisco: Jossey-Bass.

Graves, T. D. (1967). Psychological acculturation in a triethnic community. *Southwestern Journal of Anthropology, 23*, 336–350.

Green, K. C., & Astin, A. W. (1995). The mood on campus: More conservative or more materialistic. *Educational Record, 66*, 45–48.

Gregory, K., Wells, K. B., & Leake, B. (1986). Which first-year medical students expect to practice in a ghetto setting? *Journal of National Medical Association, 78*, 501–504.

Harpaz, I., & Fu, X. (1997). Work centrality in Germany, Israel, Japan, and the United States. *Cross-Cultural Research, 31*, 171–200.

Hartung, P. J., Vandiver, B. J., Leong, F.T.L., Pope, M., Niles, S. G., & Farrow, B. (1998). Appraising cultural identity in career-development assessment and counseling. *The Career Development Quarterly, 46*, 276–293.

Herring, R. D. (1996). Synergistic counseling and Native American Indian students. *Journal of Counseling and Development, 74*, 542–547.

Ho, D.Y.F. (1995). Internal culture, culturocentrism, and transcendence. *The Counseling Psychologist, 23*, 4–24.

Ho, M. K. (1987). *Family therapy with ethnic minorities*. Newbury Park, CA: Sage.

Holland, J. L. (1959). A theory of vocational choices. *Journal of Counseling Psychology, 6*, 336–342.

Holland, J. L. (1997). *Making vocational choices: A theory of vocational personalities and work environments* (3rd Ed.). Odessa, FL: Psychological Assessment Resources.

Hotchkiss, L., & Borow, H. (1996). Sociological perspective on work and career development. In D. Brown, L. Brooks, and Associates. *Career choice and development* (3rd ed., pp. 281–336). San Francisco: Jossey-Bass.

Hoyt, K. B., & Lester, J. (1995). *Survey of workers in America*. Alexandria, VA: National Career Development Association.

Hsia, J. (1988). *Asian Americans in higher education and work*. Mahwah, NJ: Erlbaum.

Hughes, E. (1958). *Men and their work*. Glencoe, IL: Free Press.

Ibrahim, F. A., Ohnishi, H., & Wilson, R. P. (1994). Career assessment in a culturally diverse society. *Journal of Career Assessment, 2*, 276–288.

Isaacson, L. E., & Brown, D. (2000). *Career information, career counseling, and career development* (7th ed.). Boston: Allyn & Bacon.

Jencks, C., Crouse, J., & Mueser, P. (1983). The Wisconsin model of status attainment: A national replication with improved measures of ability and aspiration. *Sociology of Education, 56*, 3–19.

Jepsen, D. A. (1998). *The function of work values in career decision-making: An exploratory study of college freshmen women*. Unpublished manuscript, University of Iowa, Iowa City.

Johnson, M. J., Swartz, J. L., & Martin, W. E., Jr. (1995). Application of psychological theories for career development for Native Americans. In F.T.L. Leong (Ed.), *Career development and vocational behavior of ethnic and racial minorities* (pp. 103–136). Mahwah, NJ: Erlbaum.

Judge, T. A., & Bretz, R. D., Jr. (1992). Effects of work values on job choice decisions. *Journal of Applied Psychology, 77*, 261–271.

Kluckhorn, F. R., & Strodtbeck, F. L. (1961). *Values in values orientations*. Evanston, IL: Row Paterson.

Knoop, R. (1991). Achievement of work values and participative decision-making. *Psychological Reports, 68*, 775–781.

LaFromboise, T. D., Trimble, J. E., & Mohatt, G. V. (1990). Counseling intervention and Native American tradition: An integrative approach. *The Counseling Psychologist, 18*, 628–624.

Larson, J. H., Butler, M., Wilson, N. M., Medora, L., & Allgood, S. (1994). The effects of gender on career decision problems in young adults. *Journal of Counseling and Development, 73*, 79–84.

Lebo, R. B., Harrington, T. F., & Tillman, R. (1995). Work values similarities among students from six countries. *Career Development Quarterly, 43*, 350–362.

Lee, K. C. (1991). The problem of the appropriateness of the Rokeach Values Survey in Korea. *International Journal of Psychology, 26*, 299–310.

Lent, R. W., Brown, S. D., & Hackett, G. (1996). Career development from a social cognitive perspective. In D. Brown & L. Brooks (Eds.), *Career choice and development* (pp. 373–422). San Francisco: Jossey-Bass.

Leong, F.T.L. (1991). Career development attributes and occupational values of Asian American and White high school students. *Career Development Quarterly, 39*, 221–230.

Leong, F.T.L. (Ed.). (1995a). *Career development and vocational behavior of ethnic minorities*. Mahwah, NJ: Erlbaum.

Leong, F.T.L. (1995b). Introduction and overview. In F.T.L. Leong (Ed.), *Career development and vocational behavior of ethnic and racial minorities* (pp. 1–6). Mahwah, NJ: Erlbaum.

Leong, F.T.L., & Gim-Chung, R. H. (1995). Career assessment and intervention with Asian Americans. In F.T.L. Leong (Ed.), *Career development and vocational behavior of racial and ethnic minorities* (pp. 193–226). Mahwah, NJ: Erlbaum.

Leong, F.T.L., & Leung, A. S. (1994). Career assessment with Asian-Americans. *Journal of Career Assessment, 2*, 240–257.

Leong, F.T.L., & Serifica, F. C. (1995). Career development of Asian Americans: A research area in need of a good theory. In F.T.L. Leong (Ed.), *Career development and vocational behavior of ethnic and racial minorities* (pp. 67–102). Mahwah, NJ: Erlbaum.

Leong, F.T.L., & Tata, S. P. (1990). Sex and occupational values differences among Chinese American children. *Journal of Counseling Psychology, 37*, 208–212.

Maw, I. (1982). The future autobiography: A longitudinal analysis. *Journal of College Student Personnel, 23*, 3–6.

McDiarmid, G. W., & Kleinfeld, J. S. (1986, May). Occupational values of rural Eskimos. *Journal of American Indian Education*, 23–29.

Meglino, B. M., Ravlin, E. C., & Adkins, C. L. (1989). A work values approach to corporate culture: A field test of the value congruence process and its relationship to individual outcomes. *Journal of Applied Psychology, 74,* 424–432.

Melamed, T. (1995). Career success: The moderating effects of gender. *Journal of Vocational Behavior, 47,* 295–314.

Melamed, T. (1996). Career success: An assessment of a gender-specific model. *Journal of Occupational and Organizational Psychology, 69,* 217–226.

Montalvo, F. F. (1991). Phenotyping, acculturation, and biracial assimilation of Mexican Americans. In M. Sotomayer (Ed.), *Empowering Hispanic families: A critical issue for the 90s* (pp. 176–191). Milwaukee, WI: Family Service of America.

Morrow, S. L., Gore, P. A., Jr., & Campbell, B. W. (1996). The application of the sociocognitive framework to the career development of gay men and lesbian women. *Journal of Counseling Psychology, 48,* 136–148.

NCDA. (1999). *NCDA/NOICC/Gallup survey of working America.* Tulsa, OK: Author.

Nevis, E. C. (1983). Cultural assumptions and productivity: The United States and China. *Sloan Management Review, 24,* 17–29.

Newman, J. L., Fuqua, D. R., & Seaworth, T. B. (1989). The role of anxiety in career decision making: Implications for diagnosis and treatment. *Career Development Quarterly, 37,* 221–231.

Ong, P. M. (1990). Uncertain economic progress: Racial inequality among California males. In S. Chan & J. Currie (Eds.), *Income and status differences among White and minority Americans: A persistent inequality* (pp. 29–55). Lampeter, Dyed, Wales: Edwin Mellon Press.

Osipow, S. H., & Littlejohn, E. M. (1995). Toward a multicultural theory of career development: Prospects and dilemmas. In F.T.L. Leong (Ed.), *Career development and vocational behavior of ethnic and racial minorities* (251–262). Mahwah, NJ: Erlbaum.

Pearlson, H., & Raynor, L. J. (1982). Motivational analysis of the future plans of college men: Imagery used to describe future plans and goals. In J. Raynor & E. Etin (Eds.), *Motivation, career striving and aging* (pp. 115–124). Washington, DC: Hemisphere Publishing Company.

Phillips, S. D., & Imhoff, A. R. (1997). Women and career development: A decade of research. *Annual Review of Psychology*, 48, 31–60.

Pietromonaco, P. R., & Rock, K. S. (1987). Decision style in depression: The contribution of perceived risks versus benefits. *Journal of Personality and Social Psychology*, 52, 399–408.

Ponterotto, J. G., & Casas, J. M. (1991). *Handbook of racial/ethnic minority research*. Springfield, IL: Thomas.

Posner, B. Z. (1992). Person-organization values congruence: No support for individuals differences as moderating influences. *Human Relations*, 45, 351–361.

Powell, G. N., & Butterfield, D. A. (1997). Effects of race on promotions to the top management in a federal department. *Academy of Management Journal*, 40, 112–128.

Ravlin, E. C., & Meglino, B. M. (1987). Effects of values on perception and decision-making: A study of alternative work values measures. *Journal of Applied Psychology*, 77, 666–673.

Robinson, T. L., & Ginter, E. J. (Eds.). (1999). Racism: Healing its effects [Special issue]. *Journal of Counseling and Development*, 76 (3).

Rokeach, M. (1973). *The nature of human values*. New York: Free Press.

Rotter, J. B. (1954). *Social learning and clinical psychology*. Englewood Cliffs, NJ: Prentice-Hall.

Rounds, J. B., Henley, G. A., Dawis, R. V., Lofquist, L. H., & Weiss, D. J. (1981). *Manual for the Minnesota Importance Questionnaire*. Minneapolis: University of Minnesota.

Sanderson, P. R. (1993). Untitled introduction. *The Leading Edge*, 2, 5.

Saunders, L. (1995). Relative earnings of Black and White men by region, industry. *Monthly Labor Review*, 118, 68–73.

Savickas, M. L. (1991). Improving career time perspective. In D. Brown & L. Brooks (Eds.), *Career counseling techniques* (pp. 236–249). Boston: Allyn & Bacon.

Sinha, D. (1990). Interventions for development out of poverty. In R. W. Brislin (Ed.), *Applied cross-cultural psychology* (pp. 77–97). Newbury Park, CA: Sage.

Soh, S., & Leong, F.T.L. (2001). Cross-cultural validation of Holland's theory in Singapore: Beyond structural validity of RIASEC. *Journal of Career Assessment*, 9, 115–133.

Srebalus, D. J., & Brown, D. (2001). *Introduction to the helping professions*. Boston: Allyn & Bacon.

Stimpson, D., Jensen, L., & Neff, W. (1992). Cross-cultural gender differences in preferences for a caring morality. *Journal of Social Psychology, 132*, 317–322.

Sue, D. W., & Sue, D. (1990). *Counseling the culturally different* (2nd ed.). New York: Wiley.

Super, D. E. (1953). A theory of vocational development. *American Psychologist, 8*, 185–190.

Super, D. E. (1981). Approaches to occupational choice and career development. In A. G. Watts & J. M. Kidd (Eds.), *Career development in Britain* (pp. 135–156). Cambridge, England: Hobson's Press.

Super, D. E. (1990). A life-span, life-space approach to career development. In D. Brown, L. Brooks, & Associates, *Career choice and development* (2nd ed., pp. 197–261). San Francisco: Jossey-Bass.

Super, D. E., Crites, J. O., Hummel, R., Moser, H., Overstreet, P., & Warnath, C. (1957). *Vocational development: A framework for research.* New York: Teachers College Press.

Super, D. E., & Sverko, B. (Eds.). (1995). *Life roles, values, and careers: International findings of the work importance study.* San Francisco: Jossey-Bass.

Swinton, D. H. (1992). The economic status of African Americans: Limited ownership and persistent inequality. In B. J. Tidwell (Ed.), *The state of Black America 1992* (pp. 61–117). New York: National Urban League.

Tharenou, P., & Conroy, D. (1994). Men and women managers' advancement: Personal or situational determinants. *Applied Psychology: An International Review, 43*, 5–31.

Thomason, T. C. (1995). *Introduction to counseling American Indians.* Flagstaff, AZ: American Indian Rehabilitation Research and Training Center.

U.S. Department of Labor (1995). *Employment and earnings.* Washington, DC: U.S. Department of Labor, Bureau of Labor Statistics.

Vacha-Haasa, T., Walsh, B. D., Kapes, J. T., Dresden, J. H., Thomsom, W. A., Ochos-Sargey, B., & Comacho, Z. (1994). Gender differences on the Values Scale for ethnic minority students. *Journal of Vocational Behavior, 21*, 408–421.

Vondracek, F. W., Shimizu, K., Schulenburg, J., Hostetler, M., & Sakayanagi, T. (1990). A comparison between American and Japanese students' work values. *Career Development Quarterly, 36*, 274–286.

Vroom, V. H. (1964). *Work and motivation*. New York: Wiley.

Wagoner, N. E., & Bridwell, S. D. (1989). High school students' motivation for a career as a physician. *Academic Medicine, 64*, 325–327.

Westbrook, B. W., Buck, R. W., Jr., Wynne, D. C., & Sanford, E. (1994). Career maturity in adolescents: Reliability and validity of self-ratings by gender and ethnicity. *Journal of Career Assessment, 2*, 125–161.

Wright, G.(1984). *Behavioral decision theory*. Newbury Park, CA: Sage.

Yagi, D. T., & Oh, M. Y. (1995). Counseling Asian American students. In C. C. Lee (Ed.), *Counseling for diversity* (pp. 61–84). Needham Heights, MA: Longwood.

Young, R. A. (1994). Helping adolescents with career development: The active role of parents. *Career Development Quarterly, 42*, 195–203.

Yu, L. C., & Wu, S. (1985). Unemployment and family dynamics in meeting the needs of the Chinese elderly in the United States. *Gerontologist, 25*, 472–476.

12

Status of Theories of Career Choice and Development

Duane Brown

In Chapter One, I provided some background regarding the history of theorizing about career choice and development. This brief introduction was followed by the presentations of a number of theories of career choice and development. In the third edition of this book, the theories were divided into two categories: (1) established and (2) emerging. That format was not used in this edition because most of the so-called emerging theories have become established.

This is particularly true of the social cognitive theory of Lent, Brown, and Hackett, which was presented in Chapter Seven. This theory has stimulated a great deal of research (for example, Donnay & Borgen, 1999; Luzzo & Taylor, 1994) and has been translated into practice in the form of instruments that are used as companions to the Strong Interest Inventory (Skills Confidence Inventory; Betz, Borgen, & Harmon, 1996) and the Kuder Occupational Interest Survey (Kuder Task Self-Efficacy Scale; Lucas, Wanberg, & Zytowski, 1997). The cognitive information processing model discussed in Chapter Eight by Peterson, Sampson, Reardon, and Lenz has gained attention to some degree, and the publication of the Career Thoughts Inventory (Sampson et al., 1996) may stimulate additional research, as well as application of the theory to practice. Postmodern approaches such as the one authored by Young, Valach, and Collin seem to have gained some adherents. Articles by Brott (2001) and Thorgren and Feit (2001) address the issue of assessment from postmodern perspective. Perhaps it goes without saying that Holland's theory, which was presented in Chapter Nine by Spokane and his associates, continues to be quite influential. Inexplicably, the Theory of Work Adjustment presented by Dawis in Chapter Ten has not developed adherents as one would have thought. Gottfredson's theory (Chapter Four) continues to stimulate research, and it seems likely that some of her ideas are being incorporated into the practices of career counselors. As Savickas illustrates in Chapter Five; career development theory still receives attention in both research and practice and thus is probably as viable as it was in 1996. Although other theories of career choice and development are mentioned from time to time in the professional literature, the seven theories listed here are the most influential at this time.

Cross-Cultural Sensitivity of Theories

The theory that I presented in the third edition (Brown's values-based, holistic model of career and life-role choice; Brown, 1996) has evolved to include cultural values and has narrowed to focus strictly on occupational choice, satisfaction, and success. This evolution was in response to my continued concern about what I consider to be the "white bread" nature of most of the extant theories of career choice and development and my realization that cultural values probably make a considerable difference in the career development process. Earlier (Brown, 2000) I had criticized several articles in *Career Development Quarterly* for being culturally insensitive because they attempted to apply several theories to the school-to-work transition. Lent and Worthington (2000) disagreed with my point of view, indicating that

(a) conclusions regarding the cross-cultural validity of particular career theories should be informed by empirical data, (b) it is well to avoid perpetuating uniformity myths regarding particular cultures, and (c) generic theories may help to account for the work transition of students from a variety of cultural groups and in some cases, can accommodate study of variables and processes that are assumed to be culturally specific. [pp. 382–383]

I find very little to disagree with in their statement, but it seems to me that empirical data such as those generated by Hansen, Scullard, and Haviland (2000) raise some questions about the cultural validity of Holland's theory. So does data generated by Leung and Hou (2001) and findings reported by Soh and Leong (2001) that raise questions about the construct validity of Holland's scales and the likelihood that people from other cultures who are classified using Holland's typology may have different views of occupations than white, European Americans. I also believe that career development theories that fail to take into consideration the importance of cultural context and differences in worldview perpetuate the idea that the career development processes of all groups are similar. Only the postmodern theories of career development, such as the one by Young, Valach, and Collin, can claim almost total cultural sensitivity; they make no attempt to generalize information from one person to another, let alone one group to the other. The theory that I advanced in Chapter Eleven is an attempt to advance a theory based on logical positivism that is culturally sensitive.

The Convergence of Theories Revisited

In Chapter One, I addressed the debate about whether theories of career choice and development are converging—a debate first introduced by Savickas and Lent (1994). More recently, Patton and McMahon (1999) took up this debate and argued that there has been a convergence in theorizing, at least so far as the recognition of the importance of the context in which the person functions. They suggest that four stages occur when theories converge:

1. *Rapprochement,* which they define as the cessation of competition and the development of collaborative relationships to explore the issues

2. *Convergence*, which involves the development of a common language

3. *Bridging*, which involves recognizing communalities among existing theories and developing a common set of constructs built around the common language that has developed

4. *Integration*, which involves the actual development of a single theoretical perspective

Patton and McMahon admit that, to this point at least, no overarching framework has developed. They offer systems theory as the potential integrative framework for career development theory. However, the crux of the convergence issue once again raises its head when the authors consider systems theory. The following passage from their work is illustrative:

In contrast to logical positivist models the systems worldview values the whole, a system that is more than the sum of its parts. Rather than focus on cause and effect between parts, it views patterns of interrelationships as more important. Progression within this pattern is not always linear; the complexity of a system is far too great. Rather than assuming a quantitative view of knowledge—that is knowing "more"— it views knowing in a qualitative way. [p. 135]

Perhaps career development theorizing is in the midst of a paradigm shift from logical positivism to postmodernism, as suggested by Savickas and Lent (1994) and Patton and McMahon (1999). However, Lent and his associates suggest that their social cognitive theory is a bridging theory; that may be the case. However, adherents of the theory continue to generate knowledge based on the epistemology of logical positivism. It seems to me that most career development theorists and practitioners are unready to jettison one hundred years of thought and research because of criticism from postmodern thinkers.

A Final Word

When the simplistic tripartite model of Frank Parsons (1909) is compared to the intricate theories presented in this volume, it is clear that career development theory has advanced greatly in the century since Parsons began his work in Boston. The trait-and-factor theorists have been responsible for many of the advances that have been observed, but work on the role of self-efficacy in career choice and development has made tremendous contributions to our thinking and practice. Postmodern theorists and practitioners have not derailed traditionalists, but they have caused them to reconsider the ways in which they conceptualize and practice. As Patton and McMahon (1999) and others note, there is much to be done. History suggests that we will continue to improve both our theories and our applications of them.

References

Betz, N. E., Borgen, F. H., & Harmon, L. (1996). *Skills Confidence Inventory applications and technical guide*. Palo Alto, CA: Consulting Psychologists Press.

Brott, P. E. (2001). A storied approach: A postmodern perspective for career counseling. *Career Development Quarterly, 49,* 304–313.

Brown, D. (1996). A values-based, holistic model of career and life-role decision making. In D. Brown, L. Brooks, & Associates, *Career choice and development* (3rd ed., pp. 337–332). San Francisco: Jossey-Bass.

Brown, D. (2000). Theory and school-to-work transition: Are the recommendations suitable for cultural minorities? *Career Development Quarterly, 48,* 370–375.

Donnay, D. A., & Borgen, F. H. (1999). The incremental validity of vocational self-efficacy: An examination of interest, efficacy, and occupation. *Journal of Counseling Psychology, 46,* 432–447.

Hansen, J. C., Scullard, M. G., & Haviland, M. G. (2000). The interest structure of Native American college students. *Journal of Career Assessment, 8,* 159–172.

Lent, R. W., & Worthington, R. L. (2000). On school-to-work transition, career development theories, and cultural validity. *Career Development Quarterly, 48*, 376–383.

Leung, S. A., & Hou, Z. (2001). Concurrent validity of the 1994 Self-Directed Search for Chinese high school students in Hong Kong. *Journal of Career Assessment, 9*, 283–296.

Lucas, J. L., Wanberg, C. R., & Zytowski, D. G. (1997). Development of a career self-efficacy scale. *Journal of Vocational Behavior, 50*, 437–459.

Luzzo, D. A., & Taylor, M. (1994). Effects of verbal persuasion on the career self-efficacy of college freshmen. *California Journal of Counseling and Development, 14*, 31–34.

Parsons, F. (1909). *Choosing a vocation.* Boston: Houghton-Mifflin.

Patton, W., & McMahon, M. (1999). *Career development and systems theory: A new relationship.* Pacific Grove, CA: Brooks/Cole.

Sampson, J. P., Jr., Peterson, G. W., Lenz, J. G., Reardon, R. C., & Saunders, D. E. (1996). *Career Thoughts Inventory manual.* Odessa, FL: Personality Assessment Resources.

Savickas, M. L., & Lent, R. W. (eds.). (1994). *Convergence in career development theories.* Palo Alto, CA: CPP Books.

Soh, S., & Leong, F.T.L. (2001). Cross-cultural validity of Holland's theory in Singapore: Beyond structural validity of RIASEC. *Journal of Career Assessment, 9*, 115–113.

Thorgren, J. M., & Feit, S. S. (2001). The Career-O-Gram: A postmodern career intervention. *Career Development Quarterly, 49*, 291–303.

Name Index

Subject Index